In 1984, my life changed course forever. I was diagnosed with terminal cancer and thought my life was, indeed, over. But instead, I met my husband, Robert Pirello, and things have never been the same. This new edition of my first book, like its previous incarnation, is for him—my teacher, my love, my partner and my life.

COOKING
THE
WHOLE
FOODS
WAY

Also by Christina Pirello

GLOW

COOK YOUR WAY TO THE LIFE YOU WANT

CHRISTINA COOKS

COOKING THE WHOLE FOODS WAY

THIS CRAZY VEGAN LIFE

I'M MAD AS HELL, AND I'M NOT GOING TO EAT IT ANYMORE!

COOKING
THE
WHOLE
FOODS
WAY

Your Complete, Everyday Guide to Healthy,
Delicious Eating with 500 Vegan Recipes, Menus, Techniques,
Meal Planning, Buying Tips, Wit, and Wisdom

CHRISTINA PIRELLO

Illustrations by Christina Pirello

A HOME BOOK
Published by the Penguin Group
Penguin Group (USA) Inc.
375 Hudson Street, New York, New York 10014, USA
Penguin Group (Canada), 90 Eglinton Avenue East, Suite 700, Toronto, Ontario M4P 2Y3, Canada
(a division of Pearson Penguin Canada Inc.)
Penguin Books Ltd., 80 Strand, London WC2R 0RL, England
Penguin Group Ireland, 25 St. Stephen's Green, Dublin 2, Ireland (a division of Penguin Books Ltd.)
Penguin Group (Australia), 250 Camberwell Road, Camberwell, Victoria 3124, Australia
(a division of Pearson Australia Group Pty. Ltd.)
Penguin Books India Pvt. Ltd., 11 Community Centre, Panchsheel Park, New Delhi—110 017, India
Penguin Group (NZ), 67 Apollo Drive, Rosedale, North Shore 0745, Auckland, New Zealand
(a division of Pearson New Zealand Ltd.)
Penguin Books (South Africa) (Pty.) Ltd., 24 Sturdee Avenue, Rosebank, Johannesburg 2196, South Africa

Penguin Books Ltd., Registered Offices: 80 Strand, London WC2R 0RL, England

While the author has made every effort to provide accurate telephone numbers and Internet addresses at the time of publication, neither the publisher nor the author assumes any responsibility for errors, or for changes that occur after publication. Further, the publisher does not have any control over and does not assume any responsibility for author or third-party websites or their content.

PRINTING HISTORY
HPBooks first trade paperback edition / March 1997
Revised and updated Home trade paperback edition / August 2007

Home trade paperback ISBN: 978-1-55788-517-3

The Library of Congress has cataloged the HPBooks first edition as follows:

Pirello, Christina.
    Cooking the whole foods way : your complete, everyday guide to healthy,
delicious eating with 500 recipes, menus, meal planning, techniques, buying tips,
wit and wisdom / Christina Pirello.—1st ed.
        p. cm.
    ISBN 1-55788-262-2
    1. Cookery (Natural foods). 2. Natural foods. 3. Macrobiotic diet—Recipes. I. Title.
TX741.P564 1997
641.5'63—dc20   96-23176 CIP

PRINTED IN THE UNITED STATES OF AMERICA

20 19 18 17 16 15 14 13 12 11

PUBLISHER'S NOTE: The recipes contained in this book are to be followed exactly as written. The publisher is not responsible for your specific health or allergy needs that may require medical supervision. The publisher is not responsible for any adverse reactions to the recipes contained in this book.

Most Home books are available at special quantity discounts for bulk purchases for sales promotions, premiums, fund-raising, or educational use. Special books, or book excerpts, can also be created to fit specific needs. For details, write: Special Markets, Penguin Group (USA) Inc., 375 Hudson Street, New York, New York 10014.

Contents

Acknowledgments

THERE ARE SO many people to thank in connection with this book (both the first and second editions) that I could ramble on for days . . . but don't worry, I'll be brief . . . sort of . . .

First, to my mother, who taught me everything I wanted to be and everything I didn't. She also taught me to cook from my soul and I will always be grateful. To my father, who always thinks I can do anything. To my brothers and sister, who endured countless experimental recipes as I evolved, but especially to my brother Tom, for being the best big brother a girl ever had.

To my high school art teacher, John Sebes, who introduced me to vegetarianism.

To my many teachers—Michio and Aveline Kushi, your work with macrobiotics enabled me to save my very life; Diane Avoli, Wendy Esko, Mary Kett, Carry Wolf and Geraldine Walker, your depth of understanding of food helped shape the cook I claim to be today; Tom Monte, for author encouragement and friendship; and William Tara, your enduring encouragement and mentoring taught me to listen to my heart, find my own voice and teach my own truths.

To my many computer troubleshooters, for bailing me out every time my illiteracy got me in hot water—back in the day, Diana and Dave, for your endless patience; Jim, who could teach an idiot how to operate a computer—and in this case, did just that. And to my current computer genius gurus, the cutie-pie brothers Mike and Todd . . . thank you.

To Mary and Tina, for your patient proofreading and honest, unconditional friendship.

To Christopher, for letting me pick your writer's brain more often than I care to admit. How I wish you were here now to see how far I have come in ten years. I miss you.

To Bernardo Merizalde, our family doctor and dear friend of many years. Your wise counsel has gotten me through a lot of the craziness that comes with what I do. Thanks for your patient friendship.

To Don and Juli Vitello, whose brilliant direction and even more brilliant words continue to take *Christina Cooks* to places I could never even imagine. And to everyone at Fusion (known for many years as the Telenium Group) for all your support, post-production and ability to make me look like a genius.

To my numerous students who have taught me so much over the years. You have helped me keep my mind open to the learning process, maintain a curious attitude and have the courage to experiment.

To the millions of people who watch *Christina Cooks* and write to tell me how it's going for them in the kitchen. How I love hearing from you! Keep on cooking!

To my special women friends—that little group of strong, beautiful women who not only helped me get through the rough spots of this work, but who love and support me in all my craziness . . . Cyn, Elaine, Ruth Ann, Sue, Sherry, Michele, Caryn, Lois, Gayle, Mary, Tina, Lori . . . I am sure I have missed someone, but I hope you all know who you are . . . you have my undying love and friendship.

To Michele Gambino for becoming the "glue" that holds it all together. I would be lost without you.

To Dennis, Ben, Sara, Steve (Island Man), Leslie, Donald and all my other close pals who wander in and out of my kitchen, eating and commenting with unwavering honesty on the latest dish.

To Patrick Riley and Andrew Mell, for the body work that keeps me sane when the stress nearly does me in. Your magic hands and healing hearts are much appreciated.

To Anthony Molino and Al Richezza, for keeping me fit enough to handle what comes my way. You push me to be in the best physical shape I can be and I am so grateful.

To Ray, for telling me over and over and over that I could do this. Who would have thought that by the time of this second edition, we would be eight seasons into *Christina Cooks* on National Public Television?

To Steve Feinberg, for getting this ball rolling in the first place.

To Jeanette Egan, my editor, and to everybody at the Penguin Group who made this work possible, especially John Duff. Thanks for making this novice look and sound so good. I had to leave this as is, because all these years later, you still have faith in me and it means so much to know that.

And finally, again, to my husband, Robert. Without your love and encouragement—and support—I am not sure that I would have accomplished half of what I have in this life. Your vision for us is amazing. It's true what they say: Behind every great woman is a wonderful man . . . I love you.

Thank you all.

Preface

IF YOU HAVE not met Christina Pirello or seen her on television, you are in for a treat. You will be glad you've invited Christina into your kitchen.

Each recipe is thoughtfully crafted from the most wholesome ingredients, carefully combined as only Christina could. The subtle flavors will delight your taste buds. And the rest of you will be delighted, as well, because this treasury of recipes is as healthful as it is delicious. Many people love Christina's cooking simply for the joy of good eating. But many look to her for a different reason. They want to improve their health and are looking for powerful, healing foods. If this is you, you've come to the right place. Each wonderful creation has the full measure of nature's rejuvenating powers. Perhaps your goal is simply to stay healthy and fit. Or you may want to shed a few extra pounds, or maybe more than a few. Or it may be that you need to return to health after having lost some ground. These recipes are designed with you in mind.

In our research studies, we have found that the dietary steps Christina follows can have a dramatic effect on health. Weight loss becomes almost effortless. Cholesterol levels plummet. Diabetes falls into control. People with headaches and painful joints often find surprising relief. The secret is in what she has chosen to include, foods rich in antioxidants and other healthful nutrients, as well as in what she has left out: You won't find cholesterol or animal fats lurking here. If you are new to cooking, you'll find that the recipes in *Cooking the Whole Foods Way* allow you to take very simple ingredients and make them into delicious and nutritious meals. Try the many recipes for tasty greens, colorful vegetables, whole grains and delightful desserts. And if you are an experienced chef, you'll find that you learn something new from Christina on almost every page.

Always upbeat, warm and personable, Christina is known for putting her heart into her work, and these recipes show her at her very best. Have fun with the many stories, tips and recipes, as you open the door to Christina's kitchen.

NEAL D. BARNARD, M.D.
*President, Physicians' Committee
for Responsible Medicine*

Foreword

IT'S DIFFICULT TO believe that it was only ten years ago that Christina asked me to write the foreword to the first edition of this wonderful book. Christina has filled those years with the same energy, humor and sense of purpose that propelled her then, and has accomplished much. She has moved into the broader world from her kitchen cooking classes and now shares her talents with a wide audience that expands with every year.

Her national television show has introduced wholesome cooking and natural foods to millions and won her an Emmy Award for best host. (Is an Oscar on the horizon?) She is active in several charities and has been cited by them for her wonderful enthusiasm and her ability to communicate good health in a way that is fun, easy and produces results. Her activities have involved working with the Careers Through Culinary Arts Program, an organization that inspires kids in inner-city high schools to move ahead in a positive way. In addition to all this she also has time to be an active board member of the Farm Market Trust, promoting new opportunities for farm markets in Philadelphia and serves on the Chefs' Council for Chefs for Humanity. She's a busy woman and it's good that she is. Even though huge changes have been made to improve the quality of nutrition in America, there is still much to be done.

The phenomenal growth in the consumption of natural and organic foods and the increased awareness of good nutrition is largely a result of the work of Christina and those like her. We need education and inspiration to balance the millions of dollars spent to promote an unhealthy diet. This is especially true in the case of food for kids.

When the food manufactured for the young is playfully called "junk food" and cartoon promotions lure kids (and their parents) into the land of empty calories and snacks with a negative nutritional value, we know that action is needed. When American families reclaim their kitchens back from corporate manufacturers, the reward will be a healthy society. First we need to learn how to cook meals that are tasty, appealing and nutritious; Christina is just the gal to show us what to do.

You will love this book; it is already a classic. The information and the recipes all reflect a joyous celebration of what it means to be healthy. Open the book, pull out the pots and have a wonderful time.

BILL TARA
Strathaven, Scotland

Introduction

TEN YEARS AGO, I sat down to write my first cookbook ... this cookbook. I thought it would be a snap. I had taught macrobiotic and healthy cooking for years and had literally hundreds of recipes roaming around in my head. I just had to put them on paper, right?

Anyone who has written a book can tell you it is the most cathartic experience you can have (next to childbirth) and the final product feels, in fact, like your "baby." I remember the release of this book back in 1997. I had not seen the finished product yet. I had wandered into a Borders bookstore on one of my frequent book-buying outings. I love books. As I walked into the store, I saw an end aisle display of cookbooks, with a large sign on top that read, *Local Author.* I went to check it out. What I saw stunned me ... it was an entire display of my book. I just stood there and stared. I must have been there a while, because the store manager came over, asking if he could help with something. When he realized it was me on the cover, smiling back at me, he smiled and said, "Take all the time you need. Cool, huh?" Cool did not even begin to describe the feelings. It was an excellent moment ... and when someone picked up a copy and bought it (and

it wasn't a family member), I was floored. I floated home.

I was about to begin my first season of *Christina Cooks,* set to air across the country on National Public Television and I had no idea what that would mean to my life. It has been, and continues to be, a wild ride. I have met wonderful people and have had some incredible experiences. I wouldn't change a thing.

Except maybe my thinking—a wise teacher told me that the only thing that never changes is that everything changes. How right he was, and still is. Ten years ago, I had a very different perception of what a macrobiotic lifestyle entailed. My perception has continually evolved and changed over the last ten years, bringing me to where I am now. Through my work, I have been privileged to see the many ways that food can alter lives, improve health and change communities. I have also seen new research and information and had experiences

1

that have caused me to change my views on some things. You will see those evolutionary changes in this edition of the book, from my use of oil (and what types) to my use of past forbidden ingredients, like potatoes, tomatoes, garlic and chocolate. Yes, you can enjoy these foods and still live a healthy life, but animal food, including fish … well, as Jon Stewart says, "not so much." You will no longer find fish in this book. I have lived a vegan lifestyle for nearly thirty years and I want this book to reflect my life—not some theory of macrobiotics, but macrobiotics as I live it.

The core values of what I believe a macrobiotic lifestyle to be have not changed so much, but rather, have become less theoretical and more practical. As my understanding of food increased, so did my comprehension of how to use its power. I believe, more than ever, that you are what you eat. I believe this little cliché is the simple truth. Food creates who we are, how we feel, how we act—and react.

I still believe that the kitchen is the true heart of the home. It is a place of transformation, where the food prepared creates the people who consume it. Cooks bring together ingredients, transform them into meals and create the energy that people take with them into the world. Food creates us and all that we are and will become day to day.

When I discovered macrobiotics, I was in a health crisis of mammoth proportions. I was twenty-six years old and had been diagnosed with an acute form of leukemia; I was what doctors call "terminally ill." At best, with all manner of experimental protocols, I was given six to nine months to live. I have to tell you, nothing gets your attention quite as quickly as five doctors telling you that your life is virtually over.

I will never forget the day I was diagnosed. It was a lovely spring day, sunny and fragrant with the blossoming flowers of the season. I was going to what I thought was a routine follow-up visit to a physical exam I had recently had—part of my new lease on life after the death of my mother. She had just passed away at the age of forty-nine, after a two-year struggle with colon cancer.

In retrospect, I should have seen this coming, seen the signs in my own health, but more important, I should have gauged the somber mood in the doctor's office as a portent of the bad news that was to come. But I was so filled with the spirit of the season that I blithely followed the receptionist to the conference room, fully expecting to be declared in relatively good health, although anemic, a condition that had plagued me since early childhood. I was, instead, diagnosed with terminal cancer. There is a kind of shock with a diagnosis like this that allows you to function for a while before the impact levels you.

I remember standing in the elevator, counting the floors of my descent, fighting back my panic by memorizing the pattern in the carpet, burgundy and grey fleur-de-lis. Passing through the lobby, I remember staring into a mirror and thinking that this was not the face of a dying person. I looked fine; okay, not fine, but dying? Stepping into the street, I was blinded by the sunlight and assaulted by the life that surrounded me: people going about their business as though nothing bad could happen in their lives. I wanted to scream. Instead, I returned home to my quiet apartment to examine my options.

After a sleepless night, I had reached at least one decision. I would not be returning to the doctors' offices—not on their terms, anyway. There had to be another way to approach this. I couldn't believe that my only options were devastating, experimental chemotherapies, followed by certain death.

The next day dawned clear and warm—another perfect spring day—almost mocking me, or rather, I know now, daring me. Walking to work, I decided to take the challenge. I would beat this disease, on my own, my way—no doctors, no chemical treatments. Just to get the diagnosis, I had been pushed, poked and injected in places I didn't even know I could be pushed, poked and injected. Once resolved, I realized that I was absolutely clueless as to where to start. Undaunted, I prayed for guidance and found it in the most surprising place.

Steve Feinberg was the quintessential advertising man. I was new to Philadelphia, and Steve had made it his personal business to see that my acclimation to my new home was enjoyable and easy. In a short time, we had become fast friends.

I told him about my illness and we sat in my cluttered art studio for what seemed like hours, not speaking. Finally, after the longest time, Steve looked up, a grin lighting up his face. Declaring himself the answer to my prayers, he told me about a friend of his who ate this strange diet—a macrobiotic diet—that could cure cancer. I remember thinking that as much as I loved my friend, he was nuts. Next thing I knew, I would be jetting off to Barcelona to have my blood boiled at a Jesuit monastery or some other insane, futile, pathetic attempt at saving my life. Steve met my resistance by phoning his friend and arranging for us to meet.

To say that I was leery of this meeting is an understatement. I stopped at a local natural foods store, asking what, in fact, macrobiotics was. The owner's cavalier reply was that the macrobiotic diet was some sort of fanatical approach to vegetarianism. Just great. I had been a vegetarian since I was about fourteen years old and had developed cancer, so what possible good would this diet do me? But Steve was so enthusiastic, I resolved not to disappoint him and decided to hear this fellow out. I truly had nothing to lose, after all.

My first meeting with Robert Pirello centered around the meal he had painstakingly prepared for me. His gentle manner put me instantly at ease and his confidence in the macrobiotic approach to health was infectious. My first macrobiotic meal consisted of simple miso soup with onions and daikon, a rice salad dotted with colorful blanched vegetables, arame (a sea vegetable) with sautéed carrots and onions, grilled tempeh with a light mustard sauce, corn on the cob (finally, something I recognized) and steamed collard greens. Finding the food interesting at best, I left Robert with mixed feelings about all this. He had given me *The Cancer Prevention Diet* by Michio Kushi to read, with only one request—that I read it with an open mind. No commitment, no decision. Just read.

So I did. I began with the section on leukemia, but then I read more and more and more—all night, in fact. The more I read, the more amazed I became. Finally, as the sun rose, I slammed the book shut, thinking that this was either the best-kept secret in the world, or the biggest hustle I had ever come across. I really hadn't decided which at that point.

My mind was made up the next day during lunch with Robert. While he assured me that he would help me along, with everything from the shopping to showing me a few cooking tricks, what sold me was his observation that my other options were extremely limited—namely that I had none. Laughing in spite of my predicament, I agreed to try out the macrobiotic approach to regaining my health.

And so I began my journey. Robert took me shopping at the neighborhood natural foods shop, loading my cart with foods I didn't recognize and whose names I could barely pronounce. And as much as I love a challenge, we were talking about my life here. How was I ever going to learn to prepare foods that were completely unfamiliar to me ... oh, and save my life in the process of relearning cooking? I had spent some years working as a pastry chef and caterer, but nothing I had learned in any kitchen had prepared me for this.

At first, I read everything I could get my hands on, and tried recipe after recipe, mostly failing miserably, preparing tasteless, burnt or undercooked meals. I grew quite disheartened and my health continued to decline. Robert constantly encouraged me and offered help, but I was determined to do this on my own. Then I read a book by George Ohsawa, the "father of macrobiotics," and discovered that the key to my health was in keeping things simple. So I consulted Robert, got a few quick cooking lessons from him and pared down my diet to include only the most basic, simple ingredients: whole grains, steamed greens, miso soup, small amounts of beans and sea vegetables and an occasional root vegetable dish to keep my strength up. I read cookbooks as if they were novels and began studying macrobiotics as though my life depended on it—which it did. I cooked and cooked and read and read. I mastered all the basics. Robert and I had endless discussions about what I was doing. He became my guide and my mentor. (We also fell completely in love, but that was later.) I began to see changes in my health: all positive—more vitality, more strength, incredible changes in my blood work, changes that prompted my doctors to say that I was in remission. Every blood test I took indicated incredible improvements in all of my counts: platelets, hemoglobin, white cells.

To make a long story short, after more than my fair share of ups and downs, I recovered my health completely, much to the shock and disbelief of my doctors. After a long, torturous fourteen months of cooking, improving my condition and struggling with the discharge of toxins that encompassed everything from severe nausea to blinding headaches to itchy rashes, my blood was declared perfectly normal, totally free of leukemic cells. I was cancer-free.

That was twenty-four years ago. My life was transformed in my kitchen. Since then, my path has taken me places that I could never have imagined. The things I have discovered, not only about my own health, but about life, the universe—it's as though layers of fog lift from my consciousness as I discover more and more, even now, after all these years.

But the greatest gift I have received from macrobiotics was the ability to become responsible for my own life and health ... a belief that was put to the life-and-death test once again in 1998, nearly fifteen years after my recovery from cancer. I had been teaching for several years, with the typical save-the-world passion of anyone given a second chance at life. I was working nonstop, losing sight of balance, and was exhausted. One bright April afternoon, I suffered a brainstem aneurysm, landing me in neuro-trauma intensive care for eight days. Test after test revealed that while I had suffered a rupture, the bleeding had stopped and the vein healed itself, leaving me with a pool of blood at the base of my brain and excruciating head pain. The brain surgeon told me that my condition was the result of a diet too low in fat and protein and vitamin B_{12}, which created elevated homocysteine levels, resulting in the hemorrhage. The good news was that it was also my diet that had saved my life. I just had to make some adjustments to get back on my feet, namely to add more fat and protein to what I ate. Once again, I had dodged the proverbial bullet.

And once again, I returned to the kitchen. Looking back to the beginning, as I struggled with my cooking, I struggled with my health. My health and cooking skills improved simultaneously. Later on, I discovered how to use what I had experienced and learned to regain my health once again. I seem to do my best learning when everything is at risk. I am an all-or-nothing woman, I suppose.

The key to good health is so simple that most people either miss it or don't believe it. We have complicated it so much. The single element in our lives over which we have the most control is the food we eat. The quality and quantity of the food we eat directly determines the kind of people we become. We create ourselves—our personalities, our outlook, how we act, interact and react to what life sends our way. Okay, I admit that there are other factors that contribute to who we are, but food creates a strong foundation upon which we can build. We begin to create the life we live in our kitchen.

There is more to food than food itself. There is the cook—the person who transforms ingredients into the food we eat, transforms us into the people we become. Think about it. We combine fresh, tender lettuce with crisp cucumbers and peppery radishes to create refreshing salads to cool our bodies in the summer months. Hearty winter stews give us vitality and warming strength to face the chilling temperatures of winter. Food and the way we prepare it, the wholeheartedness of spirit that we bring to each meal is what nurtures us through our lives.

When I began my cooking, I was taught mostly by my family, some of the most masterful, intuitive Italian home chefs with whom I have ever worked. There wasn't a cook in my family who could not give ingredient amounts or cooking times. They never tasted as they cooked. All my questions were met with the same response: "Listen to the food—cook with your eyes and ears and nose, not just your stomach."

"How can you tell when something is done?" I would ask my mother. "Why do you think we have forks?" was her response. My mother taught me commonsense cooking: if a sauce cooks down too much, add liquid; if an ingredient for a recipe is missing, substitute something else of a similar quality. She taught me to taste ingredients in their raw state so I would know what they would be like in a dish.

Today, people have moved away from cooking because we have made it so complicated. We have become so locked into cookbooks and recipes and styles and celebrity chefs (we're like rock stars now!) that understanding and spontaneity have been lost. It's no wonder that cooking, menu planning or dinner parties turn people into nervous wrecks, trying to orchestrate meals and praying that dishes turn out right. Just develop a basic understanding of food and how ingredients work together, and cooking becomes an act of pure joy. It becomes an art, a way that you creatively express your love for those who will enjoy your meals.

All it really takes to make cooking an exhilarating experience is an understanding of food and its energy and a mastery of a few basic cooking techniques. Becoming a student of life and listening to your intuition teaches you to create food that always turns out right— more often than not better than when you follow someone else's idea. Understanding food as energy, along with grasping some basic cooking techniques, will open up a whole new culinary world. You will find that most really great whole foods cooking comes from stretching the imagination and developing a personal style of working with the most humble ingredients. You will stop thinking about recipes and begin thinking in terms of ingredient and flavor combinations.

This is the beginning of freedom in the kitchen—and the end of cooking as a chore. Following simple techniques, using the freshest ingredients, following your taste and intuition, cooking with simplicity and common sense—these are the chief characteristics of whole foods cuisine that make life in the kitchen a joy.

I fell in love with cooking at the age of four. I remember my birthday present that year was a stool that my dad made so that I could reach the countertops to work with my mother in the kitchen. As I grew up, I discovered that I loved everything about the art of nourishing, from shopping for ingredients to preparing the food and even cleaning up—a time I used to reflect on the meal I had just served.

To this day, I love every aspect of cooking. As an artist, I find it one of the most creative outlets I know. But the real reward of cooking is that while most artistic skills require years of practice and study, cooking yields rewards immediately. And the more you cook, the greater your skills and the deeper your understanding of the energy of what you are creating.

In one corner of my kitchen, I have a floor-to-ceiling bookcase holding my prized collection of international cookbooks and magazines; everything from simple macrobiotic books to the epitome of gourmet cuisine from the greatest chefs in the world. I keep my books close at hand, because, while my own diet and understanding of food has changed dramatically, my cookbooks still serve me as constant sources of inspiration. Since learning that food is energy, that food creates who we are and how we act, these books have become more valuable to me than ever. I have learned to see recipes with new eyes, adapting and changing ingredients to create the energy I desire.

This cookbook is designed to help you understand what I have been rambling on about—understanding that the energy of food unlocks an entire world of culinary adventure. It makes cooking a natural extension of your life, not a burden to be dealt with as quickly and painlessly as possible, or worse yet, something to let someone else handle for you. I would never want to give anyone that much power over my destiny. I love being responsible for each day, each adventure, each challenge or difficulty.

Filled with delicious recipes and ideas for creating wonderful, healthy meals, this book hopefully will make you think about what you are feeding yourself and your family. I offer you what I have discovered on my journey and hope that this volume encourages you to make your own discoveries as you make your own journey. Remember that there is more to cooking than meets the eye.

Oh, one more thing: My family used to say that the best food you could ever eat is the food you prepare in your own home. So when you prepare food, see with more than your eyes, hear with more than your ears and taste with more than your appetite. Cook with respect and gratitude for all the abundance that our Mother has provided. Keep a peaceful, harmonious mind and cook wholeheartedly. To cook is to live. Enjoy all of it.

What Is Macrobiotics?

MACROBIOTICS. **WHERE DO** I begin to define this beleaguered term? Many people refer to it as whole foods cuisine, which is correct, but then again, there are a lot of approaches to whole foods that are not what we refer to as macrobiotics. Raw cuisine is whole foods based and while raw foods play a role in macrobiotics, it is not what the philosophy is about. Many vegetarian and vegan approaches are whole foods based, but are not macrobiotic, either. And yet, all types of food and eating, when done with consciousness and attention, are macrobiotic. Confused yet?

Over the years, I have been asked to define macrobiotics more times than I can count. Let me start by telling you what it is not. Macrobiotics carries with it a lot of baggage; a lot of misconceptions and myths surround its practice. Is it a religion or a cult? While it has Asian influences, it is not, in fact, Asian. It is not a deprived, nutritionally deficient diet practiced by old hippies (although some of the best teachers of the philosophy discovered it during the consciousness-altered 1960s). It is not a rice and seaweed diet, although we do eat those foods sometimes. It is not complicated to practice, clouded with exotic ingredients, bound up by all manner of esoteric rules with little flexibility. Some of the people who say that they practice macrobiotics may well give that impression, but that is their perception, not

mine . . . and certainly not the truth, at least not as I perceive it.

In truth, macrobiotics is a lifestyle that hearkens back to a more traditional and natural way of living and eating. No matter what culture, Italian, Polish, Irish, Jewish, Greek, Asian, each one is steeped in traditions that are based on a connection with nature, with the environment in which we live.

Macrobiotics is, simply stated, eating and living naturally, choosing whole, seasonal foods that are prepared in ways that are appropriate to your health and lifestyle. Period. Beside that, there is a deep philosophy about living in harmony with nature and people around you that makes macrobiotics so fundmental. Macrobiotics brings with its philosophy an understanding that food is energy, that everything we eat becomes part of us and helps create who we become. An understanding of food as energy makes it easy to create delicious, healthful meals. An understanding of food frees us from any rules or philosophic dogma because there is no more mystery. The macrobiotic approach to cooking is joyous and free of restrictions that make cooking a chore. But if you choose to not understand, then macrobiotics can seem mystical and intimidating, with dime-store philosophers asking you to believe all manner of esoteric myth as truth.

Macrobiotics is about freedom. There are no rigid techniques and rules that make cooking and the resulting cuisine more like an institution in some cultures. Macrobiotics is about intuition, about listening to that little voice inside you that tells you the truth. You know the voice, the one that society has trained us to ignore; the one that, when ignored, leads invariably to regret. With understanding, that voice is the only guide, guru, mentor or teacher that we will ever need.

Ingredients are at the core of good natural cooking. My theory is that cooking begins with the shopping. The freshness and quality of your ingredients are just as important as your cooking technique. The final outcome of the dish depends on that fact. Shopping itself should be a pleasure. I remember shopping with my mother. She never shopped with a list. Availability, the season and freshness of foods dictated our menus for each meal. She and I would go to the market, see what looked best and plan our family meals around these foods.

THE BASICS

THERE ARE FOODS, recipes and techniques that compose the basic understanding of food energy. Whenever I teach a beginning cooking class, I liken the basics to learning the art of pottery making. Before you can become truly creative at this, or at any other art or craft, you need to master some basic techniques, understand concepts and learn to work with new ingredients. If you never learn how to center a pile of clay on the potter's wheel, you can never truly branch off into wild, creative outpourings of your talents. The same goes for cooking, macrobiotic or otherwise. With a selection of simple, natural ingredients, delicious, nutritionally balanced meals can be created. The cook determines the impact of various dishes, creating the energy that will nourish the household. Strong cooking, with more salt, fire, time and pressure will concentrate the effects of foods, while lighter, fresher foods will produce a more relaxed, gentle energy quality in foods. A masterful, intuitive cook will manage these energies according to the needs and desires of those he or she cooks for.

It begins with the weather. Huh? Seasonal cooking is as basic to healthy cooking as any organic ingredient you may use. In a temperate climate (the typical four-season weather with which we are most familiar), conditions vary from cool to cold, from warm to hot. As a result, our cooking needs to change as frequently as the seasons. Spring and summer cooking, as you might guess, is lighter and fresher, taking greater advantage of the seasons' abundance of fruits and vegetables. There seems to be no end to fresh salads, dressings and quick-cooked dishes to accommodate our tastes and give us plenty of time to enjoy the outdoors. Autumn and winter focus more on heartier soups, stews and casseroles; longer-cooked grain and bean dishes, drawing from the harder, stronger root vegetables, sweet winter squash, whole beans and grains. While spring and summer take us out of the kitchen and into the garden, picking freshly grown produce and cooking it as little as possible, autumn and winter bring us back to the hearth, stewing, simmering and baking hearty, warming dishes to shield us from the harsh cold outdoors.

Now all of that is just great, if you live in one of the heavily populated temperate climates of our world. But what if you choose the world of suntans and sandals—life in a tropical region? Well, if that is the case, then you would adjust your cooking accordingly. You would focus more consistently on lighter, fresher foods, but you would also need to employ enough strong, cooked foods to keep you hale and hearty. You would choose from the foods indigenous to your home and culture. You would work with what is native to your environment.

Sound complicated? Truly, it's not. It is simply a matter of understanding that food is energy and that the energy of food creates the energy that fuels us in our lives. And if that is still confusing, simply abandon your supermarket shopping for a few weeks and shop for your food at a local farm market. Seeing what grows locally as the seasons evolve will set your feet on the path to seasonal cooking.

A healthy whole foods diet is centered around the use of whole cereal grains, fresh, seasonal vegetables, beans and bean products, sea vegetables, fresh fruits, nuts, seeds and soups.

A balanced diet, macrobiotic or otherwise needs to consist of about 50 percent whole cereal grains, 30 percent fresh vegetables (choosing from leafy greens, root and round, ground vegetables, with variety as the key ingredient), 5 percent soups and sea vegetables, 15 percent beans, bean products or other sources of protein. Any other foods, fresh fruits, nuts and seeds and fish (if desired) are generally taken as supplemental foods, in smaller amounts.

GETTING STARTED

I KNOW WHAT you're thinking: Easy for someone who has been cooking since she was four years old and she not only loves cooking, but she does it for a living. But what about those of us who can barely get a meal on the table after a day of work? She wants us to create new recipes when we can hardly get the shopping done from week to week. Well, relax. This section of the book is designed to help ease the burden of making the transition to a healthier, whole foods–based diet, from shopping to menu planning.

Shopping

Now some of you may be thinking that this could make shopping more difficult. Not true. Isn't shopping for clothing or books fun? We enjoy wandering through the shops, carefully choosing our purchases. When something looks or feels right, we know it. Simply think that way when shopping for food as well. This attitude toward food helps you to rediscover the freedom and pleasure of grocery shopping. Always remember that you are nourishing yourself. Don't you deserve the very best? Aren't we worth it?

My mother would talk to me while we did the family food shopping. Never buy food that comes prewrapped or precut, she would say. It's not fresh, so it will taste flat. She went from farmers market to farmers market, shopping only where she could touch, feel and smell the vegetables and fruits; where she knew the fish and meat was fresh. I tell you this not to reminisce, but to illustrate that shopping this way adds pleasure to thinking about and preparing your meals.

Natural cooking seems to be shrouded in mystery, reputed to employ strange, exotic ingredients cooked in bizarre ways, like stirring in a clockwise direction while standing on one foot under a full moon. Well, as much fun as that sounds, the fact is you can purchase most basic whole foods in your neighborhood supermarkets. You may need to supplement your weekly shopping with occasional trips to a natural foods store, but for the most part, you'll be able to find all that you'll need in your local market.

In larger supermarkets and gourmet stores, you'll find a wide variety of whole grains and grain products, like brown rice, barley, oats, polished rice, corn grits, cornmeal, whole wheat pastas and whole grain flours. Even buckwheat (kasha), couscous and bulgur wheat can be found in gourmet sections of markets. Dried beans abound in supermarkets, everything from lentils, to chickpeas, to black and white beans, to split peas and kidney beans, even tofu. And while these foods may not always be organic, they will nourish you and yours quite nicely.

You also don't need to go on a quest to purchase good-quality oils and condiments. Most supermarkets carry extra-virgin olive oil and other cold-pressed, unrefined oils. Nuts and seeds are readily available. You can even find some good-quality mustards, pickles, spices and herbs. Just read labels and try to avoid foods with preservatives or any chemical ingredient that you can't pronounce!

In terms of seasonings, my advice is to make that trip to the nearest natural foods store. You always want to use the best-quality seasonings, especially salt and salt products like miso and soy sauce. For your salt, you will want to choose a white, slightly moist, unrefined sea salt over any commercial brand. Why? Sea salt is simply dried from the sea, with all its nutrients intact,

while commercial brands have been chemically processed, often laced with sugar to ensure pourability and reenriched with minerals that were stripped away during processing. Soy sauce is a naturally fermented soybean-and-salt condiment. Commercial brands have been artificially fermented, colored and processed, making it quite difficult to digest and assimilate the salt. Natural soy sauces, on the other hand, have been traditionally fermented, ensuring that the salt and soybeans have been completely broken down for better digestion and superior taste. Miso can only be purchased in natural foods stores or Asian markets. I prefer the brands found in natural foods stores, because more often than not, the brands found in Asian markets have been processed with sugar, which I do not want.

The fresh produce sections of most supermarkets are like Disneyland now. The demand for fresh fruits and vegetables has turned this department into the darling of the supermarket. Here, you will find all you need to create delicious meals; most supermarkets even do an admirable job with organic and locally grown produce. Skip most of the packaged products (seriously, salad in a bag? When did we get too busy to buy a head of lettuce, rinse it under water and hand-shred it?). Go for the freshest-looking fruits and veggies you see, organic wherever possible. Organic grains, beans and produce not only taste better (really!), but they retain far more of their vital life force than other foods, more of their vitamin C and minerals than commercial fruits and veggies and so are superior to standard fare. Choosing certified organic products is a way in which you can also avoid eating foods laced with pesticides and fungicides. We have enough pollution to deal with; we don't need it in our food. And don't even think that you can't afford organic fruits and veggies. The demand has grown so much that prices have fallen very close to commercial brands.

That said, becoming familiar with your neighborhood natural foods store has its advantages as you become familiar with a new, more natural way of life. There is a whole community of people to consult for help, support and all manner of information. Many natural foods stores sponsor cooking classes and product demonstrations and provide recipe handouts to familiarize people with products. And the quality of food available in natural foods stores is usually superior to that of anything available in regular supermarkets. But I confess, I shop in both kinds of stores, as well as farm markets, to find what I want to eat.

If you choose to dive into healthy cooking (and I hope you do), you'll need to stock your refrigerator with a variety of fresh fruits and vegetables, of course. But you'll also need a few other staples in your pantry to get started. Short-grain brown rice, barley, millet, quinoa, corn grits and oats are grains that you'll want on hand at all times. A variety of dried beans, including lentils, chickpeas, cannellini, split peas, azukis and black beans will give you a good start. Finally, stock your cupboards with good-quality soy sauce, extra-virgin olive oil, cold-pressed sesame and avocado oil, sea salt and some good-quality herbs and spices, like basil, dried chiles and rosemary. Barley or brown-rice miso, umeboshi vinegar, brown-rice, red wine and balsamic vinegars should round out your pantry nicely. With these basics you can walk into the kitchen at any time and create a simple yet delicious meal in no time. I told you the transition would be painless. A well-stocked pantry allows you to grocery shop without a plan, to buy what looks freshest, to purchase on instinct—with your appetite—and plan your meals accordingly.

Equipping Your Kitchen

Any kitchen, from compact, efficient ones with barely enough room for a cutting board, to gadget-laden, spacious culinary heavens, pours forth nourishment based on the cook who works in it. The kitchen is where food is literally transformed. The warmth and love that exist in these four walls make us who we are. All it takes for any kitchen to be productive is organization and order.

Whether a novice in the kitchen or a seasoned chef, you will need a bit of reorganization to make a smooth transition to healthier cooking. First, clean the kitchen thoroughly. This kind of ritual will help you create a new atmosphere of respect for yourself and the food you will be preparing. And besides, there is nothing better to work in than a clean, orderly, pleasant environment. I personally find cooking to be much more relaxing when everything is in its place.

Create a space in which to organize your ingredients. Empty a cabinet or pantry section to accommodate your dried foods. Try to create a place where your foods can be organized together, making your job easier. Store dried foods such as grains and beans in glass jars with good seals to maintain their freshness. As much as possible, keep your ingredients close at hand, in one place, so that looking for ingredients while cooking doesn't cause you stress. I have found it easiest to keep like ingredients together—all the grains on one shelf in the pantry, beans in their own section, condiments and oils all together—so that everything is easy to locate.

Lucky for us, whole foods cooking requires very few fancy appliances. The best cookware is stainless steel, cast iron, stoneware or porcelain-covered cast iron. Aluminum and nonstick cookware are not your best choices, in my opinion, since there are conflicting studies about their safety. Some of the basic tools you will need to cook easily and well include a great vegetable-cutting knife—your most important tool (stainless steel, carbon steel or my favorite, ceramic)—a sharpening steel or stone, a large wooden cutting board (not a cheese board, a real cutting board), a vegetable brush for scrubbing, a colander and a strainer. Pots that you will find indispensable include a large soup pot, a pressure cooker (like the stainless-steel models from Kuhn Rikon . . . they are like the great sex of pots and pans) for grains, a heavy pot for bean cooking, a couple of flame deflectors, a large and small skillet—either stainless or cast iron, preferably one of each—a couple of medium and small saucepans. Rounding out your basic equipment list are wooden spoons of various shapes and sizes (like my gorgeous spoons from Jonathan's Spoons), spatulas, whisks, a vegetable peeler, a ginger grater, a steamer basket, a wok, mixing bowls, measuring cups, a food processor, a food mill and any other kitchen gadget that makes you feel comfortable.

PUTTING IT ALL TOGETHER

A BIT OF foresight can take away the anxiety that oftentimes surrounds meals and meal planning, especially when you are new to a style of cooking. Let me walk you through a typical day in my kitchen to show you, from my perspective, how thinking ahead just a bit can make cooking a part of day-to-day life.

A lot has changed for us since *Christina Cooks* began eight years ago, but much remains the same. Our day still begins early, around 7:00 a.m. Robert is up early and loves making breakfast (I do not. I like eating it!). In our office, my staff eats together for both breakfast

and lunch. So Robert is in heaven, cooking up a storm. A typical breakfast is usually a simple meal of a soft, cooked porridgelike grain, with or without vegetables, with lightly stewed vegetables as a side dish. On occasional mornings, there will be scrambled tofu, English muffins, pancakes, but always, always a side dish of lightly cooked vegetables. Once the meal is cooking, Robert jumps in the shower and gets ready for the day, while I put the finishing touches on breakfast and plan lunch for the staff—sometimes leftovers from dinner the night before can be turned into a soup or stew. Veggie burgers or hummus sandwiches, tempeh or tofu salad will be the main course and then a simple, freshly cooked vegetable dish or salad rounds out the meal.

After breakfast, the day begins with both Robert and I going nonstop. After a full day, it is off to the gym for an hour or more with my trainer and then home to get dinner on the table.

I arrive home well before my husband, around 6:30 p.m. Before I even think about cooking for us (remember, I spend my days cooking, and have just been at the gym), I take a quick shower to help wash away the day and calm my nerves so that I can cook with a clear mind and relaxed heart. The last thing I want to do is incorporate any stress from my day into our evening meal, the time of day we unwind and relax together.

The average dinner in our home consists of a simple soup of fresh vegetables, sometimes with beans and grains, sometimes not. Our main meal will include a whole grain dish of some type: brown rice, millet with vegetables, barley stew, corn polenta with a simple sauce or whole grain pasta with a sauce or vegetables. Since we both work out so hard, there is always protein in our evening meal, in the form of tofu, tempeh, beans or a bean soup (and for

Robert, often some fish). I round out the meal with a simple vegetable dish, either a root vegetable stew, fresh steamed greens, oven-roasted winter squash and onions, perhaps a sautéed sea vegetable and a fresh salad, regardless of the season. I vary the vegetables with the weather, but we find that the fresh, crisp flavor of a salad helps us feel more relaxed and fresh.

Variety is most important to me. It is the key to vitality. However, I don't have the time to cook seven or eight dishes each time I prepare dinner. While I might only prepare soup, grain and one or two other dishes, they always incorporate different ingredients and different cooking styles to ensure that we eat a wide variety of foods and get adequate nutrients as a result. This way, it doesn't matter how simple the meal is; I can rest easy knowing we get variety and proper nutrition for our lifestyle.

Preparing an average dinner in my home usually takes forty-five minutes to an hour, time well spent in my opinion. When we are properly nourished with freshly cooked, good-quality food, we become much more adept at handling all the adventures life throws at us. So when planning menus, I combine an array of ingredients in simple dishes to make sure that we get what we need to stay healthy and strong, choosing from all that nature has provided . . . whole grain; beans, tofu or tempeh; and a variety of seasonal vegetables, drawing from leafy greens, root veggies and sweet ground vegetables and fresh salad ingredients.

Leftovers and cooking ahead play a small, but important part in my cooking. I prefer to cook food fresh as much as possible, but I do not discount the value of having a container of cooked chickpeas, lentils or other beans to use as a base to create another dish. And bean soups always seem to taste better the next day. Leftover grains can easily be resteamed or cooked with fresh vegetables to create a quick, simple stew or stir-fry. And I never underestimate the benefit of tofu and tempeh as bases for quick protein dishes. Dinner can come together in a matter of minutes with some leftovers as your starting point.

THE BEGINNING

MY BEST ADVICE to novice whole foods chefs is this: Master a few basic techniques and recipes, and cook these until you are comfortable. Keep your meals simple and delicious. One or two truly satisfying dishes will go a long way toward making a smooth transition to healthier foods. After you have mastered a few techniques and have become familiar with your ingredients, let your imagination and intuition be your teacher. Relax and create.

I know what you are thinking. All this sounds great, but how exactly do you go about planning a menu? What makes a balanced meal, now that animal protein is not the featured entrée?

Dinner is always the greatest challenge for cooks—and the easiest trap to fall into, especially now, living in the age of fast-food and take-away meals. However, I also realize that it is difficult to face the task of preparing a meal from scratch every day, which is where planning comes in. Simply starting grains or beans in the morning or the evening before can simplify the act of getting dinner on the table in less than an hour, without becoming a nervous wreck.

I'm trained as a chef, so for me, timing is everything. One of my most valued skills is knowing what cooking times are required for what foods, so that my meal comes together, all dishes being ready at the same time, more or less. So, obviously, long-cooking dishes, like grains and beans start cooking first, with the lighter, fresher dishes being cooked as meal preparation progresses. I know that only seems like common sense—and it is—but it is one of those over-looked facts that people often forget . . . until it is too late and their meal prep is in chaos.

I know I said that leftovers play only a small part in my cooking, but I should clarify that a bit. When I cook a meal from scratch, some-times, there is something leftover. I use those foods to create other dishes in subsequent meals. Very often, leftover cooked beans get refried and wrapped in tortillas or stewed veg-etables serve as the base for a hearty soup. The most important thing to remember about left-overs is to add some fresh ingredient. Do some-thing with the food; don't just take leftovers from the refrigerator and eat them. Add some life to them by creating a fresh dish with the leftover foods as the base. By themselves, left-overs lack vitality and can make you tired. My own experience has shown me that when I eat a lot of leftovers, I tend to eat more. I am crav-ing the freshness that comes with cooking from scratch. Adding fresh ingredients infuses leftover food with new vitality and flavor.

Many people who work long hours have told me that their saving grace is carving out a block of time, usually on weekends, to cook a variety of food in batches—pickles, condi-ments, a big pot of beans or soup. Then on sub-sequent nights, these cooked foods become everything from croquettes to burgers, stews to stir-fry dishes. Filling in the gaps with quick-cooking foods like couscous, bulgur, tofu, and tempeh, nicely balanced with lightly cooked fresh vegetables, goes a long way to helping you put a balanced meal on the table without a lot of fuss. Don't forget the value of noodles: Many is the night that I have put a hearty meal on the table in about half an hour with noodles as the base, rounded out with fresh vegetable dishes and crusty bread.

Another tip I'd like to pass along, not only to beginning chefs but to anyone who loves to cook, is that food doesn't have to be compli-cated to be delicious. The taste comes with the skill of the cook. All fresh, natural foods have a character of their own just waiting to be brought forth in any variety of dishes. By keep-ing recipes simple, with not too many ingre-dients, your success is virtually ensured. Traditional grain and bean combinations, for instance, serve as inspiration for many con-temporary dishes. Can you think of a more sat-isfying dinner than red bean and vegetable chili served over moist corn bread or rice with freshly cooked vegetables and a light soup? Delicious foods need not be spice-laden, cooked to death or smothered in heavy, com-plicated sauces to be truly delicious. My mother used to say that all you needed to make a great meal was fresh food, lovely olive oil, garlic, lemon juice and sea salt. She said that complicated sauces and techniques were designed to disguise inferior ingredients. After all my years of cooking, I have to say . . . she was right . . . at least about that one!

Of course, I encourage you to be as creative as you wish. Combine foods as your taste dic-tates. Draw recipes from other parts of the world, and put them together to create an international meal. Don't be trapped by recipes or rigid plans. I never know how a final menu will turn out. I make a grocery list, but usually it consists of staple items that are running low in my pantry. The availability and freshness of various items will dictate what I will ultimately buy and cook. The sign of a confident cook is flexibility and the ability to adapt. Practice until you get this confidence. It is truly liber-ating, with delicious rewards for your efforts.

I have found that the best way to minimize cooking stress and to avoid obsessing about what to cook is to keep my pantry and refrig-erator well-stocked. At any given time, you should be able to walk in the door and pull together a meal in little time. Careful shopping once or twice a week really helps.

MENU PLANNING

How do you put a balanced meal together? Here are a few basic menu ideas you can use to create some simple natural meals on your own. These are designed to give you a place to begin building your own repertoire.

When preparing menus, keep in mind that the concentration should be on grain and vegetable carbohydrates and proteins from beans, bean products, fish (if you so desire) or nuts and fat. These macronutrient groups are equal in importance, but not necessarily proportion, in my meals. Prepare a wide variety of seasonal vegetables in different ways, employing long- and short-cooked dishes, with a fresh raw salad thrown in for variety and lighter energy, as your health and lifestyle allow.

When I began cooking, one of the most valuable habits I developed was jotting down my evening menus. The resulting diary not only helped me learn how to balance a meal— grains, beans, varieties of vegetables, soup—but created for me a collection of winning menu combinations that I return to when inspiration is in short supply in the kitchen or when I just want to refresh myself with some old tried-and-true ideas. It also helped me to keep track of what I was eating. It kept me "honest." When you are writing down what you are eating, you tend to be more conscious of what goes in your mouth. And when you are beginning a new way of eating, that can be important in helping you develop your discipline.

Finally, remember that whole, natural foods have innate, delicious flavors of their own. They need very little help to release their essences. So keep seasoning light and delicate to bring forth the true flavors of these foods. And then let them stand on their own in all their natural glory.

The following menu suggestions are all based on recipes that are included in this book. I hope they aid you on your journey toward a healthier way of eating.

Breakfast

Breakfast is literally breaking our overnight fast. Foods eaten for breakfast, as a result, need to help you balance your day. When we wake up, our blood sugar is a little low and we need a gentle nudge to get going, with foods that are easy to digest, not heavy foods that require a lot of work to assimilate. Whole-grain cereals, prepared as soft, creamy porridge are one of the healthiest ways to start the day. Breakfast in our house rarely includes heavy, baked flour products like bagels, muffins, or French toast and pancakes. These foods are hard and dry, make the body work very hard, and can leave us feeling very tired and short on vitality as the day wears on. But they occasionally make a nice treat.

With a little advance planning, a healthy breakfast can be ready in the time it takes you to get ready. By simply rinsing and soaking grain overnight—or in cold weather, cooking grain all night over low heat—breakfast porridge can be ready in roughly thirty minutes or less. Oatmeal, corn grits, millet, quinoa, amaranth, kasha or cracked wheat can be cooked into creamy, nutritious breakfast foods in about twenty-five minutes. Served with lightly cooked vegetables and on rare occasions, cooked fruit, like applesauce, breakfast is an easy task.

On those mornings when we have a bit more time, we like to cook whole grain cereals for a longer period of time to release a more vitalizing energy. Add five parts water to one part oats, barley, rice or any combination of whole grains and cook for about one hour to create a hearty grain porridge. These are the mornings that I might supplement this kind of dish with scrambled tofu and vegetables and a lightly cooked vegetable dish. And weekends? Those are the lazy, late-breakfast mornings for waffles or whole wheat pancakes with a sweet, fruity sauce.

Of course, there are those inevitable mornings when there is no time for anything—or maybe just a few minutes to pull together an almost-instant breakfast. On those occasions, I might make a quick dish of noodles simmered in a miso broth with vegetables or a quick porridge with leftover cooked grain with some vegetables or a whole grain English muffin or toast. Bottom line? If you have ten or fifteen minutes, you can have breakfast that doesn't have to be a dry bagel or sugary cinnamon bun on the run.

You may have noticed by this point, that fruit plays a very small part in my breakfast meals. Fruit contains a great deal of liquid and simple sugars. In general, I have found that these foods are best consumed in small amounts at breakfast. The simple sugars present in fruits wreak havoc with our blood sugar (which is low in the morning anyhow and needs stabilizing), creating mood swings and perpetuating hypoglycemia. Lots of fruit and fruit juice in the morning set you up for a roller-coaster ride of emotional and energetic ups and downs for the day.

Lunch

Usually a light and simple meal, lunch is easy. You can put together a really satisfying noontime feast from foods you prepared for dinner the evening before. These are the meals most preferred by my husband. A distance runner, he loves to sit down at lunchtime to a full meal composed of a whole grain dish, lots of fresh vegetables and a bean dish of some kind to support all of his training.

Now that my staff has grown and we are all in the office together, I prepare a "family" lunch for all of us when I am not traveling or working outside the office. A bowl of home-made soup and a sandwich can be most satisfying. Some of the office favorites include sandwiches packed with fried tofu or tempeh, smothered with sautéed onions, lettuce, sprouts and spicy mustard, coupled with corn chowder, lentil soup or mushroom-barley soup. Some days find us sitting down to a simple lunch of hearty white bean soup with a lightly cooked salad of fresh broccoli, cauliflower, carrots and leafy green vegetables. Other days find me fixing simple lunches of chickpea hummus with crisp vegetable sticks or toasted pita bread triangles. Whole grain noodles, simmered in a delicate miso broth laden with vegetables or served in a luscious tomato sauce make a lunch to satisfy the heartiest of appetites.

Dinner

Dinner presents a bit more of a challenge than other meals of the day. The family is coming home from a busy day—and they are hungry. It is up to the cook to create meals that nourish and satisfy. But it's not as difficult a task as you would think. Here are sample menus, typical of my own household. Pick and choose from these meals to create your own winning combinations.

Pay attention to the way that foods reappear in various dishes on different nights, using up leftover foods to create fresh meals. Note that soups and vegetable dishes are fresh just about every day. That's an effort worth making. The vitality and energy in these foods when cooked fresh are invaluable.

Cook for yourself and your family. Drive right past the drive-thru window if you want to live a life of health and vitality.

A WEEK OF DINNER MENUS

SUNDAY

Creamy Squash Bisque (page 76)
Pressure-cooked brown rice with millet
Black bean feijoada
Stewed root vegetables with kombu
Blanched watercress and Chinese cabbage
Creamy orange custard

MONDAY

Miso vegetable soup with noodles
Brown Rice and Millet Croquettes (page 53)
Oven-baked squash and onions
Sea Palm Salad (page 262)
Steamed leafy greens
Lemony Daikon Pickle (page 171)

TUESDAY

Fresh Corn Chowder (page 84)
Boiled brown rice with barley
Refried black beans in corn tortillas
Braised vegetable stew
Brussels sprouts with chestnuts and onions
Boiled kale and carrot matchsticks
Glazed Apples (page 318)

WEDNESDAY

Lentil-vegetable soup
Millet with squash and corn
Dried Daikon with Vegetables (page 38)
Skillet-steamed broccoli
Whole red onions with rosemary

THURSDAY

Millet–Sweet Vegetable Soup (page 81)
Brown and Wild Rice Pilaf (page 48)
Grilled tofu with sweet ginger marinade
Arame Sauté (page 199)
Sweet-and-Sour Cabbage with Tart Apples
  (page 180)
Steamed leafy greens
Italian Biscotti (page 309)

FRIDAY

Italian Minestrone (page 87)
Basil pesto noodles
Sautéed broccoli rapini with yellow summer
  squash

SATURDAY

Miso vegetable soup
Pressure-cooked brown rice with dried sweet
  corn
Nishime-Style Vegetables (page 37)
Tempeh Stroganoff (page 135)
Elegant Boiled Salad (page 248) with bal-
  samic vinaigrette
Cran-Apple Crumb Tart (page 319)

MENU TIPS

CREATING VARIETY IN daily cooking by employing a variety of ingredients is not as hard to handle as it may seem. We are all busy. We don't live in a perfect world where we can spend countless hours in the kitchen creating fresh, delicious meals from scratch. Here are a few tips that I employ on a daily basis in my own kitchen.

I usually make one soup each day and use it for two meals, with a fresh bit of something added to change it and liven it for the second meal—like another vegetable, an herb, a change in garnish.

Leftover, lightly cooked green vegetables can be tossed with pickles or fresh salad veggies and vinegar to create a light salad of sorts. Stewed or baked vegetables most often find their way into a hearty soup or stew, or can be pureed and seasoned to create a rich sauce for another dish.

Cooked grains are easily incorporated into other dishes, simply resteamed with fresh condiments, stir-fried with vegetables, cooked in a rich stock with root vegetables to create a hearty stew or made into croquettes, nori rolls, grain salads or even grain-and-vegetable burgers.

Pasta is easy. One meal serves up noodles with a rich vegetable sauce or gravy and the leftover, undressed pasta is served smothered in a delicate, vegetable-laden broth, making a fabulous one-dish meal. Leftover beans are used in soups, stews, stir-fries; pureed into flavorful pâtés and dips; and combined with veggies and a sauce to make delicious casseroles.

What I am really trying to say here is that you can create a whole range of dishes with leftovers, when you need to. I must say again that I still advocate fresh cooking wherever and whenever possible, but leftovers can be a valuable tool when used properly. Just take care that the majority of your diet isn't comprised of leftover food. Nothing replaces the vitality of fresh foods, and leftovers are only meant to supplement fresh cooking. Face it, there is no escape from cooking if you wish to achieve optimum health. But by adding fresh ingredients here and there to leftover foods, you can create different energies to nourish yourself and your loved ones.

HOW MUCH DO I COOK?

THIS GUIDE WILL provide you with a base to work from. These guidelines indicate how many people, on average, certain amounts of foods will feed. While these may vary slightly based on people's activity level and appetite, I have found the quantities to be sound in determining the quantities I need to prepare to sufficiently nourish those I cook for.

FOOD	AMOUNT	NUMBER OF PEOPLE
Whole grains	1 cup uncooked	3 or 4
Noodles	8 ounces	2
Morning porridge	1 cup grain cooked in 5 cups water	3 or 4
Soup	1 cup	1
Whole beans	1 cup	4
Tofu	1 pound	4
Tempeh	8 ounces	3 or 4
Lightly cooked leafy green vegetables	1 cup, raw	1
Stewed root vegetables	2 cups raw = 1½ cups cooked	2
Pressed salads	3 cups raw = 1½ cups pressed	2 or 3
Sea vegetables	½ cup, dried	2 or 3
Garnishes	½ to 1 teaspoon	As desired
Raw salad	2 cups mixed ingredients	1

Glossary

I CAN PRACTICALLY hear your sigh of relief when you found this section. Some of the natural ingredients I use may sound mysterious and exotic, but don't panic. While they may be new to you, it may be comforting to remember that most of the strange ingredients used in my recipes are, in fact, very traditional foods that have been used in various cultures for many, many years. Draw from these cultures to develop your own style in your healthy kitchen.

Become familiar with the more exotic foods you find in these pages. The more you cook, the more fun you will have experimenting with different foods and flavors. Preparing natural foods can be a wonderful culinary adventure. This section can help you to understand what ingredients you are buying and how to use them to create delicious, healthy meals.

Agar-agar Also called "kanten" in Asian shops, agar is a gelatinlike food made from various types of red algae. The algae fronds are harvested, dried and boiled in iron kettles. The resulting liquid is allowed to set and is then placed in the sun to dry and bleach. This process takes about ten days. After drying, the flaky gelatin is packaged, pressed in bars.

Agar flakes are made from another type of sea vegetable. A more modern product, agar flakes are easier to process and use, with more concentrated bonding properties.

Almonds Fruit kernels of the almond tree. They keep best when purchased in their thin brown skins, which protect their freshness and flavor. Also available in their skinned, blanched form; slivered; minced and ground into a flour for convenience of use. High in antioxidants and good-quality fats for health.

Amaranth A very tiny, brownish-yellow seed, high in protein and lysine. Cooked as a whole cereal grain, it has an earthy, nutty flavor and cooks quite quickly.

Amasake A fermented sweet rice drink with the texture of milk. It is a creamy base for custards, puddings and frostings, not to mention a wonderfully satisfying drink and good source of complex carbohydrates on its own.

Anasazi beans A native American burgundy-and-white bean, similar in taste and texture to pinto beans. Their slightly sweet taste makes them ideal in Mexican-style bean dishes.

Arame A large-leaf sea vegetable, arame is finely shredded and boiled before drying and packaging for selling. Since it is precooked, it requires far less cooking time than other sea vegetables and can even be marinated for salads with no cooking at all. One of the milder-tasting sea plants, it is a great source of protein and minerals like calcium and potassium.

Arrowroot A high-quality starch made from a tropical tuber of the same name, used for thickening much the same way as cornstarch is used. Arrowroot has virtually no taste and becomes clear when cooked, making it ideal as a thickener for puddings, gravies and sauces. Less expensive than kuzu, it can be used interchangeably in recipes.

Avocado oil A monounsaturated oil made from pressing whole avocados. Perfect for sautéing, frying, baking and other cooking. The mild flavor is perfect for just about any dish and its stability under heat makes it an essential cooking oil.

Azuki beans Azuki beans are small and very compact, with a deep, reddish-brown color. These tiny beans are a staple in the Far East. Originally cultivated in Japan and revered for their healing properties, they are quite low in fat and reputed to be more digestible than most other beans as well as rich sources of B vitamins (not B_{12}), potassium and iron.

Baking powder A leavening agent made up of baking soda, cream of tartar, and either cornstarch or arrowroot. Double-acting powder releases carbon dioxide on contact with liquid, creating the air pockets responsible for the light texture in baked goods. Always try to purchase non-aluminum baking powder so that sodium aluminum sulfate is not released into your foods, possibly compromising your health.

Baking powder is more perishable than you might think, not lasting much beyond the expiration date on the can. Store in a cool, dry place and purchase in small amounts for the best shelf life.

Balsamic vinegar Italian vinegar made from white Trebbiano grapes. The vinegar becomes a deep, rich amber color during aging in wooden barrels. The best balsamic vinegars are syrupy, a bit sweet, and a little more expensive than other vinegars, but well worth it. Natural balsamic vinegar is rich in live bacteria and enzymes that aid in digestion.

Bancha *See* Kukicha.

Barley Said to be the oldest cultivated grain, barley is native to Mesopotamia, where it was mainly used to make bread and ferment beer. Used by ancient cultures since the dawn of time, barley even served as currency in Sumeria. In Europe, barley has been replaced by wheat and rye but is still the staple grain of many countries in the Far and Middle East, Asia and South America. In modern cultures, barley serves to make everything from livestock feed to malted whisky to tea to miso. However, by itself, barley is a great, low-fat grain, chock-full of nutrients, and is reputed to aid the body in breaking down fat. Delicious when cooked with other whole grains and in soups and salads.

Barley malt A sweetener or grain honey made from sprouted barley that is cooked into a sweet syrup. The barley is simply steeped in water and germinated. The sprouted or malted barley is then heated to bring out the flavor and cooked until a thick syrup forms. The syrup contains dextrin, maltose, various minerals and protein. It adds wonderful depth to baked beans, roasted squash and savory baked goods.

Beans *See* individual listings.

Black-eyed peas Medium-size beans with an oblong shape, which have a distinctive black spot on their ivory surface. In the same family as yard-long beans, the pods can grow three feet in length. Native to Africa, black-eyed peas were brought to Europe and North America where they became a staple in cooking, being paired with collard greens and corn bread for a most delicious supper.

Black soybeans Rounder and more plump than black turtle beans, black soybeans are renowned in Asia for their restorative effects on the reproductive organs. Incredibly sweet and rich, but requiring roasting and long cooking time, these beans are well worth the extra effort for all the benefits of soy.

Black turtle beans A sturdy, very satisfying common bean. Earthy and mildly sweet, these beans go well with stronger, spicier seasonings, like those commonly used in Brazilian, Caribbean and Mexican dishes, and make great, creamy soups and spicy dips.

Bran A fiber-rich layer just beneath the hull of whole grains that protects the endosperm or germ. Bran is a good source of calcium, carbohydrates and phosphorous and is the main reason for eating grains in their whole form.

Brown rice vinegar A vinegar traditionally made by the agricultural communities of Japan, it is composed of brown rice, cultured rice (*koji*), seed vinegar from the previous year and well water. The vinegar is then fermented for nine to ten months. Brown rice vinegar has a sharp taste and is used for everything from salad dressings to preserving vegetables. It is also commonly used in sushi rice for flavor and for its preservative properties.

Buckwheat (Kasha) Also known as Saracen corn, buckwheat was reportedly brought to Europe by the Crusaders, although it originated in the Himalayan mountains. In botanical terms, buckwheat is not really a grain; it is actually a member of the rhubarb family, with its fruit or groats that resemble tiny, dark-colored nuts.

Grown under adverse conditions in cold weather, buckwheat is very strengthening and warming, containing more protein than most other grains as well as iron and B vitamins. A natural source of rutic acid, which aids in arterial and circulatory problems, buckwheat is used by many homeopaths for high blood pressure and other circulatory difficulties.

Cooked by itself, buckwheat makes a great porridge, grain dish or even a salad. A very traditional recipe involves sautéing onions and noodles and then tossing together with cooked kasha. Ground into flour, buckwheat is the chief ingredient used to make traditional Japanese soba noodles.

Bulgur (Cracked wheat) Made from whole wheat berries that are cracked into pieces, enabling it to cook quite quickly. A great breakfast cereal, bulgur is most commonly associated with tabbouleh, a marinated grain salad combining tomatoes, onions and cucumbers with an aromatic olive oil dressing.

Burdock A wild, hearty plant from the thistle family. According to traditional medicine, this long, dark brown root is renowned as one of nature's finest blood purifiers and skin clarifiers. A strong, dense root vegetable, burdock has a very centering, grounding energy, and is most commonly used in stews and long-simmered sautés.

Cannellini beans Creamy white oval beans most commonly used in the Italian dish *pasta e fagioli*. Their creamy texture makes them ideal for purees, dips and creamy soups.

Canola oil Expressed from rapeseeds, this light oil is substantially lower in saturated fats than any other oil and also contains omega-3 fatty acids. Virtually tasteless, this is a good oil choice for baking and salad dressings, but kind of bland for sautéing and not very stable under heat for long periods.

Capers Little pickled flower buds, most commonly used in Mediterranean cooking. Salty and briny in taste, they really add flavor to sauces and salads. If they taste too strong for you, rinse lightly before use.

Caraway seed Traditionally used in rye bread, caraway seeds have a distinctive, hearty taste, making them ideal for seasoning savory stews and other vegetable dishes. Their pungent taste is quite strong, so use sparingly.

Carob Renowned as a substitute for chocolate by natural foods enthusiasts, carob doesn't taste much like chocolate, so true devotees are rarely fooled. Carob is most commonly used in pow-

dered form, which is made from grinding roasted, tropical pods. Its natural sweet taste and dark, rich color are what gained it its reputation as a substitute for chocolate. It is higher in simple sugars than cocoa; I don't really recommend it.

Cashews A tropical nut quite high in fat, with a rich, luscious flavor for creams, nut butters and nut milks.

Chervil An aromatic herb with lacy, fernlike leaves that tastes quite like tarragon. It is best when used fresh.

Chestnuts Their rich texture and taste belie the fact that chestnuts are in fact quite low in fat, making them an ideal ingredient in many recipes. At their peak in the fall, fresh chestnuts are a wonderful addition to soups, stews and vegetable dishes, and their natural sweet taste makes them a great dessert ingredient. Dried chestnuts are available year-round and, with presoaking, achieve as creamy and sweet a taste and texture as their fresh counterparts.

Chickpeas (Garbanzo beans) Beige round beans with a wonderful nutty taste and creamy texture when cooked. Traditionally used when making hummus, a creamy spread, combining chickpeas with olive oil, tahini, lemon juice and a bit of garlic. Also wonderful in bean dishes combined with sweet vegetables or corn as well as in soups and stews.

Chiles Available fresh and dried, they range from mildly spicy to blazing hot. Remember that the real "heat" comes from the capsaicin in the seeds and spines, so removing them reduces the "fire." I recommend you wear rubber gloves when removing seeds and ribs so the oil, which contains the capsaicin, doesn't get on your hands—and then into your eyes when you rub them. It takes several hours, even with washing, to remove this oil, so trust me on this one. Ancho, chipotles, serranos, habaneros, poblanos and jalapeños are the most common varieties used in cooking today.

Chili powder A powdered blend of ground chiles, ranging from mild to hot, combined with oregano, cumin, garlic and salt. Add it slowly to dishes, adjusting the spicy taste as you go along, so your dish doesn't get too hot. The hot taste increases as you cook it.

Chocolate Do I really need to define chocolate? I suppose not, but perhaps I should define its appearances in this book. Once demonized by natural foods enthusiasts, chocolate has come into fashion as a healthful ingredient. Rich in antioxidants, iron and magnesium, chocolate releases feel-good hormones in the brain, creating a relaxed, warm condition in the body. Calorically dense, chocolate is not an everyday staple, but dark chocolate can be a valuable addition to any healthy diet.

Corn Native to South America, corn has been used for more than ten thousand years. It has become the staple grain for the entire North American continent. Today, corn is cultivated worldwide and is one of the most popular grains used in cooking.

Corn requires hot summer sun and rain to flourish, and grows quickly. Often eaten by itself, the popular corn on the cob has practically limitless other culinary uses: flour, meal, grits, tortillas, corn syrup, corn oil, bourbon and popcorn (from one variety of the grain).

Corn grits A cracked form of dried corn. Corn grits make a great polenta, creamy breakfast cereal or texturizer for soups.

Cornmeal Dried field corn ground into a coarse flour. Used to make creamier polentas, this flour is most commonly used in cornbreads, tortillas and corn chips.

Corn oil A golden-colored oil with a rich, buttery taste, ideally suited to whole-grain baking. Its full-bodied texture and light taste give baked goods a moist crumb. The biggest challenge is finding corn oil that does not contain genetically modified organisms (GMO) corn. Look for organic, if you can find it or use another oil in its place.

Couscous A staple of North Africa, this rolled durum wheat product has been stripped of its bran and germ, made into a thick paste, steamed and then dried in the form of small granules. It cooks quite quickly and its starchy texture makes it a great ingredient for loaves, patties and soups.

Crushed red pepper flakes Dried, flaked chile peppers. Used in cooking, these flakes are quite hot, since the drying has spread the capsaicin throughout the pepper.

Daikon A long, white radish root with a refreshingly clean, peppery taste. Commonly used in salads and side dishes, soups and stews. Frequently served in Asian restaurants with fish or oily dishes, since it is reputed to aid in the digestion of fat and protein as well as to help the body assimilate oil and cleanse organ tissue. Also available in dried, shredded form to be used in various stews and hearty vegetable dishes.

Dulse Dried dulse has a rich, red color, is high in potassium and comes packaged in large, wrinkled leaves. Its salty rich taste makes it a great snack right out of the package. Because it is so delicate, it actually requires little or no cooking, just a quick rinse to remove any debris on the leaves. It adds depth of flavor to hearty soups, stews, salads and bean stews.

EFAs (Essential fatty acids) Fats that we must obtain from our diet and include omega-3, omega-6 and omega-9. Omega-6 and -9 are found in most foods, but omega-3 is somewhat elusive and is only found in certain nuts, seeds and coldwater fish.

Fava beans Available both fresh and dried, favas are used extensively in Mediterranean cooking. These large, chunky beans have a rich, earthy flavor that will remind you of split peas, but they do not get quite as creamy; they retain a soft, potatolike texture.

Flageolets Light ivory beans with a very subtle taste. Highly esteemed in French cooking, these beans are best in simple recipes, which showcase their delicate flavor.

Flaxseeds Richer than soybeans in omega-3 fatty acids and rich in vitamin E, they have a sweet, nutty flavor. When boiled and whipped with unfiltered, unsweetened apple juice, they make a good binder and leavening in baked goods, in place of eggs. On their own, flaxseeds can have a laxative effect on the body and so should be consumed in moderation. Many vegans enjoy them daily for the omega-3 benefits.

Flour Flour is any ground meal of whole grains. Try to choose only whole grain flours, since these retain a bit of germ and bran and therefore are not completely devoid of nutrients. Also look for stone-ground flours, as these are not processed with extreme heat, which also can destroy nutrients. For the best shelf life, store flour in tightly sealed containers in either the refrigerator or freezer. Stored this way, most flours will keep for about a year.

Fu A meat substitute developed by vegetarian Buddhist monks, fu is made of dried wheat gluten. A good low-fat source of protein, fu can be used in various soups and stews by simply reconstituting it in water.

Ginger A golden-colored, spicy root vegetable with a variety of uses in cooking. It imparts a mild, peppery taste to cooking and is commonly used in stir-fries, sautés, sauces and dressings. Shaped like the fingers of a hand, ginger has the reputation of stimulating circulation with its hot taste. A very popular remedy in Oriental medicine for helping with everything from joint pain to stomachaches and acid indigestion.

Gluten The protein found in wheat, although it is also found in smaller amounts in other grains like oats, rye and barley. When kneaded in dough, gluten becomes elastic and holds air pockets released by the leavening, helping bread to rise.

Gluten is also used to prepare *seitan*, a meat substitute made from wheat gluten.

GMO The acronym GMO stands for "genetically modified organism," and was first used years ago to designate microorganisms that had had genes from other species transferred into their genetic material by the then-new technique of "gene-splicing." Applied to crops, the term refers to any genetic plant type that has had a gene or genes from a different species transferred into its genetic material using accepted techniques of genetic engineering, and where such introduced genes have been shown to produce a gene product (a protein).

Great Northern beans Medium-size white beans, they hold their shape very well in cooking, making them ideal ingredients in bean salads as well as in heartier bean dishes that complement their subtle flavor.

Hato mugi barley Also known as "Job's Tears," this grain is large pearl barley with beige, translucent skin. A good source of iron, protein and calcium, hato mugi is reputed in Asia to create beautiful, flawless skin, due to its ability to cleanse the blood and remove hard fat deposits from beneath the skin.

Hazelnuts (Filberts) Shaped like a large chickpea, hazelnuts have a very bitter outer skin that needs to be removed before eating. These guys love chocolate.

Herbs Simply defined, herbs are the leaves and stems of certain plants used in cooking because of their unique, aromatic flavors. Available fresh or dried, herbs add rich, full-bodied taste to soups, stews and salad dressings among other things. When using fresh herbs, remember to use three to four times the amount of dried, as drying concentrates their natural flavor. Try to buy your herbs in natural foods stores, since you can be assured that these herbs are not irradiated, as most commercial brands are.

Hiziki (Hijiki) Sold in its dry form, hiziki resembles black angel hair pasta. It is one of the strongest-tasting of all sea plants; soaking it for several minutes before cooking can gentle its briny flavor. It is one of the richest sources of useable calcium in the plant kingdom with a whopping 1,350 mg of calcium per ½ cup uncooked hiziki, with no saturated fat. So it is worth getting used to.

Horseradish A root vegetable known for its sharp, hot taste. Actually a member of the mustard family, horseradish adds real zing to any dish. It is truly wonderful freshly grated and stirred into bean dishes or grain salads, or served with fish.

Kidney beans Available in a variety of shapes and colors, kidney beans are most commonly recognized in their deep-red all-American shape. Full-flavored and hearty, kidney beans hold up incredibly well in chilies, stews, soups, salads and casseroles.

Kombu (Kelp) A sea vegetable packaged in wide, dark, dehydrated strips that will double in size upon soaking and cooking. Kombu is a great source of glutamic acid, a natural flavor enhancer, so adding a small piece to soups and stews deepens flavor. It is also generally believed that kombu improves the digestibility of grains and beans when added to these foods in small amounts.

Kukicha A Japanese tea made from the stems and twigs of the tea bush.

Kuzu (Kudzu) Kuzu is a high-quality starch made from the root of the kuzu plant. A root native to the mountains of Japan (and now in the southern United States), kuzu grows like a vine with tough roots. Used primarily as a thickener, this strong root is reputed to strengthen the digestive tract due to its alkaline nature.

Legumes A large plant family including beans, lentils, peanuts and peas.

Lentils An ancient legume that comes in many varieties, from common brown-green to red to yellow to lentils le puys (a tiny sweet French variety, which is great in salads). Very high in protein and minerals and with a full-bodied, peppery taste, lentils are good in everything from stews and soups to salads and side dishes.

Lima beans Also known as "butter beans," these popular white beans are most commonly used in their dried form, although fresh lima beans are exquisite. Lima beans have a very delicate outer skin, so they seem to do best when cooked in salted water (unlike other beans), which helps hold their skin in place. Once the skins loosen, the limas turn to mush—although then you can use them to cream soups or make dips.

Baby lima beans are simply smaller, with tougher skins and a sweeter taste.

Maple syrup A traditional sweetener made by boiling sugar maple sap until it becomes thick. The end product is quite expensive because it takes about thirty-five gallons of sap to produce one gallon of maple syrup. The syrup is available in various grades of quality from AA to B: AA and A are quite nice for sauces and dressings, but I use grade B in baking. I have found the higher grades can result in hard baked goods.

I do not often use maple syrup, since it is a simple sugar, releasing quickly in the bloodstream, thus wreaking havoc with blood sugar.

Millet Native to Asia, millet is a tiny grain that once equaled barley as the chief staple of Europe. It was very popular in Japan before the cultivation of rice, and is still the staple grain of China, India and Ethiopia.

Millet is a tiny round grain grown in cold weather. An effective alkalizing agent, it is the only whole grain that does not produce stomach acids, so it aids spleen and pancreas function as well as stomach upset.

Millet is very versatile, making delicious grain dishes, creamy soups, stews and porridges, stuffings and loaves. With its sweet, nutty taste and beautiful yellow color, millet complements most foods well, but goes best with sweet vegetables like squash and corn.

Mirin A Japanese rice wine with a sweet taste and very low alcohol content. Made by fermenting sweet brown rice with water and koji (a cultured rice), mirin adds depth and dimension to sauces, glazes and various other dishes and can be used as a substitute for sherry in cooking.

Miso A fermented soybean paste used traditionally to flavor soups but prized throughout Asia for its ability to strengthen the digestive system. Traditionally aged miso is a great source of high-quality protein. Available in a wide variety of flavors and strengths, the most nutritious miso is made from barley and soybeans, and is aged for at least two years—this is the miso used most extensively in daily cooking. Other varieties of misos are used to supplement and to create different tastes in different dishes.

Miso is rich in digestive enzymes, but these enzymes are quite delicate and should not be boiled. Just lightly simmering miso activates and releases the enzymes' strengthening qualities into food.

Mochi Mochi is made by cooking sweet brown rice and then pounding or extruding it to break the grains, a process that results in a very sticky substance. Flat packages of mochi can be purchased in most natural foods stores. Mochi can be used to create creamy sauces, to give the effect of melted cheese, to make dumplings in soups, or simply cut into small squares and pan-fried, creating tiny turnoverlike puffs, a rich source of complex carbohydrates.

Mung beans Tiny pea-shaped, deep-green beans, these are most popular in their sprouted forms, although they cook up quickly, making delightful soups, purees and Indian *dahls*. Mung bean sprouts are a delicious addition to any salad or stir-fried dish.

Mustard Mustard in a jar is made by blending dried mustard seeds with vinegar and various spices. The best-quality mustards are Dijon or those that have been stone ground; these are made from coarse seeds and have a heartier texture.

Navy beans Also called pea beans, these are cream-colored, egg-shaped beans that are the quintessential baked bean. They generally require long, slow cooking, but hold up well in the pressure cooker. I have found that they do not have a substantial enough flavor for salads, so I use other white beans for those dishes.

Noodles (Pasta, macaroni) Pasta, macaroni or noodles are made by combining flour, salt and water into limitless shapes and sizes. Try to choose pastas made from organic flours, preferably whole grain and without eggs for a healthier product. These are made from the endosperm of the wheat and contain protein and carbohydrates as well as essential fiber, minerals and B vitamins. However, even refined semolina pastas have a place in a whole foods diet, lending light taste and texture when desired.

Nori (Sea laver) Usually sold in paper-thin sheets, nori is a great source of protein and minerals like calcium and iron. Most well-known as a principal ingredient in sushi, nori has a mild, sweet flavor, just slightly reminiscent of the ocean. Great for garnishing grain and noodle dishes or floating in soup.

Nut butters Thick pastes made from grinding nuts. While rich in fiber and protein, nut butters are also excellent sources of good-quality fat. Nut butters have intense, rich flavors and are great in sauces, dressings and baked goods.

Nuts *See also individual listings.* Nuts are true powerhouses of energy. Bear in mind that, in most cases, nuts have the strength to grow entire trees, so imagine what impact they have on us, giving us great strength and vitality. They are wonderful in small amounts for taste and richness (they are calorically dense) and for a lift of energy.

Oats Native to Central Europe and used since Neolithic times, oats are rich in B vitamins and contain one of the highest amounts of protein of any grain in addition to iron and calcium. Reputed to have a high-fat content (which they do), oats contain soluble gums that bind cholesterol in the intestines, preventing its absorption by the body, making it a heart-healthy grain.

Most commonly used in modern cultures as oatmeal, a process by which the oat groats are rolled or steel cut, oats are most delicious when used in their whole state. I use oatmeal flakes mostly to cream soups and thicken sauces as well as in breads, cookies and croquettes.

Ocean ribbons A brownish-green sea vegetable in the kelp family, normally packaged in long, thin strips/ribbons. It has a sweeter taste than kombu and cooks a bit more quickly.

Oil Oils are rich liquids extracted from nuts, seeds, grains and fruit (like olives and avocados). A highly refined food source, oils add a rich taste to foods, making dishes more satisfying and creating a warming, vitalizing energy and soft, supple skin and hair. Try to choose oils that are expelled or cold-pressed, since these oils were extracted by pressing and not by extreme heat, which can render oil carcinogenic. I try to limit my oil use to only a few of the more digestible varieties, like toasted sesame, light sesame, avocado and olive oil (usually only extra virgin, which is the oil extracted from the first pressing of the olives, and therefore the best quality), occasionally adding canola oil to a recipe. Oils should be stored in a cool place, but it is not necessary to refrigerate them to prevent rancidity.

Olives Olives are native to semitropical climates and are used in Mediterranean cooking to add an appealing punch to grain, vegetable and bean salads. There are almost limitless varieties available, so you can satisfy your taste by choosing anything from the intensely flavored, oil-cured ripe olives, to purple Greek kalamata olives, to green Spanish olives. Rich in monounsaturated fats and minerals, pantothenic acid and niacin, olives are a nutritious treat.

Organic Organic agriculture is an ecological production management system that promotes and enhances biodiversity, biological cycles and soil biological activity. It is based on minimal use of off-farm inputs and on management practices that restore, maintain and enhance ecological harmony.

Peanuts Although considered a nut, peanuts are in fact legumes and are a good source of protein. Unlike other legumes, peanuts are very high in fat. Since peanuts are one of the most chemically treated of all crops, try to choose organic peanuts for use. Peanuts are also prone to a carcinogenic mold called *aflatoxin*, especially if they are stored under humid conditions, so choose peanuts from the arid climate

of the Southwest, like Valencia peanuts, to minimize this risk.

Pecans Among the highest in fat, these nuts are one of the most delicious for baking in cookies, pies and cakes.

Pignoli (Pine nuts) Incredibly luscious nuts that are quite expensive, due to the labor-intensive process involved in their harvesting from pinecones. High in oil and rich in taste, pine nuts add great depth to pasta and grain pilafs. Roasting them enhances their rich taste, making them delightful in any dish.

Pinto beans The most famous Southwestern bean, pintos were actually named by the Spanish, who used the word meaning "painted" for them because of the red-brown markings on their beige surface. Their nutty taste holds up well in stews, chilis and baked bean dishes.

Quinoa A tiny seedlike grain native to the Andes Mountains. Pronounced "keen-wah," this small grain packs a powerhouse of protein and numerous amino acids not normally found in large amounts in most whole grains, particularly lysine, which aids digestion. Quinoa grains are quite delicate, so nature has coated them with an oily substance called *saponin*. If the grain isn't rinsed well, it can have a bitter taste. Quinoa has a lovely, nutty taste and cooks quickly, qualities that make it a great whole grain addition to your menus.

Rice The staple grain of many cultures, rice is low in fat and rich in vitamins, amino acids and minerals, like calcium, protein, iron and B vitamins. Rice as we know it was reportedly cultivated in India, spreading from there to Asia and the Middle East.

In its whole form, rice is a near-perfect

food. High in moisture, rice acts as a gentle diuretic, balancing the moisture content of the body and encouraging the elimination of any excess. Polished or white rice, while delicious on occasion, is pretty much devoid of nutrition. Brown rice should be used as the staple grain.

The most common strains of rice include short-grain, medium-grain and long-grain. Short-grain, the hardest and most compact variety, is best suited to cooler, temperate climates, while medium- and long-grain rice are used in warmer climates and during the summer months. Other gourmet varieties of rice have become popular in today's cooking. These include arborio, basmati, texmati, wehani, black japonica and red rice. Sweet brown rice, a glutinous variety of brown rice, is commonly used not only as a grain dish but also in *mochi*, a cake formed by pounding and drying cooked sweet rice.

There are limitless uses for rice in daily cooking: It can be pressure-cooked, steamed, boiled, fried, baked, roasted, sautéed and used in breads, sushi, casseroles, sautés, pilafs or stuffings.

Rice milk A creamy liquid made by cooking ten parts water to one part rice for one hour, the resulting rice is pressed through a cheesecloth, creating "milk." It is also packaged commercially.

Rice syrup (Brown rice syrup, yinnie, rice malt) The Japanese call this "liquid sweetness." Rice syrup is a thick, amber syrup made by combining sprouted barley with cooked brown rice and storing it in a warm place. Fermentation begins and the starches in the rice convert to maltose and some other complex sugars, making this syrup a wonderfully healthy sweetener. Complex sugars release slowly into the bloodstream, providing fuel for the body rather than wreaking havoc on the blood sugar.

Rice syrup's wonderful, delicate sweetness makes it ideal for baked goods and other desserts.

Risotto A generic term for a creamy, almost soupy rice dish native to northern Italy. Traditionally made with a specific short-grain white rice called arborio, the perfect risotto is creamy and soupy, while the rice retains a bit of chewy texture.

Rye The Romans began cultivating this Asian grain, thought to be a weed by the Greeks. By the Middle Ages, rye was a staple grain in most of Europe.

As opposed to use in its whole form, rye is most commonly used in flour form to make rich, hearty breads. Similar to wheat in composition, rye is a bit less glutinous and, like wheat, can be used by itself to make breads.

Rye is completely delicious when cooked with rice and makes a great whole grain dish.

Salt Not all varieties of salt is are a good thing. The quality of the salt we use is quite important; the best to use is white, unrefined sea salt with no additives. Unrefined salts are rich in the trace minerals that are destroyed in processed salt.

Sea vegetables The exotic vegetables that are harvested from the sea coast and nearby rocks are high in protein and rich in minerals. Readily available in dehydrated form in natural foods stores, sea vegetables are not yet widely used in American cooking, but are growing in popularity for their nutritional benefits and interesting taste.

Seeds In a word, seeds are powerhouses. (Remember that they are the source of entire plants, even trees in some cases.) That's a lot of energy in a little seed. They are good sources of protein and calcium, but because of their high oil content, seeds spoil relatively quickly and keep best refrigerated. The most popular seeds in natural foods cooking include pumpkin seeds (pepitas), poppy seeds, sunflower seeds and sesame seeds.

Seitan (Wheat gluten) Most commonly called "wheat meat," seitan is made from wheat gluten. Made by kneading the bran and starch out of flour, raw seitan is rather bland, so most commercial brands are simmered in savory broth before sale. A wonderful source of protein, it is low in calories and fat and is very popular in Asian "mock-meat" dishes as well as in hearty stews and casseroles.

Sesame tahini A thick, creamy paste made from ground hulled sesame seeds, it is used for flavoring everything from sauces to salad dressings to dips, spreads and baked goods. Available in natural foods stores and Middle Eastern markets, this spread has a delicate, nutty flavor that adds luxurious taste to any recipe.

Shiitake mushrooms Gaining popularity over the last several years for their power to lower cholesterol and cleanse blood, shiitake mushrooms can be found in just about any natural foods store and gourmet shop. They have an intensely earthy taste, so a few go a long way. It is necessary to soak the dried ones until tender, fifteen to twenty minutes before cooking, and I usually trim off the stems to avoid bitter flavor. They are wonderful in soups, stews, gravies and sauces and as bouillon flavoring.

Shiso (Beefsteak leaf) A lovely herb with large, reddish leaves. A very popular staple in Japanese cooking, shiso is often used in pickling,

most commonly in umeboshi plum pickling. Shiso is rich in calcium and iron.

Shoyu (Soy sauce) A confusing term because it is the generic term for Japanese soy sauce as well as the term for a specific type of traditionally made soy sauce, the distinguishing characteristic of which is the use of cracked wheat as the fermenting starter, along with soybeans. The best shoyu is aged for at least two years. This is lighter seasoning than tamari.

Soba A noodle made from buckwheat flour. Some varieties contain other ingredients, like wheat flour or yam flour, but the best-quality soba are those made primarily of buckwheat flour.

Somen Japanese angel hair. A very fine, white or whole grain wheat flour noodle that cooks very quickly, somen are traditionally served in a delicate broth with lightly cooked fresh vegetables.

Soybeans The base bean for many natural foods products, from miso to soy sauce to tofu and tempeh to soymilk to soy flour. On their own, soybeans are rather bland and hard to digest, and so are more commonly used in other products. However, when cooked on their own—long and slow cooking is the only way—soybeans can be most delicious.

Soyfoods A catchall term for the wide range of foods that have soybeans as their base, including soymilk, tofu, soy flour, tempeh, soy sauce, tamari, shoyu, miso, soy cheese, soy oil, etc.

Soy sauce Traditional soy sauce (the same as shoyu) is the product of fermenting soybeans, water, salt and wheat. Containing salt and glutamic acid, soy sauce is a natural flavor enhancer. The finest soy sauces are aged for one to two years, while commercial soy sauce is synthetically aged in a matter of days, producing a salty, artificially flavored condiment.

Spices Spices are highly aromatic seasonings that come from the seed, root, bark and buds of plants, while herbs are obtained from the leaves and stems. Spices generally give food a very strong flavor and energy, and can be quite stimulating to our vitality. Use of spices can be very helpful in getting energy moving when it's stagnant or "stuck." Spices become stale when kept for more than six months, so it is advisable to buy them in small quantities that you will use in that time period. Store spices and herbs in well-sealed containers in a cool, dark place to retain potency.

Split peas These dried peas, most commonly available in yellow or green, make wonderful creamy soups.

Tamari A fermented soy sauce product that is actually the liquid that rises to the top of the keg when making miso. This thick, rich flavor enhancer is nowadays produced with a fermentation process similar to that of shoyu, but the starter is wheat-free. Tamari is richer, with a full-bodied taste, and contains more amino acids than regular soy sauce. I prefer the heavier taste of tamari for heartier, winter cooking.

Tempeh A traditional, Indonesian soy product created by fermenting split, cooked soybeans with a starter. As the tempeh ferments, a white mycelium of enzymes develops on the surface, making the soybeans more digestible as well as providing a healthy range of B vitamins, except B_{12}. Found in the refrigerator or freezer section of natural foods stores, tempeh is great in everything from sandwiches to salads to stews to casseroles.

Toasted (dark) sesame oil An oil extracted from toasted sesame seeds that imparts a wonderful, nutty flavor to quick sautés, stir-fries and sauces, but should not be cooked over high heat for a long period. I use it as a finishing oil and in dressings.

Tofu (Soybean curd) Fast becoming a popular low-fat food in our fat-crazed world, tofu is a wonderful source of protein and phytoestrogens, and is both inexpensive and versatile. Rich in calcium and cholesterol-free, tofu is made by extracting curd from coagulated soymilk and then pressing it into bricks. For use in everything from soups and stews to salads, casseroles and quiches or as the creamy base to sauces and dressings.

Udon Flat noodles, much like fettuccine. Udon comes in a variety of blends of flours, from all whole wheat to brown rice to lotus root to unbleached white flour. I prefer the whole wheat variety.

Umeboshi plums (Ume plums) Japanese pickled plums (actually, green apricots) with a fruity, salty taste. Pickled in a salt brine and shiso leaves for at least one year (the longer, the better), ume plums are traditionally served as a condiment with various dishes, including grains. Ume plums are reputed to aid in the cure of a wide array of ailments—from stomachaches to migraines—because they alkalize the blood. These little red plums (made red from the shiso, which adds vitamin C and iron) make good preservatives. The best-quality plums are the most expensive ones, but they are used in small amounts, so one jar will last a long time.

Umeboshi paste A puree made from umeboshi plums to create a concentrated condiment. Use this sparingly, as it is quite salty, but it is a great ingredient in salad dressings and sauces.

Umeboshi vinegar A salty liquid left over from pickling umeboshi plums. Used as a vinegar, it is good in salad dressings and pickle making.

Vanilla (Pure vanilla extract) A smoky, smooth flavoring made by extracting the essence from vanilla beans and preserving it in alcohol and water, although nowadays you can obtain vanilla preserved without alcohol. Pure vanilla extract is a bit expensive, but a small bit goes a long way, so splurge and get the best. By the way, inexpensive, artificial vanilla is made from vanillin, a by-product of paper making—appetizing, no?

Vegetable stock A flavorful broth made by simmering any variety of finely cut vegetables until they release their flavor and nutrients into the water. A great base for soups and sauces, a good stock is usually made from a combination of vegetables and small quantities of herbs to create a full-bodied broth.

Vinegar *See also individual vinegars.* A fermented condiment familiar to most people. There is an entire world of vinegars to explore—and a variety of uses for them, way beyond salad dressings. While lots of vinegars exist, they can be very acidic, so I limit my use to brown rice vinegar (page 22), sweet brown rice vinegar (both made from fermented brown rice and sweet brown rice), umeboshi vinegar (above), balsamic vinegar and, occasionally, a fruity vinegar, like raspberry or champagne vinegar.

Wakame (Alaria) A very delicate member of the kelp family, wakame is most traditionally used in miso soups and tender salads. It requires only a brief soaking and short cooking time, and has a very gentle flavor, so it is a great way to add sea vegetables to your diet.

Wasabi A very potent root, comparable in taste to horseradish. Rather fiery, wasabi adds quite a kick as a condiment or as an ingredient, so use it sparingly until you become familiar with its potency.

Wheat Called the "staff of life," wheat has been the mainstay of foods in temperate climates since the dawn of time. As long ago as 4000 BCE, Egyptians were cultivating yeast and baking exotic breads for their royalty. From there, wheat spread throughout the Roman Empire and eventually the rest of the world.

There are many strains of wheat, classified according to hardness or softness, which reflects the percentage of protein. Hard winter wheat is high in gluten and is best for breads, while softer wheats work best in cakes and pastries. Hard durum wheat and its by-product, semolina, are the principal ingredients in most pasta and macaroni. White flour, bleached and unbleached, has been stripped of most of its nutritional value and makes the soft, puffy pastry and bread commercially produced today.

Whole wheat berries are difficult to digest in their whole form but can be soaked and cooked with other whole grains to create delicious dishes.

Whole wheat flour A flour ground from whole wheat berries that is high in gluten. Good, stone-ground flour retains much of its germ and bran, and thus much more of its nutrients than its unbleached white counterpart, making it a healthier choice for bread baking.

Whole wheat pastry flour A flour ground from a softer strain of wheat that is low in gluten. It is more finely milled than regular whole wheat flour, making it an excellent choice for pastry, cookie, cake and muffin baking.

Zest Also called the peel, the zest is the thin, colored layer of skin on citrus fruit, which imparts a fragrant essence of the fruit into cooking.

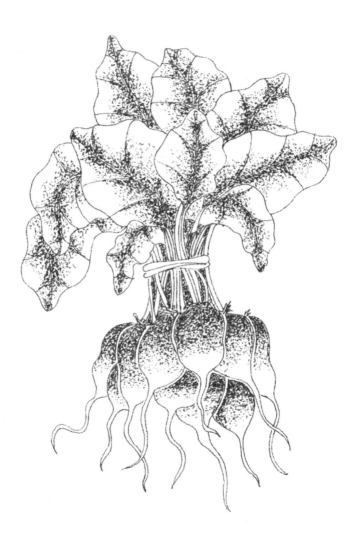

The Basics

THERE ARE SOME dishes basic to macrobiotic cooking that seem to be unique to this style of cuisine. These dishes encompass the very foundation of food energy—the most central theories surrounding macrobiotic cooking—of how food creates who we are and how we act. Mastering these dishes and understanding their energy is the basis upon which you can build an entire whole foods repertoire. Only in understanding can you find true freedom.

When you truly understand the effects of food and cooking, in terms of energy, you can branch out and use foods to create the person you want to be, achieving what it is you desire in life. Sound amazing? Think about it: What single other factor in life creates who we are and how we act as much as the food we consume? It is the one aspect of our lives where we have the most control. Wise use of food helps us become all that we can possibly be in life.

Use these dishes as your jumping-off point to creating a delicious, healthy repertoire of foods.

Basic Miso Soup

Miso is a fermented soybean paste used to flavor various dishes, but most widely used as bouillon would be to season soups. Miso's natural fermentation process creates a combination of enzymes that strengthen and nourish the intestinal tract. As a result, the blood that nourishes the balance of the body is stronger. The quality of our blood creates the people we are, and the health we possess. The best-quality misos are those aged over two or more summers. Basic miso soup encompasses the use of miso, of course, a small amount of sea vegetables to mineralize the blood and a variety of fresh vegetables. The balance of these ingredients creates a strengthening energy vital to life.

The key to basic miso soup is that it be a light broth, like consommé with vegetables. The flavor should be delicate and not too salty. Any soup or stew can be seasoned with miso. But keep it light and fresh tasting, simple and delicious. Vary the veggies each day.

This simple yet elegant broth is traditionally served in Japanese households for breakfast. With just a few ingredients, this warming broth is a great way to start the day—a great energy-booster, that is, if you can get past the idea of soup for breakfast!

MAKES ABOUT 4 SERVINGS

3 cups spring or filtered water
3 (1-inch) pieces wakame, soaked until tender (about 3 minutes) and diced
Several pieces each of a few vegetables, such as onion slices, daikon matchsticks, carrot rounds, finely shredded Chinese cabbage or head cabbage and finely diced winter squash
¾ to 1½ teaspoons barley or brown rice miso
1 to 2 fresh green onions, thinly sliced, for garnish

Bring water and wakame to a boil over medium heat. Reduce heat to low, cover and simmer about 3 minutes. Add vegetables and simmer, covered, over low heat 3 to 4 minutes, until just tender.

Remove a small bit of hot broth, add miso and stir until dissolved. Stir miso mixture into the soup and simmer, uncovered, without boiling, 3 to 4 minutes more. Garnish with green onions and serve hot.

■ **NOTES** It is very important that you do not boil the miso. The beneficial enzymes present need warmth to activate, but boiling them will destroy their benefits, leaving you only with the flavor.

Garnishing isn't arbitrary or done simply because it makes soup look beautiful, which,

of course it does. Garnishing adds a final touch of fresh, light energy to a soup that has cooked over fire for several minutes. All soups need that kind of freshness. You can use anything raw and fresh, such as green onions, parsley sprouts or grated carrot, daikon or fresh ginger, to name just a few options.

Pressure-Cooked Short-Grain Brown Rice

Because whole grains are important macronutrient, complex carbohydrates, they are foods that should be present in some form at just about every meal. Also rich in protein, vitamins and minerals, these foods possess a sweet taste and provide a lasting and sustained energy. These are the foods that will help you sail through your day, easily facing life's little adventures with grace and style. The light fatigue you will feel at the end of a busy day will be the result of actually accomplishing something, not the result of dropping blood sugar levels, which can make us feel exhausted.

While there are many ways to cook whole grains, the most nourishing method, in my opinion (and that is all you really get in this book!), is pressure cooking. With this method, foods cook at a temperature higher than boiling, from inside out, making the grain very digestible and minimizing the loss of nutrients to steam, so that most of the grain's nutritive properties are retained. Pressure cooking imparts a strength to whole grains that can't be achieved by using any other method. Cooking grains under pressure creates a great vitality in us. Pressure cooking combines great contracting energy in the bottom of the pot with balanced energy midpot and expanded, light energy at the top of the pot, where the steam is contained.

One thing to remember: Brown rice needs to be soaked before cooking to neutralize the phytic acid that can inhibit our ability to assimilate calcium. Soaking the grain and then discarding the soaking water does the trick.

This particular method of pressure cooking is the one I have found most strengthening for my family. There are many twists on pressure cooking, and I recommend you try a variety of them to see which method suits you best.

MAKES 3 TO 4 SERVINGS

1 cup organic short-grain brown rice
1½ cups spring or filtered water
Pinch sea salt

Rinse rice by placing it in a bowl with enough water to cover. Gently swirl with your hands to loosen any dust. Pour through a fine strainer to drain. Soak in fresh water to cover, for at least 1 hour. Drain well.

Combine rice and the water in a pressure cooker and cover loosely. Bring to a boil over medium heat. Add salt and seal the lid. Increase the heat to high and bring the pot to full pressure. Allow the pot to cook at full pressure 30 to 60 seconds. Reduce heat to low, place over a flame deflector and cook over low heat 25 minutes. Turn off heat and allow pressure cooker to stand, undisturbed, 25 minutes. Remove pot from stove and open pressure cooker. Stir rice well and transfer to a serving bowl.

Nishime-Style Vegetables

Nishime or water-braising of vegetables, calls for large pieces or chunks of root or hard ground vegetables cooked over low heat until they are tender and sweet. The steam generated in this method of cooking allows the veggies to cook in their own juices, eliminating the need for anything more than just a little added water. A light seasoning toward the end of cooking brings out their full-bodied flavor and natural sweetness. Vegetables cooked in this manner are quite soft and juicy, giving us a very warming, strengthening energy. A great dish for creating vitality.

A small piece of kombu in the bottom of the pot brings out the sweetness of the veggies, naturally tenderizes them by virtue of its glutamic acid and lightly mineralizes the dish, helping to create strong blood.

Nishime dishes may be very simple, consisting of one root vegetable braised to sweet perfection to hearty stews made up of any number of vegetables. Here is one of my favorites, with a few variations to get you started.

MAKES 3 TO 4 SERVINGS

1 (1-inch) piece kombu
2 dried shiitake mushrooms, soaked until
    tender, thinly sliced
1 carrot, cut into large chunks
1 cup (1-inch) cubed winter squash
1 onion, cut into thick wedges
Spring or filtered water
Soy sauce

In a heavy pot, place kombu and layer the vegetables in order listed above or arrange the vegetables in a pot in individual sections. Add enough water just to cover the bottom of the pot and bring to a boil over medium heat. Reduce heat to low, cover and cook until vegetables are just tender, about 25 minutes. Season vegetables lightly with soy sauce and simmer 10 minutes more, until all liquid has been absorbed into the vegetables. If water evaporates too quickly during cooking, add a little more and reduce the heat, because it is cooking too quickly. Transfer to a bowl and serve.

■ **VARIATION** Other nishime combinations that are real winners include: carrot, burdock and onion; onion, Brussels sprouts and corn-on-the-cob pinwheels; leek, parsnip and turnip; onion and squash; onion, squash and green cabbage wedges; daikon and lotus root. Most often I add the small piece of kombu and shiitake, but it is okay to leave these out when you feel like it.

Squash, Azuki Beans and Kombu

A very strengthening dish, especially for the kidneys. The small red azuki beans are extremely low in fat, while power-packed with potassium and other valuable nutrients. Combine them with mineral-packed kombu and the naturally sweet squash to help stabilize the blood sugar, and you have a dish that creates great vitality and strength.

MAKES ABOUT 4 SERVINGS

1 (1-inch) piece kombu
½ cup azuki beans, sorted, rinsed and soaked 1 hour
2 cups spring or filtered water
1 cup diced winter squash
Soy sauce

Place kombu in the bottom of a heavy pot. Top with beans and spring water. Bring to a boil over high heat and cook, uncovered, about 10 minutes. Reduce heat to low, cover and cook until beans are almost done, 40 to 50 minutes.

Add squash and cook, covered, until squash and beans are tender, about 25 minutes. Season lightly with soy sauce and simmer until all liquid has been absorbed by the beans. Transfer to a serving bowl and serve.

■ **VARIATION** Add or substitute other vegetables like onions, carrots or parsnips—any sweet root vegetable will do. And when the weather is particularly chilly, I add a bit of fresh-grated ginger juice for added warmth and a little spice. The sweet taste can be accented with 1 to 2 teaspoons barley malt when seasoning the dish.

Dried Daikon with Vegetables

A deep-cleansing dish. Fresh daikon has the energy to help the body assimilate and discharge excess fluids, fats and proteins. Dried daikon concentrates that energy, aiding deeper organs in their cleansing process. The sweet taste of the carrot and onion in this dish helps create a calming, strengthening energy, gently mineralized by ever-faithful kombu.

MAKES ABOUT 4 SERVINGS

1 (3-inch) piece kombu, soaked about 5 minutes or until tender and sliced into thin strips
1 or 2 dried shiitake mushrooms, soaked until tender and thinly sliced
½ cup dried daikon, soaked about 10 minutes or until tender
1 small onion, cut lengthwise into thin half-moon slices
1 carrot, cut into thin matchsticks
Spring or filtered water
Soy sauce

Place kombu in the bottom of a small skillet. Top with mushrooms, daikon, onion and carrot. Add water to half cover ingredients, using a combination of soaking liquid (from mushrooms only) and fresh water. Bring to a boil, cover and cook over low heat, 35 minutes. Season lightly with soy sauce and simmer about 10 minutes more. Remove the cover and simmer until any remaining liquid has been absorbed into the dish. Transfer to a serving bowl and serve.

Pressed Salad

A quick wilted vegetable dish that gives you the freshness of raw salad, but is processed just enough with salt or vinegar to break down the tough outer cellulose layer, which can make raw vegetables so difficult to digest. Use 1/2 teaspoon sea salt or umeboshi vinegar per cup of vegetables. Pressing also eliminates a lot of the excess liquids in raw vegetables, which can make us feel very cold during winter months. The secret to this dish is slicing the vegetables as thinly as you can. This helps them press quickly so that they retain their fresh quality.

MAKES ABOUT 3 SERVINGS

1 cup finely shredded Chinese cabbage
2 to 3 green onions, cut into thin diagonal slices
1 to 2 red radishes, very thinly sliced
½ cucumber, very thinly sliced in rounds, do not peel unless cucumber is not organic
1 carrot, cut into very fine matchsticks
1 tablespoon umeboshi vinegar or 2 teaspoons sea salt and 1 tablespoon fresh lemon juice
1 tablespoon balsamic vinegar

Place all vegetables in a medium bowl and toss well with vinegars, rubbing the vegetables through your fingers to work the vinegars into their surfaces. Place a plate on top of the salad with a light weight (like a bottle of apple juice) on top and press 20 to 30 minutes.

Squeeze out the fluid that accumulates in the salad and, if the salad is too salty, gently rinse to soften the taste.

Kinpira

This is an incredible dish whose name means "golden pieces." Vegetables are sautéed over high heat very quickly, with lots of hot spice. Kinpira-style cooking is very vitalizing. Burdock is the most strengthening root vegetable known to man. Other plants do not grow within a four-foot radius. If burdock encounters rock in its growth path, it grows right through it, and is thus by nature a very centering, strengthening vegetable. Burdock helps us focus and take aim at our goals. Very strong, burdock needs the gentle, sweet taste of carrots to balance its strength.

MAKES 3 TO 4 SERVINGS

1 tablespoon light sesame oil
1 cup matchstick pieces burdock
Sea salt
Generous pinch crushed red pepper flakes
1 cup matchstick pieces carrot
Soy sauce
1 green onion, thinly sliced on the diagonal

Heat sesame oil in a heavy skillet over medium heat. Add burdock, a pinch of salt and red pepper flakes and sauté until coated with oil, about 3 minutes. Stir in carrot and sauté 3 minutes. Season to taste with soy sauce and sauté 2 minutes. Stir in green onion and transfer to a serving platter.

Nabe

Nabe, pronounced "na-bay," is a quick and fresh style of meal preparation that involves actually cooking at the table, usually in a large, open, specially designed ceramic or metal nabe pot. This style of cooking has lots of advantages: It is easy on the cook and as fresh as you can possibly get. Your food certainly can't lose much vitality when you are cooking it just as you eat it! This kind of freshness is not only delicious but also imparts a terrific vitality.

The great majority of nabe meals involve thinly sliced vegetables and some form of protein, a dipping sauce and a small portion of cooked grain or noodles on the side. I usually choose lighter veggies for these meals—anything from sliced leafy greens, Chinese cabbage, head cabbage, leeks, dandelion greens, small broccoli florets, rapini, mushrooms, green beans, sugar snap peas, snow peas, slivered Brussels sprouts, green onions, chives and onions. I also love adding the flavors of thin slices of winter squash, daikon, carrot and corn-on-the-cob pinwheels, because they are so incredibly sweet when cooked this way. And on occasion, I add small pieces of fresh tofu or tempeh, mochi or fu. Sometimes when I entertain dinner guests who may not be vegetarian, some shrimp or chunks of white fish can be lovely, but that requires a separate burner and another pot, so that the whole dish does not taste like fish.

Sound like a lot of food? Well, nabe can be as simple or as complicated as you like. The greater the variety of ingredients you choose, however, the greater the vitality you will receive from this type of meal. And actually, the only real work involved here is in slicing and dicing the vegetables and cooking the accompanying grain dish.

Putting a nabe meal together is simple. Prepare a grain side dish, like brown rice, quinoa with corn or noodles. While the grain is cooking, begin preparing your vegetable platter for the meal. Then fill the nabe pot with fresh spring or filtered water and one or two dried shiitake mushrooms. (Sometimes I add a small piece of kombu as well, but no other seasoning is needed for this broth.) When the mushrooms are soft, slice them thinly and return them to the broth.

Set the table with bowls at each place, dipping sauce and a burner in the center of the table. Arrange your platter and utensils around the burner.

When everything is prepared, sliced and diced, heat the broth to boiling on the stove, bring it immediately to the table and keep it cooking at a low boil over medium heat on the burner. Begin adding sliced vegetables to the pot, cooking each one for anywhere from several seconds to a couple of minutes. You want the veggies to be just tender, not too soft. Don't add so many vegetables to the pot that you lose the boil; just add a few pieces at a time. Take a small amount of grain, a bowl of dipping sauce and eat to your heart's content!

The dipping sauces you create are the seasoning for nabe meals, so don't be afraid of them. Give them interesting strong flavors. I like to use a wide variety of dipping sauces, from hot to spicy to citrusy to hearty. Some dipping sauces I use on a regular basis include tamari broth with grated fresh ginger, miso broth with lemon juice and sesame seeds, tamari broth with hot chiles, leftover miso soup with green onions and grated daikon. During the summer months, umeboshi vinegar combined with fresh orange juice is really refreshing. Use the proportions that taste good to you and experiment to find your favorite.

Amazing Grains

GRAIN. **IT'S INTERESTING** how even the word evokes feelings of simplicity, elegance, beauty and humility. Simply stated, whole grains and grain products are the cornerstone of any healthy, whole foods diet. There is an old saying, "Man cannot live by bread alone." But he sure can live well on grain! Yes, we need to supplement whole grains with fresh fruits and vegetables, beans, nuts and seeds, and even a small amount of fish, if you so desire. With the abundant variety of grains available to us, however, we could, in theory, survive on whole grains alone. Grains are the link between the plant and animal kingdoms from which we, as humans, draw life.

So are grains the all-around perfect food? Just about. The majority of nutrients that the human organism needs to sustain life are fully present in whole grains. Water, protein, vitamins, minerals, complex carbohydrates, fats and fiber compose this miraculous food that not only reproduces itself a thousand times over (with little assistance from us), but can be stored and transported literally without damage or spoilage.

In traditional cultures, grain was always associated with the fruitful forces of Mother Nature. To these peoples, grain was the key to opening consciousness, carrying the force of life through its deep roots in the earth up through its stem to its fruit, opened to the heavenly force of the sun. In modern botani-

cal thinking, there are about 8,000 species of grasses that are categorized as "grain." Of these, human beings eat only a few, although we have come to think of other plant varieties as "grains" because of the similarities in their characteristics and energetic qualities.

What does whole grain mean anyway? This name refers to a seed's anatomical structure—the pericarp, endosperm and germ. So, any reference to whole grains means that the entire grain structure is being used; there has been no polishing, rolling, purling or stripping of the seed. All of the nutritive parts of the grain are intact for consumption.

And don't even start with me about the whole carbohydrate thing. Sure, simple carbs like white flour, sugar and bread will make you fat faster than you can say carbohydrate, but whole grains (complex carbohydrates) will nourish you like no other food group. The brain needs glucose to function, but it is the quality of the glucose source that matters. Complex or long-chain carbohydrates, like the kind that dominate whole grains break down slowly in the bloodstream, do not trigger an excessive insulin release and give us energy resources to draw on for hours. Eating brown rice, millet, barley, quinoa, whole grain breads and pasta in balanced proportions are the key to reaching and maintaining your ideal weight and more important, your health.

When shopping for whole grains, look for well-shaped, uniform (size, shape and color) grains. I personally prefer organic grains to commercial varieties. Because grain is such an important part of a healthy diet, it only makes sense to obtain the very best quality. And since grain absorbs so much from the soil, any pesticide residue present in the earth will find its way into our grains; and therefore, our bodies.

Once purchased, I advise storing grains in tightly sealed glass jars in a cupboard or pantry—or any cool and dry place. I have gotten into the habit of adding a whole bay leaf to each jar to discourage grain moths. At first, with so many grains available to us, you may wish to label each jar, so you will remember what is what until grains become familiar to you.

In general, cooking styles for grains will vary—amounts of water, cooking time and so forth. You will see many different methods employed in the following recipes. What remains constant is rinsing grains. Grains will develop a light dust over their surface as they sit because of naturally occurring oxidation. A light rinsing process will ensure the natural, sweet, nutty taste of your cooked grains. First, quickly sort through the grain for any tiny stones or debris. Then,

place the grain in a bowl, cover with water, swirl gently with your fingers to loosen dirt and pour through a fine strainer. You may wish to repeat the process a couple of times if the water is particularly cloudy.

The energy and spirit of whole grains keep me enchanted almost more than the delicious flavors. They possess an inner strength that comes from the harmony of water, earth, sun and air—nature's basic elements of life. By utilizing the whole grain, these powerful energetic qualities are passed on to us, nourishing us completely and restoring us to that same harmony with nature.

A diet centered around the grain family will awaken our spirits and open our consciousness to all that the universe has to provide. Our instinct and intuition will guide our choices, making our lives happier and healthier and free from the petty stresses of daily living that seem to so debilitate people these days.

Looking at grains, we see a great variety available to us. I dare say that, to a newcomer, a natural foods store with row after row of grain products can be quite daunting. But instead of giving in to anxiety, let this abundance reawaken the very essence of humanity in you—your creativity. And again, always choose organic grains over commercially grown and processed ones whenever possible. Organic foods nourish us better because they are allowed to flourish naturally, possess greater concentrations of certain vitamins and minerals and they also support the earth that gives them life—and it is always better to choose life.

Let these recipes serve only as your inspiration. All that follows are simply tools to create dishes to nourish the body and spirit. For more information on the vast varieties of grains available to us, check the Glossary (pages 20 to 34).

Mochi

Made from sweet brown rice, mochi is so versatile you can use it in sauces, stews, casseroles and soups; as a cheese alternative; and on its own. While you can purchase it packaged, nothing compares to homemade mochi. Make the effort; it really is worth it.

MAKES ABOUT 10 OUNCES

2 cups sweet brown rice, rinsed, soaked for at least 1 hour, drained and soaking water discarded
3 cups spring or filtered water
2 pinches sea salt
Brown rice flour

Place rice and water in a pressure cooker and soak 6 to 8 hours more. Bring to a boil, loosely covered. Add salt, seal, and bring to full pressure. Place over a flame deflector, reduce heat to low and cook 45 minutes. Remove pot from heat and allow pressure to reduce naturally. Transfer grain to a heavy clay or wooden bowl.

Take a large pestle and moisten it. Begin pounding the cooked rice, periodically dipping the pestle in water to prevent the rice from sticking. Continue pounding about 1 hour, until all the grains of rice appear to be broken and the rice is very sticky. Sprinkle a baking sheet with rice flour and spread mochi evenly over the sheet. Cover with a straw mat and allow to dry 1 to 2 days before cutting into pieces and wrapping in plastic. Mochi will keep, refrigerated, about 10 days.

■ **VARIATION** Do not dry the mochi. Place freshly pounded mochi in a moistened plastic container. Cover and refrigerate. The mochi will be a little softer, but just as good.

Short-Grain Brown Rice with Squash

This is a staple in our house during the fall and winter, when the squash is so sweet that you'd swear it was sugared if you didn't know better. A delicious breakfast dish when cooked soft, it creates very warming energy, nourishing our middle-body organs, like the spleen, pancreas and stomach. This also makes a richly flavored dinner grain as well.

MAKES 4 OR 5 SERVINGS

2 cups short-grain brown rice, rinsed, soaked for at least 1 hour, drained and soaking water discarded
1 cup cubed winter squash
3 cups spring or filtered water
2 pinches sea salt
1 tablespoon barley miso
1 sheet toasted nori, slivered
2 to 3 sprigs flat-leaf parsley, finely minced, for garnish

Combine rice, squash and water in a pressure cooker and cook over medium heat, uncovered, until mixture comes to a boil. Add salt. Seal and bring to full pressure. Place over a flame deflector; reduce heat to low and cook 50 minutes.

Meanwhile, puree miso in a small amount of water and simmer it 3 to 4 minutes. When the rice is cooked, remove it from heat and allow pressure to reduce naturally. Stir pureed miso into hot rice and transfer to a serving bowl. Serve garnished with nori and parsley.

Fried Rice and Vegetables

A familiar favorite, this vegetarian version relies on an abundance of fresh vegetables and flavorful seasoning to create a low-fat, delicious alternative to the oily and salty take-out standard.

MAKES 4 OR 5 SERVINGS

1 to 2 teaspoons dark sesame oil
3 or 4 slices fresh ginger, cut into thin
   matchsticks
1 to 2 cloves fresh garlic, slivered
Sea salt
¼ cup each sliced onion, carrot matchsticks,
   burdock matchsticks, thinly sliced button
   mushrooms and shredded cabbage
1 to 2 cups cooked short-grain brown rice
1 to 2 stalks broccoli, broken into florets,
   stems peeled and thinly sliced
Soy sauce
Brown rice vinegar
2 to 3 sprigs flat-leaf parsley, for garnish

Heat oil in a skillet over medium–low heat. Add ginger, garlic and a pinch of salt and cook, stirring, until golden. Add onion and another pinch of salt and cook, stirring, until onion is translucent, about 5 minutes. Add carrot, burdock and mushrooms and another pinch of salt and cook, stirring occasionally, until coated with oil. Finally, stir in cabbage and another pinch of salt and cook, stirring, until cabbage begins to wilt, about 5 minutes.

Spread vegetables evenly over the skillet and top with cooked rice, then broccoli florets and stems. Sprinkle lightly with soy sauce. Gently add about ⅛ inch of water to allow everything to steam together, cover and cook over medium heat about 10 minutes, until all liquid is absorbed and broccoli is cooked. Turn off heat and season to taste with rice vinegar. Stir

well, transfer to a serving bowl and garnish with parsley sprigs.

Fried Rice with Sweet Pineapple

There's fried rice and then there's *this* fried rice. The pineapple adds not only sweetness and a light energy, but enzymes to help us digest the grain and tofu. Brilliant!

MAKES 4 TO 6 SERVINGS

Avocado oil
3 or 4 slices fresh ginger, cut into fine
   matchstick pieces
2 or 3 cloves fresh garlic, finely minced
1 small leek, split lengthwise, rinsed well and
   thinly sliced on the diagonal
Soy sauce
3 to 4 dried shiitake mushrooms, soaked until
   tender and thinly sliced
1 carrot, cut into fine matchstick pieces
¼ small head green cabbage, finely shredded
Mirin
½ pound extra-firm tofu, cut into small cubes
1½ cups cooked short-grain brown rice
Spring or filtered water
Toasted sesame oil
Brown rice vinegar
2 cups cubed fresh pineapple
2 or 3 fresh green onions, thinly sliced on the
   diagonal

Place a small amount of oil, the ginger, garlic and leek in a deep skillet over medium heat. When the vegetables begin to sizzle, add a dash of soy sauce and sauté 2 to 3 minutes. Stir in mushrooms and carrot and another dash of soy sauce and sauté 2 minutes. Add cabbage, a dash of soy sauce and a generous splash of mirin. Sauté until the cabbage just wilts. Top with tofu and brown rice. Season lightly with soy sauce and add about ½ cup water. Cover, reduce heat to low and cook until water is absorbed into the dish, 7 to 10 minutes.

Remove from heat and stir in a modest drizzle of sesame oil, brown rice vinegar and pineapple. Serve garnished with green onions.

Bill's Squash and Millet Casserole

Once a year, I am invited to teach in Portland, Maine, and it is a party from start to finish. Two of the reasons for that atmosphere are my hosts, Bill and Marie Wood, who generously open their home to me when I am there, making sure I get rest and lots of great food. They both are amazing in the kitchen and this breakfast was my favorite on my last visit. Way to go, Bill!

MAKES 4 OR 5 SERVINGS

1 cup yellow millet, rinsed very well
Spring or filtered water
Sea salt
1 small butternut squash, peeled, seeded and
    cubed
Scant pinch ground cinnamon
1 pound soft tofu, coarsely crumbled
Soy sauce

Place millet and 5 cups water in a saucepan and bring to a boil over medium heat. Add a pinch of salt, cover and reduce heat to low. Cook until millet is soft and water is absorbed, about 30 minutes.

While the millet cooks, place squash in a saucepan with about ½ inch water. Add a pinch

of salt and cinnamon and bring to a boil over medium heat. Cover and reduce heat to low. Cook until squash is quite soft, about 20 minutes. Drain away any remaining water and mash with a fork until mixture is smooth.

While the millet and squash cook, mix tofu with a light seasoning of soy sauce, just to create some flavor.

Preheat oven to 350F (175C) and lightly oil a 2-quart baking dish. Spread one-third of the millet on the bottom of the dish, top with half of the squash and then half of the tofu. Spread one-third of the millet evenly over the tofu. Spread the remaining tofu and squash in layers over the millet. Spread remaining millet over the top of the casserole, cover and bake 30 to 35 minutes to set the casserole. Serve hot or warm.

Millet and Veggie Burgers

This is such an easy dish to put together for lunches or snacks, or on those nights when you would love to just send out for a pizza instead of cooking a well-balanced, healthy meal. These burgers satisfy the cook's need for ease of preparation, without compromising your food choices.

MAKES ABOUT 4 SERVINGS

1 to 2 teaspoons avocado oil, plus additional
    for pan-frying
3 to 4 slices fresh ginger, cut into thin
    matchsticks
Sea salt
1 cup millet, rinsed
3 cups boiling spring or filtered water
½ cup *each* diced onion, carrot and celery
¼ cup minced fresh flat-leaf parsley
½ cup yellow cornmeal, plus additional for
    dredging

Heat oil in a pot over medium heat. Add ginger and a pinch of salt and cook 2 to 3 minutes. Remove ginger from oil. Add millet and cook, stirring, until millet is coated with oil and gives off a nutty fragrance. Carefully add boiling water, season lightly with salt to taste and reduce heat to low. Cover and simmer 35 minutes. Add onion, carrot and celery, re-cover and simmer about 5 minutes. Remove from heat and stir in parsley and cornmeal. Allow mixture to stand 10 to 15 minutes before forming into burgers.

Shape millet mixture into thick patties. Dredge in cornmeal to coat. Heat about ⅛ inch avocado oil in a skillet over medium heat. Fry patties until golden, about 3 minutes on each side. Remove from skillet and drain on paper towels to absorb any excess oil. Serve as you would any conventional burger.

Chilled Asian Rice

It may sound like just another brown-rice-and-tofu salad, but this delicious version of Asian take-out fare contains less salt and fat than its restaurant counterpart. It is a great, easy recipe for using up leftover grain as well.

MAKES 4 TO 5 SERVINGS

8 ounces extra-firm tofu, cubed

MARINADE
1 to 2 teaspoons light sesame oil
Juice of 1 lemon
Juice of 1 lime
2 cloves fresh garlic, finely minced
1 tablespoon fresh ginger juice (see Note, page 164)
2 teaspoons soy sauce

1 teaspoon brown rice vinegar
1 tablespoon brown rice syrup
Spring or filtered water

7 or 8 snow peas, cut into thin slices, blanched
1 celery stalk, cut into large dice
½ red bell pepper, roasted over a flame, peeled, seeded and diced (see Note, page 262)
2 cups cooked medium- or long-grain brown rice
2 tablespoons minced, pan-roasted walnut pieces (see Note, below)
1 to 2 fresh green onions, thinly sliced on the diagonal, for garnish

Place tofu in a shallow dish. Whisk together marinade ingredients, adding enough water to create a thin consistency. The flavors in the marinade can be as mild or strong as you like, so adjust the seasonings to your taste; because the tofu takes on the flavors of the marinade. (Err to the mild side on the taste here.) Pour marinade over tofu and allow to stand 10 to 15 minutes.

Combine vegetables, rice, walnuts, tofu and marinade. Serve garnished with green onions.

■ **NOTE** To pan-toast nuts and large seeds, such as pumpkin or sunflower, place in a dry skillit over medium to medium-low heat. Toast until golden and fragrant, about 5 minutes, stirring. Toast small seeds, such as sesame, or chopped nuts for about 4 minutes. Immediately remove toasted nuts or seeds from hot skillet to prevent burning.

Quinoa Salad

Quinoa is far from a new grain. Dating back to native South American cooking, this delicious, nutty grain is quite high in protein, cooks quickly and has a very strengthening, calming effect on the body, making it a great all-around carb. Available at most natural foods stores, quinoa is a great addition to your grain repertoire, especially if you are active and looking for a little more protein.

MAKES 4 OR 5 SERVINGS

2 cups spring or filtered water
Sea salt
1 cup quinoa, rinsed very well
1 cup fresh or frozen corn kernels
1 cup fresh or frozen green peas
1 small cucumber, peeled, seeded and diced
1 to 2 celery stalks, diced
Juice of ½ lemon
Juice of ½ orange
2 teaspoons soy sauce
2 tablespoons extra-virgin olive oil
7 to 8 fresh mint leaves, minced
4 to 5 fresh basil leaves, minced

Bring water and a pinch of salt to a boil over medium heat. Add quinoa and bring back to the boil. Cover, reduce heat and simmer until all the liquid is absorbed and the quinoa is fluffy, 25 to 30 minutes.

Bring another pot of water to a boil over high heat. Add corn and cook 2 minutes. Remove with a slotted spoon, drain well and transfer to a mixing bowl. Add peas to boiling water and boil 30 seconds. Drain well and add to corn. Add quinoa, cucumber and celery to corn mixture, mixing well to combine ingredients.

Whisk together the lemon and orange juices, soy sauce and olive oil in a small bowl; add mint and basil to taste. Adjust seasonings to suit your taste. Pour dressing over hot quinoa mixture and toss to combine. Serve immediately or the quinoa will take on too much moisture and become soggy.

Roasted Vegetable and Corn Chili

This thick, rich, elegant-tasting version of a classic recipe employs corn grits as an unusual alternative to the beans usually found in vegetarian versions of meatless chili. Serve with crusty whole-grain bread and lightly boiled or steamed veggies to round out your meal.

MAKES 4 OR 5 SERVINGS

1 to 2 yellow squash, cut into cubes
1 red bell pepper, cut into large dice
1 portobello mushroom, stem removed and
**   cap cut into large dice**
1 cup coarsely chopped button mushrooms
Extra-virgin olive oil
Sea salt
1 yellow onion, finely diced
3 cloves fresh garlic, finely minced
Scant pinch crushed red pepper flakes
Generous pinch *each* ground cumin and
**   ground ginger**
3 to 4 fresh plum tomatoes, coarsely chopped
**   (do not peel or seed)**
½ cup fresh or frozen corn kernels
Spring or filtered water
Generous pinch chili powder
1 cup corn grits

Preheat oven to 450F (220C). Toss the squash, bell pepper and mushrooms in a little olive oil to lightly coat. Spread on a baking sheet and sprinkle lightly with salt. Roast about 20 minutes, tossing occasionally, until lightly browned. Remove from oven and set aside.

Heat 2 tablespoons olive oil in a large, heavy Dutch oven (enamel-covered cast iron is great) over medium heat. Add the onion, garlic and a pinch of salt and sauté until fragrant, 2 to 3 minutes. Stir in red pepper flakes, cumin and ginger and cook 1 to 2 minutes more. Add tomatoes, corn, 3 cups of water, a pinch of salt and chili powder to taste. (The flavor of chili powder gets stronger as it cooks, so err on the mild side in the beginning. You can always spice things up later.) Fold in corn grits and roasted vegetables, cover partially and simmer, stirring occasionally, over low heat until thick, about 1 hour. Add water as needed as the chili cooks. The finished product should be creamy and thick, but not pasty.

Sweet-and-Sour Corn Salad

The quintessential symbol of summer, this wonderful grain is packed with vitamins, minerals and protein. Growing high and proud, corn is at its best during the warmest summer weather. It gives us great vitality and helps us adapt more smoothly to the warm temperatures of the season. This salad is a different take on the use of corn: The mustard-flavored sweet-and-sour sauce enhances the flavor of the corn just perfectly. It is great served over a bed of lightly steamed leafy greens.

MAKES 4 OR 5 SERVINGS

4 ears fresh corn, kernels removed
1 red bell pepper, roasted over a flame,
peeled, seeded and diced (see Note, page
262)
½ cucumber, seeded and diced, but not
peeled (unless it has been waxed)
3 to 4 green onions, cut into thin diagonal
slices
¼ cup minced fresh flat-leaf parsley

SWEET-AND-SOUR SAUCE
1 tablespoon brown rice syrup
Juice of ½ lemon
2 tablespoons spring or filtered water
1 tablespoon soy sauce
2 tablespoons brown rice vinegar
4 teaspoons prepared mustard
1 tablespoon extra-virgin olive oil

Bring a small pot of water to a boil and add the corn kernels. Return to a boil and drain immediately. (This will enhance the sweet flavor of the corn and make it tender.) Toss together the corn, bell pepper, cucumber, onions and parsley in a large bowl.

Combine the sauce ingredients in a small bowl and whisk until blended. Adjust seasonings to your taste. Stir sauce into the vegetables and allow to marinate about 30 minutes so the flavors can develop.

Brown and Wild Rice Pilaf

No grain section would be complete without a pilaf recipe. This popular style of serving whole grains is a chewy, crunchy symphony of flavors, textures and colors.

<small>MAKES 4 OR 5 SERVINGS</small>

1 teaspoon extra-virgin olive oil
1 small onion, finely diced
2 cloves fresh garlic, finely minced
Sea salt
2 tablespoons slivered almonds
1 cup thinly sliced button mushrooms,
   brushed clean
1 cup fresh corn kernels
1 medium carrot, cut into large dice
1 cup brown basmati rice, rinsed well, soaked
   for at least 1 hour
¼ cup wild rice
2½ cups spring or filtered water
2 to 3 sprigs flat-leaf parsley, for garnish

In a deep, heavy pot, heat the oil over medium heat. Add the onion, garlic and a pinch of salt and cook until fragrant, 2 to 3 minutes. Add the almonds and cook, stirring, until coated with oil. Stir in the mushrooms, corn, carrot and a pinch of salt and cook 1 to 2 minutes more. Spread the vegetables evenly over the bottom of the pot and top with the basmati and wild rices.

Gently add the water and bring to a boil. Add 1 or 2 pinches of salt. Reduce heat, cover, and simmer over low heat about 45 minutes, until all the liquid is absorbed and the rice is fluffy. Remove pot from heat and allow to stand, covered, 5 minutes. Stir well and transfer to a serving bowl. Garnish with parsley sprigs.

■ **NOTE** A trick to help you know when the rice is ready: When the cooking time is about up, use the handle end of a wooden spoon to drill a hole into the rice and if there is no water in the hole, the rice is done. If there is still water, then the rice still needs to cook.

Cynthia's Chili with Polenta Croutons

Meatless meals have predominated cooking throughout most, if not all, cultures. This peasant cuisine is again becoming fashionable as modern people discover that vegetarian meals are satisfying and simple to prepare. I worked as head chef a number of years ago in a natural foods restaurant where the following chili recipe was developed by the owner, Cynthia Tice. It is the best I have ever tasted. Its thick texture and authentic, spicy flavor will win raves. Trust me, no one will miss meat in this meal. Serve with crusty whole grain bread and lightly cooked vegetables.

<small>MAKES 5 TO 6 SERVINGS</small>

1 (1-inch) piece kombu
½ cup each pinto beans and kidney beans,
   rinsed well and soaked for 1 hour (soaking
   is optional)
Spring or filtered water
Generous pinch of cumin powder
1 to 2 teaspoons chili powder
Extra-virgin olive oil
2 cloves fresh garlic, finely minced
Generous pinch crushed red pepper flakes
½ cup each diced onion, celery, winter squash
   and carrot
Sea salt
1 cup millet, rinsed well
1 recipe Old World Polenta (page 63), cut into
   1-inch squares

Place kombu in the bottom of a pressure cooker. Add beans and 3 cups fresh water. Bring to a boil, uncovered, over medium heat and cook at a rolling boil about 10 minutes. Seal and bring to full pressure. Reduce heat to low and cook 40 minutes. Remove pot from heat and allow pressure to reduce naturally. Open the pot, stir in cumin and chili powder to taste and simmer 5 minutes, uncovered.

In a soup pot, heat about 1 tablespoon of olive oil over medium heat. Add garlic, red pepper flakes, onion, celery, squash, carrot and a pinch of salt and sauté until shiny with oil. Top with millet and, finally, the cooked beans. Add enough water to generously cover all ingredients and sprinkle lightly with salt. Cover and bring to a boil over medium heat. Reduce heat and cook until millet is creamy and chili is thick with a "meaty" texture, 35 minutes.

Heat enough olive oil in a skillet over medium heat to cover the bottom. Add polenta squares and cook, turning, until golden brown on both sides. Garnish each bowl of chili with a few polenta squares and serve.

■ **VARIATION** You may also use canned organic beans instead of cooking your own to save cooking time in this recipe.

Bulgur with Skillet Veggies

A simple and satisfying one-dish meal. Serve with a fresh salad and a light soup to create the perfect quick dinner.

MAKES 4 OR 5 SERVINGS

1 to 2 teaspoons extra-virgin olive oil
1 onion, finely diced
1 clove fresh garlic, finely minced
Sea salt
1 cup bulgur wheat
2 cups spring or filtered water
2 cups thinly sliced fresh cremini or button mushrooms
1 cup small cauliflower florets
1 carrot, cut into thin matchsticks
7 or 8 Brussels sprouts, halved and thinly sliced lengthwise
Generous pinch dried rosemary
1 tablespoon kuzu or arrowroot, dissolved in a little cold water
2 tablespoons slivered almonds, pan-toasted (see Note, page 55), for garnish

Place oil, onion and garlic in a deep skillet over medium heat. When the onion begins to sizzle, add a pinch of sea salt and sauté until translucent, 2 to 3 minutes. Add bulgur and cook, stirring constantly, about 2 minutes. Gently add water and a pinch of salt and bring to a boil. Cover, reduce heat and cook until liquid is absorbed, about 15 minutes.

While the bulgur cooks, place another skillet over medium heat, and arrange mushrooms, cauliflower, carrot and Brussels sprouts each in their own sections avoiding overlap in the skillet. Add enough water to half cover, sprinkle lightly with salt, and bring to a boil. Cover, reduce heat and simmer until cauliflower is crisp-tender, about 6 minutes. Add rosemary to taste and stir in kuzu mixture. Cook, stirring, until liquid is slightly thickened. Transfer bulgur to a serving bowl. To serve, spoon bulgur into individual bowls and top with vegetables and almonds.

Barley and Corn Salad

A lovely summer combination, this salad joins the cooling, dispersing energy of barley with the energizing power of fresh summer corn, all generously dressed in a refreshing lime vinaigrette.

MAKES 4 OR 5 SERVINGS

2 cups spring or filtered water
Sea salt
1 cup pearl barley, sorted and rinsed
1 to 2 ears fresh corn, kernels removed
1 small red onion, finely diced
1 small cucumber
¼ cup extra-virgin olive oil
2 to 3 tablespoons umeboshi vinegar (see Note, opposite)
2 teaspoons brown rice syrup
Juice of 1 lime
1 to 2 tablespoons prepared mustard
¼ cup minced fresh flat-leaf parsley

Bring water and a pinch of salt to a boil in a medium saucepan over medium heat. Slowly add barley. Cover, reduce heat to low, and cook 20 to 25 minutes. Add corn kernels and onion, season to taste with salt and continue cooking until barley is tender and liquid is absorbed, about 15 minutes. Transfer to a mixing bowl to cool.

While the barley mixture cools, peel, seed and dice cucumber.

In a small bowl, combine the oil, vinegar,

rice syrup, lime juice, mustard and a little salt. Whisk until blended. The dressing should have a refreshing, yet spicy taste. Toss the barley mixture and dressing together. Fold in cucumber and parsley. Allow the salad to marinate in the refrigerator about 30 minutes before serving.

■ **NOTE** If you cannot find umeboshi vinegar, substitute fresh lemon juice and adjust the taste of the dressing by adding a little more salt.

Wild Rice with Apples

Wild rice is not actually a whole grain but an aquatic grass seed still harvested by hand. It has a wonderful, nutty flavor. Mix in crisp, tart apples and a warm orange dressing for a taste sensation.

MAKES 4 OR 5 SERVINGS

1 cup brown basmati rice, rinsed well and soaked for at least 1 hour
1 cup wild rice, rinsed well
2½ cups spring or filtered water
Sea salt
½ cup fresh orange juice
1 tablespoon extra-virgin olive oil
1 tablespoon brown rice syrup
Grated zest of 1 orange
Juice of 1 lemon
1 tart apple (such as Granny Smith), cored and diced
1 celery stalk, diced

Drain basmati rice very well after soaking. Place both rices and water in a pressure cooker and bring to a boil, uncovered, over medium heat. Add a couple of pinches of salt, seal and bring to full pressure. Place over a flame deflector, reduce heat to low and cook 45 minutes.

Remove pot from heat and allow pressure to reduce naturally. Transfer rice to a serving bowl, fluffing with a fork.

While the rice is cooking, warm orange juice, olive oil, rice syrup, orange zest and a pinch of salt in a small pan over low heat. Remove from heat and stir in lemon juice and apple. Toss rice and celery with apple and orange dressing and serve warm.

Asian-Style Millet

Millet is one of the natural wonders of the culinary world. It is one of the most versatile grains, with a delicious, nutty flavor. It cooks up creamy and stew-like or you can pan-roast it to make it fluffy and light, enhancing and supporting the other flavors in the dish, as in this elegant, exotic grain dish.

MAKES 4 OR 5 SERVINGS

1 cup millet, rinsed well
3 cups spring or filtered water
Soy sauce
1 to 2 teaspoons dark sesame oil
3 to 4 slices fresh ginger, finely minced
2 cloves fresh garlic, finely minced
1 small carrot, finely diced
2 to 3 green onions, cut into thin diagonal slices
1 teaspoon fresh ginger juice (see Note, page 164)
1 teaspoon brown rice syrup
1 tablespoon brown rice vinegar
2 tablespoons peanuts, pan-toasted (see Note, page 46)

Heat a deep, dry skillet over medium heat. Drain millet well before toasting so that it toasts evenly and doesn't burn. Add to skillet and toast until millet puffs and begins to pop, about 5 minutes. Add water and a sprinkle of soy sauce and bring to a boil. Reduce heat, cover and simmer until the liquid is nearly absorbed, 30 minutes. Remove from heat and allow to stand, covered, 10 minutes. Fluff with a fork and transfer to a serving bowl.

Heat sesame oil in a skillet over medium heat. Add minced ginger and garlic and cook 2 to 3 minutes. Add carrot and green onions and cook until tender, 2 to 3 minutes. Sprinkle with a little soy sauce and stir in ginger juice and rice syrup. Remove from heat and stir in rice vinegar and peanuts. Fold into hot millet. Serve warm, as millet tends to stiffen as it cools.

Amaranth and Corn

An ancient grain revisited. It was cultivated by the Aztecs, but was also widely used in China and in South and Central America. Commonly ground into flour, amaranth is also a wonderful whole grain dish, but it only recently came back into vogue as a grain. It has a strong, earthy, sweet flavor that matches perfectly the sweetness of fresh corn.

MAKES 3 TO 4 SERVINGS

1 cup amaranth, rinsed and drained through a very fine strainer
½ cup fresh or frozen corn kernels
2¼ cups spring or filtered water
Pinch sea salt

Combine amaranth, corn and water in a medium pan over medium heat and bring to a boil. Add salt. Cover, reduce heat and simmer until all the liquid is absorbed and the grain is creamy, 25 to 30 minutes.

■ **VARIATION** This grain dish combines very well with hato mugi barley, also known as

Job's tears. Cooked in the same manner as the recipe indicates, simply add ¼ cup barley to the amaranth and increase the water by a little over ½ cup.

Quinoa with Tempeh and Cilantro

Truly a fast food, quinoa cooks up very quickly, unfolding like a spiral as it cooks. As in this recipe, quinoa partners very well with more cooling vegetables and helps to create some wonderful, nutty grain dishes.

It is especially important to rinse quinoa well before cooking, because the grains are covered with a coating of a substance called saponin, which protects the delicate grains. If not rinsed off, this substance can make your cooked quinoa taste bitter.

MAKES 4 OR 5 SERVINGS

1 cup quinoa
2 cups spring or filtered water
Pinch sea salt
Avocado or light olive oil, for deep-frying
1 (8-ounce) package tempeh, cubed
1 tablespoon extra-virgin olive oil
1 clove fresh garlic, finely minced
6 to 7 green onions, cut into thin diagonal slices
Soy sauce
2 teaspoons brown rice syrup
2 celery stalks, finely diced
Juice of 1 lime
¼ cup fresh cilantro, very finely minced

Place quinoa in a fine strainer and rinse well. Place in a pot with water and bring to a boil. Add salt. Cover, reduce heat and simmer until liquid is absorbed and quinoa is fluffy, about 30 minutes. Set aside.

Heat about 1 inch of avocado oil in a heavy skillet or pan over medium heat. Test the oil temperature by dropping in a piece of tempeh. If it sinks and comes immediately back to the top, the oil is hot enough to deep-fry properly. (Remember the point of frying is to add richness to your diet and to give you the strong kind of energy present only in foods cooked very quickly over high heat.) Deep-fry the tempeh cubes until golden brown. Drain on paper towels and set aside.

Heat olive oil in a skillet over medium heat. Add garlic, green onions, a little soy sauce and rice syrup. Cook until onions are bright green, about 3 minutes. Stir in celery, quinoa and tempeh and toss well. Remove from heat and stir in lime juice and cilantro. Serve warm.

Brown Rice and Millet Croquettes

Tired of simply resteaming leftover grain, putting it into soup or, even worse, throwing it away after a few days? Well, this recipe is for you. All you need to make croquettes is some cooked grains, some oil and about a half hour prep time. The amounts suggested are really just a guide. Grain ratios may vary, depending on what you have available. The same goes for vegetables.

MAKES 3 OR 4 SERVINGS

½ cup cooked brown rice
½ cup cooked millet
¼ cup combined finely diced onion and carrot
¼ cup fresh or frozen corn kernels (optional)
Fine yellow or white cornmeal
Avocado or olive oil, for shallow-frying or pan-frying

Combine grains and vegetables in a large bowl. With moist hands, form the mixture into small rounds, thick discs or oblong fingers. Pour some cornmeal onto a plate and gently pat croquette until completely coated. (This will hold the croquette together as well as give it a crispy outer coating.)

To shallow-fry, heat about 1 inch of oil in a heavy skillet or pan over medium heat. Fry each croquette until golden brown, turning as needed to cook evenly. Drain well on paper towels to remove excess oil. If pan-frying, heat less than ¼ inch of oil in a skillet over medium heat. Fry the croquettes on each side until golden. Drain well on paper towels.

These are great served with Creamy Sesame Dressing (page 271), Garlic, Mushroom and Leek Sauce (page 276), in a simple broth or with a dipping sauce consisting of soy sauce, water and fresh ginger juice or lemon juice.

■ **VARIATION** Don't limit youself to this combination. Any cooked whole or cracked grains will make delicious croquettes. Rice with bulgur, millet with couscous, barley and corn—the list is virtually endless.

Bulgur, Mushroom and Greens Salad

In the summer months, it is really nice to lighten things up a bit with quick-cooking cracked grains. This delicious salad combines a variety of flavors to create a nutty, sweet-and-sour medley.

MAKES 3 OR 4 SERVINGS

2 cups spring or filtered water
Sea salt
1 cup bulgur
2 tablespoons extra-virgin olive oil
½ cup diced onion
**1 cup button mushrooms, brushed clean and
    thinly sliced**
**6 or 7 leaves arugula, dandelion or
    watercress, rinsed**
1 cup seedless grapes
Juice of 1 lemon
**2 tablespoons slivered almonds, pan-toasted
    (see Note, opposite)**

Bring water and a pinch of salt to a boil in a medium pan over medium heat. Add bulgur, cover and reduce heat. Cook until water is absorbed and bulgur is fluffy, 20 minutes.

Heat oil in a skillet over medium heat. Add onion and a pinch of salt and cook until onion

is translucent, about 5 minutes. Add mushrooms and a pinch of salt and sauté until limp. Hand-shred greens into small pieces, add to the skillet and cook until greens just wilt, about 2 minutes. Add grapes and stir well. Remove from heat and stir in lemon juice. Toss with bulgur and almonds and transfer to a serving bowl.

- **NOTE** Pan-toast almonds in a dry skillet over medium heat, stirring constantly, until fragrant, about 5 minutes.

Nutty Rice and Broccoli

Another take on a basic grain dish. See? The variations really are endless . . .

MAKES 6 TO 8 SERVINGS

2 cups medium grain brown rice, rinsed well, soaked for at least 1 hour
2½ cups spring or filtered water
2 pinches sea salt
2 cups broccoli florets
¼ cup finely diced carrot
¼ cup finely diced red onion
½ cup walnut pieces, coarsely chopped
1 teaspoon barley miso, dissolved in a little warm water
Grated zest of 1 lemon

Drain rice well after soaking. Combine rice and water in a pressure cooker. Bring to a boil, loosely covered, over medium heat. Add salt, seal and bring to full pressure. Place over a flame deflector, reduce heat to low and cook 25 minutes. Turn off heat and allow pressure cooker to stand undisturbed for another 25 minutes. Remove from heat.

While the rice is cooking, bring a pan of water to a boil. Separately, cook broccoli, carrot

and onion in boiling water until crisp-tender, and drain well. Mix vegetables together in a medium bowl. Set aside.

Heat a dry skillet over medium heat. Add walnuts and pan-toast until fragrant, about 5 minutes, stirring. Transfer to a food processor with dissolved miso and pulse until a coarse paste forms. Stir vegetables, walnut paste and lemon zest into rice. Transfer to a serving bowl and serve hot.

Brown Rice Risotto

Traditionally made in northern Italy from a glutinous white rice, this risotto is a whole grain version. A few alterations in ingredients and cooking methods result in a rich and creamy dish, much like the classic version.

MAKES 4 OR 5 SERVINGS

1½ cups medium-grain brown rice, rinsed well
2 teaspoons extra-virgin olive oil
Sea salt
¼ cup mirin or white wine
¾ cup spring or filtered water
2 to 3 cloves fresh garlic, finely minced
½ yellow onion, finely diced
5 cups Vegetable Stock (page 74)
¼ cup thinly sliced leek, rinsed well
½ cup diced carrot

Soak rice in water to cover, 6 to 8 hours. Drain and discard the soaking water. Heat 1 teaspoon of the oil in a deep skillet over medium heat. Add rice and a pinch of salt and cook, stirring, until coated with oil. Stir in mirin and water, cover and cook, stirring frequently, over medium heat. As soon as rice absorbs the liquid, stir in garlic and onion and mix well. Begin adding vegetable stock in ½-cup amounts, stirring frequently, but cook rice covered, instead of the traditional method of cooking risotto in an uncovered pan. As rice absorbs liquid, continue adding stock and stirring frequently until all the stock has been used, 40 to 45 minutes. Taste the rice to be sure that it is tender before removing from heat.

Heat the remaining oil in a skillet over medium heat. Add leek and a pinch of salt and cook, stirring, until limp. Add carrot and a pinch of salt and cook until tender. Stir vegetables into the risotto. Serve immediately.

Basic Risotto

Rather than pasta, grain is more dominant in the cuisine of northern Italy. Risotto is traditionally made with white, glutinous arborio rice. Its name refers to the cooking method as well as to the dish itself. The trademark creamy texture is achieved by slowly adding liquid, usually a savory stock, in small increments, cooking the rice over medium heat and stirring constantly. Straying from these basics can result in tough, uncooked risotto or gluey, sticky risotto—neither of which is desirable.

MAKES 3 OR 4 SERVINGS

4 cups Vegetable Stock (page 74) or spring or filtered water
1 tablespoon extra-virgin olive oil
1 to 2 cloves fresh garlic, minced
1 small onion, finely diced
Pinch sea salt
1 cup arborio rice, rinsed well
1 cup white wine
1 to 2 tablespoons unsweetened soymilk
2 to 3 sprigs flat-leaf parsley, finely minced

Warm stock over low heat and keep warm.
Heat oil in a deep skillet over medium heat.

Add garlic, onion and salt and cook, stirring, until onion is softened, about 3 minutes. Add rice and cook, stirring, 2 to 3 minutes. Add wine and cook, stirring often, until absorbed into rice.

Stir in soymilk for added richness. Remove from heat and stir in parsley. Transfer to a serving bowl and serve immediately.

Roasted Beet Risotto

I was never a fan of beets. I did not like how sweet they were—I know, crazy, right? But then a friend of mine taught me this dish and I realized I had been missing out on some amazing flavor and glorious color.

MAKES ABOUT 4 SERVINGS

2 medium beets, unpeeled, rinsed well
4 cups spring or filtered water
Sea salt
Extra-virgin olive oil
1 small red onion, diced
1 cup arborio rice (do not rinse)
⅓ cup dry white wine
2 to 3 tablespoons unsweetened soymilk
1 or 2 sprigs flat-leaf parsley, finely minced, for garnish

Preheat oven to 425F (220C). Wet a sheet of parchment paper and wring out excess water. Lay a double-thick sheet of foil on a work surface with parchment paper on top. Lay beets on paper and wrap foil and parchment tightly around beets. Bake 1 to 1½ hours, until tender. Cool slightly before opening foil. When the beets have cooled enough to handle, peel and dice. Set aside.

Make the risotto: Place water and a pinch of salt over low heat, covered and keep it warm during cooking. Place a small amount of oil and onion in a deep skillet over medium heat. When the onion begins to sizzle, add a pinch of salt and sauté 2 to 3 minutes. Stir in rice and sauté 1 minute. Stir in wine and cook over low heat, stirring constantly, until the wine is absorbed. Begin adding warm water, by ladles to the rice, stirring frequently and only adding more water as it is absorbed. Continue this process until the rice is creamy and tender, about 25 minutes. Stir in beets, salt to taste and soymilk and cook, stirring, until any remaining liquid is absorbed. Transfer to a serving bowl and garnish with parsley.

Butternut Squash Risotto

The squash adds a rich golden color and delightful sweet taste to basic risotto . . . and cooking it in a pressure-based risotto cooker sweetens it even more by making it s-o-o-o easy to make.

MAKES 4 OR 5 SERVINGS

1 medium butternut squash, seeds removed and cut into 8 pieces
1 tablespoon extra-virgin olive oil
3 shallots, peeled and minced
Sea salt
1 cup arborio rice, rinsed
½ cup white wine
2 cups Vegetable Stock (page 74) or spring or filtered water
Generous pinch grated nutmeg
2 sprigs basil, leaves minced, plus 1 small sprig, for garnish

Steam the squash over boiling water 10 to 15 minutes or until soft. Scoop meat out of skin and mash. Set aside.

Heat olive oil in a deep skillet over medium heat. Add the shallots and a generous pinch of salt and cook, stirring, 2 to 3 minutes. Add rice and cook, stirring, 2 to 3 minutes. Stirring constantly, add wine and cook until wine is almost absorbed into rice. Stir in squash puree. In ½-cup amounts, slowly add warm stock to rice and cook, stirring constantly, until liquid is absorbed. Continue this process until all stock is used and rice is creamy and tender, about 25 minutes. Stir in nutmeg and minced basil to taste. Serve hot, garnished with basil sprigs.

■ **NOTE** The Kuhn Rikon Risotto Cooker makes fabulous risotto without all the stirring. Cook the shallots and salt and add wine and squash to the risotto cooker as above. Seal the lid and bring to full pressure. Reduce heat to low and cook for 7 minutes. Remove from heat and allow pressure to reduce.

Any risotto recipe can be adapted and cooked in this fashion with rich, creamy results.

Mushroom-Leek Risotto

The mushroom flavor is enhanced by the homemade stock and fresh mushrooms.

MAKES 4 OR 5 SERVINGS

5 to 6 cups Mushroom Stock (page 75)
2 tablespoons extra-virgin olive oil
1 or 2 cloves fresh garlic, finely minced
½ small leek, rinsed well, thinly sliced
Sea salt
1 cup thinly sliced button mushrooms, brushed free of dirt
½ cup thinly sliced porcini mushrooms, brushed free of dirt
1 cup arborio rice, rinsed
1 cup white wine
¼ cup minced fresh flat-leaf parsley

Heat stock in a medium saucepan and keep warm over low heat.

Heat 1 tablespoon of the olive oil in a deep skillet over medium heat. Add garlic and sauté for 30 seconds; do not burn. Add leek and a pinch of salt and cook, stirring, until leek is bright green and softened. Add mushrooms and a pinch of salt and cook, stirring, until softened. Transfer mixture to a small bowl and set aside.

In the same skillet, heat remaining oil over medium heat. Add the rice and cook, stirring, 2 to 3 minutes. Stirring constantly, add the wine and cook, stirring, until wine is almost absorbed. In ½-cup amounts, slowly add warm stock to rice and cook, stirring constantly, until liquid is absorbed. Continue this process until all of stock is used and rice is creamy and tender, about 25 minutes. Stir in sautéed vegetables and parsley. Serve hot.

Corn and Shallot Risotto

This is a perfect summer dish when corn is at its peak.

MAKES 4 OR 5 SERVINGS

5 cups Corn Stock (recipe below)
1 tablespoon extra-virgin olive oil
2 to 3 shallots, peeled and finely minced
2 cloves fresh garlic, finely minced
Sea salt
1 cup arborio rice, rinsed
¼ cup mirin
Spring or filtered water
2 ears fresh corn, kernels removed, or 1 cup frozen corn
Fresh rosemary leaves and sprigs

Heat stock in a large pot and keep warm over low heat.

Heat the olive oil in a deep skillet over medium heat. Add shallots, garlic and a pinch of salt and sauté until fragrant, 2 to 3 minutes. Add rice and cook, stirring, 2 to 3 minutes. Stir in mirin and ½ cup water and cook, stirring constantly, until liquid is absorbed.

In ½-cup amounts, slowly add warm stock to rice and cook, stirring constantly, until liquid is absorbed. Continue this process until all of stock is used and rice is creamy and tender, about 25 minutes.

Bring a pot of water to a boil. Add corn kernels to water and bring back to a boil to bring out corn's sweetness; drain. Stir corn and about ⅛ teaspoon fresh rosemary leaves into rice. Serve hot, garnished with rosemary sprigs.

Corn Stock

MAKES ABOUT 6 CUPS

1 teaspoon avocado oil
1 onion, finely diced
Sea salt
3 to 4 ears fresh corn, kernels removed, cobs reserved
8 to 9 cups spring or filtered water
2 bay leaves

Heat oil in a large pot over medium heat. Add onion and a pinch of salt and cook, stirring, 2 to 3 minutes. Add corn kernels and cook, stirring, until coated with oil. Add water, corn cobs and bay leaves and bring to a boil. Reduce heat and simmer, uncovered, for 1 hour. Season lightly with salt and simmer an additional 10 minutes. Strain the stock, pressing as much liquid as possible from the vegetables before discarding them.

Baked Risotto with Italian Herbs

A variation on the stovetop theme . . . great rich taste with no stirring.

MAKES 4 OR 5 SERVINGS

5 to 6 cups Vegetable Stock (page 74)
1 tablespoon extra-virgin olive oil
1 small onion, finely minced
2 cloves fresh garlic, finely minced
Sea salt
1 cup arborio rice
Equal amounts (about ½ teaspoon *each*) of minced fresh flat-leaf parsley, basil, rosemary and oregano
½ cup spring or filtered water
½ cup white wine
Juice of ½ lemon

Preheat oven to 350F (175C). Lightly oil a shallow baking dish and set aside. Heat stock in a large pot and keep warm over low heat.

Heat the olive oil in a skillet over medium heat. Add onion, garlic and a pinch of salt and sauté until softened, 2 to 3 minutes. Add rice and cook, stirring, 2 to 3 minutes. Stir in herbs. Spoon into prepared dish. Combine water, wine and stock and pour over rice mixture. Stir well, cover tightly and bake 25 to 30 minutes or until liquid is absorbed and rice is tender. Remove from oven and allow to stand, undisturbed, 5 minutes. Stir in lemon juice and serve hot.

Curried Corn with Chiles

Sweet corn and spicy chiles come together to create the perfect blend of flavors for a side dish that will win you raves. The flavors and textures produce a dish that is as lovely to eat as it is to look at.

MAKES 4 TO 6 SERVINGS

2 tablespoons extra-virgin olive or avocado oil
1 bunch green onions, minced
1 tablespoon ground coriander
2 teaspoons ground cumin
2 teaspoons curry powder
Generous pinch crushed red pepper flakes
1 (14-ounce) can unsweetened coconut milk
1 cup unsweetened soymilk
Grated zest of 1 lemon
Sea salt
4 cups fresh or frozen corn kernels
2 large poblano chiles, roasted over a flame, peeled, seeded and diced (see Note, page 262)
2 or 3 sprigs cilantro, finely minced

Place oil and green onions in a deep skillet over medium heat. When the green onions begin to sizzle, stir in coriander, cumin, curry powder, red pepper flakes and ½ cup of the coconut milk. Reduce heat and cook 3 minutes, stirring often.

Stir in remaining coconut milk, soymilk and lemon zest, season to taste with salt and cook, stirring often, 2 to 3 minutes. Stir in corn and cook, stirring often, until heated through, 3 to 4 minutes. Stir in chiles and cilantro and cook 1 minute. Transfer to a serving platter and serve immediately.

Quinoa and Potato Croquettes with Mango Salsa

An athlete's dream. Combining protein-rich quinoa with potatoes creates a dish that balances carbs and protein like no other. Add the salsa to the mix and you have spice to stimulate circulation and just enough sweetness to keep your healthy body relaxed.

MAKES ABOUT 5 SERVINGS

MANGO SALSA

1 ripe mango, peeled, seeded and cut into
    small dice
½ red onion, cut into small dice
1 small jalapeño chile, finely minced
1 clove fresh garlic, finely minced
Sea salt
1 teaspoon hot sauce
1 cup cooked black beans, drained
Juice of 1 lemon
Extra-virgin olive oil

CROQUETTES

2 cups spring or filtered water
1 Yukon Gold potato, peeled, diced
1 cup quinoa, rinsed very well
Sea salt
Extra-virgin olive oil
3 green onions, finely diced
4 sprigs parsley, minced
1 jalapeño chile, seeded, finely minced
½ teaspoon ground cumin
½ teaspoon dried oregano
Cracked black pepper
2 cloves fresh garlic, finely minced
½ cup pureed silken tofu
3 tablespoons grated vegan mozzarella
    cheese alternative
Whole wheat bread crumbs

Make salsa: Combine mango, onion, chile and garlic in a small mixing bowl. Season with salt to taste and stir in hot sauce, black beans, lemon juice and a generous drizzle of oil. Mix well, cover and set aside for flavors to meld.

Make croquettes: Bring water to a boil in a saucepan over medium heat and add potato and quinoa. Add a pinch of salt, cover and bring to a boil. Reduce heat to low and cook until quinoa has absorbed the water and has opened, about 20 minutes.

Meanwhile, place a small amount of oil in a skillet over medium heat. Add green onions, parsley, chile, cumin, oregano, pepper and garlic and sauté 1 to 2 minutes. Transfer to a mixing bowl.

When quinoa and potato are cooked, mash mixture with a fork to break up the potato. Combine with onion mixture and fold in tofu and cheese alternative. Mix very well. Form quinoa mixture into 2-inch patties.

Heat about 1 tablespoon of oil in a skillet over medium heat. Dredge croquettes in bread crumbs. Fry until golden on each side, about 2 minutes per side, turning once to ensure even browning. Transfer to a platter and spoon salsa on top of croquettes.

Polenta with Spicy Puttanesca Sauce

Puttanesca is a classic Italian sauce invented in Naples by ladies of the night (or so the story goes). It was said that this spicy sauce was quick to make and kept the ladies' energy high for their . . . profession. Served over mild-mannered polenta, the flavors of the sauce are showcased beautifully. I left out the traditional anchovies for obvious reasons.

MAKES 4 OR 5 SERVINGS

4 cups spring or filtered water
Pinch sea salt
1 tablespoon extra-virgin olive oil
1 cup yellow cornmeal
2 to 3 tablespoons unsweetened soymilk

PUTTANESCA SAUCE
Extra-virgin olive oil
2 or 3 cloves fresh garlic, crushed
Sea salt
Generous pinch crushed red pepper flakes
½ red onion, diced
1 (28-ounce) can diced tomatoes, undrained
3 to 4 tablespoons capers, drained, but not
**   rinsed**
12 to 18 oil-cured black olives, pitted and
**   coarsely chopped**

Whisk water, salt, oil and cornmeal in a large saucepan and place over medium heat. Cook, stirring constantly, until mixture comes to a boil. Reduce heat to low and cook, stirring frequently, until the center of the polenta pops and bubbles, about 25 minutes. Stir in soymilk to finish.

Make sauce: Place a small amount of oil and the garlic in a skillet over medium heat. When the garlic begins to sizzle, add a pinch of salt, red pepper flakes and onion and sauté 1 to 2 minutes. Add tomatoes with their juices, capers and olives and stir well. Season lightly with salt and cook, stirring occasionally, 5 minutes.

To serve, spoon polenta into individual bowls and spoon sauce over top.

Farro Salad, Umbria Style

Farro is my favorite whole grain, bar none. I was in Umbria the first time I tasted this ancient grain, and I fell in love. Don't let anyone fool you by saying you can use spelt or barley in place of farro. While lovely, they could not be more different. Trust me, seek out farro at an Italian specialty store. It's worth the search.

MAKES ABOUT 4 SERVINGS

3 cups spring or filtered water
1 cup farro, rinsed well
Sea salt
3 tablespoons extra-virgin olive oil, plus extra
**   for drizzling**
1 tablespoon red wine vinegar
½ cup fresh or frozen fava beans or baby lima
**   beans**
½ cup fresh or frozen baby green peas
2 cups baby arugula
3 plum tomatoes, diced (do not seed)
3 sprigs basil, leaves removed, left whole

Place water and farro in a saucepan over medium heat and bring to a boil. Add a generous pinch of salt, cover partially and reduce heat to low. Cook until farro has absorbed all liquid, about 25 minutes. Remove from heat and stir in oil, vinegar and a light seasoning of salt to taste.

While the farro cooks, bring a pot of water with a pinch of salt to a boil. Add fava beans and boil 3 minutes. Add peas and cook 1 minute more. Drain well and cool in a bowl of iced water to stop the cooking. Drain again. Gently fold fava beans and peas into farro mixture.

To serve, arrange arugula on a serving platter and drizzle lightly with olive oil. Just before serving, stir tomatoes and basil into farro, taking care not to break the grain or peas too much in the mixing. Spoon onto arugula and serve.

Millet-Tofu Stew

Truly one of the great comforting dishes of all time with its creamy texture laden with sweetly satisfying squash, laced with tiny cubes of tofu, and wrapped in the nutty taste of millet.

Millet tends to hold on to dust, so be sure to rinse it.

MAKES 4 OR 5 SERVINGS

1 cup millet
1 cup cubed winter squash
½ cup small cubes extra-firm tofu
5 cups spring or filtered water
1 teaspoon barley miso
1 to 2 green onions, thinly sliced on the
   diagonal, for garnish

Place millet in a bowl, cover with water and gently swirl with your hands to loosen any dirt. Drain and repeat two or three times or until the water is relatively clear.

Layer squash and tofu in a heavy pot and top with millet. Gently add water, cover and bring to a boil over medium heat. Reduce heat and simmer until liquid is absorbed and millet has a creamy texture, about 30 minutes. Dissolve miso in a small amount of warm water and gently stir into millet. Simmer 2 to 3 minutes. Remove from heat and stir briskly. Squash will break apart and disperse throughout the millet. Serve hot, garnished with green onions.

Smashing Corn Casserole

This truly deluxe casserole is a snap to make and a hit with everyone who has tasted it. It blends the sweet taste of fresh corn, tangy roasted red bell peppers, rich sesame tahini and the protein and phytochemical kick of tofu.

MAKES 4 OR 5 SERVINGS

1 (1-pound) package firm tofu, crumbled
⅓ cup sesame tahini
Soy sauce
About ½ cup yellow cornmeal
Pinch sea salt
Spring or filtered water
2 ears fresh corn, kernels removed and husks
   reserved
2 red bell peppers, roasted over a flame,
   peeled, seeded and diced (see Note, page
   262)

Preheat oven to 375F (190C). Lightly oil a deep casserole and set aside. Mix the tofu and tahini together until blended and season lightly with soy sauce. Set aside. In a medium bowl, mix cornmeal, salt and enough water to make a thick, flavorful paste. You will need about 1½ cups of this mixture. Fold in corn kernels and set aside.

Line the prepared casserole dish with several clean corn husks, allowing them to hang over the sides a bit. Begin layering by spreading some cornmeal mixture on the husks. Next, add some of the tofu mixture and sprinkle generously with some of the bell peppers. Continue layering until the dish is full, ending with cornmeal mixture on the top. Fold the husks over the casserole and press into the topping to hold them in place. Cover and bake 35 minutes or until firm. Remove cover and return to oven to brown the top slightly. Serve immediately.

Millet-Corn Loaf

This is a really unique way to serve this lovely grain. Millet takes on a delightful, creamy texture that will cause the grain to set up as it cools—ideal for a loaf like this.

MAKES 5 TO 6 SERVINGS

1 small onion, finely diced
1 small carrot, finely diced
1 ear of fresh corn, kernels removed, or 1 cup
    frozen corn
1½ cups millet, rinsed well
6 cups spring or filtered water
Sea salt
2 to 3 green onions, thinly sliced on the
    diagonal
2 tablespoons umeboshi vinegar
3 tablespoons sesame tahini

In a heavy pot, place diced onion, carrot, corn and millet. Add water and a pinch of salt. Cover and bring to a boil over medium heat. Reduce heat and simmer 25 to 30 minutes. Season lightly with salt and simmer 5 minutes. Stir in green onions and remove from heat.

Preheat oven to 300F (150C). Lightly oil a loaf pan and set aside. Whisk together vinegar and tahini and stir into cooked millet mixture. Press mixture into prepared pan and bake, uncovered, 15 minutes. Allow to cool slightly before slicing so the loaf can set up.

To serve, cut into slices and serve with a light sauce or lightly pan-fry before serving.

■ **NOTE** If you cannot find or do not have umeboshi vinegar, substitute fresh lemon juice and adjust your seasoning of salt to your taste.

Old World Polenta

I hated polenta as a child. Well, okay, it wasn't the polenta I actually hated, but the process. My mother liked to make it the old-fashioned way—stirred for hours over low heat while it thickened and finally pulled away from the pan and could be turned out to set. And yes, you guessed it: All us kids got to do the stirring. Sure, the resulting dish was delicious, but we were exhausted! Well, I have since learned that you can make an equally delicious polenta just as light and airy in no time at all.

MAKES 5 OR 6 SERVINGS

5 cups spring or filtered water
Sea salt
1 tablespoon extra-virgin olive oil
½ cup fresh corn kernels
1 cup yellow corn grits
Fresh basil, finely minced (optional)
Fresh Basil Pesto (page 278), Creamy
    Mushroom Sauce (page 274), Roasted
    Pepper Sauce (page 277) or other sauce
    (optional)

Lightly oil a shallow casserole and set aside. In a deep pot, over medium heat, bring water, salt, oil, corn and grits to a rolling boil, whisking

constantly. Reduce heat to very low and cook, stirring frequently, until the center of the polenta "burps," about 25 minutes. Stir in basil (if using). Turn into prepared dish and allow to stand until set, about 30 minutes. Slice and serve with sauce (if using).

■ **VARIATION** If serving the polenta with a sauce, I usually omit the herbs, so that flavors don't compete. If I want a smooth, airy, almost quichelike polenta, I omit the corn kernels. However, if I am serving polenta on its own, then I cook it with not only the herbs and corn, but also some finely diced green onions and minced parsley.

Miso-Millet Stew

A hearty, warming breakfast dish, this is sure to get your day off to a great start.

MAKES 4 OR 5 SERVINGS

½ teaspoon avocado oil
1 small onion, finely diced
Sea salt
1 small parsnip, finely diced
1 cup millet, rinsed well
¼ cup dried sweet corn
5 cups spring or filtered water
2½ teaspoons barley miso
Mirin

Heat oil in a heavy pot over medium heat. Add onion and a pinch of salt and cook, stirring, until onion is translucent, about 2 minutes. Add parsnip and a pinch of salt and cook, stirring, until coated with oil. Top with millet and corn and slowly add water. Cover and bring to a boil. Reduce heat and simmer, 25 to 30 min-

utes. Dissolve miso in a small amount of warm water, stir into stew and simmer, uncovered, 4 to 5 minutes. Remove from heat and stir in a splash of mirin. Transfer to a serving bowl and serve.

Mochi Melt

Miss melted cheese? Try this incredibly rich and easy-to-make alternative. Sure to cure the dairy blues . . .

MAKES 4 OR 5 SERVINGS

1 teaspoon extra-virgin olive oil
½ leek, rinsed well and thinly sliced
1 to 2 cloves fresh garlic, thinly sliced
1 cup thinly sliced button mushrooms
1 carrot, cut into thin matchsticks
1 cup matchsticks daikon
½ cup finely shredded green cabbage
1 cup cauliflower florets
Sea salt
1 cup broccoli florets
1 to 2 cups thin strips Mochi (page 43)
½ cup spring or filtered water

Heat oil in a large skillet over medium heat. Add leek and garlic and cook, stirring, until fragrant, about 3 minutes. Add vegetables, except broccoli, in the order listed in the recipe and stir-fry until tender, but not quite cooked through, seasoning lightly throughout cooking with salt as each ingredient is added. Spread vegetables evenly over the bottom of the skillet and top with broccoli. Begin placing thin strips of mochi over the entire surface. When the vegetables are completely covered with mochi, gently pour water down the side of the skillet to allow everything to steam. Cover and cook over medium heat about 10 minutes, until mochi melts completely. Serve immediately.

Kasha with Noodles

A very traditional recipe cooked in a very healthy manner. It is so wonderful to go back and find all of these traditional foods that work so well in our return to a more natural style of cooking.

MAKES 3 OR 4 SERVINGS

1 cup blonde kasha, rinsed and drained
2 cups spring or filtered water
Sea salt
1 small onion, cut into thin half-moon slices
1 cup uncooked whole grain noodles, spirals,
    bow-ties or elbows
Fresh sauerkraut, for garnish

Add kasha to a large dry pot over medium heat and pan-roast, stirring occasionally, until darker golden in color and very fragrant, 2 to 3 minutes.

Bring water and a generous pinch of salt to a boil. Add onion and simmer 2 minutes. Pour water and onion over kasha and return to a boil. Reduce heat to low, cover and cook until liquid is absorbed, 15 to 20 minutes. Remove from heat and allow to stand, undisturbed, 5 minutes.

While the kasha is cooking, bring a pot of water to a boil and cook noodles until just tender. Drain well.

Toss kasha and onion with noodles, mix well and transfer to a serving bowl. Serve garnished with sauerkraut.

■ **NOTE** You can purchase toasted kasha and eliminate the step of pan-toasting.

Nori Maki

I remember the first time I attempted to make this traditional Japanese dish. Trying to follow very complicated and confusing instructions, I ended up rolling the bamboo sushi mat into the roll. I gave in to defeat that time and did not attempt to make this easy-to-assemble (really!) rice dish until my husband showed me how. Let's see if I can instruct you more clearly. I have certainly made all the mistakes you can make . . .

MAKES 4 OR 5 SERVINGS

2 sheets toasted sushi nori
About 1 cup cooked brown rice

FILLING
2 to 3 blanched carrot spears
2 to 3 thinly sliced green onion spears
Prepared mustard
Fresh sauerkraut

Pickled ginger or dipping sauce of soy sauce,
    water, ginger and diced green onion

Take either a bamboo sushi mat or a cotton dish towel and place it in front of you on a dry work surface. If using a mat, make sure that the bamboo pieces are horizontal (so it can roll up). Next, place the nori, shiny side down, on the mat.

Press rice evenly and firmly over nori sheet, leaving about 1 inch of nori exposed at the edges closest to and farthest from you. Make sure the rice covers the nori completely from side to side. Rice should be about ¼ inch thick.

Place filling ingredients on the rice on the edge closest to you. A thin line of filling will suffice: a carrot and onion spear, a thin line of mustard and sauerkraut. Then, using the mat as a guide, roll the nori maki, jelly-roll style, completely encasing the rice and filling in nori.

When completely rolled, wrap the mat around the maki and gently press to seal the roll. Remove the mat and with a sharp, wet knife, slice the nori roll, crosswise, into 8 nori rounds, each about 1 inch thick. Arrange on a serving platter and serve with pickled ginger.

■ **NOTE** Nori maki fillings are only limited by what you can imagine . . . from bean puree to leftover pickles to veggies and peanut butter, the combinations are deliciously endless.

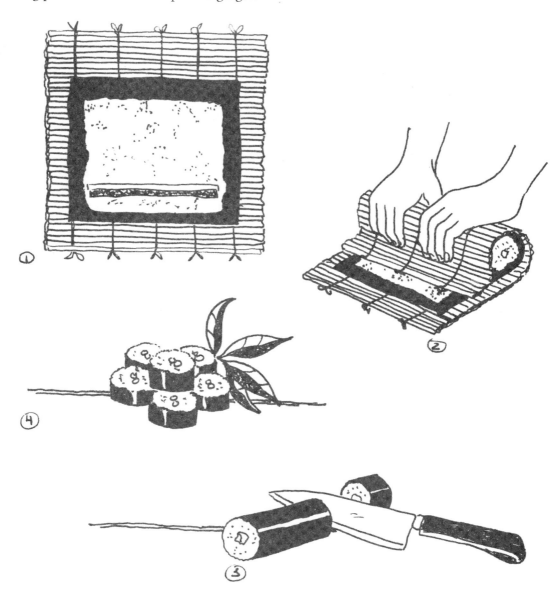

Spanish-Style Paella

I love to play with traditional recipes, making them work for me within my own understanding of cooking and food energy. This delicious version of paella has no meat, fowl or fish, but is packed with flavor. You won't miss anything. This hearty rice dish can stand on its own as a meal with some lightly steamed vegetables on the side.

MAKES 4 OR 5 SERVINGS

1½ cups short-grain brown rice, rinsed,
    soaked for 1 hour and drained
Avocado or olive oil for deep-frying
4 ounces tempeh, cut into ¼-inch cubes
1 teaspoon extra-virgin olive oil
1 to 2 cloves fresh garlic, finely minced
1 onion, finely diced
1 or 2 celery stalks, diced
1 carrot, diced
1 cup diced fresh burdock
2 cups spring or filtered water
Sea salt
Minced fresh flat-leaf parsley
Freshly grated fresh ginger and juice (see
    Note, page 164)

Add rice to a dry skillet over medium heat and pan-roast, stirring occasionally, until light brown and fragrant, 2 to 3 minutes. Set aside.

Heat 1 inch of avocado oil in a deep saucepan over medium heat. When the oil is hot, deep-fry tempeh until golden brown, about 2 minutes. Set aside to drain on paper towels.

Heat olive oil in a pressure cooker over medium heat. Add garlic and onion and cook, stirring, until fragrant, about 3 minutes. Add celery, carrot and burdock and stir to combine. Top with rice and tempeh and gently add water. Sprinkle lightly with salt, seal the lid

and bring to full pressure. Place over a flame deflector, reduce heat to low and cook 45 minutes. Remove pot from heat and allow pressure to reduce naturally. Open carefully, stir in parsley, to taste, and fresh ginger pulp and juice to taste and transfer to a serving bowl.

Sweet Rice with Chestnuts

Winter cooking just wouldn't be the same without chestnuts. In desserts, soups, bean and grain dishes or on their own, lightly roasted, they impart a delicate sweetness that brings a smile to everyone's lips. In this dish, combining chestnuts with sweet rice creates a comfortable warming energy just right for cold winter months, not to mention that this combination nourishes the middle organs of the body—the stomach, spleen and pancreas, helping to alleviate symptoms of hypoglycemia.

MAKES 3 OR 4 SERVINGS

½ cup dried or fresh chestnuts (see Note,
    page 68)
1½ cups sweet brown rice, rinsed well,
    soaked for 1 hour and drained
2½ cups spring or filtered water
Sea salt

If using dried chestnuts, dry-roast them in a skillet over medium heat until fragrant and then soak them 6 to 8 hours before using. This extra bit of effort ensures their sweetness.

Place chestnuts and rice in a pressure cooker with water. Cover loosely and bring to a boil over medium heat. Add 2 pinches of salt, seal the lid and bring to full pressure. Place over a flame deflector, reduce heat to low and cook 45 minutes. Remove pot from heat and allow pressure to reduce naturally. Gently stir to combine rice and chestnuts. Transfer to a serving bowl.

- **NOTE** If using fresh chestnuts for this dish, cut a cross in the flat side of each and roast in a 350F (175C) oven about 20 minutes. Allow to cool enough to handle and peel. You may also boil the chestnuts 15 minutes before peeling.

Millet "Mashed Potatoes"

I am not much into disguising healthy foods to look like their conventional counterparts: like tofu lasagna, etc. The diner is always disappointed, and more than that, our approach to food will never change if habits don't change. So while this grain dish is very unlike mashed potatoes as you may know them, its creamy, rich texture and mellow flavor make it a wonderful alternative to its creamy, simple carb and usually fat-laden counterpart.

MAKES 4 OR 5 SERVINGS

1 onion, finely diced
1 cup cauliflower florets
1 cup millet, rinsed well
4 to 5 cups spring or filtered water
1 teaspoon sweet white miso
¼ cup minced fresh flat-leaf parsley
Creamy Mushroom Sauce (page 274) or your
favorite gravy

Place onion in the bottom of a heavy pot. Add cauliflower and then millet. Gently add water, trying not to disturb the layers. (The layering effect allows the flavors of the vegetables to cook into the grain without stirring.) Cover and bring to a boil. Reduce heat and cook over low heat until liquid has been absorbed and millet is soft, 25 to 30 minutes. Dissolve the

miso in a small amount of warm water. Stir mixture into millet and simmer 3 to 4 minutes more. Whisk briskly to create creamy texture, fold in parsley and serve topped with sauce.

Holiday Rice

Nothing spices up a vegan holiday meal more than a deliciously festive whole grain entrée. This combination of fragrant basmati, tangy tangerines and aromatic pine nuts creates something so good that you know it's a triumph. The dressing should be a light essence added to the cooked rice. A small amount will go a long way.

MAKES 3 OR 4 SERVINGS

1½ cups brown basmati rice, rinsed, soaked
for 1 hour and drained
½ cup wild rice, rinsed
2½ cups spring or filtered water
Sea salt
¼ cup fresh tangerine juice
½ cup dried currants
2 tangerines
2 tablespoons pine nuts
2 to 3 tablespoons extra-virgin olive oil
2 tablespoons sweet brown rice vinegar

Combine both rices in a pressure cooker with water. Cover loosely and bring to a boil. Add salt, seal the lid and bring to full pressure. Place over a flame deflector, reduce heat to low and cook 25 minutes. Turn off heat and allow pressure cooker to stand undisturbed for another 25 minutes.

Meanwhile, heat the tangerine juice in a small saucepan until hot and pour it over the currants to soften them. Peel and section the tangerines, being careful to remove all the skin and threads to avoid a bitter taste. Lightly pan-toast the pine nuts in a dry skillet over medium heat until fragrant, 2 to 3 minutes, and set aside.

Open the lid of the pressure cooker and stir in currants and juice, tangerine segments, olive oil and rice vinegar. Stir well and transfer to a serving bowl. Just before serving, stir in pine nuts.

Polenta with Mushroom Ragout

A more traditional style of polenta, this version is a thick, creamy mixture served in bowls. Top it off with this thick, reduced vegetable sauce for a real winning combination. A bit time-consuming to make, however, the sauce can be made up to two days in advance and refrigerated. It may thicken, so you may need to thin it with water when reheating for use.

MAKES 5 TO 6 SERVINGS

1 to 2 teaspoons extra-virgin olive oil
1 or 2 cloves fresh garlic, finely minced
1 or 2 small carrots, finely diced
2 celery stalks, finely diced
½ red bell pepper, roasted over a flame, peeled, seeded and finely diced (see Note, page 262)
Sea salt
1 to 2 cups quartered button mushrooms, brushed free of dirt
3 or 4 dried shiitake or porcini mushrooms, soaked in warm water until tender, liquid reserved and mushrooms coarsely diced

POLENTA
5 cups spring or filtered water
Sea salt
Extra-virgin olive oil
1 cup yellow cornmeal

Heat the olive oil in a deep skillet over medium-high heat. Add garlic and cook until fragrant, 1 to 2 minutes. Add carrot, celery, bell pepper and a generous pinch of salt and cook, stirring, about 3 minutes. Add button mushrooms, reduce heat to medium and cook until mushrooms exude liquid. Add dried mushrooms and cook, uncovered, until all the liquid evaporates, about 10 minutes. Add mushroom soaking water, plus some additional water to almost half-cover the vegetables. Cover pan and bring to a boil. Reduce heat and simmer about 2 hours, stirring occasionally, until the sauce thickens.

Meanwhile, to prepare polenta, bring the 5 cups water, a generous pinch of salt and a splash of olive oil to a boil in a deep pot over medium heat. Slowly add cornmeal, through your fingers (like rain, my grandmother would say), stirring constantly. Cook, stirring constantly, until polenta becomes very thick and pulls away from the sides of the pan, usually 20 to 30 minutes but up to 1 hour. Ladle into individual serving bowls. Ladle ragout over polenta and serve hot.

Corn with Green Onions and Bell Peppers

From the nightshade family, peppers can be highly acidic for our blood and aggravate some people's symptoms of arthritis. But when they are roasted and cooked, that affect is nearly eliminated, and in some recipes, I can't think of any other vegetable to get that delicious, strong, smoky taste. So indulge yourself . . .

MAKES 4 OR 5 SERVINGS

1 red bell pepper, skin lightly oiled
1 yellow bell pepper, skin lightly oiled
1 to 2 teaspoons extra-virgin olive oil
1 or 2 green onions, minced
Sea salt
4 ears fresh corn, kernels removed

Place whole peppers over a flame and roast until the outer skin turns completely black. Place them in a paper sack, seal tightly and allow to steam about 10 minutes to loosen the skin. Then rub the peppers gently between your fingers to remove the skins. Seed the roasted peppers and finely dice.

Heat oil in a skillet over medium heat. Add green onions and cook 1 minute. Add bell peppers and a pinch of salt. Add corn and salt to taste and cook 10 minutes, stirring occasionally. Transfer to a bowl and serve hot.

■ **NOTE** Lightly oiling the outer skin of the pepper makes for much easier peeling after roasting.

Barley with Winter Vegetables

I know, I know, I told you that barley has great dispersing energy and can help to keep you cool in warm weather. So why am I pairing it with warming winter vegetables? Well, the energies harmonize very well to create a very warming stew that's not too heavy and balances with the heavier, well-cooked foods that make up winter cooking. That's why.

MAKES 4 OR 5 SERVINGS

2 (1-inch) pieces kombu
2 cups whole barley, rinsed and soaked 6 to 8
    hours and drained

6 cups spring or filtered water
Sea salt
1 onion, finely diced
½ cup ½-inch cubes rutabaga
½ cup ½-inch cubes turnip
1 small carrot, cut into ½-inch cubes
½ cup thinly sliced fresh burdock
2 to 3 dried shiitake mushrooms, soaked and
    thinly sliced
2 stalks celery, thinly sliced

Place kombu in a heavy pot and add barley and water. Cover and bring to a boil over medium heat. Reduce heat to low, add salt and simmer 40 minutes. Layer vegetables, except celery, on top of barley in the order listed. Re-cover pot and simmer until barley is creamy and vegetables are soft, 40 to 45 minutes. Stir in celery and transfer to a serving bowl. Serve hot.

Millet Pie

Millet takes on a creamy texture when cooked, and, upon cooling, it is easily molded into shapes, lending itself nicely to a variety of uses. One delicious way to add millet to your diet is to create a piecrust for a rich vegetable filling.

MAKES ABOUT 6 SERVINGS

MILLET CRUST
3 cups spring or filtered water
Pinch of sea salt
1 cup millet, rinsed and drained

VEGETABLE FILLING
1 to 2 teaspoons extra-virgin olive oil
1 or 2 cloves fresh garlic, finely minced
2 to 3 shallots or 1 onion, finely diced
Soy sauce

1 carrot, cut into large dice
½ cup large dice daikon
½ cup large dice small turnip
½ cup large dice winter squash
1 to 2 cups small cauliflower florets
2 cups peeled and finely diced broccoli stems
1 cup small broccoli florets
1 cup fresh or frozen corn kernels
Spring or filtered water
Generous pinch of fresh or dried ground
  rosemary
3 to 4 leaves fresh leafy greens (kale, collards
  or other greens), finely chopped
1 tablespoon kuzu or arrowroot, dissolved in
  2 tablespoons water

Lightly oil a 9-inch pie plate and set aside. To prepare the crust, bring water and salt to a boil, add the millet and return to a boil. Reduce heat, cover and simmer until creamy, about 30 minutes. Remove from heat and whisk briskly to increase creaminess. Allow to cool only enough to be able to handle the

mixture, stirring frequently to prevent the millet from setting up. When cool enough to handle, press the millet into prepared pie plate, taking care to create an even crust on the bottom and sides. Set aside while preparing the filling.

Preheat oven to 375F (190C). To prepare the filling, heat olive oil in a skillet over medium heat. Add garlic, shallots and a sprinkle of soy sauce and cook until limp, about 3 minutes. Add carrot, daikon, turnip, squash, cauliflower and broccoli stems and cook 2 or 3 minutes. Add broccoli florets, corn and about 1 cup water. Add rosemary and sprinkle with soy sauce. Cover and cook over medium-low heat about 10 minutes. Add chopped greens and simmer, covered, until bright green, about 5 minutes. Stir in dissolved kuzu and cook, stirring, 3 minutes or until a thin glaze forms over the vegetables.

Spoon the filling into the crust and bake about 30 minutes, until the filling is set and the millet crust turns a nice golden color. Serve warm.

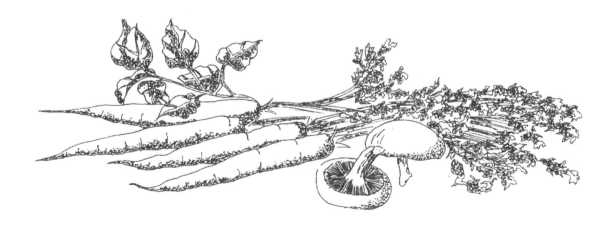

Savory Soups and Stews

SOUP MAKING HAS always been a kind of ritual in my kitchen. I can remember the aromas coming from the bubbling pots on my mom's stove. She had a way of combining the most humble ingredients to make the most delicious soups and stews. She understood that the key to really good soup is determined by the quality and freshness of what goes into the pot—never any limp, old vegetables for her. I learned well. I love soup.

I find it interesting that meals begin with soup. Have you ever wondered why? It is a symbolic return to the sea, where life began. Also, a bowl of soup is soothing and relaxing. It stimulates the appetite and relaxes our digestive system in preparation for the meal to come. Soup can even help us to eat a bit less at the meal, by as much as 110 calories.

Soup creates the atmosphere for the entire meal. An ideal soup complements the meal with its taste, texture, aroma and color. If a meal is hearty and complex, it is always a pleasure to begin the meal with a simple, elegant broth or clear soup. A light and simple meal might be given some substance by beginning with a thick vegetable, bean or grain stew.

Seasonal balance also plays a large role in soup making. In cooler weather, I tend more toward warming soups that include a greater portion of root vegetables, richer ingredients

and stronger seasoning. During the warmer months of the year, I make more cooling soups, even chilled soups, to complement the weather. Lighter ingredients, like noodles, leafy greens and delicately cut vegetables, along with more delicate seasonings and reduced cooking time will actually help to beat the heat.

The variety of soups we can prepare is virtually limitless. There are a few basic, yet essential techniques that, if mastered, will give you the confidence you need to really experience the pleasure of making soup. Remember that repetition is our greatest teacher. Find a few favorite recipes and make them several times to build your confidence. Then, change ingredients around. Vary the beans and vegetables. Add whole or cracked grains. Season with any variety of herbs and spices. Sauté the vegetables before adding water. The possibilities of soup are endless. Scavenging around the refrigerator, you will come up with enough fresh ingredients to make a wonderfully delicious soup.

Some Basic Techniques

Soups need to begin with base or foundation flavors. I begin a lot of my soups by either sautéing or simmering onions, shallots or leeks, and often a bit of garlic. A pinch of sea salt at this point seals in the vegetables' flavors while drawing out some vegetables' juices, thereby creating a richer flavor.

When seasoning soups, don't wait until the last minute. Herbs, spices and salty seasonings need time to develop and blend with the other flavors in the soup. You may even want to add seasoning several times during cooking so that the flavors gradually mature until they are exactly as you desire. Common choices for seasoning are good-quality soy sauce or sea salt, both of which I simmer for at least seven minutes to develop the flavors. Fresh herbs and garnish will serve you best if added just prior to serving.

Generally, miso is added only toward the end of cooking—the last three to four minutes, to be exact. Miso adds a full-bodied taste to any soup, but its real benefits come from its delicate enzyme content. These beneficial enzymes are good for intestinal and immune system strength. However, the enzymes are fragile. When seasoning with miso, take care not to boil the soup; the enzymes need heat to activate, but boiling will destroy them, so instead just simmer miso about four minutes.

I don't often add wine or mirin to soups, but occasionally these more exotic ingredients can add a depth to soup that is impossible to achieve any other way. I save this type of seasoning for special occasions.

I mostly begin my soups with fresh spring or filtered water, but sometimes I like to make stocks. They give the soup a full-bodied taste that is simply amazing. When adding stock to soup, go slowly. Adding stock gradually ensures that the soup will retain its richness and texture. A too-thin soup can be flavorless and flat. Remember that even simple brothlike soups should have a full flavor.

Soups based on beans or whole grains can be hearty or incredibly light. It all depends on the seasoning and quantities of ingredients. I usually cook bean soups for a long time, unseasoned, adding vegetables gradually so that I can achieve a variety of vegetable textures—some very tender, some just tender, some a bit crispy for lightness. The key to good bean soup is cooking the beans long enough. The softer the better; even mushy is good. A bay leaf or two, or some fresh herbs, will transform the bean cooking water into a delicious broth. Bean soups are one exception to the seasoning rule. Season toward the end of cooking, so that the beans become very tender. If you salt beans too early in the cooking, they will contract and resist moisture, remaining hard.

Whole grains add hearty flavor and creamy texture to soups, making them the world's greatest comfort foods. Pasta, rice, barley and millet add delicious flavors as well. I usually cook pasta separately so that my broth doesn't get too starchy or overly thick with pasta. Whole grains are added to soups during cooking, depending on the time required for each grain to soften. While grains cook in soups, their natural starches bind the broth, giving the soup body and a creamy consistency. Remember that grains expand during cooking, so use them sparingly so that you don't end up with a pot of soft grain mush instead of a hearty soup.

Last, invest in a few really good soup and stockpots. They will come in handy more often than you can imagine. And get a food mill. This simple kitchen gadget will become indispensable. It's great for smoothing the texture of soups. I use mine all the time in place of a food processor. The soups that come through a food mill are smoothly elegant.

Stocks

Stock is the full-bodied broth that ties a soup together, complementing the ingredients and making the soup whole. I work mostly with three different stocks, going from one to the next to build a variety of soups: a mushroom stock, an onion stock and a basic vegetable stock. I don't always begin soup with a stock. Many times, I like to begin fresh with water and work from there, but occasionally I like the variety in tastes you can achieve with stock.

To make a good stock, remember that the broth will taste exactly like the ingredients you are using, so this is not the place to use up stale, limp vegetables that you just can't bear to discard. Flavorful, fresh vegetables are essential for a delicious broth. Trim away any dry or yellowed bits on vegetables and do not use onion skins and roots in the stock. They can turn the broth bitter. However, keep the papery skin on garlic cloves to keep the flavor gentle. Herbs can be used, stems and all, to get the full benefit of their delicate tastes. And of course, vegetables that are cut to expose the greatest surface area will make the most flavorful broth, so dicing or slicing into very thin pieces will work best.

When I start the stock, I simmer onions or leeks in a small amount of water or sauté them in oil or water with a pinch of salt to enrich their flavor. Then I add the balance of ingredients and water, bring the mixture to a boil, reduce the heat and simmer it, uncovered, for about one hour to develop and concentrate the flavors.

Stock will keep, refrigerated, for a day or two. After that, it can turn sour. However, stocks will keep almost indefinitely in the freezer. Just allow any frozen stock to thaw and then warm it before using. Cold stock can inhibit the cooking process of the soup and compromise the flavors.

Vegetable Stock

This serves as the foundation of many of my soups. It is quite versatile, as I vary the vegetables, seasonings and herbs, but the technique remains constant. I usually avoid members of the cabbage family because their strong flavors can create a stock that will overwhelm rather than support your soups.

MAKES ABOUT 6 CUPS

1 onion, cut into thin half-moon slices
Several green onions or a small leek, rinsed and finely diced
2 cloves fresh garlic, unpeeled
Sea salt
8 or 9 cups spring or filtered water
1 or 2 carrots, finely diced
2 celery stalks, finely diced
1 cup button mushrooms, brushed clean and halved
1 or 2 bay leaves
2 sprigs flat-leaf parsley
Fresh basil or rosemary sprigs (optional)

Add onions, garlic, salt and about ½ cup of the water to a soup pot over low heat. Simmer about 15 minutes. Add the remaining water and other ingredients and bring the stock to a boil. Reduce heat to low and cook, uncovered, about 1 hour. Pour the stock through a strainer, pressing as much liquid as you can from the vegetables before discarding them.

- ■ **VARIATION** Sauté the onions in extra-virgin olive or avocado oil instead of simmering them in water.

Mushroom Stock

This is a rather strong-tasting stock. Use it for heartier soups and for sauces or gravies as well as for some grain dishes. Dried mushrooms give the broth tremendous flavor. On their own, fresh mushrooms will create too weak a flavor.

MAKES ABOUT 6 CUPS

1 onion, cut into thin half-moon slices
8 or 9 cups spring or filtered water
Several green onions or a small leek, cleaned and finely diced
2 or 3 dried shiitake mushrooms, soaked until tender and thinly sliced
Sea salt
2 cups button or cremini mushrooms, brushed clean and thinly sliced
1 carrot, finely diced
2 bay leaves
2 sprigs flat-leaf parsley

Combine onion and about ½ cup of the water in a soup pot over low heat and simmer 1 to 2 minutes. Add green onions and shiitake mushrooms and soaking water with a pinch of salt, and simmer 15 minutes. Add the remaining water and other ingredients and bring to a boil. Simmer, uncovered, over low heat, about 1 hour. Strain the stock, pressing as much liquid as possible from the vegetables before discarding them.

Onion Stock

This sweet stock can be delicate or strong, depending on the quantity and freshness of the onions used. Remember that stale onions will give your stock a strong and bitter taste instead of a delicately sweet, aromatic flavor. The optional corn cobs add additional sweetness.

MAKES ABOUT 6 CUPS

½ teaspoon extra-virgin olive oil
6 or 7 onions, cut into thin half-moon slices
1 leek, cut in half lengthwise, rinsed well and finely diced
Sea salt
8 to 9 cups spring or filtered water
2 or 3 corn cobs with kernels removed and used in other recipes (optional)
2 or 3 celery stalks, finely diced
2 bay leaves
Sprigs flat-leaf parsley

Heat olive oil in a soup pot over medium-low heat. Add onions and leek with a pinch of salt and cook, stirring occasionally, until translucent and fragrant, about 5 minutes. Add a small amount of the water and simmer over low heat 15 minutes. Add remaining water and other ingredients and bring to a boil. Reduce heat to low and simmer, uncovered, about 1 hour. Strain the stock, pressing as much liquid as possible from the vegetables before discarding them.

Creamy Parsnip Soup

This is a delicious winter soup. Its smooth and creamy consistency lends quite an elegant touch to a holiday or any other meal.

MAKES 4 OR 5 SERVINGS

4 to 5 cups spring or filtered water
2 or 3 shallots, peeled and finely diced
2 cups finely diced parsnips
2 teaspoons white miso
2 or 3 green onions, thinly sliced, for garnish

Bring 1 cup of the water to a boil in a soup pot over medium-low heat. Add shallots and simmer 4 to 5 minutes. Add parsnips and the remaining water and bring to a boil. Reduce heat, cover and cook over low heat 25 minutes.

Remove a small amount of broth, add miso and stir until dissolved. Stir mixture into soup and simmer 3 to 4 minutes. Put soup through a food mill or puree in a food processor until a creamy consistency. Serve garnished with green onions.

Creamy Squash Bisque

Any sweet winter squash works in this recipe. This bisque is so satisfyingly sweet that you could serve it for dessert.

MAKES 4 OR 5 SERVINGS

2 to 3 pounds winter squash (butternut,
**   delicata or buttercup)**
5 cups Vegetable Stock (page 74)
½ cup unfiltered, unsweetened apple juice
3 tablespoons brown rice syrup or honey
1 teaspoon fresh ginger juice (see Note, page
**   164)**
Pinch grated nutmeg
Sea salt
Mint sprigs, for garnish

Preheat oven to 450F (230C). Halve the squash, place on a baking sheet, cut side down, and bake until tender when pricked with a fork, 35 to 45 minutes.

Cool squash slightly. Remove and discard seeds. Puree pulp in a food mill or food processor. Gradually stir in enough stock until mixture is smooth. Transfer to a soup pot over low heat and add the remaining stock, apple juice, rice syrup, ginger juice and nutmeg. Lightly season with salt and simmer, covered, 10 to 15 minutes. Serve garnished with mint sprigs.

Winter Vegetable–Bean Stew

Any beans work well in this hearty recipe, but I think that white beans are the prettiest. I love to serve this stew on cold nights with crusty whole grain bread and lightly cooked vegetables for a warming, easy-to-make meal.

MAKES ABOUT 4 SERVINGS

2 teaspoons extra-virgin olive oil
1 leek, halved lengthwise, well rinsed and
**   sliced into 1-inch pieces**
2 cloves fresh garlic, finely minced
2 tablespoons whole wheat pastry flour
1 bay leaf
1 cup cubed winter squash
1 small sweet potato, cut into large dice
2 carrots, cut into large dice
2 parsnips, cut into small, irregular pieces
1 cup cauliflower florets
5 cups Vegetable Stock (page 74)
½ cup white cannellini beans, cooked without
**   seasoning until tender**
2 to 3 teaspoons white miso
1 cup broccoli florets
1 or 2 green onions, thinly sliced, for garnish

Heat olive oil in a soup pot over medium-low heat. Add leek and garlic and cook, stirring, for 2 minutes. Slowly stir in flour and cook, stirring constantly, until leek is coated. Add bay leaf, squash, sweet potato, carrots, parsnips and cauliflower and gently add stock. Bring to a boil. Stir in beans and return to the boil. Reduce heat to low, cover and cook 35 to 40 minutes. Remove a small amount of broth, add miso and stir until dissolved. Stir mixture into soup. Add broccoli and simmer until broccoli turns bright green, about 4 minutes. Serve garnished with green onions.

Tomato Soup

I can hear all the hardcore macrobiotic readers now, gasping in horror as I cook with infamous tomatoes. Tomatoes got a bad rap because they have an acidic nature, and they may not be the best choice for some people who have health conditions until their health has returned. But for those healthy and hale readers who love tomatoes, there is no reason not to enjoy their yumminess and the many nutritional benefits these lovely fruits provide, from magnesium to lycopene and vitamin C.

MAKES 3 OR 4 SERVINGS

2 tablespoons extra-virgin olive oil
2 cloves fresh garlic, finely minced
1 small red onion, finely diced
2 cups diced tomatoes, fresh or canned
2 cups soymilk
1 carrot, left whole
1 bay leaf
About 1 teaspoon sea salt
Generous pinch cracked black pepper
3 to 4 sprigs basil, for garnish

Heat oil, garlic and onion in a soup pot over medium heat. When the onion begins to sizzle, sauté until translucent, 2 minutes. Stir in tomatoes and bring to a boil. In a separate pot, heat soymilk and stir into tomato mixture. Add carrot and bay leaf. Cover, bring to a boil, reduce heat and cook 15 minutes. Season with salt and pepper and simmer 7 to 10 minutes to develop the flavor. Remove and discard carrot and bay leaf and serve garnished with fresh basil sprigs.

■ NOTES The whole carrot, as well as the bay leaf, is added to the soup to help neutralize the acidic nature of tomatoes.

For a smooth, creamy bisque, transfer the soup to a food processor or food mill and puree until smooth.

Veggie Vichyssoise

This elegant soup will turn any simple dinner into a magical feast. Richly flavored, simple to make and so comforting, this bisque will have your guests moaning with pleasure.

MAKES 4 OR 5 SERVINGS

2 tablespoons avocado oil
3 small to medium leeks, split lengthwise, rinsed free of dirt and diced
1 small onion, diced
2 cups thinly sliced peeled potatoes
2 cups spring or filtered water
1½ cups unsweetened soymilk
Sea salt
Cracked black pepper
4 or 5 fresh chives, minced, for garnish

Place oil in a soup pot and sweat leeks and onion over medium heat until quite soft, but not browned, about 7 minutes. Stir in potatoes, water and soymilk, cover and bring to a boil. Reduce heat to low and simmer 30 minutes. Season to taste with salt and pepper, keeping the flavor light. Simmer 5 minutes more to develop flavors. Transfer soup, by ladles, to a food processor or blender and puree until smooth. Serve garnished with chives.

Italian Wedding Soup

Minestra Maritata, the Italian name for this classic soup, actually has nothing to do with the happy day, but instead is one soup in a long list of meat-and-vegetable soups designed to be a complete meal, often the only meal of the day. The name is derived from the marriage of meat and vegetables. Once I knew there was no superstition in this recipe . . . and that my marriage was safe from curses, I had no trouble creating a vegetarian version.

MAKES 4 OR 5 SERVINGS

1 recipe Meatless Balls (page 205)

Extra-virgin olive oil
1 small onion, diced
Sea salt
1 stalk celery, diced
1 small carrot, diced
1 cup shredded green cabbage
1 small bunch escarole, rinsed well and shredded
4 cups Vegetable Stock (page 74) or spring or filtered water
2 tablespoons sweet white miso
2 or 3 sprigs parsley, finely minced, for garnish

Prepare the Meatless Balls, but roll them into miniature versions.

Place a small amount of oil and the onion in a soup pot over medium heat. When the onion begins to sizzle, add a pinch of salt and sauté 3 minutes. Stir in celery, carrot and a pinch of salt and sauté 2 minutes. Stir in cabbage and a pinch of salt and sauté until cabbage wilts. Stir in escarole and sauté until wilted. Add stock, cover and bring to a boil. Reduce heat to low and cook 15 minutes. Remove a small amount of broth, add miso and stir until dissolved. Stir into soup and simmer for 3 minutes.

To serve, place a couple of Meatless Balls in individual soup bowls and ladle broth over top with a sprinkle of parsley. Serve any extra meat-balls on the side.

Matzo Ball Soup

I know what you're thinking . . . impossible. Well, I won't even tell you how many batches of leaden matzo balls I threw out before I got them right. But this is a lovely soup for those special holidays . . . or any day, really.

MAKES 5 OR 6 SERVINGS

MATZO BALLS
1½ cups matzo meal (whole grain is available
  in some stores)
12 ounces silken tofu
⅓ cup extra-virgin olive oil
½ cup sparkling water
Sea salt
Cracked black pepper
2 or 3 sprigs flat-leaf parsley, finely minced
Spring or filtered water

SOUP
6 cups Vegetable Stock (page 74)
3 cloves fresh garlic, thinly sliced
1 small onion, diced
2 stalks celery, diced
1 carrot, diced
2 to 3 tablespoons sweet white miso
2 or 3 sprigs flat-leaf parsley, coarsely
  chopped, for garnish

Make the matzo ball mixture first, as it has to chill for at least an hour before proceeding with the recipe.

Place matzo meal in a mixing bowl. In a blender, puree tofu, oil, sparkling water and salt and pepper to taste until smooth. Fold tofu mixture and parsley into matzo meal, mixing until well combined. Cover tightly and refrigerate for at least an hour, but overnight is the best.

When you are ready to make the soup and finish the matzo balls, bring a pot of water to a boil with a generous pinch of salt. Remove the matzo mixture from the refrigerator and form into balls, about 1½ inches in diameter. Place prepared matzo balls on parchment paper and continue forming until all the matzo mixture is used. Carefully drop the matzo balls into the boiling water, cover and reduce the heat to medium. Cook the matzo balls 35 to 40 minutes; try not to uncover the pot before 35 minutes are up.

While the matzo balls cook, make the soup: Combine all ingredients, except miso and parsley, in a soup pot. Bring to a boil, cover and reduce heat to low. Cook until vegetables are tender, about 15 minutes. You may strain the veggies out of the soup and serve only the broth, which is traditional, but I love to keep the vegetables in the soup. Remove a small amount of hot broth, add miso and stir until dissolved. Stir into soup and simmer over low heat 3 to 4 minutes.

To serve, ladle 3 matzo balls into individual serving bowls and spoon soup over top. Garnish with parsley and serve immediately.

Sweeter Than Sweet Carrot Soup

Carrot soup, the ultimate comfort food, creamy, sweet, delicious, warming and relaxing. What could be sweeter? This carrot soup . . .

MAKES ABOUT 6 SERVINGS

Extra-virgin olive oil
½ red onion, diced
Sea salt
¼ teaspoon ground coriander
¼ teaspoon ground cumin
¼ teaspoon sweet paprika
Generous pinch chili powder
2½ cups diced carrots
3 cups spring or filtered water
1 cup unsweetened soymilk
2 to 3 tablespoons brown rice syrup
Very thin fresh lemon slices and sprigs flat-
    leaf parsley, for garnish

Place a small amount of oil and onion in a soup pot over medium heat. When the onion begins to sizzle, add a pinch of salt and sauté 1 to 2 minutes. Stir in spices and sauté 30 seconds. Stir in carrots and add water, soymilk and rice syrup. Cover and bring to a boil. Reduce heat to low and cook until carrots are tender, about 35 minutes.

Transfer soup, by ladles to a food mill, chinois or blender and puree until smooth. Return to low heat until ready to serve. To serve, ladle into individual bowls and garnish with a floating lemon slice and parsley sprig.

White Bean Soup with Almond Pistou

A healthy twist on a classic French soup. While the bean soup has always been great for us, the original pistou was the problem. This one has the powerful protein and good-quality fat of almonds as the base and no dairy to clog things up.

MAKES 4 TO 6 SERVINGS

1 tablespoon extra-virgin olive oil
4 shallots, finely diced
3 cloves fresh garlic, finely minced
Sea salt
2 stalks celery, diced
1 carrot, diced
1 cup dried cannellini beans
3 cups unsweetened soymilk
1 cup spring or filtered water
1 bay leaf

PISTOU
½ cup blanched almonds
2 cloves fresh garlic, sliced
1 cup loosely packed basil leaves
2 teaspoons sweet white miso
4 tablespoons extra-virgin olive oil
1 teaspoon brown rice syrup

Place oil, shallots and garlic in a medium soup pot over medium heat. When the shallots begin to sizzle, add a pinch of salt and sauté until the shallots are translucent, about 2 minutes, taking care not to burn the garlic. Stir in celery and sauté just until shiny with oil. Stir in carrot and sauté until shiny with oil. Spread vegetables over the bottom of the pan and top with beans. Add soymilk, water and bay leaf, cover and bring to a boil over medium heat. Reduce heat to low and cook until the beans are quite soft, about 60 minutes.

While the soup cooks, make the pistou: Place all ingredients in a food processor and puree until smooth.

To serve, remove bay leaf and ladle soup into individual bowls, and swirl a hearty dollop of pistou into each bowl.

- **NOTE** You can speed up the cooking time of the soup by using canned organic beans. The soup will cook in 20 minutes.

Cream of Mushroom Soup

If you think going vegan will leave your culinary life devoid of rich, creamy soups, think again. And easy? Wait till you taste this!

MAKES 6 OR 7 SERVINGS

7 tablespoons extra-virgin olive oil
2 cloves fresh garlic, finely minced
1 onion, finely diced
Sea salt
1 pound fresh button mushrooms, diced, plus
**   4 whole mushrooms**
2 ounces dried porcini mushrooms, soaked
**   until tender, diced**
5 tablespoons whole wheat pastry flour
3 cups Mushroom Stock (page 75)
3 cups unsweetened soymilk
4 tablespoons mirin or white wine
2 tablespoons sweet white miso
2 or 3 sprigs flat-leaf parsley, finely minced,
**   for garnish**

Place 4 tablespoons oil, garlic and onion in a soup pot over medium heat. When the onion begins to sizzle, add a pinch of salt and sauté 2

to 3 minutes. Stir in mushrooms and a pinch of salt and sauté 5 minutes. Stir in flour and cook, stirring into a thick paste, like a roux. Whisk in stock, soymilk and wine and cook, stirring frequently, until the soup returns to a boil. Reduce heat to low and simmer 7 to 10 minutes, stirring frequently to avoid lumps. Remove a small amount of hot broth, add miso and stir until dissolved. Stir into soup and simmer 3 to 4 minutes more.

While the miso simmers in the soup, remove the stems from remaining mushrooms and slice caps. Heat the remaining oil in a skillet and sauté the mushrooms until golden, about 3 minutes. Serve the soup garnished with mushrooms and parsley.

Millet–Sweet Vegetable Soup

This deliciously satisfying soup is comfort in a cup. The creamy texture of stewed millet combined with the delicate sweet taste of the vegetables gives this soup the ability to center and ground us by stabilizing our blood sugars.

MAKES 4 SERVINGS

½ cup millet
¼ cup *each* finely diced onion, green
**   cabbage, winter squash and carrot**
5 cups spring or filtered water
2 teaspoons barley miso
1 or 2 green onions, thinly sliced, for garnish

Rinse millet by placing in a glass bowl and covering with water. Gently swirl grain with your hands to loosen any dust. Drain well and repeat rinsing until the water runs clear.

Layer onion, cabbage, squash, carrot and then millet in a soup pot. Add enough water to just cover, taking care to preserve the layering as much as possible. Cover and bring to a boil over medium heat. Add remaining water. Reduce heat to low and simmer soup 30 minutes. Remove a small amount of broth, add miso and stir until dissolved. Stir mixture into soup and simmer 3 to 4 minutes. Serve garnished with green onions.

Minute Miso Soup

Okay, so it really takes 6 minutes to make this soup, but it's still quick and easy.

MAKES ABOUT 4 SERVINGS

3 cups spring or filtered water
1 (3-inch) piece wakame, soaked and diced
1 small onion, cut into thin half-moon slices
1½ teaspoons barley miso
Small handful fresh flat-leaf parsley, minced

Bring water to a boil in a medium saucepan over medium heat. Add wakame and simmer 1 minute. Add onion and simmer 1 to 2 minutes more. Remove a small amount of broth, add miso and stir until dissolved. Stir mixture into soup and simmer 3 to 4 minutes more. Serve garnished with parsley.

French Onion Soup

Without cheese, I achieve richness in this soup by sautéing the onions until nearly caramelized, sometimes for as long as 25 minutes. It's well worth the effort.

MAKES 4 OR 5 SERVINGS

1 tablespoon extra-virgin olive oil
8 to 10 onions, thinly sliced lengthwise
Pinch sea salt
5 cups spring or filtered water
Several pieces brown rice mochi, cut into ¼-inch cubes
2 tablespoons barley miso
2 tablespoons minced fresh flat-leaf parsley
Sourdough bread croutons (see Note below)

Heat olive oil in a soup pot over low heat. Add onions and salt. Cook, stirring occasionally, until lightly browned and reduced in bulk, 25 to 30 minutes. Gently add water and bring to a boil. Reduce heat, cover and cook about 15 minutes. Add mochi cubes. Remove a small amount of broth, add miso and stir until dissolved. Stir back into soup and simmer about 4 minutes more, until mochi melts and becomes creamy. Do not boil. Serve garnished with parsley and a few croutons.

■ **NOTE** The best croutons are made from slightly stale bread that is cubed and dried in a warm oven until crispy. Or deep-fry bread cubes just before serving the soup.

Sunny Buckwheat Soup

This unique soup combines sweet vegetables with the nutty flavor of buckwheat groats, whose creamy consistency gives this soup a full-bodied taste and texture sure to please.

MAKES 4 SERVINGS

½ cup buckwheat groats
4 to 5 cups spring or filtered water
1 small onion, finely diced
Sea salt

2 cups finely diced green cabbage
1 carrot, finely diced
2 to 3 sprigs flat-leaf parsley, finely minced

Pan-toast the buckwheat in a dry skillet over medium heat until fragrant and lightly browned, 2 to 3 minutes.

Bring a small amount of the water to a boil in a soup pot over medium heat. Add onion with a pinch of salt and cook 3 to 4 minutes. Add remaining water and vegetables, except parsley, and bring to a boil. Add buckwheat. Return to a boil, cover and cook over low heat 15 minutes or until creamy. Season to taste with salt and simmer 10 minutes more. Serve garnished with parsley.

Buckwheat Noodle Soup

I love this soup. It's like a meal in a bowl. It doesn't hurt that I adore pasta on any level, either. Round out your meal with some lightly steamed green vegetables or a fresh salad.

MAKES 4 SERVINGS

2 teaspoons avocado oil
1 small onion, finely diced
4 to 5 cups spring or filtered water
1 cup thin rounds daikon
1 carrot, cut into thin rounds
1 cup shredded Chinese cabbage
3 or 4 Brussels sprouts, quartered
2 teaspoons white miso
8 ounces buckwheat noodles (soba), cooked
    until al dente
2 to 3 green onions, thinly sliced on the
    diagonal, for garnish

Heat oil in a soup pot over medium-low heat. Add onion and cook, stirring, 3 to 4 minutes.

Gently add water and bring to a boil. Add vegetables. Return to a boil, cover and cook over low heat 10 minutes. Remove a small amount of broth, add miso and stir to dissolve. Stir mixture into soup and simmer about 4 minutes more. Do not boil.

Divide noodles among individual soup bowls and ladle soup over noodles. Serve garnished with green onions.

Jim's Lemon–Zucchini and Leek Soup

This lovely soup was adapted by a good friend of mine from a recipe in *Gourmet* magazine. Healthful, delicious versions of rich recipes are his trademark.

MAKES ABOUT 4 SERVINGS

1 tablespoon extra-virgin olive oil
2 or 3 cloves fresh garlic, finely minced
1 onion, finely diced
Sea salt
1 pound leeks, sliced lengthwise, rinsed well
    and cut into ¼-inch pieces
1 pound zucchini, cut into ¼-inch-thick
    rounds, then halved
3 to 4 cups spring or filtered water
1 (2-inch) piece kombu, soaked briefly and
    diced
4 ounces tofu, crumbled
2 tablespoons sweet white miso
Juice of 1 lemon
Lemon slices, for garnish

Heat olive oil in a soup pot over medium-low heat. Add garlic and onion with a pinch of salt and cook 3 to 4 minutes. Add leeks, zucchini and a pinch of salt and sauté until just tender, about 5 minutes. Add enough water to just cover the veggies, add kombu and bring to a boil over high heat. Cover and cook over low heat 30 minutes.

Add remaining water and crumbled tofu and simmer 10 minutes more. Puree soup until smooth and return to pot. Remove a small amount of hot broth, add miso and stir until dissolved. Stir mixture into the soup and simmer 3 to 4 minutes more. Remove from heat and stir in lemon juice to taste. Serve warm or chilled, garnished with lemon slices.

Mushroom-Barley Soup

A hearty, rich soup that can be a meal all by itself. The creamy consistency of barley balanced by the smoky, natural flavor of mushrooms makes a lovely combination. I love to serve this soup on chilly autumn days with crusty whole grain bread and a freshly cooked vegetable medley.

MAKES ABOUT 4 SERVINGS

1 cup pearl barley
1 tablespoon extra-virgin olive oil
1 onion, cut lengthwise into thin slices
5 to 6 cups Mushroom Stock (page 75)
4 or 5 dried shiitake mushrooms, soaked until tender and thinly sliced
1 cup button mushrooms, brushed clean and thinly sliced
Sea salt
2 celery stalks, thinly sliced on the diagonal
2 green onions, thinly sliced on the diagonal, for garnish

Rinse the barley by placing it in a bowl and covering with water. Swirl gently with your hands and drain.

Heat oil in a soup pot over medium-low heat. Add onion and cook, stirring, until translucent, about 5 minutes. Add stock and barley and bring to a boil over high heat. Stir in mushrooms, reduce heat and cook, covered, about 30 minutes, until barley becomes soft and creamy. If the soup begins to stick, you may need to cook the soup on a flame deflector. Season to taste with salt and simmer 10 to 15 minutes more. Stir in celery for some crunch and serve garnished with green onions.

Fresh Corn Chowder

If you love corn, don't miss this one. Jam-packed with succulent corn, this soup is the epitome of light summer cooking.

MAKES 4 SERVINGS

½ teaspoon avocado oil
1 small onion, finely diced
5 cups spring or filtered water
3 to 4 ears fresh corn, kernels removed and cobs reserved
2 or 3 small Yukon Gold potatoes, finely diced
Sea salt
2 to 3 teaspoons kuzu or arrowroot, dissolved in 4 tablespoons cold water
Several sprigs flat-leaf parsley

Heat oil in a soup pot over medium-low heat. Add onion and cook, stirring, until translucent, about 3 minutes. Add water and corn cobs and boil 3 to 4 minutes. Remove the cobs from the soup and discard. Add corn kernels and potatoes and return the soup to a boil. Reduce heat, cover and cook over low heat 20 to 25 minutes. Season lightly with salt and simmer 7 to 10 minutes more. Stir in dissolved kuzu and cook, stirring, until soup thickens slightly. Serve garnished with parsley.

■ **VARIATION** Create a soup with a velvety texture by partially pureeing the soup.

Creamy Carrot Bisque

A creamy, sweet beginning to any meal . . . any time of the year. It is most delicious warm in cool weather, and refreshing when chilled and garnished with fresh lemon slices to help beat the heat of summer.

MAKES ABOUT 4 SERVINGS

1 tablespoon extra-virgin olive oil
1 clove fresh garlic, finely minced
3 to 4 shallots, finely diced
Sea salt
3 to 4 cups diced carrots
4 to 5 cups spring or filtered water
2 tablespoons white miso
Fresh dill sprigs, for garnish

Heat olive oil in a soup pot over medium-low heat. Add garlic and shallots with a pinch of salt and cook, stirring, 3 to 4 minutes. Add carrots and another pinch of salt and cook, stirring, until coated with oil. Add water and bring to a boil over high heat. Reduce heat, cover and simmer over low heat until carrots are tender, 20 to 25 minutes. Put soup through a food mill or puree in a food processor until smooth and return to the pot. Remove a small amount of broth, add miso and stir until dissolved. Stir mixture into soup and simmer 3 to 4 minutes more. Serve garnished with fresh dill sprigs

Japanese Noodle Soup with Tofu

A traditional Japanese-style soup that is easy to make and quite delicious.

MAKES 4 SERVINGS

4 cups spring or filtered water
1 (2-inch) piece kombu
1 dried shiitake mushroom
Soy sauce
1 cup ¼-inch cubes tofu
8 ounces udon or somen noodles, cooked al
    dente, drained and rinsed
1 to 2 green onions, cut into thin diagonal
    slices
½ sheet nori, shredded

Bring water to a boil in a soup pot. Add kombu and shiitake mushroom, cover and simmer 10 minutes. Remove kombu and mushroom and lightly season liquid with soy sauce. (You have just made a traditional Japanese broth called *dashi*, which is used as a soup base or dipping sauce in many recipes.) Stir in tofu cubes. Simmer 10 minutes more. Divide cooked noodles among individual soup bowls and ladle soup over noodles. Serve garnished with green onions and shredded nori.

■ **VARIATION** If desired, thinly slice the kombu and shiitake mushroom and add back to the soup.

Sweet-and-Sour Soup

Another favorite from Asia. My version is rich in flavor, but not fat and salt. I like to serve this soup with homemade dumplings or wontons.

MAKES 4 SERVINGS

1 teaspoon dark sesame oil
1 onion, finely diced
4 to 5 cups Vegetable Stock (page 74)
3 celery stalks, cut into thin diagonal slices
1 carrot, finely diced
2 stalks broccoli, cut into small florets with
    stems peeled and diced
1 tablespoon brown rice syrup
2 tablespoons mustard powder
Sea salt
1 tablespoon brown rice vinegar
1 to 2 green onions, thinly sliced, for garnish

Heat oil in a soup pot over medium–low heat. Add onion and cook until translucent, about 5 minutes. Add stock and bring to a boil. Add celery, carrot and broccoli stems. Reduce heat, cover and cook over low heat 10 minutes. Stir in rice syrup, mustard powder and a light seasoning of salt. Add broccoli florets and simmer 5 minutes more. Remove from heat and stir in rice vinegar. Serve garnished with green onions.

■ **VARIATION** If serving this soup with wontons or dumplings, add them just before the last 5 minutes of cooking, so they are soft, but not doughy.

Fresh Corn on a Green Field

I discovered this recipe quite a long time ago in an out-of-print cookbook, *Cooking for Life* by Michel Abeshara, a longtime macrobiotic teacher and counselor who wrote one of the loveliest cookbooks I have ever used. I hope you enjoy it as much as I have over the years.

MAKES 4 SERVINGS

1 teaspoon light sesame oil
1 leek, sliced lengthwise, rinsed well and
    finely diced
Sea salt
4 to 5 cups spring or filtered water
2 ears fresh corn, kernels removed and cobs
    reserved
1 (2-inch) piece wakame, soaked briefly and
    finely diced
2 or 3 celery stalks, finely diced
2 cups thinly sliced kale
1 tablespoon kuzu or arrowroot, dissolved in
    4 tablespoons cold water
Small handful fresh flat-leaf parsley, finely
    minced, for garnish

Heat oil in a soup pot over medium–low heat. Add leek with a pinch of salt and cook, stirring, 3 to 4 minutes. Add water and bring to a boil. Add corn cobs and boil 3 to 4 minutes. Carefully remove cobs and discard. Add corn kernels, wakame and celery, cover and cook over low heat 15 minutes. Season lightly with salt and simmer 5 minutes more. Add kale and stir in dissolved kuzu. Cook, stirring, until soup thickens slightly. Serve garnished with parsley.

Cantaloupe Soup with Blueberries

If you love fruit, this summer refresher is for you. Serve as a starter for a brunch or as an interesting beginning to any warm-weather feast.

MAKES 4 SERVINGS

1 ripe peach, peeled, pitted and finely diced
1 cantaloupe, peeled, seeded and finely diced
1 cup unfiltered, unsweetened apple juice
Pinch sea salt
Juice of 1 lemon
1 teaspoon pure vanilla extract
Fresh blueberries, for garnish
Fresh mint leaves, for garnish

Place peach and cantaloupe in a soup pot with apple juice and salt. Cook over medium heat, covered, about 10 minutes. Remove from heat. Transfer to a food processor and puree until smooth. Stir in lemon juice and vanilla, pour into a bowl and cover. Chill thoroughly before serving, about 2 hours. Serve garnished with blueberries and mint leaves.

Zuni

A simple soup, traditionally served in Japan on the New Year for good fortune, this elegant soup is lucky any time of year.

MAKES 4 SERVINGS

4 to 5 cups spring or filtered water
1 (3-inch) piece wakame, soaked until tender and diced
1 cup thin rounds daikon
4 to 6 (1-inch) brown rice mochi cubes

2 teaspoons barley miso
1 or 2 green onions, thinly sliced diagonally, for garnish

Bring water to a boil in a small soup pot over medium–low heat. Add wakame and simmer over low heat 3 to 4 minutes. Add daikon and mochi and cook over low heat, covered, until mochi has softened, about 7 minutes. Remove a small amount of broth, add miso and stir until dissolved. Stir mixture into soup and simmer 3 to 4 minutes more. Serve garnished with green onions.

Italian Minestrone

My mom used to make this hearty soup; it was one of my dad's favorite dishes. I can still see him sitting at the head of the table, a heel of bread in one hand, spoon in the other, intent on not leaving a drop behind.

MAKES 4 TO 6 SERVINGS

¼ cup *each* dried chickpeas, kidney beans and white beans, sorted, rinsed well and soaked together 1 hour
1 tablespoon extra-virgin olive oil
2 to 3 cloves fresh garlic, finely minced
1 onion, finely diced
Sea salt
2 celery stalks, diced
2 to 3 ripe tomatoes, coarsely chopped
1 carrot, diced
Generous pinch dried basil
4 cups spring or filtered water
1 bay leaf
1 cup tiny pasta (orzo, acini, pastina), cooked al dente and rinsed
Several leaves broccoli rapini, diced

Drain beans, discarding soaking water.

Heat oil in a soup pot over medium-low heat. Add garlic and onion and a pinch of salt and cook about 3 minutes. Add celery, tomatoes, carrot, basil and a generous pinch of salt. Cook, stirring, until coated with oil. Add beans, water and bay leaf. Bring to a boil, cover and simmer over low heat until beans are tender, 1 to 1½ hours. Season with salt to taste and simmer 10 minutes more. Remove bay leaf. Stir in cooked pasta and rapini, simmer 1 minute to cook rapini and serve hot.

■ **VARIATION** I cook the pasta separately for this soup, because my mother believed that cooking pasta in the soup made the broth too starchy and the pasta too mushy. But you may cook it in the broth, if you wish. The resulting soup will be much thicker.

Clear Daikon Consommé

This elegant soup is the ideal starter for a rich meal that may contain heartier foods, like long-cooked beans, a fish entrée or perhaps some foods cooked with rich sauces or oils. Daikon helps the body to assimilate and process fat and protein, so this light broth can be more than just a delicious beginning to your meal.

MAKES 4 SERVINGS

4 cups spring or filtered water
1 cup thinly sliced daikon
1 to 2 tablespoons umeboshi vinegar
1 or 2 green onions, thinly sliced, for garnish

Bring water to a boil in a soup pot over medium heat. Add daikon, cover and simmer over low heat until tender, 7 to 10 minutes.

Remove from heat and season to taste with vinegar. Serve garnished with green onions.

■ **NOTE** This soup is delicious served hot or chilled during the summer—in fact, it can really help you beat the heat, because of the alkalizing effect of the umeboshi vinegar, along with the cooling effect of the daikon.

Flageolet Bean Soup

Flageolet are French greenish-white beans, found in most gourmet shops. They have the loveliest subtle flavor. However, you may make an equally delicious soup with white navy beans. I like to serve this very pretty, delicately flavored soup in the spring and early fall.

MAKES 4 OR 5 SERVINGS

1 (½-inch) piece kombu
1 onion, finely diced
1 clove fresh garlic, finely minced
½ cup flageolet beans, rinsed well
Dried rosemary leaves
2 bay leaves
Spring or filtered water
3 to 4 cups Vegetable Stock (page 74)
Sea salt
3 or 4 slices whole grain sourdough bread, cubed
2 teaspoons extra-virgin olive oil
1 cup diced fresh tomato, for garnish
2 tablespoons minced fresh flat-leaf parsley

Place kombu in a heavy pot and top with onion, garlic, beans, a generous pinch of rosemary, bay leaves and enough water to just cover ingredients. Boil 10 minutes. Reduce heat to low, cover and cook until beans are tender, about 1 hour. Drain away any remaining liquid and puree the beans and vegetables in a food mill or food processor until smooth. Return mixture to the pot and whisk in stock until you achieve desired consistency. Season to taste with salt and simmer for 10 minutes.

Meanwhile, preheat oven to 300F (150C). Arrange bread cubes in a single layer on an ungreased baking sheet and bake until dry and crisp, about 10 minutes.

Heat oil in a skillet. Add bread cubes and cook, stirring occasionally, until cubes are light golden. Drain on paper and set aside.

Serve the soup hot, garnished with diced tomatoes, parsley and several sourdough croutons per bowl.

Simple Vegetable Soup

This basic vegetable soup makes a great lunch when partnered with a sandwich and some lightly cooked vegetables. More than just an energizing meal, soup can be a quick-fix solution to menu planning in our busy lives. Mixing and matching soups and sandwiches is a great way to add variety to your noontime meals.

MAKES 5 OR 6 SERVINGS

½ cup thinly sliced onion
4 cups Mushroom Stock (page 75) or spring or filtered water
1 carrot, cut into thin diagonal slices
1 cup thinly sliced daikon
2 teaspoons avocado oil
1 cup button mushrooms, brushed clean and thinly sliced
½ red bell pepper, sliced into thin ribbons
½ teaspoon fresh ginger juice (see Note, page 164)

Soy sauce
4 to 6 snow peas, sliced into thin matchsticks

Combine onion and enough stock to just cover in a soup pot and simmer 3 to 4 minutes. Add remaining stock and bring to a boil. Stir in carrot and daikon, cover and cook over low heat about 5 minutes.

Meanwhile, heat oil in a skillet over medium-low heat. Add mushrooms and bell pepper and cook until just tender, about 4 minutes. Add vegetables to soup, season with ginger juice and soy sauce and simmer 5 minutes more. Serve garnished with snow pea matchsticks.

Florentine Rice Soup

When I lived in Tuscany several years ago, I discovered that rice is much more popular there than pasta. I spent a lot of time with the people I worked with, and one of our favorite things to do together was, yes, you guessed it, cook! This fabulous soup has changed and evolved over the years, but I still get nostalgic for life in Italy whenever I make it.

MAKES 5 OR 6 SERVINGS

1 cup white or arborio rice
Sea salt
2½ cups spring or filtered water
2 teaspoons extra-virgin olive oil
2 cloves fresh garlic, finely minced
3 to 4 shallots, finely minced
4 to 5 cups Vegetable Stock (page 74)
3 or 4 kale leaves, finely minced

Rinse rice very well to prevent it from becoming sticky when it is cooked. Place rice in a bowl with enough water to cover and gently swirl with your hands. Drain through a fine strainer and repeat process until water rinses away relatively clear.

Place rice in a pot with a pinch of salt and water and bring to a boil, uncovered. Cover pot. Reduce heat to low and cook until liquid has been absorbed, about 30 minutes. Transfer rice to a bowl, cover and set aside.

In a soup pot, heat oil over medium-low heat. Add garlic and shallots and cook 2 to 3 minutes. Add stock and cooked rice and bring to a boil. Cover and simmer over low heat about 10 minutes, stirring frequently to prevent sticking. Season lightly with salt and simmer 5 minutes more. Stir in kale just before serving and simmer 1 to 2 minutes.

Chilled Cucumber Bisque

A quick and easy, light summer soup, this is a great addition for an outdoor summer buffet.

MAKES 4 OR 5 SERVINGS

1 teaspoon avocado oil
1 small leek, sliced lengthwise, rinsed well
   and finely diced
2 to 3 cups peeled, seeded and diced
   cucumber
1 tablespoon fresh dill, finely minced
Sea salt
2 cups spring or filtered water
1 cup soy or rice milk
2 tablespoons kuzu or arrowroot, dissolved in
   4 tablespoons cold water
Juice of 1 lemon
Fresh lemon slices, for garnish
Dill sprigs, for garnish

Heat oil in a soup pot over medium-low heat. Add leek and cook, stirring, 2 to 3 minutes.

Add cucumber, minced dill and a pinch of salt and cook 2 to 3 minutes more. Add water and milk and bring to a boil. Cover and cook over low heat until vegetables are tender, about 5 minutes. Stir in dissolved kuzu and cook, stirring, until soup thickens slightly, about 3 minutes. Remove from heat and stir in lemon juice. Chill thoroughly, about 2 hours, before serving garnished with fresh lemon slices and dill sprigs.

Greek Lentil Soup

I spent only three days in Greece, but realized immediately that you only need three minutes to fall completely in love with the country, the culture, the people, and the food. I got this recipe from an elderly Greek chef during my brief stay. The changes I have made over the years have kept the essence of this lovely, saffron-scented soup intact.

MAKES 5 OR 6 SERVINGS

1 tablespoon extra-virgin olive oil
1 onion, cut into large dice
2 to 3 cloves fresh garlic, finely minced
1 small leek, sliced lengthwise, rinsed well
   and cut into large dice
Sea salt
2 celery stalks, cut into large dice
1 carrot, cut into large dice
1 cup green lentils, sorted and rinsed well
5 cups spring or filtered water
1 (1-inch) piece kombu or bay leaf (see Note,
   opposite)
About 1 teaspoon saffron, ground between
   your fingertips
Grated zest and juice of 1 lemon
1 cup whole grain sourdough croutons (see
   Note, page 82)

Heat olive oil in a soup pot over medium-low heat. Add onion, garlic, leek and a pinch of salt and cook, stirring, 3 to 4 minutes. Add celery and carrot and cook 3 to 4 minutes more. Top with lentils and stir briefly, just to coat the lentils with oil. Add water and kombu and bring to a boil. Cover and cook over low heat until lentils are soft, 35 to 40 minutes. Season to taste with salt and saffron (a little goes a long way, so use saffron sparingly) and simmer 20 minutes. Remove from heat and stir in lemon zest and juice. Serve garnished with several croutons per bowl.

■ **NOTE** If using bay leaf, remove from soup and discard before serving.

Arroz con Chícharos

This Mexican recipe is also known as *sopa seca,* which means "dry soup," because much of the broth is soaked up by the rice, making a thick, rich stew. Serve with tortilla chips and a fresh salad for a very satisfying meal.

MAKES 5 OR 6 SERVINGS

2 tablespoons avocado or olive oil
1 onion, cut into half-moon slices
2 to 3 cloves fresh garlic, thinly sliced
2 carrots, cut into large dice
2 to 3 teaspoons chili powder or to taste
1½ cups long-grain brown rice, rinsed well
5 cups spring or filtered water
Sea salt
1 cup fresh or frozen green peas
1 cup diced fresh tomatoes, for garnish

Heat oil in a soup pot over medium heat. Add onion and garlic and cook, stirring, until

translucent, about 2 minutes. Add carrots and chili powder and cook, stirring, until all vegetables are coated. Stir in rice. Gently pour in water and bring to a boil. Cover and cook over low heat until rice is soft and the consistency is creamy, 40 to 45 minutes. Season lightly with salt, stir in peas and simmer 5 minutes more. Serve garnished with tomatoes.

Chickpea Stew

A thick and creamy stew that is a meal on its own. On chilly days I usually serve this stew followed by a simpler meal of sautéed noodles and vegetables or a salad.

MAKES 5 OR 6 SERVINGS

1 onion, finely diced
1 clove fresh garlic, finely minced
5 cups Vegetable Stock (page 74)
½ cup yellow corn grits
2 cups cooked chickpeas
1 cup finely shredded green cabbage
2 teaspoons white miso
1 or 2 green onions, thinly sliced, for garnish
Extra-virgin olive oil

Combine onion, garlic and a small amount of stock in a soup pot over medium heat. Bring to a boil, reduce heat and simmer 3 to 4 minutes. Add remaining stock and return to a boil. Stir in grits, chickpeas and cabbage, cover and cook over low heat 40 minutes, stirring frequently to prevent corn grits from scorching. Remove a small amount of broth, add miso and stir until dissolved. Stir mixture into soup and simmer 3 to 4 minutes. Serve garnished with green onions and a light drizzle of olive oil.

Red Lentil–Corn Chowder

Adding fresh vegetables and tiny pasta makes this even better and a fabulous change from the lentil soup we all knew and loved growing up.

MAKES 4 OR 5 SERVINGS

1 tablespoon extra-virgin olive oil
3 to 4 shallots, peeled and finely minced
Several pinches ground cumin
1 cup dried red lentils, rinsed well
4 cups spring or filtered water
1 medium zucchini, large dice
½ red bell pepper, roasted over a flame, peeled, seeded and diced (see Note, page 262)
2 cups fresh corn kernels
1 cup cooked tiny pasta (orzo, pastina, acini)
2 tablespoons barley miso
1 teaspoon red wine vinegar
Small handful fresh flat-leaf parsley, minced
Sprigs flat-leaf parsley, for garnish

Heat oil in a soup pot over medium-low heat. Add shallots and cumin and cook, stirring, until shallots are limp, 3 to 4 minutes. Add lentils and water and bring to a boil. Add zucchini, bell pepper and corn, cover and cook over low heat until lentils are very soft, 20 minutes.

While soup simmers, cook pasta in boiling salted water according to package directions until al dente. Drain pasta.

Remove a small amount of broth from soup, add miso and stir until dissolved. Stir mixture into soup and simmer 3 to 4 minutes more. Remove soup from heat and stir in cooked pasta, vinegar and minced parsley. Serve garnished with parsley sprigs and a side of crusty whole grain bread.

Anasazi Bean Stew

I love to serve this unique stew with cornmeal dumplings. It is so savory and rich that I usually round out the meal with a fresh salad.

MAKES 4 OR 5 SERVINGS

1 (1-inch) piece kombu
1 cup Anasazi beans, rinsed well
4 or 5 cups spring or filtered water
1 small leek, sliced lengthwise, rinsed well and diced
2 celery stalks, diced
1 medium carrot, diced
1 cup diced daikon
1 cup diced winter squash
2 or 3 bay leaves
Dried rosemary leaves
2 or 3 ripe tomatoes, diced
Sea salt
Balsamic vinegar
Cornmeal Dumplings (recipe opposite)
Extra-virgin olive oil

Layer kombu, beans and 3 cups of the water in a soup pot and bring to a boil over high heat. Boil, uncovered, 10 minutes. Add vegetables, bay leaves and a generous pinch of rosemary. Return to a boil, cover and cook over low heat until beans are very tender, about 45 minutes. Stir in remaining water (to desired consistency) and tomatoes and season lightly with salt. Simmer 10 minutes more. Remove from heat and stir in a light sprinkle of vinegar. Ladle stew into individual soup bowls and serve topped with dumplings and a drizzle of olive oil.

Cornmeal Dumplings

MAKES 4 TO 6 DUMPLINGS

½ cup whole wheat pastry flour
½ cup cornmeal
Pinch sea salt
¼ teaspoon baking powder
4 ounces firm tofu

Combine flour, cornmeal, salt and baking powder in a medium bowl. Puree tofu with a small amount of water until a smooth paste forms. Fold into cornmeal mixture until ingredients are well incorporated and the dough gathers easily into a thick batter.

Bring a pot of spring or filtered water to a boil. Drop dumpling batter, by large spoonfuls, into the pot and simmer about 10 minutes over low heat. Test for doneness by removing a dumpling and slicing it in half. The inside should be moist and breadlike.

Orange-Squash Soup

This is the sweetest, most delicious squash soup. The delicate zest of fresh orange makes this an attention-getting starter.

MAKES 4 OR 5 SERVINGS

2 teaspoons avocado oil
1 onion, diced
Sea salt
Grated zest of 1 orange
2 small butternut squash, seeded, peeled and
    diced
4 cups spring or filtered water
1 tablespoon sweet white miso
Juice of 1 orange
Fresh orange slices, for garnish

Heat oil in a soup pot over medium-low heat. Add onion and a pinch of salt and cook, stirring, until translucent, about 3 minutes. Stir in zest and squash and cook, stirring, until coated with oil. Add water and bring to a boil. Cover and cook over low heat until squash is tender, about 20 minutes.

Transfer soup to a food mill or food processor and puree until smooth. Remove a small amount of soup, add miso and stir until dissolved. Stir mixture into soup and simmer 3 to 4 minutes more. Whisk in additional water, if necessary, to create a thinner soup. Remove from heat and stir in orange juice while soup is still hot. Serve garnished with fresh orange slices.

Dulse and Leek Soup

I learned this soup from my Irish grandmother. I remember she found it quite amusing when I "discovered" dulse, a sea vegetable that Irish cooks have been using for thousands of years. So much for reinventing the wheel.

MAKES 4 OR 5 SERVINGS

1 small leek, sliced lengthwise, rinsed well
    and diced
4 cups spring or filtered water
½ cup dried dulse
⅔ cup rolled oats
2 tablespoons white miso
Green onions, thinly sliced, for garnish

Combine leek and enough water to just cover in a soup pot over medium heat. Bring to a boil and simmer over low heat 3 to 4 minutes. Add remaining water and bring to a boil.

Sort through dulse and shred. Do not soak. Add dulse and oats to boiling broth, cover and cook over low heat 15 minutes. Remove a small amount of broth, add miso and stir until dissolved. Stir mixture into soup and simmer 3 to 4 minutes more. Serve garnished with green onions.

- **VARIATION** During winter weather, I cook this soup for about 1 hour using whole oats, instead of rolled oats, to create a more warming, hearty soup.

Italian Vegetable Stew

This Tuscan specialty is really lovely. I make it with everything: during the summer, fresh fava beans make a most delicious soup; in cooler weather, dried cannellini beans. My vegetarian version gets its full-bodied flavor from a rich vegetable stock.

MAKES 4 OR 5 SERVINGS

1 tablespoon extra-virgin olive oil
1 cup dried cannellini beans, rinsed well
1 pound fresh or frozen green peas
1 to 2 cloves fresh garlic, finely minced
1 onion, cut into large dice
4 cups Vegetable Stock (page 74)
1 bay leaf
¼ cup mirin or white wine
Sea salt
Juice of 1 lemon
3 or 4 leaves of kale, finely chopped

Heat oil in a soup pot over medium-low heat. Add beans and cook, stirring, 1 to 2 minutes. Stir in peas, garlic and onion. Add stock and bay leaf and bring to a boil. Add mirin, cover and cook over low heat until beans are soft, about 45 minutes to 1 hour. Season lightly with salt and simmer 10 minutes more. Remove from heat and stir in lemon juice and kale. Serve hot.

Italian Cabbage Soup

This lovely peasant soup is another jewel from my mother's kitchen, although, as kids, we didn't quite see it that way; a simple soup like this was an indication of just how limited our resources were that week. It was only later in life that I learned that I get the most pleasure from simple things.

MAKES 4 OR 5 SERVINGS

1 tablespoon extra-virgin olive oil
2 cloves fresh garlic, thinly sliced
1 onion, finely diced
Sea salt
1 cup very finely shredded green cabbage
4 to 5 cups spring or filtered water
½ cup yellow corn grits
Sprigs flat-leaf parsley, for garnish

Heat oil in a soup pot over medium-low heat. Add garlic and cook until just brown; do not burn. Add onion and a pinch of salt and cook, stirring, until translucent, about 3 minutes. Stir in cabbage and a pinch of salt and cook, stirring, until coated with oil. Carefully add enough water to just cover ingredients and boil gently 3 to 4 minutes. Add remaining water and return to a boil. Stir in corn grits, whisking constantly. Reduce heat to low and add a pinch of salt. Cover and cook, stirring very frequently to prevent scorching, about 35 minutes. The soup will take on a very creamy consistency. Season lightly with salt and simmer 5 to 7 minutes more, stirring frequently. Serve garnished with parsley sprigs.

Beans, Beans, Beans

I HAVE TO be honest and tell you that I put off writing this section of the book for as long as I could. Not that I don't love beans; I do, but as a culture, we're protein maniacs. I hear the same lament more times than I care to relate: "Where do vegetarians get their protein?" "Will I get enough protein if I give up meat?" Well, I am here to tell you that in all the years I have been vegetarian, I have never met a protein-deficient person—ever.

The truth is, all grains, vegetables, nuts, seeds and, yes, beans, contain protein. The best news is that all of those are vegetable-quality proteins, which means that we can assimilate it easily and utilize it completely. In our fragmented, vitamin-obsessed thinking, we have lost sight of the fact that we do not require as much protein to satisfy our bodies' needs as we have been led to believe by clever marketing. In traditional cuisines, protein-rich foods, like animal food or even beans, were used in small amounts, composing less than 10 percent of daily intake— this was not because of concern about protein overconsumption, but rather due to availability. These foods were added to the diet for richness and for the energy they provide naturally. People labored physically harder than we do today and required the kind of stamina that went along with their work. But the people of these cultures knew instinctively that only small

amounts of these foods were required to obtain the desired effects. It is only in our modern culture that we have centered our daily diet around protein-rich animal foods, so much so that when we consider eliminating animal protein from our diet, we become fearful of protein deficiency and loss of strength.

Beans have been cultivated around the world since ancient times. It seems that, along with vegetables, they have always been served as a traditional complement to whole cereal grains. For example, in South and Central America, cooked beans wrapped in corn tortillas were a dietary staple. In India, dahl, a thick sauce made from dried peas or lentils, was served with rice or chapatis. Far Eastern cuisine traditionally pairs whole grain rice with azuki, soy or mung beans. In Africa, chickpeas and black-eyed peas are served as accompaniments with couscous or cracked wheat. And in

Europe, broad beans and lentils are the natural companions of barley, farro and rice.

Modern culture has turned its back on most traditional cuisines in favor of convenient, quick foods. The result has been that we, as a species, have become weaker and have more difficulty digesting food, especially whole foods. This is manifested by the great number of people who have difficulty assimilating whole beans and bean products. We need to understand that animal foods and dairy foods are very taxing to our digestive tract, leaving it weak, overworked and in some cases, flaccid. This results in the tract's loss of ability to contract and push food through. So sometimes the change to a whole foods diet can result in digestive trouble, especially when those whole foods are beans.

What is the best way to handle this problem of digesting beans? Do we just grin and bear it until we become a bit stronger? Do we eliminate beans from our diet? (A grim thought.) Or are there ways of preparing beans to make them easier on our digestive systems, while still preserving the benefits of these nutrient-rich foods? Of course there are. We'll get to them.

Importance of Beans in the Diet

Why eat beans in the first place? Beans and bean products are proportionately higher in fat and protein than whole cereal grains and lower in carbohydrates. Combined with grains, beans make a complete protein, providing all of the amino acids needed by the body to function properly. Beans are also quite high in nutrients like calcium, phosphorus, iron, niacin, thiamin and vitamin E. While relatively low in vitamin A, legumes contain phosphatides, which increase our absorption of beta-carotene (the precursor to vitamin A found in yellow and orange vegetables and considered a strong anticancer factor), making vegetable and bean combinations an ideal food.

Beans are completely cholesterol free and contain only unsaturated fat. Also high in minerals, recent studies have shown that a diet including beans and bean products, particularly soyfoods, greatly reduces arteriosclerotic lesions and high cholesterol levels. European doctors have reported that patients eating a diet rich in soyfoods significantly reduced the risk of heart disease. And tempeh, which contains the microorganism bacillus subtilis, has strong antibiotic effects as well.

Beans and bean products have another benefit as well: They provide slow, steady energy—fuel, if you will—by releasing nutrients slowly into the bloodstream. The result is that the quality of the blood is strengthened, as well as the lymph and other body fluids. Remember that the blood nourishes every organ and organ system in the body; so if blood quality is good and strong, it only follows that the body will be strong, too.

So if the only bad news about beans is digestibility, then we'll just have to get you over that one, because these are valuable nutrients that you just can't pass up.

Buying and Storing Beans

Before we talk about cooking beans, let's consider which characteristics we should look for when buying them. Quality is important, and since beans are often rotated with other crops, it is important to consider the quality of the growing soil. In my opinion, organic beans are always the best choice; they are not grown in chemically depleted soil and thus give us more strength and nutrients, particularly minerals, drawn from the earth.

After harvest, beans are cleaned, dried and packaged. Good processing loses only about 10 percent to damage. Once at the market, you should look for beans that are well formed, uniform in size and shape, smooth skinned, full-bodied and shiny. Any deformities like spots, wrinkles, flecks, cracks and pits mean that the beans have lost their vitality. And if you don't believe me, take a cracked or broken bean and try to sprout it. It will not grow; no life force exists. Dried beans should also be hard, shattering when bitten into. If the beans only dent, they have not been properly dried and will not yield a hearty taste.

After purchase, store beans in tightly sealed glass jars and keep in a cool, dry place like a pantry. Preserved and stored in this manner, beans will retain their vitality for many years. Different varieties of beans should be stored separately from one another. As with grains, I also like to keep a bay leaf in each jar of beans to ensure freshness.

So what are the best types of beans to purchase for regular use? Generally, I like to choose smaller beans that are lower in fat for daily use, occasionally supplementing with larger, broader beans. As an additional supplement, I use bean products like tofu and tempeh. For more information about individual beans, check the listings in the glossary.

Cooking Beans

Okay, so now you've made the decision to include more beans and bean products in your diet. You've gone out and bought a variety of beans and stocked your pantry. So now what? Well, here are some of the most common methods for cooking beans for the best flavor and digestibility.

Before cooking beans, quickly sort through them to remove any visible stones or damaged beans. (Don't get crazy with this, just a quick sort to remove debris.) Then gently rinse the beans in a colander to remove any surface dust.

I used to soak beans before cooking. I don't anymore . . . or if I do, it is only for an hour. Let me tell you a story. I was cooking for one of our tour groups (my husband and I run a small travel company that hosts healthy vacations) in a small inn in central Tuscany. We had taken over the entire *agriturismo* and one of the perks was that we had the professional kitchen all to ourselves. The regular cook was an elderly Italian woman who checked in on me daily to be sure I was not destroying her kitchen (as I would do, to be frank . . .). One morning, she came in as I was draining the soaking water from chickpeas. She asked me what I was doing. When I explained that I had soaked the beans for several hours before cooking, she asked if I liked my guests . . . because I was going to give them bad digestion by soaking beans. I told her that soaking also shortened cooking time. She smiled, called me *stupida* in an affectionate way and suggested that we cook beans together with identical recipes and see the outcome. To make a long story short, her beans had a richer taste and no one became "musical" after eating them. I thought about it and realized that soaking caused the beans to lose flavor and enzymes, and the cooking time between the two recipes varied only by a few minutes. I have not soaked a bean since. However, if you just can't break the habit, try soaking for only an hour. Life just became so much easier, didn't it?

When ready to cook the beans, discard the soaking water (if you are still soaking) and begin the cooking process with fresh water.

Next, take a deep, heavy pot and place a one-inch piece of kombu or one bay leaf per cup of beans on the bottom. This small piece of sea vegetable or bay leaf mineralizes and softens the beans, rendering the fat and protein more digestible (both are rich sources of monosodium glutamic acid, a natural "tenderizer"). Add the beans and water and bring the pot to a rolling boil. The last step in making beans most digestible is to allow the beans to boil rapidly for five to seven minutes before covering and cooking over low heat until done. This final precaution helps cook away any remaining "gas" from the beans.

Following these simple steps prior to cooking beans can really help alleviate the digestive problems commonly associated with them. The last step in your insurance policy comes when the beans are fully prepared. Chew them very well. That exercise is the very best advice I can give you for bean eating. Saliva secreted during chewing is the best aid to digestion.

So, now, what are the best cooking methods for beans? Well, in order for beans to thoroughly cook inside and out, it is best to cook beans for as long as possible over low heat. There is a wide variety of seasonings, including miso, soy sauce, sea salt, mirin, wine, barley malt and sometimes a bit of oil, depending on what taste you want in the final dish. Sometimes I add vegetables at the beginning of cooking to create a creamy stew; other times I add the vegetables toward the end of cooking so that each retains its own character and holds its shape. Or I may use dried vegetables in a bean stew. Finally, I frequently serve bean dishes garnished with something a bit spicy or hot, such as grated daikon, fresh ginger or horseradish or diced green onions or chives. Many times I will separately sauté a variety of vegetables, possibly with cumin or other spice, and stir them into completely cooked beans for

yet another type of bean dish. So, you see, preparing beans is still another area of creativity in the kitchen.

Some of the more common methods for cooking whole beans properly include:

Shock Method

Shocking, a traditional method for cooking beans, comes to us from Asia. Place rinsed beans in a heavy, cast-iron pot with 2½ cups of water for each 1 cup of beans. Cook the beans over low heat, uncovered, until they boil. After a few minutes at a boil, set a drop lid (a lid that sets loosely inside the pot) inside the pot on top of the beans. After the beans are covered, the water will return to a strong boil, causing the cover to jiggle. Remove the lid and add cold water down the side of the pot until the boiling stops, then replace the lid. Repeat the process each time the beans return to a boil until they are about 80 percent cooked when tasted for tenderness. At that point, remove the lid, add any desired vegetables and allow the beans to cook over medium heat until both are tender. Season to taste and simmer away any remaining liquid. This method brings out the natural sweet taste of beans, giving you perfectly tender and delicious beans every time.

Boiling

Add 3 to 3½ cups water to 1 cup rinsed beans. After bringing beans to a boil, cover them and cook over low heat until tender. Season and continue cooking until completely done.

Pressure Cooking

The fastest method for cooking beans is to pressure-cook them. This method is a great time-saver and gives large amounts of energy to the dish. The water ratio remains the same, as does the use of kombu or bay leaf.

Canned Beans

If cooking beans simply cannot fit into your busy schedule, there are canned organic beans now available in most natural food stores. Granted, they won't be quite as delicious as beans cooked from scratch, but in a pinch, they do quite nicely. Before use, rinse the beans free of the liquid in the can, as this fluid can give the beans a stale taste. Any whole-bean recipe here can be made with canned beans; simply eliminate the bean-cooking steps in the cooking process.

Crispy Pea Fritters

This recipe is based on a Cuban delight that I loved when I lived in Miami. Called *bollitos de caritas* (little face fritters), these black-eyed pea treats were sold by just about every street vendor and shopkeeper in Little Cuba. I love them served with a hot dipping sauce. They have a truly vitalizing effect—from hot onions, aromatic garlic and the strong fire of frying—with a steady energy base provided by the beans.

MAKES 4 OR 5 SERVINGS

1 bay leaf
1 cup dried black-eyed peas, sorted and rinsed
3 cups spring or filtered water
1 red onion, finely diced
2 or 3 cloves fresh garlic, finely minced
¼ cup finely minced fresh flat-leaf parsley
½ to 1 teaspoon sea salt
¼ cup whole wheat pastry flour

¼ cup yellow cornmeal
1 teaspoon baking powder
Avocado oil, for frying

Place bay leaf in a heavy pot with peas and water. Bring to a boil over medium heat and boil, uncovered, 5 to 7 minutes. Reduce heat, cover and simmer until peas are tender, 45 minutes to 1 hour. Drain the peas and transfer to a food processor or hand grinder and puree to a mashed-potato consistency. Spoon into a bowl and fold in onion, garlic and parsley. Add salt to taste and mix well.

In a small bowl, combine flour, cornmeal and baking powder with a pinch of salt. Stir into the pea mixture, making a stiff dough. Form the mixture into small, thick rounds, like silver-dollar pancakes.

Heat about ¼ inch oil in a deep skillet over medium heat and pan-fry each fritter until golden brown in color, about 2 minutes per side, turning. Remove from oil and drain on paper towels before arranging on a platter. Serve hot as a side dish or as a snack with a spicy dipping sauce.

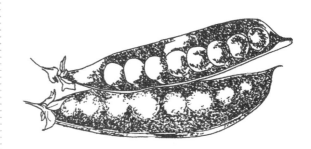

Country Bean Pâté

If you make this dish, be sure to have plenty of great bread to spread it on. It will go so fast, your head will spin. I like to lightly oil the bread and broil it until crispy brown before serving it with this creamy, incredibly easy to make, low-fat dip. It's an ideal party dish that actually allows the cook to enjoy as well.

MAKES 4 TO 6 SERVINGS

2 cups cooked white navy beans, drained
1 small onion, diced
2 cloves fresh garlic, minced
½ cup whole wheat bread crumbs
2 teaspoons prepared mustard
Juice of 1 lemon
2 tablespoons extra-virgin olive oil
1 teaspoon brown rice syrup
½ teaspoon each dried basil and dill weed
Sea salt
Lettuce leaves

Place all ingredients except lettuce in a food processor, seasoning with salt to taste, and puree until smooth. Transfer mixture to a serving bowl lined with crisp greens, cover tightly with plastic wrap and chill thoroughly before serving.

Sautéed Broad Beans

My grandfather loved fresh fava beans fixed this way. Hard to come by these days, fresh fava beans can be found in ethnic markets. Frozen, shelled fava beans are available in most supermarkets. This dish imparts a lovely, steady energy that is enhanced by the freshness and lighter tastes of the vegetables.

MAKES 3 OR 4 SERVINGS

1 tablespoon extra-virgin olive oil
Several leaves fresh basil, minced, or generous pinch dried basil
1 leek, cut lengthwise, rinsed well and thinly sliced
1 clove fresh garlic, finely minced
2 cups fresh shelled fava beans
Spring or filtered water
1 red bell pepper, roasted over a flame, peeled, seeded and diced (see Note, page 262)
1 or 2 small zucchini, diced
1 or 2 tomatoes, coarsely chopped
Sea salt
¼ cup finely minced fresh flat-leaf parsley

Heat oil in a saucepan over medium heat. Add basil, leek and garlic and sauté 1 to 2 minutes. Add beans and cook, stirring, to combine. Add water to cover and bring to a boil. Reduce heat to low, cover and simmer until beans are tender, about 15 minutes. Add bell pepper, zucchini, tomatoes and a light seasoning of salt. Cook 15 to 20 minutes. Remove from heat and stir in parsley. Transfer to a bowl and serve hot.

Savory Black Beans with Squash

A rich and savory stew, nicely scented with lots of garlic and ginger and brimming with sweet winter squash. It has a warm, vitalizing energy to make you feel strong and steady.

MAKES 4 OR 5 SERVINGS

1 (1-inch) piece kombu
1 cup dried black turtle beans, sorted and rinsed
3 cups spring or filtered water

2 teaspoons avocado oil

5 or 6 cloves fresh garlic, finely minced

4 or 5 slices fresh ginger, finely minced

3 or 4 shallots, minced

Generous pinch cumin

2 or 3 celery stalks, diced

2 or 3 cups small cubes winter squash

Spring or filtered water

1 tablespoon barley miso

4 or 5 green onions, thinly sliced, diagonally, for garnish

Place kombu in a heavy pot and add beans and water. Bring to a boil over medium heat and boil, uncovered, 10 minutes. Reduce heat, cover and simmer until beans are tender, 45 minutes to 1 hour. Transfer to a heat-resistant bowl, draining away any remaining cooking liquid.

In the pot used for cooking the beans, heat oil over medium heat. Add garlic, ginger, shallots and cumin and cook, stirring, 1 to 2 minutes. Add celery and squash. Add enough water to just cover vegetables and simmer, covered, until squash is tender, about 10 minutes. Add cooked beans. Do not stir. Remove about 1 tablespoon cooking broth and mix with miso until dissolved. Stir mixture into the bean stew and simmer, uncovered, about 4 minutes. Remove from heat and fold in green onions. Transfer to a bowl and serve hot.

Black Soybean Relish

The great thing about black soybeans is that as they cook, they create their own gravy. In addition to being a deliciously satisfying stew, this dish has celery and dried daikon, which, coupled with the beans, create cleansing energy. In Oriental medicine, this dish was believed to have the ability to cleanse stagnated fat and mucus from the reproductive organs.

MAKES 4 OR 5 SERVINGS

1 cup dried black soybeans, sorted, rinsed and towel-dried

1 (1-inch) piece kombu

3 to 4 cups spring or filtered water

1 onion, diced

2 or 3 celery stalks, diced

½ cup dried daikon, soaked until tender and diced

2 or 3 tablespoons barley miso

¼ cup minced fresh flat-leaf parsley

In a hot, dry skillet, dry-roast soybeans over medium heat, stirring constantly, until slightly puffed and skins have split, 4 to 5 minutes.

Place kombu in a heavy pot and add beans and water. Bring to a boil over medium heat and boil, uncovered, 10 minutes. If a thick foam appears, simply skim it from the pot with a slotted spoon. Reduce heat, cover, and simmer until beans are slightly tender, 1 to 1½ hours.

Add vegetables to the top of the pot. Re-cover and cook 30 minutes. Remove about 1 tablespoon cooking broth and mix with miso until dissolved. Stir mixture into beans and cook, uncovered, until any excess liquid has been absorbed and beans are creamy, stirring often. Remove from heat and stir in parsley. Spoon into a bowl and serve hot.

Spicy Black Beans and Peppers

Another take on black beans from my life in Florida, this dish was originally a Spanish recipe. Cuban cuisine added a bit of ginger and spice to produce a real attention-getter . . . and a great dish for creating strong, fiery energy.

MAKES 4 OR 5 SERVINGS

1 bay leaf
1 cup dried black turtle beans, sorted and
 rinsed
3 cups spring or filtered water
Sea salt
2 tablespoons extra-virgin olive oil
1 red onion, diced
4 or 5 slices fresh ginger, finely minced
3 cloves fresh garlic, finely minced
1 to 2 chiles, seeded and minced
2 ripe tomatoes, diced (do not peel or seed)
2 red bell peppers
¼ cup finely minced fresh flat-leaf parsley

Place bay leaf in a heavy pot and add beans and water. Bring to a boil over medium heat and boil, uncovered, 10 minutes. Reduce heat, cover, and simmer until beans are tender, about 1 hour. Season with salt to taste and simmer 10 minutes. If too much liquid remains, allow the beans to cook, uncovered, until liquid evaporates.

Meanwhile, heat oil in a skillet over medium heat. Add onion, ginger, garlic and chiles and cook, stirring, until softened, 2 to 3 minutes. Stir in tomatoes and a light seasoning of salt. Simmer until tomatoes have broken down, about 4 minutes.

While the beans and vegetables cook, lightly oil the skins of the peppers. Place whole peppers over an open gas flame until the outer skin is charred black. Transfer to a paper sack, seal tightly and allow peppers to steam 10 minutes. Gently rub charred skin from peppers, removing all charred skin. Cut in half and remove seeds. Dice peppers and toss with vegetables.

When beans are completely cooked, discard bay leaf and toss with vegetables and parsley. Transfer to a serving bowl and serve hot with corn tortillas or with crisp corn chips for dipping.

■ **NOTE** If you do not have a gas stove, roast the peppers by oiling them, splitting them in half lengthwise and laying them cut side down on a baking sheet, seeds intact. Place them under a hot broiler and broil until the skins are charred and then follow the rest of the directions.

Oiling the outer skin of the peppers makes for easier peeling.

Red Lentil–Walnut Pâté

This is a great dip for parties. I love to serve it with toast points or toasted pita bread chips. Lightly toasted walnuts give this dish such a rich taste that you'd best make a lot; it's usually the first dish to disappear. Full of energizing qualities, this pâté will make for an active social gathering.

For this recipe, I always pan-toast the nuts instead of oven-roasting them. They have a much nicer flavor when cooked that way.

MAKES 6 TO 8 SERVINGS

2 cups dried red lentils, sorted and rinsed
 well
1 bay leaf
4 cups spring or filtered water
Sea salt
1 teaspoon extra-virgin olive oil
1 onion, diced
2 to 3 cloves fresh garlic, minced
Generous pinch dried basil
1½ cups walnut pieces, lightly pan-toasted
 (see Note, page 46)
¼ cup minced fresh flat-leaf parsley
1 teaspoon umeboshi vinegar or lemon juice
1 tablespoon balsamic vinegar

Place lentils, bay leaf and water in a heavy pot over medium heat. Bring to a boil and boil, uncovered, 10 minutes. Reduce heat, cover and simmer until lentils are very creamy, 25 to 35 minutes. Season lightly with salt and simmer 5 minutes.

Meanwhile, heat oil in a skillet over medium heat. Add onion, garlic, basil and a light seasoning of salt and cook, stirring, until softened, 3 to 4 minutes. Set aside.

Discard bay leaf. Transfer cooked beans, vegetables, walnuts and parsley to a food processor. Puree until smooth and creamy. Spoon into a serving bowl and sprinkle with umeboshi and balsamic vinegars. Mix well and serve surrounded with toast points.

Baked Beans

I'll be honest: I was never a fan of baked beans. My mother made them for summer picnics and for winter dinners and I just did not get it. They did not do it for me until I was asked to make them for a potluck. A little research and some creative adapting and I came up with this recipe, a popular item in our house these days. Go figure . . .

MAKES 6 TO 8 SERVINGS

2 cups dried cannellini beans, sorted and rinsed
6 cups spring or filtered water
2 bay leaves
2 to 3 tablespoons extra-virgin olive oil
1 large red onion, diced
3 cloves fresh garlic, thinly sliced
Sea salt
4 (8-ounce) cans tomato paste
1 (8-ounce) can diced tomatoes
⅓ cup barley malt
2 teaspoons dried mustard

Cracked black pepper
Scant pinch ground nutmeg
Scant pinch ground cinnamon
Scant pinch smoked paprika

Lightly oil a large casserole and set aside. Place beans and water in a heavy pot with bay leaves and bring to a boil over medium heat. Reduce heat to low, cover and cook until tender, about 1 hour. Drain and transfer beans and bay leaves to prepared casserole.

Preheat oven to 300F (175C).

Heat oil in a skillet over medium heat; add onion and garlic. When the onion begins to sizzle, add a pinch of salt and sauté until translucent, 3 to 4 minutes. Stir mixture into beans.

Whisk together tomato paste, diced tomatoes, barley malt, mustard, a light seasoning of salt and pepper and spices. Mix into the beans until well incorporated.

Cover and bake 3½ hours, stirring frequently and adding a small amount of water, if needed, to keep the beans moist as they bake. Remove cover and bake 30 minutes more to firm up the beans.

Pinto Burgers with Bean "Mayo"

A protein lover's dream, this burger. Made from mineral-rich pinto beans laced through with lots of veggies and smothered in a delicious mayo made from white beans . . . and did I mention that there is no saturated fat to go with all this protein?

MAKES 4 TO 6 BURGERS

BURGERS
½ cup diced red onion
½ cup whole wheat bread crumbs
¼ cup minced fresh cilantro
2 tablespoons minced jalapeño chile
2 tablespoons soy mayonnaise
1 teaspoon hot sauce
½ cup pureed silken tofu
Sea salt
Cracked black pepper
2 cups cooked pinto beans, coarsely mashed
     with a fork
1 cup fresh or frozen corn kernels

BEAN "MAYO"
1 cup cooked white beans
1 tablespoon fresh lemon juice
1 tablespoon red wine vinegar
2 teaspoons brown rice syrup
½ teaspoon sea salt
¼ teaspoon dry mustard
⅔ cup avocado oil
Unsweetened soymilk

Extra-virgin olive oil
4 or 5 leaves kale, washed and shredded
Sea salt
Whole grain burger buns

Make burgers: Combine onion, crumbs, cilantro, chile, mayonnaise, hot sauce and tofu in a mixing bowl. Season to taste with salt and pepper. Fold in beans and corn until ingredients are fully combined. Form the mixture into burger-sized patties. Arrange on a plate, cover and refrigerate for 10 minutes to set the patties.

Make "mayo:" Place all the ingredients, except oil and soymilk, in a blender. Puree, while slowly pouring in the oil to create a smooth mayonnaise texture. Slowly add a small amount of soymilk to thin mixture to your taste. Transfer to a bowl, cover and set aside to allow flavors to develop.

Place a small amount of oil in a skillet over medium heat. Lay patties in skillet and cook, about 4 minutes per side, until browned. Transfer to a plate. Place a small amount of oil in the same skillet and add kale. Sauté kale until just wilted, about 2 minutes. Sprinkle with salt and sauté 1 minute more.

Assemble the burgers: Lay a patty on the bottom half of a bun, spoon some kale on top. Spread the cut side of the top half of the bun with bean "mayo" and press gently on top of burger. Serve immediately.

Lemon-Lime Hummus with Oven-Roasted Pita Chips

A citrusy twist on a culinary classic. I love how the citrus not only makes for a sparkling flavor, but helps us digest the protein and fat of the hummus.

MAKES 4 TO 5 SERVINGS

4 cloves fresh garlic, chopped
½ teaspoon sweet paprika, plus extra for
     sprinkling

2 cups cooked chickpeas, drained
⅓ cup fresh lemon juice
⅓ cup fresh lime juice
½ cup sesame tahini
5 to 6 tablespoons extra-virgin olive oil, plus
    extra for drizzling
Sea salt
½ teaspoon ground cumin
½ teaspoon chili powder
Unsweetened soymilk
8 pita bread rounds, each cut into 8 triangles
Kalamata olives, for garnish

Place all ingredients, except bread and olives, in a food processor, seasoning with salt to taste. Puree until smooth, slowly adding small amounts of soymilk to thin hummus to desired consistency.

Preheat the oven to 350F (175C). Prepare the pitas by drizzling with olive oil and sprinkling with paprika. Bake until the pita triangles are crisp.

Spoon hummus into a bowl, garnished with olives and pita triangles on the side.

Not Your Mamma's Meat Loaf

My father loved meat loaf. I did not, but then again, I was the world's fussiest eater as a kid, so I didn't like anything. My mother cooked for my father's taste and this was one of his favorites. A lot of years and changes later . . . and here is my version. Even my dad likes it.

MAKES 6 TO 8 SERVINGS

1 cup brown or green lentils, sorted and
    rinsed

3 cups spring or filtered water
1 bay leaf
1 small red onion, finely diced
2 cloves fresh garlic, finely minced
1 small carrot, finely diced
1 cup quick-cooking oats
¾ cup grated vegan mozzarella cheese
    alternative
¼ cup whole wheat bread crumbs
⅔ cup tomato sauce
1 tablespoon barley malt
1 teaspoon dried basil
Sea salt
Cracked black pepper

Place lentils, water, bay leaf, onion and garlic in a saucepan over medium heat. Bring to a boil, cover and reduce heat to low. Cook until lentils are soft, about 35 minutes. Remove and discard bay leaf and drain away any remaining cooking liquid. Transfer lentil mixture to a mixing bowl.

Preheat oven to 350F (175C) and lightly oil a 9 × 5-inch loaf pan.

Stir carrot, oats, cheese alternative and bread crumbs into lentils. Whisk together tomato sauce, barley malt, basil and salt and pepper to taste and fold into lentil mixture.

Spoon lentil mixture into prepared loaf pan and press the top firmly with a spatula. Bake 35 to 45 minutes, until the top of the loaf is firm and beginning to brown. Remove from oven and cool about 10 minutes before inverting loaf onto a platter.

Pan-Fried Burritos

What could be better than burritos stuffed with richly flavored, spicy beans? Pan-fried burritos stuffed with richly flavored, spicy beans, silly!

MAKES 4 SERVINGS

SALSA

2 ripe tomatoes, finely diced

½ red onion, finely diced

1 red bell pepper, roasted over a flame, peeled, seeded and diced (see Note, page 262)

2 cloves fresh garlic, finely minced

1 serrano chile, finely minced, including seeds

Sea salt

Extra-virgin olive oil

BURRITOS

Extra-virgin olive oil

3 cloves fresh garlic, thinly sliced

1 red onion, cut into small dice

Sea salt

1 carrot, cut into small dice

2 stalks celery, cut into small dice

Pinch ground cumin

Generous pinch crushed red pepper flakes

1 cup cooked black turtle beans, drained

1 cup cooked red azuki beans, drained

4 (10-inch) whole wheat tortillas

5 to 6 ounces vegan Monterey Jack cheese alternative, grated

½ cup avocado oil

Make salsa: Combine first 5 ingredients in a mixing bowl. Season to taste with salt and drizzle lightly with olive oil. Mix well, cover tightly and set aside while prepping the filling so flavors can develop.

Make the burrito filling: Place a small amount of oil, garlic and onion in a deep skillet over medium heat. When the onion begins to sizzle, add a pinch of salt and sauté 1 to 2 minutes. Stir in carrot, celery and a pinch of salt and sauté 1 to 2 minutes. Stir in cumin and red

pepper flakes, season lightly with salt and sauté 1 minute more. Stir in beans, season to taste with salt and cook, stirring constantly, until beans are warmed through, about 3 minutes.

Lay a tortilla on a dry work surface. Spoon one-fourth of the filling onto tortilla and spread evenly, leaving a 1-inch border all around. Sprinkle with one-fourth of the cheese alternative. From the side nearest you, roll, jelly-roll style, to create the burrito. Set aside, seam side down. Repeat with remaining tortillas, cheese alternative and filling.

Heat oil in a large skillet over medium heat. Lay 2 burritos in hot oil, seam side down, and fry until golden on the undersides, 1 to 2 minutes. Turn the burritos carefully and brown on the other side. Drain on paper and repeat with remaining 2 burritos.

To serve, arrange burritos on a platter and spoon salsa over top.

Stuffed Roasted Red Peppers

I love roasted peppers . . . in any form, in any recipe. But when I figured out that I could stuff them with my favorite black bean recipe, I was in heaven. I hope you like them, too.

MAKES 4 MAIN-COURSE SERVINGS, OR 8 STARTER COURSES

STUFFING

Extra-virgin olive oil

2 to 3 cloves fresh garlic, finely minced

½ red onion, finely diced

Sea salt

Generous pinch crushed red pepper flakes

1 carrot, finely diced
2 or 3 stalks celery, finely diced
1 cup fresh or frozen corn kernels
2 to 3 teaspoons mirin or white wine
1½ cups cooked black beans, drained

PEPPERS
4 red bell peppers
Extra-virgin olive oil

Red Wine Sauce (optional, recipe follows)

Prepare stuffing: Place a small amount of oil, garlic and onion in a small skillet over medium heat. When the vegetables begin to sizzle, add a pinch of salt and red pepper flakes and sauté 1 to 2 minutes. Add carrot, celery and a pinch of salt and sauté 1 to 2 minutes more. Stir in corn, season lightly with salt and add mirin. Cover and cook over low heat 3 to 4 minutes. Stir in beans until ingredients are well combined. Transfer to a mixing bowl to cool.

Lightly oil each pepper and place over an open flame on the stove. Turn each pepper, charring the skins completely. When the peppers are blackened, transfer them to a paper sack and seal shut to steam the skins from the peppers. After 10 minutes, carefully remove the peppers and, with your fingers, gently remove the charred skin, taking care to keep the peppers intact. Once all the charred skin is removed, carefully pull the seeds out of the tops of the peppers, keeping the peppers intact. Clean any remaining seeds from the peppers.

Preheat oven to 300F (150C). Carefully spoon filling into each pepper, filling abundantly, but taking care not to split them open. Place stuffed peppers on a baking sheet and bake about 10 minutes, until warmed through. Serve drizzled with a fruity olive oil or Red Wine Sauce.

Red Wine Sauce

MAKES 3 TO 4 CUPS SAUCE

Extra-virgin olive oil
1 red onion, chopped
6 cloves garlic
2 cups hearty red wine
3 to 5 fresh tomatoes, chopped
2 (28-ounce) cans pureed tomatoes
2 bay leaves
¼ teaspoon dried thyme
1 teaspoon dried oregano
½ teaspoon dried basil
Sea salt
Handful crushed red pepper flakes
Cracked black pepper

Place a generous amount of oil and onion in a skillet over medium heat. Sauté 2 to 3 minutes. Crush the garlic and add directly to the onion. Stir 1 to 2 minutes. Add the red wine and bring mixture to a boil.

Stir in fresh and canned tomatoes and herbs. Return the sauce to a boil, reduce heat and let simmer, stirring frequently until the sauce has reduced to desired consistency, 5 minutes. Remove the bay leaves and season with salt and peppers.

Vitality Stew

This black soybean stew is like rocket fuel in a pot. I have adapted this recipe from a dish I learned from Aveline Kushi, America's preeminent macrobiotic cooking teacher, during my studies of macrobiotic cooking. This stew creates great strength and vitality. It is a bit of work, but worth the effort.

MAKES 4 OR 5 SERVINGS

**1 cup dried black soybeans, rinsed and towel-
   dried**
1 (1-inch) piece kombu
3 cups spring or filtered water
**¼ cup dried daikon, soaked until tender and
   diced**
**2 or 3 pieces dried tofu, soaked until tender
   and diced**
½ cup diced fresh daikon
1 carrot, diced
¼ cup diced fresh lotus root
¼ cup diced burdock
2 tablespoons barley miso
Fresh ginger juice (see Note, page 164)
4 or 5 green onions, thinly sliced, diagonally

In a hot, dry skillet, pan-toast soybeans over medium heat until slightly puffed and the skins split, 3 to 4 minutes. Place kombu in a pressure cooker and add beans and water. Bring to a boil and cook 5 minutes, uncovered. Seal pressure cooker and bring to full pressure. Cook over low heat 35 minutes. Remove from heat and allow pressure to reduce naturally.

In a heavy pot, place dried daikon, then tofu. Open pressure cooker and reserve cooking liquid. Using a slotted spoon, add beans to dried vegetables. Add fresh daikon, carrot, lotus root and burdock. Using cooking liquid, add enough liquid to the pot to half cover ingredients. Bring

to a boil, cover and cook over low heat until vegetables are tender, 30 to 40 minutes.

Remove about 1 tablespoon cooking broth and mix with miso until dissolved. Stir into stew with ginger juice to taste and simmer 5 to 10 minutes, until all liquid has been absorbed. Stir in green onions, transfer to bowl and serve warm.

Lentils with Squash

A simple bean stew, but a welcoming dish on a chilly night. The peppery lentils are nicely balanced by the deliciously sweet squash and onion, all simmered together in a bubbling stew, creating a warming, comforting dish.

MAKES 3 OR 4 SERVINGS

1 bay leaf
1 cup dried lentils, sorted and rinsed
3 cups spring or filtered water
1 onion, diced
2 to 3 cups ½-inch cubes winter squash
Sea salt or soy sauce
Balsamic vinegar

Place bay leaf, lentils and water in a heavy pot. Bring to a boil over medium heat and boil, uncovered, 10 minutes. Cover and cook over low heat 35 minutes. Add onion and squash and cook until squash is tender, about 15 minutes. Season lightly with sea salt and simmer 10 minutes. All liquid should be absorbed and the stew should be creamy. Remove from heat and sprinkle lightly with vinegar. Mix well, transfer to a bowl and serve hot.

Baked Beans with Miso and Apple Butter

A sweet and savory bean casserole, inspired by Ann Marie Colbin. Lightly spiced with stone-ground mustard and dotted with sweet vegetables, it is a real treat anytime.

MAKES 4 OR 5 SERVINGS

1 (1-inch) piece kombu
1 cup dried pinto beans, sorted and rinsed
3 cups spring or filtered water
1 red onion, diced
1 red bell pepper, roasted over a flame, peeled, seeded and diced (see Note, page 262)
1 carrot, diced
1 stalk celery, diced
2 tablespoons barley miso
⅓ cup unsweetened apple butter
3 teaspoons stone-ground mustard
2 tablespoons brown rice syrup
1 tablespoon brown rice vinegar

Place kombu in a heavy pot and add beans and water. Bring to a boil over medium heat and boil, uncovered, 10 minutes. Reduce heat, cover and simmer 45 minutes. Drain, reserving 1 cup cooking liquid.

Preheat oven to 350F (175C). Lightly oil a deep casserole. In a small bowl, combine remaining ingredients and reserved cooking liquid. Stir cooked beans into apple butter mixture until combined. Spoon into prepared casserole, cover and bake 1½ hours. Remove cover and return to oven 10 minutes to set casserole. Serve hot.

■ **NOTE** You can shorten cooking time for this recipe by using canned organic beans and using 1 cup fresh water in place of the bean cooking water.

Lentils with Braised Vegetables and Thyme

Peppery lentils are nicely offset by sweet, braised winter vegetables and delicately scented with thyme, providing the kind of energetic boost everyone wants.

MAKES 4 OR 5 SERVINGS

1 cup dried lentils, sorted and rinsed
1 onion, diced
1 carrot, diced
3 cups spring or filtered water
1 bay leaf
Sea salt
1 tablespoon extra-virgin olive oil
4 or 5 cloves fresh garlic, finely minced
4 or 5 shallots, peeled and diced
Several sprigs thyme or a few generous pinches of dried thyme
1 cup matchstick-size pieces butternut squash
7 or 8 button mushrooms, brushed clean and thinly sliced
2 or 3 zucchini, cut into thin matchsticks
1 or 2 celery stalks, cut into thin diagonal slices
1 cup Vegetable Stock (page 74) or spring or filtered water
1 to 2 tablespoons balsamic vinegar
Green onions, thinly sliced diagonally, for garnish

Place lentils, onion, carrot and water in a heavy pot. Bring to a boil over medium heat and boil, uncovered, 10 minutes. Add bay leaf, reduce heat, cover and cook until lentils are tender, 40 to 50 minutes. Season with salt to taste and cook about 10 minutes, or until all liquid has been absorbed.

Meanwhile, heat oil in a heavy skillet over medium heat. Add garlic and shallots and a pinch of salt and sauté until fragrant, 2 to 3 minutes. Add thyme and cook 1 minute. Stir in butternut squash, mushrooms, zucchini, celery and a pinch of salt and cook 2 to 3 minutes. Gently add stock, balsamic vinegar and season lightly with salt and cook over low heat, uncovered, until all liquid has been absorbed and vegetables are tender. Remove from heat, cover and set aside 10 to 15 minutes so flavors can develop.

Just before serving, stir braised vegetables into cooked lentils, remove bay leaf and serve warm, garnished with green onions.

Frijoles Borrachos

Here is another Cuban recipe adapted from my days in Miami. I guess you can tell by now that I loved the Latin influence in Florida. There is a vibrancy and exuberance in all aspects of Latin life, especially in the cuisine, that I have always found irresistible. The name of this recipe translates to mean "drunken beans," because they are simmered in beer for a long time. Combined with crisply sautéed tempeh (bacon in the original version) and vegetables, this dish goes well with crunchy tortilla chips.

MAKES 4 OR 5 SERVINGS

1 tablespoon extra-virgin olive oil
2 or 3 cloves fresh garlic, finely minced
1 red onion, diced
Sea salt
1 hot chile, seeded, finely minced
4 ounces tempeh, crumbled
1 cup dried pinto beans, sorted and rinsed

1 bay leaf
1 (12-ounce) bottle dark beer
2 or 3 ripe tomatoes, diced (do not peel or seed)
1 cup spring or filtered water
Generous pinch oregano
Generous pinch cumin
3 or 4 green onions, minced

Heat oil in a heavy pot over medium heat. Add garlic, onion and a pinch of salt and cook, stirring, 2 to 3 minutes. Add chile and tempeh and cook until tempeh is golden brown and crispy. Add beans and push bay leaf to the bottom of the pot. Slowly add beer, tomatoes, water, oregano and cumin. Boil, uncovered, 10 minutes. Reduce heat, cover, and simmer over low heat until beans are very tender, 1½ to 2 hours. Season lightly with salt and simmer 10 minutes. The beans should be very creamy, almost pureed. Remove and discard bay leaf. Gently stir in green onions and transfer to a bowl. Serve warm.

Red Lentil Loaf

One taste of this savory loaf and you will forget all about meat loaf.

MAKES 6 TO 8 SERVINGS

1 cup dried red lentils, sorted and rinsed
2 cups spring or filtered water
1 (1-inch) piece wakame, soaked
1 tablespoon extra-virgin olive oil
2 cloves fresh garlic, finely minced
2 to 3 shallots, minced
1 carrot, diced
2 celery stalks, diced
Generous pinch dried basil
Soy sauce
1 cup organic rolled oats

1 teaspoon umeboshi vinegar
1 to 2 teaspoons balsamic vinegar

Combine lentils, water and wakame in a saucepan. Bring to a boil over medium heat and boil, uncovered, 10 minutes. Reduce heat, cover and cook over low heat until liquid is absorbed and lentils are creamy, 25 to 35 minutes.

Meanwhile, heat oil in a skillet over medium heat. Add garlic and shallots and cook, stirring, 2 to 3 minutes. Add remaining vegetables and cook, stirring, 3 to 4 minutes. Stir in basil and season lightly with soy sauce. Simmer 2 to 3 minutes and remove from heat.

Preheat oven to 350F (175C). Lightly oil an 8 × 4-inch loaf pan and set aside. Combine lentils with vegetables and rolled oats, reserving a small amount of oats to sprinkle on top of the loaf. Season to taste with vinegars and press mixture into oiled loaf pan. Sprinkle remaining oats on top and bake 20 to 25 minutes, until the loaf is firmly set. Remove from oven and allow to stand 5 to 10 minutes before slicing. Serve warm or at room temperature as a side dish to a meal or as a pâté with toast points.

Red Bell Peppers Stuffed with Black Beans

I like to serve these peppers with a side of mildly hot salsa and a crisp fresh salad for a delicious, easy-to-make lunch or brunch. Beans with the zip of hot flavor lift our energy and make us more outgoing as well as stronger.

MAKES 5 MAIN-COURSE SERVINGS

1 bay leaf
1 cup dried black turtle beans, sorted and
   rinsed

3 cups spring or filtered water
Sea salt
5 red bell peppers
Extra-virgin olive oil
1 red onion, diced
2 cloves fresh garlic, finely minced
1 to 2 teaspoons chili powder
Generous pinch *each* powdered cumin and
   basil
1 cup cooked short-grain brown rice
1 to 2 teaspoons balsamic vinegar
3 or 4 green onions, minced
5 tablespoons grated vegan Monterey Jack
   cheese alternative

Place bay leaf in a heavy pot and add beans and water. Bring to a boil over medium heat and boil, uncovered, 10 minutes. Reduce heat, cover and cook over low heat until beans are tender, about 45 minutes. Season lightly with salt and cook 10 minutes.

Cut bell peppers in half lengthwise and remove seeds and tops. Place in a skillet with ½ inch water and steam until crisp-tender, about 5 minutes. Rinse under cold water and set peppers aside.

Preheat oven to 350F (175C). Lightly oil a baking sheet and set aside. Heat about 1 tablespoon oil in a skillet over medium heat. Add onion, garlic and a pinch of salt and cook, stirring, until translucent, about 5 minutes. Add chili powder, cumin, basil and a pinch of salt and cook 3 to 4 minutes. Stir in rice until ingredients are well incorporated. Season to taste with salt. Remove and discard bay leaf. Add beans, balsamic vinegar and green onions and stir well.

Fill the pepper halves with the rice and bean mixture. Sprinkle ½ tablespoon cheese alternative on each pepper half. Place on prepared baking sheet and bake until peppers are tender and topping has melted, about 15 minutes. Arrange on a platter and serve hot.

Black Bean Tacos

Back we go to Miami or perhaps Mexico, although the Cuban version of these spicy tacos has always been my favorite.

MAKES 5 OR 6 SERVINGS

1 tablespoon extra-virgin olive oil
4 to 5 cloves fresh garlic, minced
1 hot chile, such as serrano, seeded and minced
1 red onion, diced
Sea salt
Generous pinch dried basil
1 carrot, diced
1 to 2 cups button mushrooms, brushed clean and thinly sliced
2 cups cooked dried black turtle beans
½ to 1 teaspoon chili powder
Spring or filtered water
2 tablespoons barley or red miso, dissolved in small amount warm water
Several chapati breads, lightly steamed, or taco shells
2 to 3 ripe tomatoes, diced (do not peel or seed)
Shredded romaine lettuce

Heat oil in a deep skillet over medium heat. Add garlic, chile and onion and cook, stirring, 2 to 3 minutes. Add basil, carrot and mushrooms and cook, stirring, 2 to 3 minutes. Partially mash beans and add to skillet with chili powder. Add about ⅛ inch of water, cover and simmer over low heat 15 minutes. Stir miso mixture into beans. Simmer 3 to 4 minutes more. Spoon beans into chapati breads and garnish with tomatoes and lettuce. Serve warm.

Baked Pinto Beans

A spicy take on baked beans, this is a great picnic dish, with just the right touch of freshness to keep it light for summer weather.

MAKES 4 OR 5 SERVINGS

1 (1-inch) piece kombu
1 cup dried pinto beans, sorted and rinsed
3 cups spring or filtered water
1 small onion, diced
2 or 3 celery stalks, diced
1 carrot, diced
1 cup fresh corn kernels

SPICY TOMATO SAUCE
1 tablespoon extra-virgin olive oil
3 to 4 cloves fresh garlic, finely minced
1 (16-ounce) can crushed tomatoes
2 tablespoons brown rice syrup
Sea salt
Generous pinch *each* dried oregano and basil
1 teaspoon umeboshi vinegar
2 teaspoons barley miso

Place kombu in a heavy pot and add beans and water. Bring to a boil over medium heat and boil, uncovered, 10 minutes. Reduce heat, cover and cook over low heat until beans are tender, 45 to 60 minutes. Drain beans, reserving 1 cup of the cooking liquid.

Preheat oven to 350F (175C). Lightly oil a deep casserole and set aside. Combine beans, onion, celery, carrot and corn in a bowl and set aside.

To make the sauce: Combine oil, garlic and tomatoes in a deep skillet over medium heat. Simmer for 3 minutes. Stir in rice syrup, a pinch of salt, oregano, basil and vinegar and simmer 5 minutes more.

Dissolve miso in reserved bean cooking liquid. Stir miso mixture and tomato sauce into bean mixture and spoon the mixture evenly into the prepared casserole. Cover and bake 1½ hours. Remove cover and bake until beans are creamy and set, about 15 minutes. Serve warm or hot.

Plantain-Bean Casserole

On a trip to St. Thomas, I taught a cooking class using native Caribbean produce to create a whole foods meal. It was quite a challenge, using foods that I was completely unfamiliar with in old, standard recipes, but incredibly fun. This recipe is based on a very traditional bean stew that is truly delicious . . . and a great balance of stamina and freshness—perfectly suited to a tropical clime.

MAKES 5 OR 6 SERVINGS

2 tablespoons extra-virgin olive oil
6 cloves fresh garlic, finely minced
1 red onion, diced
1 cup cooked chickpeas
1 cup cooked pinto beans
2 cups small cubes winter squash
2 small chayote, cut into small cubes
2 cups diced celery root
2 cups diced, peeled plantain
6 plum tomatoes, coarsely chopped
Sea salt
3 to 4 cups spring or filtered water
¼ cup minced fresh cilantro (optional)

Preheat oven to 350F (175C). Lightly oil a casserole and set aside. Heat oil in a skillet over medium heat. Add garlic and onion and cook, stirring, 2 to 3 minutes. Mix together chick-peas, beans, onion mixture, winter squash, chayote, celery root, plantain, tomatoes and salt to taste. Add water and sprinkle with cilantro (if using). Spoon into prepared casserole and

cook, uncovered, 3 hours, stirring gently every half hour and adding water as needed, or until creamy and thick. Serve hot over a cooked whole grain with a side of lightly cooked vegetables.

Polenta-Topped Kidney Bean Casserole

Crispy polenta tops a creamy kidney bean casserole, laden with savory vegetables and scented with spices.

MAKES 5 OR 6 SERVINGS

2 tablespoons extra-virgin olive oil
2 or 3 cloves fresh garlic, finely minced
1 red onion, diced
Several sun-dried tomatoes, soaked until tender, and diced
1 red bell pepper, roasted over a flame, peeled, seeded and diced (see Note, page 262)
1 yellow bell pepper, roasted over a flame, peeled, seeded and diced (see Note, page 262)
2 hot chiles, seeded and minced
2 zucchini, diced
2 cups cooked kidney beans, drained and partially mashed
Generous pinch dried basil
Sea salt

POLENTA TOPPING
2½ cups spring or filtered water, plus extra for casserole
Pinch sea salt
½ cup yellow corn grits
½ cup fresh or frozen corn kernels
Extra-virgin olive oil

Preheat oven to 375F (175C). Lightly oil a deep casserole and set aside.

Heat oil in a deep skillet over medium heat. Add garlic and onion and cook, stirring, 2 to 3 minutes. Add sun-dried tomatoes, bell peppers and chiles and cook, stirring, 2 minutes. Add zucchini and cook, stirring, 2 minutes. Top cooked vegetables with beans, basil and a light seasoning of salt. Stir until ingredients are well incorporated. Set aside.

Meanwhile, prepare polenta: Bring water, salt and grits to a boil in a heavy pot. Whisk until the mixture boils. Whisk in corn and a drizzle of oil and cook over low heat until polenta pulls away from the pan and the middle "burps," about 25 minutes, stirring frequently to prevent sticking.

Spoon bean mixture into casserole and add about ¼ inch of water. Spoon polenta evenly over beans and vegetables and bake, uncovered, about 30 minutes, until casserole is bubbling and thick and the polenta is golden and crispy. Serve hot.

Pum Buk

This is a traditional Chinese side dish served around the New Year for good fortune. Sweet and satisfying, this dish will make you so steady, you will have no choice but to have good luck.

MAKES 4 OR 5 SERVINGS

½ cup dried chestnuts, soaked 6 to 8 hours
    and drained well
½ cup dried azuki beans, sorted and rinsed
1 cup sweet brown rice, rinsed well, soaked 1
    hour and drained well
3 cups cubed winter squash
2½ cups spring or filtered water
Pinch sea salt

Combine all ingredients in a pressure cooker. Seal lid and bring to full pressure over medium heat. Reduce heat, place over a flame deflector and cook over low heat 50 minutes. Remove from heat and allow pressure to reduce naturally. Stir briskly to create a creamy texture, transfer to a bowl and serve immediately.

Tasty Tofu, Tempeh and Seitan

SOYBEANS, LONG ASSOCIATED with healthful eating, have always, in traditional cuisine, been processed in some way or another before consumption by humans, because they are so difficult to digest. It actually takes more effort by our bodies to digest these beans than the energy they provide. The processing gives us a variety of delicious, versatile products, including tofu and tempeh.

Let's address the soy issue from the top. When I wrote this book ten years ago, soy was being touted as the "perfect food." Since that time, controversy has risen around soy, so let's clear it all up right now, shall we?

Soybeans are the wonder food they are reputed to be . . . fabulous sources of protein and minerals and low in fat. In addition, the fat they contain is great for our health. Tofu contains all nine essential amino acids found in animal protein (with no cholesterol). Research has shown that eating twenty-five grams of soy protein (like that in tofu) in place of animal protein every day can lower cholesterol levels by 5 to 10 percent. Even the FDA has published the claim that diets low in saturated fat and cholesterol, and include twenty-five grams of soy protein per day, may reduce the risk of heart disease.

Soy's real claim to fame, and ironically the source of the controversy, are a group of nutrients known as isoflavones, which include phytoestrogens, trace substances in plant foods, like soybeans and some whole grains that mimic and supplement the action of our body's own hormone, estrogen. Said to reduce the symptoms of PMS and menopause, including hot flashes, vaginal dryness, cramps and all the other delights associated with these conditions, soy protein went from being the Clark Kent of the culinary world to Superman in no time.

So where did the soy controversy begin? When soy gained its "miracle" food reputation, manufacturers and marketers began including soy protein in everything from tofu to hand cream, creating too much of a good thing. In many cases, the soy used was an isolated soy protein that can have adverse effects on our health and is even believed to be carcinogenic. So like everything else in life, eat the whole soybean or products made from whole soybeans and eat them in moderation. A little goes a long way.

Tofu

Tofu or bean curd is the name given to the pressed curd of the soybean. Processing involves adding a coagulating agent to cooked, ground soybeans, which causes the curd to separate and rise to the top of the cooking pot. The curd is then removed and pressed to the desired firmness; tofu can be found in a variety of firmness, from silken and soft to extra firm.

A rather bland, cool character, tofu is packed with nutrition. High in protein, a rich source of good quality fat, choline, and phytoestrogens, tofu has a reputation for being effective in helping to build muscle (protein, after all), improving memory, relieving symptoms of PMS, relaxing muscle tension, relieving "hot flashes" and helping to create strong bone mass before menopause—not to mention helping to simulate regulated estrogen levels after menopause.

This important food has little personality by itself, but when combined with stronger oils, seasonings or vegetables, it immediately comes to life, bursting with flavor. It seems to wait for stimulation through other foods with more defined characteristics. Most people, however, are not quite sure what to do with this gelatinous white block of food. And that's okay. That's why you have me and this book, so you won't miss out on this amazing ingredient. So read on.

By nature, tofu has a cooling, dampening effect on the body, making it very helpful in reducing fever and inflammations—and even as a topical remedy for minor burns and abrasions. It holds coldness and can be used as an

ice pack, effectively reducing any inflammation symptoms of sprains and swellings; it is not only a great food, but an essential member of your first-aid kit! However, remember that with its cooling effect, too much tofu can dampen or cool your energy, so you don't want to overuse it in your cooking, serving it only once or twice a week. Much more than that will leave you growing fatigued more easily than you should.

Tempeh

Coming to us by way of Indonesia, tempeh is a whole fermented soy food with a chewy texture and delectable, unique flavor. It makes for a most satisfying entrée for a meatless meal.

Eating tempeh has many benefits. Tempeh contains a microorganism called bacillus subtilis, which has been found effective in relieving symptoms of cirrhosis of the liver, diabetes, intestinal disorders and iron-deficient blood. Because it is fermented, tempeh is especially helpful in promoting healthy digestion, which in turn strengthens the quality of the blood, lymph and other body fluids. Its fermented quality can also make it a bit easier to digest than other soyfoods, and that is always a good thing.

Tempeh can be stewed, fried, steamed or roasted. Combined with grains and vegetables, tempeh makes a great foundation for any number of stews, stir-fries, kabobs, sandwiches or salads.

Seitan

Seitan is actually a wheat product rather than a bean product. So why is it in the chapter that features mostly soybean products? Well, the truth is, no one is really sure how to categorize seitan. Though it has wheat as its source, after its processing, seitan is such a great source of concentrated protein that you would not want to serve it as a grain dish, but rather as your protein or bean dish in a meal. Hence, most cooks, including me, usually place seitan recipes with other beans and bean-product recipes.

Seitan is made from hard whole wheat flour, which is combined with water to create a dough not unlike bread dough. Then, alternating between warm and cool water, the dough is kneaded under water until the germ and bran of the flour is rinsed away, leaving only a ball of gluten. This gluten is then cooked in a savory broth, creating the product we recognize as seitan.

Very meaty in texture and rich in flavor, seitan goes well in any number of recipes, but seems to shine in stews, oven-baked casseroles—when it is grilled or broiled—or when sautéed with onions for a great sandwich filling.

Seitan can be tough for many people to digest, so I like to serve it with lots of vegetables to help the process along and to lighten it up a bit. Its "heavy" nature makes it an occasional ingredient in my house, but experiment and see what works for you.

Tofu "Cream Cheese"

This is a great alternative to dairy products. Completely cholesterol-free, this version retains all of its creamy texture and rich taste without a lot of fat. I love to serve it at brunches with toasted bagels or whole grain toast.

MAKES 5 OR 6 SERVINGS

1 pound soft tofu
2 teaspoons umeboshi paste
1 teaspoon sesame tahini

2 or 3 green onions, minced
1 or 2 celery stalks, diced
1 carrot, grated
¼ cup fresh minced flat-leaf parsley
Juice of ½ lemon

Bring a pot of water to a boil, add tofu and cook 5 minutes. Drain tofu and process in a food processor with umeboshi paste and tahini until smooth. Adjust seasoning to your taste. Fold in vegetables, parsley and lemon juice, transfer to a serving bowl and chill thoroughly before serving.

Tofu Vegetable Roll

This is a great appetizer. I love to serve it chilled as a starter to a summer meal. It's light and refreshing, pretty on a serving platter and, best of all, a breeze to make.

MAKES 4 TO 6 SERVINGS

1 pound extra-firm tofu
½ red bell pepper, roasted over a flame, peeled, seeded and minced (see Note, page 262)
1 small carrot, minced
½ bunch watercress, minced
Soy sauce

Puree tofu in a food processor to a smooth, thick paste. Fold in bell pepper, carrot, watercress and soy sauce to taste and mix well.

Using a bamboo sushi mat, spread tofu mixture about ¼ inch thick directly on the mat, leaving 1 inch exposed on the sides of the mat farthest from you and closest to you. With the mat as a guide, roll the tofu into a tight cylinder, wrapping the mat completely around the roll, but not into it. Place in a bamboo steamer over boiling water and steam 10 to 15 minutes. Unroll the mat and slice the tofu roll into 1-inch-thick rounds. Repeat process until all ingredients are used up. Arrange rolls on a serving platter and serve at room temperature or chilled.

Creamy Olive Dip

Strong and aromatic, this dip is great served with toast points or pita chips. Its salty, rich taste makes for an active, social get-together.

MAKES 4 TO 6 SERVINGS

¼ cup extra-virgin olive oil
3 or 4 cloves fresh garlic, minced
8 ounces firm tofu, boiled 5 minutes and
　drained
Juice of 1 lemon
Pinch sea salt
10 to 12 oil-cured black olives, pitted and
　minced
⅛ cup capers, drained well

Heat oil in a small skillet over medium heat. Add garlic and cook until fragrant, 1 to 2 minutes. Place tofu, oil with garlic, lemon juice and salt in a food processor and puree until smooth. Transfer to a mixing bowl and gently fold in olives and capers. Chill thoroughly before serving.

Chinese Firecrackers

I love to serve this hot and spicy appetizer at parties. Tofu's high protein content and the stimulating energy of the ground chiles make for animated conversation and a most lively gathering!

MAKES 4 OR 5 SERVINGS

Avocado oil, for deep-frying
1 pound extra firm tofu, cut into ½-inch cubes
　and patted dry

FIRECRACKER SAUCE
3 tablespoons soy sauce
2 tablespoons brown rice syrup
2 tablespoons brown rice vinegar
1 tablespoon chili powder
Scant pinch cayenne
Scant pinch ground ginger
1 cup spring or filtered water
1 tablespoon kuzu or arrowroot, dissolved in
　small amount cold water

Green onions, sliced diagonally, for garnish

Heat about 3 inches of oil in a deep saucepan over medium heat. Add tofu cubes and deep-fry until golden brown and crispy. Drain on paper towels and set aside while preparing the sauce.

Prepare sauce: Combine soy sauce, rice syrup, rice vinegar, chili powder, cayenne, ginger and water in a small saucepan over medium heat. When warmed through, stir in dissolved kuzu and cook, stirring, until sauce is thick and clear. Stir in tofu cubes until well coated with sauce and serve garnished with green onions.

Tofu Cheese

If you hate the thought of giving up cheese, this recipe is for you. Rich, creamy and savory, this sharp-tasting, pickled tofu can stand on its own in place of any cheese in recipes ranging from creamy white sauces to thin squares on a cracker, to whipped cream cheese—without the negative effects of dairy products. You have to experience this one for yourself.

Experiment with different misos to create an incredible variety of flavors.

MAKES ABOUT 1 POUND

1 to 1½ cups white miso
1 pound extra-firm tofu

Spread about ¼ inch of miso on a piece of cheesecloth (much larger than the tofu brick) on a plate. Press tofu on top of miso. Cover the rest of the tofu with a ¼-inch-thick coating of miso. (Any tofu left exposed will spoil.) Wrap the cheesecloth up around the tofu, covering it completely. Set aside in a cool place to ferment (not in the refrigerator). Tofu may pickle anywhere from 12 hours to 4 days, depending on how strong you would like the flavor to become.

During fermentation, there will be a delicate beerlike aroma around the tofu. This means that the fermentation process is active. When the tofu cheese is ready, simply scrape miso completely from the tofu, reserving the miso to use in sauces or salad dressings. Rinse tofu gently under cool water to remove any remaining miso residue and use as you wish as a cheese substitute in any recipe.

Broiled Tofu with Walnut-Miso Sauce

Delightfully easy to make and sinfully rich tasting, this dish will change your mind about tofu.

MAKES 6 SERVINGS

1 pound extra firm tofu, cut into 6 (⅓-inch-thick) slices

WALNUT-MISO SAUCE
½ cup walnut pieces
3 tablespoons barley miso
3 tablespoons spring or filtered water
1 teaspoon brown rice syrup

Preheat broiler. Lightly oil a baking pan. Lay tofu slices on a clean kitchen towel and pat dry. Place slices in pan and broil until golden on one side, 4 to 5 minutes. Turn and repeat on the other side. Remove from baking pan and set aside to cool.

Prepare sauce: Lightly pan-toast walnuts in a dry skillet over medium heat until fragrant, about 4 minutes. While warm, grind into a fairly fine meal in a food processor. Add miso, water and rice syrup and process to a thick paste. Spread a thin layer of sauce over each slice of tofu, place on baking sheet and return to the broiler 1 minute. Serve warm or at room temperature.

■ **VARIATION** I like to spread the walnut sauce on 3 tofu slices and top with the remaining 3 slices, making "sandwiches." Then wrap a thin vegetable strip (blanched leek or green onion strip) around each one to make packages.

Mushroom-Broccoli Quiche

Real men *do* eat quiche, especially this one. This is so creamy and rich, you won't believe it's tofu. Laced with fresh broccoli and smoky mushrooms throughout, this quiche is a meal in itself.

MAKES 6 TO 8 SERVINGS

WHOLE WHEAT CRUST

1½ cups whole wheat pastry flour

¼ cup avocado oil

Pinch sea salt

¼ cup cold spring or filtered water

FILLING

2 tablespoons extra-virgin olive oil

2 cloves fresh garlic, finely minced

1 onion, finely diced

1 cup mushrooms, brushed clean and thinly
   sliced

1 to 2 stalks broccoli, cut into tiny florets

1½ pounds firm tofu

3 tablespoons sesame tahini

2 tablespoons fresh lemon juice

1 teaspoon brown rice syrup

Soy sauce

2 tablespoons black or tan sesame seeds, for
   garnish

Prepare crust: Preheat oven to 350F (175C). Combine flour, oil and salt with a fork until the mixture is sandy in texture. Add water and continue to mix until the dough begins to form a ball. Do not overmix or use your hands during this stage of dough preparation, as it can result in a tough, heavy crust. Gather dough between hands and knead 3 to 4 times to shape into a ball. Roll dough out between 2 sheets of waxed paper or pastry cloth into a thin crust.

Transfer to a 9-inch pie plate and, without stretching dough, press it into pan. Trim away any excess crust, leaving about ¼ inch hanging over the edge of the pie plate. Fold the excess back toward the inside of the pan, pinching between thumb and fingers to create a scalloped-edged crust. Prick crust with a fork several times over the surface. Bake 15 to 17 minutes, until dough is set. Set aside to cool while preparing the filling.

Make filling: Heat oil in a skillet over medium heat. Add garlic and onion and cook, stirring, 2 to 3 minutes. Add mushrooms and cook, stirring, until limp. Set aside.

Bring a small pot of water to a boil and quickly cook broccoli until bright green but still crispy, 1 to 2 minutes. Drain and set aside.

Place tofu, tahini, lemon juice, rice syrup and a generous dash of soy sauce in a food processor and puree until smooth. Transfer to a bowl and fold in broccoli and sautéed vegetables. Spoon mixture evenly into pie shell, sprinkle sesame seeds lightly around the rim of the quiche, and bake until quiche is firm and edges are light golden, about 30 minutes. Remove from oven and allow to stand about 15 minutes before serving.

Stuffed Tofu Agé

This is a traditional Asian way to serve tofu. Pretty ingenious, too, I might add. What you do is deep-fry the tofu and then, to remove any excess oily taste, the pockets are simmered in a savory broth. Talk about rich flavor! The stuffing is up to you. I serve them smothered in Sweet-and-Sour Sauce. Fabulous.

MAKES 4 TO 6 SERVINGS

1 pound firm tofu, cut into 8 triangular
   wedges

Avocado oil, for deep-frying

Spring or filtered water

Soy sauce

1 (2-inch) piece kombu

4 or 5 slices fresh ginger

About ½ cup sautéed, curried vegetables,
   pickled sea vegetables, sautéed corn and

shallots or sautéed diced mushrooms, for filling
Sweet-and-Sour Sauce (page 48)

Make a slit along the longest side of each tofu wedge for the stuffing, being careful not to slice all the way through. Heat about 3 inches of oil in a saucepan over medium heat until it is very hot. (You will know the oil is ready when patterns form in the bottom of the pot.) Add tofu, 3 to 4 wedges at a time, and deep-fry until deep golden brown, 3 to 4 minutes. Drain on paper towels.

Bring a medium pot of water to a boil, season lightly with soy sauce, and add kombu and ginger. Carefully drop tofu wedges into broth and simmer over low heat, uncovered, 30 minutes. Drain tofu wedges and discard broth.

Allow tofu to cool enough to touch while preparing filling. When wedges have cooled enough to handle, gently pull open slits and press filling inside. Arrange on a serving platter and just before serving, ladle warm Sweet-and-Sour Sauce over each pocket.

Steamed Tofu Rolls

This is a really pretty dish with round white pinwheels of tofu dotted with sautéed, diced vegetables. Wrapped in thin sheets of rich, black nori, these beauties are as much fun to eat as they are to serve. The light energy provided by the tofu and lightly cooked veggies makes this an ideal summer side dish.

MAKES 4 TO 6 SERVINGS

2 teaspoons light sesame oil
4 or 5 slices fresh ginger, minced
1 onion, finely diced
Soy sauce

1 carrot, finely diced
1 cup button mushrooms, brushed clean and finely diced
1 pound extra-firm tofu
2 to 3 sheets toasted nori

Heat oil in a skillet over medium heat. Add ginger, onion and a splash of soy sauce and cook, stirring, 3 to 4 minutes. Add carrot and mushrooms and a splash of soy sauce and cook, stirring, 2 to 3 minutes or until vegetables are limp.

Crumble tofu into a fine meal into a bowl. Stir in sautéed vegetables and a little soy sauce to taste.

Place a sushi mat on a flat surface and lay a sheet of nori, shiny side down, on top. Gently spread tofu mixture ¼ inch thick evenly over surface of nori, leaving 1 inch of nori exposed at the far end to help seal the roll. Using the mat as a guide, gently but firmly roll the tofu roll, jelly-roll style, sealing it at the end with the exposed nori. Remove mat and repeat with remaining ingredients.

Place rolls in a bamboo steamer over a pot of boiling water and steam over high heat, uncovered, 10 to 12 minutes. Remove rolls from heat and cool 5 to 10 minutes before slicing into 1-inch-thick rounds. Arrange on a platter and serve at room temperature or chilled.

Tofu-Millet Stew

Real comfort food. A creamy, golden stew, this stew has tiny cubes of tofu throughout. We love to serve this for breakfast, especially on chilly fall and winter mornings, when the warming energy of millet is especially nice to have around.

MAKES 4 OR 5 SERVINGS

1 cup yellow millet, rinsed well
8 ounces firm tofu, cut into ¼-inch cubes
1 cup small cubes winter squash
5 cups spring or filtered water
Pinch sea salt
Green onions, for garnish (optional)

Combine all ingredients, except green onions (if using), in a heavy pot and bring to a boil. Cover and cook over low heat until all liquid is absorbed and millet has a creamy consistency, about 30 minutes. Remove from heat and stir briskly. Transfer to a bowl and serve immediately, garnished with sliced green onions (if using).

Any leftover stew can be pressed into a loaf pan and, when set, sliced and lightly pan-fried.

Yu-Dofu

Since tofu is a traditional staple food in Asia, it's no wonder so many tofu recipes have an Asian flair to them. This is a very traditional one-dish meal that is usually served family style, with everyone dipping into the pot as they eat. It is so easy, there is no excuse *not* to cook anymore!

MAKES 4 OR 5 SERVINGS

1 pound extra-firm tofu, cut into 1-inch cubes
1 cup finely shredded Chinese cabbage
1 (2-inch) piece kombu, soaked briefly and cut into thin matchsticks
1 carrot, cut into thin matchsticks
1 cup thin matchstick pieces daikon
4 dried shiitake mushrooms, soaked until tender and thinly sliced
Spring or filtered water
Soy sauce
1 small bunch watercress, rinsed and drained

In a wide pot or deep skillet, arrange tofu and each vegetable, cabbage through mushrooms, in its own section. Add water to generously half-cover ingredients, cover and bring to a boil over medium heat. Reduce heat and simmer, covered, over low heat 10 minutes. Season lightly with soy sauce and simmer, covered, 5 to 7 minutes more. Remove from heat, add watercress, cover and allow to stand 1 minute, to wilt watercress. Serve at once with a side dish of cooked whole grains or noodles.

■ **VARIATION** Sometimes, for added richness, I deep-fry the tofu before proceeding with the yu-dofu.

Sweet Marinated Tofu with Spicy Peanut Sauce

I love tofu dishes. They are so good, and with tofu's neutral nature, a simple sauce can transform it into a most delicious dish. The cooling, relaxing energy of these recipes is ideal for our stress-filled lives. I like to serve the marinated slices of tofu on a pool of thick sauce, garnished with green onion slices.

MAKES ABOUT 4 SERVINGS

1 pound extra-firm tofu, cut in half and then into ½-inch-thick slices
2 tablespoons soy sauce
2 or 3 teaspoons brown rice syrup
¼ cup avocado oil
2 teaspoons prepared mustard
2 tablespoons fresh ginger juice (see Note, page 164)
3 or 4 cloves fresh garlic, crushed
1 cup spring or filtered water

SPICY PEANUT SAUCE

2 teaspoons avocado oil
1 tablespoon grated onion
1 clove fresh garlic, finely minced
2 teaspoons chili powder
1 cup unsweetened peanut butter
Soy sauce
1 tablespoon brown rice syrup
Juice of 1 lemon
Spring or filtered water

Place tofu slices on a clean kitchen towel and pat excess water off the surface. Whisk together remaining ingredients for a marinade and pour into a small saucepan. Bring to a boil, reduce heat and simmer, uncovered, 10 minutes. Place tofu pieces in a shallow dish and spoon hot marinade over top, covering completely. Allow to marinate at least 1 hour before serving or up to 12 hours in the refrigerator.

Prepare sauce: Heat oil in a small pan. Add onion, garlic and chili powder and cook, stirring, over medium heat 2 to 3 minutes. Add peanut butter, a dash of soy sauce and rice syrup. Stir well and simmer over very low heat 5 minutes. Remove from heat, stir in lemon juice and enough water to make the sauce as thick or thin as you desire. Serve tofu at room temperature with sauce.

Tofu Pot Pie

I learned this recipe from Sarah LaPenta, a cooking instructor from Connecticut. I assisted her at a conference in a cooking class on fun foods. Here is my version of this easy-to-make family casserole that will win you raves.

MAKES 6 TO 8 SERVINGS

2 recipes Whole Wheat Crust (page 120)
2 tablespoons avocado oil
1 pound extra-firm tofu, cut into ¼-inch cubes
1 cup diced onion
Sea salt
1 carrot, diced
1 to 2 cups small broccoli florets
1 cup fresh or frozen corn kernels
1 cup fresh or frozen green peas
1 cup small cauliflower florets
Soy sauce
1 to 2 cups spring or filtered water
2 tablespoons arrowroot or kuzu, dissolved in small amount cold water
Generous pinch ground ginger

Prepare pastry dough and roll each one between waxed or parchment paper. Set aside.

Heat 2 teaspoons of the oil in a skillet over medium heat. Add tofu cubes and cook, turning often, until evenly browned. Set aside.

Heat remaining oil in another skillet over medium heat. Add onion and a pinch of salt and cook, stirring, 2 to 3 minutes. Add remaining vegetables and a pinch of salt and cook, stirring, until crisp-tender, 2 to 3 minutes. Add tofu cubes, season lightly with soy sauce, and add water to scantly cover ingredients. Bring to a boil over medium heat, reduce heat to low and stir in dissolved kuzu. Cook, stirring, until a thin glaze forms over the entire mixture, about 3 minutes. Stir in ginger, remove mixture from heat and set aside.

Preheat oven to 350F (175C). Place 1 crust in pie plate and without stretching dough, press into pan, allowing excess to hang over the rim. Prick surface with a fork in several places. Spoon filling into pie shell and lay second crust over top. Press edges of both crusts between fingers and thumb, creating a crimped, sealed edge. Pierce the top crust in several places to allow steam to escape. Bake 40 to 45 minutes, until crust is golden and filling is bubbling. Remove from oven and allow to stand 5 to 10 minutes before slicing. Serve hot.

Tofu Chili

Frozen tofu creates a texture that is similar to that of ground meat in traditional chili con carne. Coupled with lots of beans and vegetables in a savory chili broth, this Southwestern-style dish is a real winner, with a rich, strengthening energy.

MAKES 4 OR 5 SERVINGS

1 pound extra-firm tofu
Sea salt
2 tablespoons natural peanut butter
2 cloves fresh garlic, crushed
Generous pinch ground cumin
Scant pinch of ground ginger
Spring or filtered water
1 tablespoon extra-virgin olive oil
1 red bell pepper, roasted over a flame,
**   peeled, seeded and diced (see Note, page**
**   262)**
1 small poblano chile, seeded, diced (see
**   Note, opposite)**
1 teaspoon chili powder
1 red onion, diced
1 carrot, diced
1 cup diced winter squash (like butternut)
1 or 2 celery stalks, diced
1 cup cooked pinto beans, drained
1 cup cooked red kidney beans, drained
1 to 2 cups Vegetable Stock (page 74)
¼ cup minced fresh flat-leaf parsley, for
**   garnish**

Cut tofu into ½-inch-thick slices and place on a tray in the freezer until firmly frozen, about 2 hours. Thaw tofu pieces, squeeze out the fluid, and coarsely crumble.

Preheat oven to 375F (175C). Lightly oil a baking sheet and set aside. Mix together a generous pinch of salt, peanut butter, garlic, cumin and ginger, thinning with a small amount of water to make a thick sauce. Stir tofu into peanut butter mixture until sauce is completely absorbed. Spread tofu evenly on prepared baking sheet and bake about 20 minutes. Stir well and bake another 10 minutes. Set aside.

Heat oil in a soup pot over medium heat. Add bell pepper, chile, chili powder, onion and a pinch of salt and cook, stirring, 3 to 4 minutes. Add remaining vegetables and a pinch of salt and sauté 2 to 3 minutes more. Add beans and enough stock to just cover ingredients. Bring to a boil, season to taste with salt and stir in baked tofu. Cover and simmer over low heat 10 to 15 minutes more. Serve hot, garnished with parsley.

■ **NOTE** To increase the heat of a fresh chile, leave the seeds and inner veins intact.

Braised Tofu with Mango on Arugula

I love to serve this dish to people who say they hate tofu. The combination of flavors and textures takes their mind off their tofu-phobia as they are consumed by culinary bliss.

MAKES 4 SERVINGS

¼ cup soy sauce
1¼ cups unsweetened pineapple juice
Juice of 2 fresh limes or lemons
4 whole cloves fresh garlic, plus one clove,
**   minced**

1 (2-inch) piece fresh ginger, cut into 4 equal
   pieces
8 ounces extra-firm tofu, cut into thick slices
¼ cup minced red onion
1 medium jalapeño chile, stemmed, seeded
   and minced
1 teaspoon Dijon mustard
½ teaspoon sea salt
1 tablespoon chopped fresh cilantro
3 tablespoons sesame oil
½ pound baby arugula
1 large mango, peeled, pitted and sliced into
   ¾-inch strips

Place soy sauce, ¼ cup pineapple juice, half the lime juice, whole garlic cloves and ginger in a saucepan. Whisk well. Add tofu and bring to a boil. Reduce heat to low and simmer for 5 minutes. Remove tofu carefully and set aside. With a slotted spoon, remove garlic and ginger and discard.

Add onion to cooking liquid and simmer for 1 minute. Drain onion, discarding marinade and place onion in a small bowl.

Place remaining pineapple juice in a small saucepan and simmer over medium heat until reduced by half, about 15 minutes. Remove from heat and whisk in chile, mustard, salt, cilantro and 1 tablespoon of the oil. Set aside.

Place remaining oil in a skillet over medium heat and lay tofu in oil. Braise tofu until browned on both sides, turning once to ensure even browning, about two minutes per side. Remove from skillet and set aside.

Place arugula and onion in a bowl and toss with dressing to coat. Arrange on a platter with tofu and mango on top.

Pan-Fried Beggar's Purses

The perfect finger food for a party or a great starter course, for a little kick of protein.

MAKES 5 OR 6 SERVINGS

Extra-virgin olive oil
4 cloves fresh garlic, minced
1 red onion, cut into small dice
Soy sauce
Generous pinch crushed red pepper flakes
1 small leek, split lengthwise, rinsed well and
   cut into small dice
Mirin or white wine
8 ounces extra-firm tofu, coarsely crumbled
10 to 12 wonton wrappers
10 to 12 green onions, split lengthwise, ends
   trimmed and blanched 30 seconds
4 or 5 chives, cut into 4-inch lengths, for
   garnish

Place a small amount of oil, garlic and onion in a skillet over medium heat. When the onion begins to sizzle, sprinkle with soy sauce and red pepper flakes and sauté 2 to 3 minutes. Stir in leek, sprinkle with soy sauce and sauté 2 minutes. Sprinkle generously with mirin and stir in tofu. Season to taste with soy sauce and reduce heat to low. Cover and cook, stirring occasionally, 3 to 4 minutes. Set aside to cool.

Lay a wonton wrapper on a dry work surface and spoon about 2 tablespoons of filling onto the center. Roll, jelly-roll style, and lay on seam side. Using steamed green onions, tie each end of the wrapper, creating an oblong "package." Set aside and repeat with remaining wonton wrappers and filling.

Place enough oil to lightly cover the bottom of a skillet and place over medium-high heat. Lay beggar's purses in hot oil and cook, turning as they brown, until browned evenly. It is best to fry in batches, because if the packages are arranged too tightly in the pan, you will not be able to turn them without breaking.

When the beggar's purses are properly browned, drain them on paper towels, arrange on a platter, garnish with chives and serve hot.

■ **NOTE** You may serve the purses on their own or with a spicy dipping sauce of your choice.

Garbanzo, Baked Tofu and Eggplant Pita Sandwiches

A protein-packed sandwich to keep you strong and healthy. This nutrient-rich pocket is perfect for an active athlete who doesn't want to be weighed down by animal protein.

MAKES 6 SERVINGS

2 to 3 tablespoons extra-virgin olive oil
2 small Japanese eggplants, unpeeled, cut into ¾-inch cubes
1 red onion, diced
Sea salt
Cracked black pepper
Generous pinch crushed red pepper flakes
1½ cups cooked chickpeas, drained
White wine
1 tablespoon fresh lemon juice
4 tablespoons finely minced fresh mint
3 to 4 slices baked extra-firm tofu, finely shredded
3 pita rounds, split in half, warmed in oven to soften

Place olive oil in a deep skillet over medium heat. When the oil is hot, sauté eggplant and red onion with a pinch of salt, a light sea-soning of pepper and crushed red pepper flakes until quite soft and beginning to brown, about 7 minutes. Stir in chickpeas and wine and simmer until warmed through, 3 to 4 minutes. Remove from heat and stir in lemon juice, mint and tofu. Season to taste with salt and pepper and toss well to combine. Spoon filling generously into pita halves and serve hot.

■ **NOTE** To bake tofu, preheat oven to 400F (205C). Lay slices on a baking sheet and lightly brush soy sauce and sesame oil on both sides of slices. Allow to marinate for 10 minutes and then bake until golden brown, 20 to 25 minutes. You may also purchase packaged baked tofu in a natural foods store.

Tofu Cutlets with Blueberry Chutney

Before you run from the room screaming, try this recipe! Different, yes. Delicious, absolutely!

MAKES 3 TO 6 SERVINGS

BLUEBERRY CHUTNEY
2 cups fresh or frozen blueberries
⅓ cup brown rice syrup
½ medium red onion, cut into fine dice
¼ cup golden raisins
3 tablespoons red wine vinegar
2 teaspoons fresh ginger juice (see Note, page 164)
⅓ teaspoon sea salt
Generous pinch ground cinnamon
Generous pinch crushed red pepper flakes
2 cloves fresh garlic, minced

CUTLETS

4 tablespoons extra-virgin olive oil
¾ teaspoon dried basil
¾ teaspoon dried oregano
6 (½-inch) slices extra-firm tofu
3 cloves fresh garlic, finely minced
Sea salt
Cracked black pepper

Prepare the chutney: Combine all ingredients in a saucepan and bring to a boil. Reduce heat to medium-low and simmer until thickened, stirring occasionally, about 20 minutes.

While the chutney cooks, prepare the cutlets: Combine 2 tablespoons of the oil, basil and oregano and spread over tofu. Set aside to marinate 10 minutes.

Place remaining oil and garlic in a skillet over medium heat. When garlic begins to sizzle, sauté 1 minute. Do not burn. Lay tofu cutlets in oil and season with salt and pepper to taste. Braise on each side until golden and crispy, 3 to 4 minutes per side.

To serve, arrange tofu cutlets on a platter and spoon chutney over top.

Tofu with Red Chili Sauce and Vegetables

Tofu is the perfect backdrop to strong flavors, and oh, how it loves spicy taste. Try this dish out on someone who is not so sure they love tofu . . . you will have a convert on your hands. And tofu lovers? Pure heaven.

MAKES 4 TO 6 SERVINGS

RED CHILI SAUCE
1 cup brown rice syrup
1 tablespoon red chili powder

Pinch sea salt

8 ounces extra-firm tofu, cut into ½-inch-thick slices
4 tablespoons avocado oil
2 tablespoons soy sauce
½ red onion, sliced into very thin rings
1 bunch watercress, rinsed well, tips of stems trimmed
2 teaspoons shelled hempseeds, lightly pan-toasted

DRESSING
2 tablespoons sesame tahini
1 teaspoon brown rice vinegar
1 teaspoon brown rice syrup
Grated zest of 1 lime
1½ teaspoons soy sauce
Spring or filtered water

Prepare red chili sauce: Place rice syrup, red chili powder and a pinch of salt in a small saucepan over low heat. Simmer, stirring constantly, 3 to 4 minutes, to develop flavors.

Slice tofu and wrap in a kitchen towel to absorb water.

Heat oil, 4 tablespoons of the red chili sauce and soy sauce in a skillet over medium heat. Lay tofu slices in hot mixture and cook until browned on the underside. Carefully, turn tofu slices and brown on the other side, 2 to 3 minutes per side.

While the tofu cooks, bring a small pot of water to a boil and quickly blanch the onion. Using a slotted spoon, remove onion and place in a mixing bowl. In the same water, blanch watercress until it just wilts, about 1 minute. Drain and cut into bite-size pieces. Mix with onion. Stir in hempseeds and arrange on a serving platter. Arrange tofu on top of greens.

Prepare dressing: Whisk all ingredients together, adding water just to thin dressing to desired consistency. Spoon dressing over warm salad and serve immediately.

Tofu Larb with Red Peppers, Mushrooms and Cabbage

Never heard of "larb," you say? This traditional Indonesian dish is usually made with shredded beef or pork, but in my version, tofu is the star of the show . . . I mean, the larb.

MAKES ABOUT 4 SERVINGS

2 tablespoons avocado oil
2 or 3 serrano or jalapeño chiles, seeded and
    minced (about 2 tablespoons)
1 red bell pepper, roasted over a flame,
    peeled, seeded and thinly sliced (see Note,
    page 262)
Sea salt
1 carrot, cut into fine matchstick pieces
¼ head green cabbage, finely shredded
5 or 6 green onions, thinly sliced on the
    diagonal
3 cloves fresh garlic, finely minced
1 tablespoon Thai chili paste
2 tablespoons brown rice syrup
8 ounces extra-firm tofu, cubed
Soy sauce
½ cup fresh mint, shredded
½ cup fresh cilantro, shredded
Juice of 1 fresh lime
Avocado oil, for frying
1 (8-ounce) package bifun noodles (see Note
    below)
½ cup unsalted roasted peanuts, coarsely
    chopped

Heat avocado oil in a wok or deep skillet over medium heat. Add chiles, bell pepper and a pinch of salt and sauté 2 minutes. Stir in carrot and cabbage and sauté until just limp. Stir in green onions and garlic and sauté 1 minute. Whisk together chili paste and rice syrup and stir into vegetables. Stir well to combine. Gently stir in tofu and season to taste with soy sauce. Cover and reduce heat to low. Simmer until tofu is warmed through, 3 to 4 minutes. Remove from heat and stir in mint, cilantro and lime juice.

While the tofu and vegetables are cooking, heat about 2 inches oil in a wok over medium heat until very hot. Increase the heat to high and drop noodles into hot oil. They will puff up and sizzle. Remove carefully from hot oil and arrange on a platter. Spoon tofu larb over noodles and sprinkle with roasted peanuts. Serve immediately.

■ **NOTE** Bifun noodles are made of rice flour and potato starch. They are also called rice stick noodles or rice vermicelli.

Sesame Chile Tempeh with Gingered Watermelon Salsa

The perfect main course to grace your summer table. Hot and spicy, cooled by watermelon, this dish has it all . . . protein, minerals, vitamins and flavor to spare!

MAKES 4 OR 5 SERVINGS

2 tablespoons soy sauce
1 tablespoon Thai chile paste
2 cloves fresh garlic, finely minced

2 tablespoons sesame oil

1 tablespoon avocado oil, plus more for frying

8 ounces tempeh, cut into 2-inch-square pieces

SALSA

2 cups seeded, cubed watermelon

½ yellow bell pepper

3 or 4 green onions, thinly sliced

1 teaspoon finely minced fresh cilantro

1 teaspoon grated fresh ginger

2 teaspoons mirin

1 teaspoon fresh lime juice

Sea salt

1 jalapeño chile, seeded and minced

Combine soy sauce, chile paste, garlic and sesame and avocado oils and whisk until smooth. Transfer to a self-sealing plastic bag and add tempeh. Let marinate at least 1 hour in the refrigerator.

While tempeh marinates, prepare salsa: Mix together watermelon, bell pepper, green onions, cilantro, ginger, mirin, lime juice, salt to taste and chile. Toss carefully to combine, taking care not to break watermelon.

Place a generous amount of avocado oil in a skillet over medium heat. When the oil is hot, fry tempeh (reserve any remaining marinade) until golden brown, turning once to ensure even browning, 2 to 3 minutes per side.

To serve, lay tempeh on a platter and spoon any remaining marinade over top. Mound salsa on top and serve immediately.

Savvy Shepherd's Pie

This hearty casserole is a great centerpiece dish for any cold-weather meal. My version is light on meat (actually, none . . .) and saturated fat and topped with mashed sweet potatoes for added antioxidants as well as sweet flavor. Pretty savvy, those shepherds . . .

MAKES 4 OR 5 SERVINGS

4 or 5 sweet potatoes, peeled and cubed

Spring or filtered water

Generous pinch sea salt

2 teaspoons brown rice syrup

Scant pinch ground nutmeg

1 cup unsweetened soymilk

FILLING

Extra-virgin olive oil

8 ounces tempeh, coarsely crumbled

Soy sauce

1 small yellow onion, diced

3 cloves fresh garlic, finely minced

Sea salt

1 small carrot, diced

1 cup fresh or frozen corn kernels

2 or 3 portobello mushrooms, brushed free of dirt and coarsely chopped

White wine

1 cup fresh or frozen peas

Creamy Mushroom Sauce (page 274) (optional)

Place sweet potatoes in a saucepan with ½ inch water. Add salt, rice syrup and nutmeg and bring to a boil. Cover and reduce heat to low. Cook until potatoes are quite soft, about 20 minutes. Drain away any remaining liquid and mash, slowly adding soymilk to create a smooth mashed sweet potato mixture. Cover and set aside.

Preheat oven to 350F (175C), lightly oil a 2-quart baking dish and set aside.

Make filling: Place a small amount of oil in a deep skillet over medium heat. Cook tempeh, stirring constantly, with a splash of soy sauce, until golden brown, about 5 minutes. Stir in onion and garlic and a pinch of salt and sauté 2 minutes. Stir in carrot, corn and a pinch of salt and sauté 2 minutes. Stir in mushrooms, a generous splash of wine and a light seasoning of salt and sauté until wine is absorbed into the mixture. Stir in peas and cook until bright green, about 1 minute.

Spoon tempeh and vegetables evenly into prepared casserole and spread mashed sweet potatoes evenly over top. Bake, uncovered, 25 to 30 minutes, until the sweet potatoes are lightly browned at the edges. Serve hot, with Creamy Mushroom Sauce (if using).

Bean and Tempeh Ragout

There's nothing like a hearty stew to warm you to the bone when the weather outside is frightful. I love the combination of beans and tempeh with lots of veggies. The protein that I need is all here, and the energy is lifted and refreshed by the vegetables so you'll never feel heavy and lethargic.

MAKES ABOUT 4 SERVINGS

Extra-virgin olive oil
½ red onion, diced
Sea salt
4 ounces cubed fried tempeh (see Note, below)
1 small zucchini, quartered lengthwise and cubed
3 cloves fresh garlic, minced
6 cups coarsely chopped kale
½ cup white wine or spring or filtered water
2 cups cooked or canned cannellini beans, drained
1 (14-ounce) can diced tomatoes, undrained
Cracked black pepper
Parsley sprigs, for garnish

Place a small amount of oil and onion in a large skillet over medium heat. When the onion begins to sizzle, add a pinch of salt and sauté 1 minute. Stir in tempeh and sauté 1 minute. Stir in zucchini, garlic and a pinch of salt and sauté 2 minutes. Add kale, wine, beans and tomatoes with their juices, season with salt and pepper to taste and bring to a boil. Reduce heat to low, cover and cook 10 to 15 minutes. Serve garnished with parsley.

■ **NOTE** To fry tempeh, heat a generous amount of oil in a skillet over medium-high heat and lay tempeh cubes in oil. Cook until browned and crispy on each side, turning once to ensure even browning, 2 to 3 minutes per side.

Sausage and Pepper Sandwiches

What? You think I have lost my mind? Not really, just creating a healthy twist on one of my all-time-favorite sandwiches!

MAKES 4 SANDWICHES

Extra-virgin olive oil
1 red onion, cut into thin half-moon slices
Sea salt
3 red peppers, roasted over a flame, peeled, seeded and thinly sliced (see Note, page 262)
2 green peppers, roasted over a flame, peeled, seeded and thinly sliced (see Note, page 262)
4 soy sausages, links halved lengthwise
4 whole grain hoagie rolls, split lengthwise

Place a small amount of oil in a skillet over medium heat. Add onion and a pinch of salt and sauté until wilted, about 2 minutes. Stir in bell peppers, season with salt to taste and sauté 2 minutes more. Transfer to a bowl and wipe out skillet.

Place a small amount of oil in the same skillet over medium heat and lay sausage, cut sides down, in skillet. Cook, undisturbed, until browned on the cut side, about 2 minutes. Turn and brown lightly on the other side. Transfer to a plate and wipe out skillet one more time.

Lay rolls, cut sides down, in the skillet and cook over medium-low heat until the bread browns lightly. Remove from skillet.

To assemble, lay 2 sausage halves in a roll, smother with peppers and onions and serve.

Vegetarian Black Bean Chili

Nothing makes game day quite like a steaming bowl of chili, and you can have it with all the flavor, spice, texture and comfort you love—with none of the saturated fat—in this version of a classic dish.

MAKES 4 OR 5 SERVINGS

MARINADE
2 cups strongly brewed grain coffee
4 chopped oil-packed, sun-dried tomatoes
2 cloves fresh garlic, finely minced
1 jalapeño chile, finely minced, with seeds
¼ red onion, finely diced
1 tablespoon hot sauce
Sea salt
Cracked black pepper

8 ounces tempeh, cut into small cubes
Extra-virgin olive oil
2 cloves fresh garlic, thinly sliced
1 red onion, diced
Sea salt
2 serrano chiles, seeded, minced
1 (28-ounce) can diced tomatoes
2 cups cooked black turtle beans, drained
2 sprigs cilantro, finely minced

Make marinade: Combine all ingredients, adding salt and pepper to taste. Mix very well. Pour marinade over tempeh and set aside to marinate about 30 minutes.

Place a small amount of oil, garlic and onion in a soup pot over medium heat. When the onion begins to sizzle, add a pinch of salt and sauté 2 to 3 minutes. Stir in chiles and tomatoes. Add black beans, tempeh and marinade. Stir gently, cover and bring to a boil. Reduce heat to low and cook 35 minutes, until the vegetables, tempeh and beans are quite soft. Season to taste with salt and cook 5 minutes more. Serve garnished with cilantro.

Grilled Cheese Sandwiches

Grilled cheese sandwiches have been my favorite lunch since I was a kid. When I decided to go vegan, I thought that my days of real "happy meals" were over. Then I found some truly lovely vegan cheeses and I was back in business!

MAKES 2 SANDWICHES

4 slices whole grain bread
Vegetarian buttery spread (like Earth Balance)
4 slices vegan mozzarella cheese alternative
4 slices ripe tomatoes

Preheat a lightly oiled skillet or griddle pan over low heat.

Lay 2 slices of bread on a dry work surface and lightly spread both sides of the slices with the spread. Arrange 2 slices of cheese alternative on each bread slice and top each with 2 slices of tomato. Lightly spread both sides of the remaining bread slices with vegetarian spread and press together. Lay the 2 sandwiches in the skillet and press down firmly with a spatula. Allow to grill until lightly browned, 2 to 3 minutes. Turn sandwiches, press with spatula again and cook until lightly browned, 2 to 3 minutes. Remove from pan, slice in half diagonally and serve immediately.

Tropical Tempeh Grill

When I was in St. Thomas, the native produce was so lush and abundant that I simply could not resist it. So I didn't. I looked through lots of local cookbooks and discovered so many ways to incorporate all of these exotic, delicious foods into my own recipes.

MAKES 4 OR 5 SERVINGS

Juice of 2 or 3 limes
¼ cup plus 2 tablespoons brown rice syrup
Generous dash soy sauce
2 to 3 tablespoons light sesame oil
2 cloves fresh garlic, finely minced
2 teaspoons fresh ginger juice (see Note, page 164)
8 ounces tempeh, cut into 1-inch-thick slices
1 onion, finely chopped
1 cup cubed fresh pineapple
1 cup cubed fresh papaya
1 red bell pepper, roasted, peeled, seeded and minced (see Note, page 262)
Pinch sea salt

Spring or filtered water
1 to 2 tablespoons arrowroot or kuzu, dissolved in small amount cold water
Generous splash fresh lemon juice
Cooked rice, to serve

Whisk together lime juice, ¼ cup rice syrup, soy sauce, oil, garlic and ginger juice. Pour mixture over tempeh and marinate 35 minutes. Drain tempeh. Heat a griddle over medium heat. Add tempeh and cook, turning, until golden on both sides, about 3 minutes per side. Drain on paper towels and set aside.

Combine onion, pineapple, papaya, bell pepper, remaining 2 tablespoons rice syrup, and salt in a saucepan. Add enough water just to cover and bring to a boil. Cover and cook over low heat until fruit is soft, but not mushy, 5 to 7 minutes. Stir in dissolved arrowroot and cook, stirring, until slightly thickened. Remove from heat and stir in lemon juice and tempeh. Transfer to a bowl and serve over rice.

Tempeh with Corn and Onion

Tempeh is delicious deep-fried and then stewed in a rich sauce. Frying tempeh forms a crispy, outer coating with a moist, chewy center. In this recipe, I combine the distinctive flavor of tempeh with stewed onion and fresh sweet corn. Because it's fermented, tempeh makes digesting protein so easy.

MAKES 4 OR 5 SERVINGS

Avocado oil, for deep-frying
8 ounces tempeh, cut into 1-inch cubes
1 red onion, cut into thick half-moon slices
1 cup fresh or frozen corn kernels
1 cup spring or filtered water

Soy sauce
1 to 2 teaspoons fresh ginger juice (see Note,
    page 164)
2 tablespoons arrowroot or kuzu, dissolved in
    small amount cold water
2 to 3 sprigs flat-leaf parsley, finely minced

Heat 3 inches of oil in a heavy pot over medium heat. Add tempeh, increase heat to high, and deep-fry until golden brown, about 2 minutes. Drain on paper towels and set aside.

In a deep skillet, layer onion, corn and tempeh. Add water and bring to a boil. Reduce heat, cover and simmer over low heat until onion is very soft, about 15 minutes. Season lightly with soy sauce and ginger juice and simmer 5 minutes. Stir in dissolved arrowroot and cook, stirring, until slightly thickened. Remove from heat and gently fold in parlsey. Transfer to a bowl and serve immediately.

Tender Tempeh with Basil

Indonesia meets Italy in this recipe. Combining the distinctive flavor of tempeh with the delicate taste of fresh basil makes for an explosion of sensations in your mouth as well as a light energy that will put pep in your step.

MAKES 4 OR 5 SERVINGS

2 tablespoons extra-virgin olive oil
8 ounces tempeh, crumbled
2 cloves fresh garlic, finely minced
1 red onion, cut into large dice
Sea salt
1 carrot, cut into large dice
1 or 2 celery stalks, cut into large dice
1 red bell pepper, roasted over a flame,
    peeled, seeded and diced (see Note, page
    262)

2 cups button mushrooms, brushed clean and
    thinly sliced
2 to 3 sprigs basil, leaves removed and
    shredded
Spring or filtered water
1 tablespoon arrowroot or kuzu, dissolved in
    small amount cold water
Pasta, cooked al dente, to serve
2 to 3 sprigs flat-leaf parsley, minced, for
    garnish

Heat 1 tablespoon of the oil in a skillet over medium heat. Add tempeh and cook, stirring occasionally, until golden and crispy, about 4 minutes. Remove tempeh and set aside.

In the same skillet, heat remaining oil. Add garlic, onion and a pinch of salt and cook, stirring, 2 to 3 minutes. Add carrot, celery, bell pepper, mushrooms, basil and a pinch of salt and cook 3 to 4 minutes. Season with salt to taste. Add tempeh and enough water to scantly half-cover ingredients and bring to a boil. Reduce heat, cover and cook over low heat 15 minutes. Stir in dissolved arrowroot and cook, stirring, until slightly thickened, about 3 minutes. Serve over pasta, garnished with parsley.

Tempeh Brochettes

Marinated tempeh is perfect for grilling. Its own distinctive flavor is enhanced by the variety of flavors in the marinade, then grilled to golden perfection and skewered with fresh summer veggies. A cookout dish to die for.

MAKES 4 OR 5 SERVINGS

2 to 3 teaspoons soy sauce
⅓ cup mirin or white wine
⅓ cup fresh orange juice
2 tablespoons dark sesame oil
1 tablespoon brown rice syrup
1 or 2 cloves fresh garlic, crushed
1 teaspoon fresh ginger juice (see Note, page 164)
Generous pinch crushed red pepper flakes
8 ounces tempeh, cut into 1-inch cubes
1 red bell pepper, cut into 1-inch pieces
1 yellow bell pepper, cut into 1-inch pieces
1 red onion, cut into 6 wedges
2 zucchini, cut into 1-inch-thick rounds
2 yellow summer squash, cut into 1-inch-thick rounds
7 or 8 button mushrooms, brushed clean and left whole
1 to 2 cups 1-inch cubes cantaloupe

For marinade, whisk together soy sauce, mirin, orange juice, sesame oil, rice syrup, garlic, ginger juice and pepper flakes. Arrange tempeh in a shallow dish, cover with marinade and allow to stand at room temperature about 1 hour, stirring occasionally.

Preheat grill. Drain tempeh, reserving marinade. Thread tempeh, veggies and melon alternately on skewers, leaving a tiny space between each piece to allow for quicker, more even cooking. Brush brochettes lightly with reserved marinade.

Arrange the brochettes on grill rack with a small space between them. Grill 7 to 8 minutes, turn each brochette, brush with marinade and grill the other side for an additional 7 to 8 minutes. Brochettes are ready when the tempeh and vegetables are crispy and beginning to blacken, but are still tender at their centers. Serve hot.

Steamed Spring Rolls with Citrus-Mustard Sauce

No one handles tempeh quite like Indonesia, and lightly steamed spring rolls have a freshness about them that makes this a protein dish that won't weigh you down.

MAKES 4 SERVINGS

2 teaspoons dark sesame oil
8 ounces tempeh, cut into 2 × ¼-inch strips
½ cup mung bean sprouts
4 green onions, cut into 3-inch pieces
½ cup finely shredded Chinese cabbage
½ red bell pepper, roasted over a flame, peeled, seeded and cut into thin 3-inch strips (see Note, page 262)
Juice of 1 lemon
8 dried rice-paper spring roll wrappers

CITRUS-MUSTARD SAUCE
3 tablespoons prepared Dijon mustard
3 to 4 tablespoons sesame tahini
2 green onions, minced
Juice of 1 lime
Juice of 1 orange
1 teaspoon brown rice syrup
Dash soy sauce
2 teaspoons dark sesame oil

1 teaspoon fresh ginger juice (see Note, page 164)
Spring or filtered water

Heat sesame oil in a skillet over medium heat. Add tempeh and cook, turning, until golden brown on all sides, about 2 minutes per side. Drain and set aside. Toss sprouts, green onions, cabbage and bell pepper with lemon juice in a medium bowl.

Soften rice wrappers by soaking in cold water 5 minutes or by moistening with a wet sponge until pliable. Lay rice wrappers with one corner pointing toward you. Arrange one-eighth of vegetables (about 3 tablespoons) and a strip of tempeh close to the middle of the wrapper. Fold over the corner near you, then the two side corners. Gently roll toward the far corner. The spring roll wrapper will seal itself as you roll it. Arrange rolls in a bamboo steamer basket and steam over boiling water 10 minutes. Transfer rolls to a serving platter and set aside while preparing the sauce.

Prepare sauce: Combine all sauce ingredients, except water, in a small saucepan over low heat. Cook 3 to 5 minutes, or until warmed. Add a small amount of water to thin the sauce to desired consistency. Serve sauce in individual bowls for dipping either warm or chilled if made ahead.

Tempeh Stroganoff

A hearty winter bean dish. Aromatic tempeh, deep-fried until crispy and smothered in a creamy white mushroom sauce, is just about as unbeatable a combination as I can imagine. Oh, and do yourself a real favor and serve this dish over fettuccine or brown basmati rice with a side dish of lightly cooked green vegetables—a fabulous warming winter supper.

MAKES 4 OR 5 SERVINGS

Avocado oil, for deep-frying
8 ounces tempeh, cubed
2 teaspoons light sesame oil
1 or 2 cloves fresh garlic, finely minced
4 or 5 slices fresh ginger, finely minced
1 onion, cut into thin half-moon slices
Sea salt
2 to 3 tablespoons whole wheat pastry flour
6 to 8 dried shiitake mushrooms, soaked until tender and thinly sliced
5 or 6 button mushrooms, brushed clean and thinly sliced
2 cups spring or filtered water
Soy sauce
Wide noodles or basmati rice, cooked, to serve
2 to 3 sprigs parsley, left whole, for garnish

Heat 3 inches of avocado oil in a deep pot over medium heat. Add tempeh and deep-fry until golden and crispy, about 2 minutes. Drain on paper towels and set aside.

Heat sesame oil in a skillet over medium heat. Add garlic, ginger, onion and a pinch of salt and cook, stirring, 3 to 4 minutes or until softened. Stirring constantly, slowly add flour to skillet. Add mushrooms and a pinch of salt and stir well. Slowly add water, stirring constantly so mixture doesn't get lumpy. Add tempeh, season lightly with soy sauce, cover and simmer over low heat 25 minutes, stirring occasionally to prevent sticking. The mixture will thicken as it simmers, forming a rich, creamy sauce. Remove skillet from heat and stir gently. Arrange cooked noodles on a serving platter and top with stroganoff and parsley. Serve hot.

Tempeh-Stuffed Cabbage Rolls

This is a delicious, easy dinner dish. Smothered in a rich, mushroom gravy and filled with savory tempeh and melted mochi, this version of cabbage rolls will become a standard in your mealtime repertoire, providing stamina and energy from that winning combination of grain and beans.

MAKES 4 TO 6 SERVINGS

8 ounces tempeh, steamed 10 minutes and cooled
½ cup minced red onion
1 carrot, minced
About 8 large cabbage leaves, lightly blanched
4 ounces brown rice mochi, thinly sliced into 1-inch pieces
Spring or filtered water
5 or 6 button mushrooms, brushed clean and thinly sliced
Soy sauce
1 teaspoon arrowroot or kuzu, dissolved in small amount cold water

Crumble tempeh into a bowl. Stir in onion and carrot. Lay each cabbage leaf flat and spoon a small amount of tempeh filling (about ¼ cup) onto the center of the leaf. Top filling with 2 or 3 pieces of mochi. Roll the cabbage, folding in the edges to seal the roll. Repeat until all leaves and filling are used up.

Arrange cabbage rolls in a skillet, packed tightly together. Add enough water to half-cover rolls, top with a layer of mushrooms and bring to a boil. Reduce heat, cover and cook over low heat 10 minutes. Season lightly with soy sauce and simmer 5 minutes.

Gently lift cabbage rolls from pan, leaving mushrooms behind as much as possible, and arrange rolls on a serving platter. Stir dissolved arrowroot into remaining cooking liquid and mushrooms and cook, stirring, until slightly thickened, about 3 minutes. Spoon sauce over cabbage rolls and serve hot.

Tempeh Melt

Move over, tuna melt . . .

MAKES ABOUT 4 SERVINGS

2 tablespoons avocado oil
1 red onion, diced
1 red bell pepper, roasted over a flame, peeled, seeded and diced (see Note, page 262)
Soy sauce
1 or 2 small zucchini, diced
1 cup finely shredded green cabbage
8 ounces tempeh, coarsely crumbled
Spring or filtered water
4 ounces brown rice mochi, grated

Heat oil in a deep skillet over medium heat. Add onion, bell pepper and a splash of soy sauce and cook, stirring, until softened, 3 to 4 minutes. Add zucchini, cabbage and a splash of soy sauce and cook until cabbage is limp, about 5 minutes. Sprinkle tempeh over vegetables, add ¹⁄₁₆ inch of water, and season lightly with soy sauce. Cover and cook over low heat 10 minutes. Sprinkle grated mochi over tempeh and vegetables, re-cover, and simmer over low heat until mochi has melted and water is absorbed, 5 to 7 minutes. Serve hot.

Where's the Beef? Stew

My dad was a butcher, so growing up our dinner table was all about meat. I hated it, but we didn't have a lot of choices so I ate what was on the table. One thing I did love was beef stew. I loved the veggies, the potatoes, the tomatoes (we're Italian; there were tomatoes in everything!). There's no beef in this version, but it is a hearty, yummy stew in its own right.

MAKES 4 TO 5 SERVINGS

⅓ cup arrowroot
Sea salt
Cracked black pepper
1 pound seitan, cut into 1-inch cubes
3 tablespoons extra-virgin olive oil
3 red onions, quartered
4 carrots, chunk cut
2 parsnips, chunk cut
1 (28-ounce) can diced tomatoes, undrained
2 bay leaves
Spring or filtered water
4 medium Yukon Gold potatoes, cubed
1 cup frozen green peas

Combine arrowroot with a generous pinch of salt and pepper. Dredge seitan in arrowroot mixture and set aside.

Heat oil in a heavy pot and pan-fry seitan pieces until the coating is crispy, about 5 minutes. Add onions, carrots, parsnips, tomatoes and bay leaves. Season lightly with salt and pepper and add water to almost cover ingredients. Bring to a boil, cover, reduce heat to low and cook 20 minutes. Add potatoes, adjust seasonings to your taste and cook until potatoes are tender, about 20 minutes more. Add more water, if needed, to maintain a stewlike consistency. Remove bay leaves, stir in peas and cook

5 minutes more. Stir gently to combine and serve hot.

Chickenless Pot Pie

Pot pie has to be one of the world's greatest comfort foods, but the average chicken pot pie has so much saturated fat and so many calories, you'll take little comfort there. In this version, we have lots of veggies, a flaky crust and all the comforts of home with no compromise to your health.

MAKES 6 TO 8 SERVINGS

2 recipes Pastry Dough (page 304)

FILLING
Extra-virgin olive oil
2 cloves fresh garlic, thinly sliced
1 small red onion, cut into thin half-moon
    slices
Sea salt
¼ cup whole wheat pastry flour
2 vegetable bouillon cubes
3 cups unsweetened soymilk
1 tablespoon white miso
2 stalks celery, diced
1 carrot, diced
1 small yellow squash, diced
1 small zucchini, diced
1 cup fresh or frozen peas
2 cups shredded seitan
½ teaspoon ground sage

Prepare pastry and roll out between waxed or parchment paper into 2 (11-inch) rounds.

Prepare filling: Place about 3 tablespoons oil, garlic and onion in a deep skillet over medium heat. When the onion begins to sizzle, add a pinch of salt and sauté 2 to 3 minutes. Stir in flour and cook, stirring to create a thick paste. Whisk in bouillon cubes and soymilk and cook, whisking constantly, until the mixture thickens, about 3 minutes. Stir in vegetables, seitan, sage and salt to taste until all ingredients are well incorporated. Cover and set aside.

Preheat oven to 375F (190C). Lay one of the dough rounds over a deep 9-inch pie plate and, using your knuckles, press the pastry to conform to the pan, trying not to stretch it too much. Allow excess pastry to hang over the sides of the pan. Using a fork, pierce in several places. Spoon filling evenly into the pie shell. Lay second dough round over the filling. Trim excess of both crusts even with the rim of the pan. Press the edges of the pie crusts together to seal. Using your thumb and forefinger, crimp the edge of the crust. With a sharp knife, make 4 slits in the top of the pie to allow steam to escape.

Bake 35 to 40 minutes, until the crust is golden and firm and the filling is bubbling. Remove from oven and allow to stand at least 10 minutes before serving.

Winter Seitan Pie

My inspiration for this pot pie came from Meredith McCarty, one of the most talented whole foods cooks in the world, in my humble opinion. She has an intuitive cooking style that has created some of the richest, most delicious dishes I have ever tasted.

MAKES 5 OR 6 SERVINGS

4 cups spring or filtered water
1 cup diced green cabbage
1 small carrot, cut into large dice

1 small parsnip, cut into large dice
1 turnip, cut into large dice
1 yellow onion, cut into large dice
1 cup bite-size chunks seitan
1 tablespoon soy sauce
1 teaspoon avocado oil
⅓ cup whole wheat pastry flour, mixed with a little cold water

CRUST
¾ cup whole wheat pastry flour
¼ cup yellow cornmeal
Pinch sea salt
Pinch dried rosemary
2 tablespoons avocado oil
¼ cup cold spring or filtered water

Lightly oil a deep-dish pie pan and set aside. Bring water to a boil in a large pot and cook each vegetable separately (in the order listed above) until almost done. Reserve cooking water in pot. Combine vegetables with seitan in a bowl and set aside.

Add soy sauce and avocado oil to vegetable cooking water and cook over low heat 5 minutes. Stirring constantly, slowly add flour mixture. Cook, stirring, until thickened, about 3 minutes. Pour mixture over vegetables and seitan and stir well. Spoon this mixture into prepared pie pan.

Preheat oven to 350F (175C).

Prepare crust: Combine flour, cornmeal, salt and rosemary in a small bowl. Stir in oil and water with a fork and mix well. Knead briefly to form a ball. Roll out dough, between waxed paper, into a thin round. Cut crust into thin strips and arrange over top of vegetables in a lattice pattern, tucking edges of strips into the filling. Bake about 40 minutes, until filling is bubbling and top of pie is golden brown and firm. Serve hot.

Seitan in Rainbow Sauce

I like to serve this really pretty, simple-to-make dish during the summer months when vegetables are the most plentiful, not to mention at peak flavor. The vegetables cook only long enough to tenderize them slightly. Combining the wonderful textures of golden-fried seitan and crispy, summer veggies is perfect. Seitan is a heavier protein and the light veggies lift the energy of the dish, so you feel strong and steady, not heavy or stuffed.

MAKES ABOUT 4 SERVINGS

Avocado oil, for deep-frying
1 pound seitan, cut into thin strips
About ¼ cup yellow cornmeal
2 to 3 cups Vegetable Stock (page 74)
½ red bell pepper, roasted over a flame,
    peeled, seeded and cut into thin strips (see
    Note, page 262)
2 green onions, cut into long, thin diagonal
    slices
1 red onion, cut lengthwise into thin slices
1 lemon, peeled and cut into thin slices
2 teaspoons arrowroot or kuzu, dissolved in
    small amount cold water

Heat 3 inches of oil in a deep pot over medium heat. While oil is heating, dredge seitan strips in cornmeal. Add seitan to oil and deep-fry until golden and crispy. Drain on paper towels and set aside.

Bring stock to a boil over medium heat. Stir in vegetables and lemon and simmer 1 or 2 minutes. Stir in dissolved arrowroot and cook, stirring, until mixture is thickened, about 3 minutes. Arrange seitan on a serving platter and spoon sauce over top. Serve immediately with some freshly cooked vegetables or a crisp salad.

Seitan-Barley Stew

When barley cooks for a long time, it takes on a delightfully creamy texture and its natural, uplifting, dispersing energy makes it a complement to the heavier protein of seitan. I serve big, steaming bowls of this stew in the winter, with a crisp side salad for a most satisfying dinner.

MAKES ABOUT 4 SERVINGS

1 onion, cut into large dice
2 or 3 celery stalks, cut into large dice
2 cups cubed winter squash
1 cup cubed cabbage
½ cup whole barley, rinsed and soaked 6 to 8
    hours
1 cup bite-size chunks seitan
Spring or filtered water
2 tablespoons barley miso
3 or 4 green onions, thinly sliced, diagonally,
    for garnish

In a soup pot, layer onion, celery, squash, cabbage, barley and seitan. Add water to half-cover ingredients and bring to a boil. Reduce heat, cover and cook over low heat until barley is very creamy, 1 to 1½ hours. Remove about 1 tablespoon cooking broth and mix with miso until dissolved. Stir mixture into stew and simmer 3 to 4 minutes. Serve hot, garnished with green onions.

Chinese Orange Seitan

Seitan is a very common meat substitute in Asian cuisine. Meaty in texture and savory in flavor, it is a perfect catalyst for sauces and the perfect companion for crisply cooked Oriental-style vegetables, which provide a lightness to balance its more dense nature. Serve over rice or pasta.

MAKES ABOUT 4 SERVINGS

½ cup fresh orange juice
Soy sauce
¼ cup spring or filtered water
2 teaspoons arrowroot
1 teaspoon fresh ginger juice (see Note, page 164)
Dash of umeboshi or red wine vinegar
2 teaspoons brown rice syrup
2 tablespoons light sesame oil
1 pound seitan, cut into strips
2 tablespoons dark sesame oil
4 or 5 slices fresh ginger, finely minced
2 cloves fresh garlic, finely minced
4 or 5 green onions, cut into 1-inch pieces
1 carrot, cut into thin matchsticks
1 or 2 stalks broccoli, broken into florets
½ red bell pepper, roasted over a flame, peeled, seeded and cut into thin strips (see Note, page 262)

4 or 5 button mushrooms, brushed clean and thinly sliced
¼ pound fresh snow peas, trimmed and left whole

For sauce, combine orange juice, 2 teaspoons soy sauce, water, arrowroot, ginger, vinegar and rice syrup in a bowl and set aside.

Heat 1 tablespoon of the oil in a wok over medium heat. Add seitan strips and stir-fry until browned, 3 to 4 minutes. Remove from wok and set aside.

In the same wok, heat remaining oil. Add ginger, garlic, green onions and a splash of soy sauce and stir-fry 1 to 2 minutes. Add carrot, broccoli and a splash of soy sauce and stir-fry 2 to 3 minutes. Stir in bell pepper, mushrooms and a splash of soy sauce and stir-fry 2 to 3 minutes. Add snow peas and cooked seitan. Stir sauce mixture and add to wok. Cook, stirring, until clear and thickened, about 3 minutes. Serve hot.

Eat Your Veggies!

IN THE LAST several years, society has come to rely on animal foods as the mainstay of most meals. I am not sure how we got here. Are these foods easier to prepare? Not really. Is it the belief that you can obtain great strength from these incredibly dense sources of fat and protein? Maybe. Is it that they are more readily available and familiar than, say, broccoli? Nope. There are cultural myths that tell us that being able to have lots of meat was a sign of affluence, so we piled on the meat, but I'm not sure about that reason either. Regardless of the reason, we are where we are . . . and it's not the best place to be, culinarily speaking, for our health.

The excessive consumption of animal foods requires extended exertion of our organ systems simply to assimilate these foods and process them into energy we can use. Interestingly, we can derive the same amount of energy from vegetable foods with substantially less work.

Which brings us to vegetables. Having long suffered under the myth that anything good for you must taste just awful, I am here to tell you that veggies not only are delicious and beautiful to serve, but they are some of the most nutritionally sound foods we can consume, chock-full of all the vitamins, minerals and other nutrients we need to maintain good health.

Vegetables are never boring. If you let the seasons dictate which vegetables to eat, you will find that variety is rarely a problem and that vegetables taste best when grown as nature intended, picked at the height of ripeness and cooked as soon as possible after picking.

Choosing Vegetables

So now that you've committed (you are committed, right?) to at least trying to eat more vegetables, what do you buy? What do you look for? How do you know you are choosing good quality? Let's start with what to buy. Always try to choose seasonal and, whenever possible, locally grown produce, preferably organic if it is available. You substantially reduce your intake of harmful pesticides by doing so, and you won't believe the difference in the taste of foods allowed to grow unhampered by chemicals. "Organic," now certified by the FDA so that the standards are consistent countrywide, means food grown free of chemical intervention of any kind: pesticides, fungicides, hormones, antibiotics, sewage sludge, etc. Unless food meets these standards, they can not bear the label indicating organic certification.

That said, when it comes to locally grown vegetables and fruit, ask the farmer before you simply stop purchasing his produce. In many cases, a small family farm cannot afford the federal cerfication fee to have their produce certified, but they may grow and produce according to the standards, so check in with your local farm markets to get a real handle on how your food is being grown.

Choose a good variety of vegetables, combining root vegetables (like carrots, turnips, parsnips, burdock, rutabaga), round and ground vegetables (like squash, onion, broccoli, cabbage, Brussels sprouts, cauliflower, Chinese cabbage), lots of hearty and delicate leafy greens (like kale, collards, mustards, watercress, escarole, arugula, lettuces, bok choy, rapini) and some herbs and grasses . . . and whatever you love. A most important tip: Make a new rule to purchase a fruit or vegetable that you don't know during every shopping trip. Take it home and play in the kitchen with a new flavor and ingredient. The worst that can happen is you'll hate it; you'll have my permission to order out . . . that night!

Macrobiotics is an all-encompassing way to nourish your body, but some nutritional myths have come to be regarded as truth, so let's get past those right now. It was held (and for some people, still is . . .) that there are some vegetables that you need to minimize for health. In some cases, this may be true, but for very specific reasons and we will get to those in a minute. But the problem is not in eating vegetables—it's *not* eating them that is doing us in.

Spinach and chard, as well as chives, parsley and purslane are rich sources of oxalic acid, a compound that can inhibit the body's ability to assimilate calcium efficiently, so if you are struggling with bone loss, you may want to keep these at a minimum. However, when oxalic-rich vegetables are combined with other vegetables, the acid can be gentled, so if you can't live without spinach and parsley (and who can?), just don't eat them alone. See? I told you . . . no harm with veggies.

The nightshade family of vegetables, including tomatoes, potatoes, bell peppers and eggplant, all contain mildly toxic acids that seem to affect people with arthritis in an adverse way. But before you close the book and walk away, read on. While this acid is strong enough to repel insects in the soil, it is easily neutralized with cooking, marinating, drying, juicing or roasting. However, for some with particularly acute symptoms of arthritis, these may still be a source of aggravation and you will need to minimize them or avoid these vegetables completely. For the rest of us, they are so nutrient-rich that to eliminate them from your diet would be, well . . . just silly.

And then there are tropical vegetables and fruit. Grown in hot climates, nature designed these foods to cool the body in hot weather. They are light, juicy and sweet. For some people, year-round consumption of oranges, grapefruit, papaya, banana, mango, yucca, plantain and other tropical treats can leave them feeling chilled in cold weather. They are also quite rich in simple sugars, wreaking havoc on the immune function, which is not a great idea in the winter. These particular vegetables and fruits can also cause the blood to become acidic, rather than slightly alkaline, resulting in all sorts of ailments that modern people have come to accept as "normal" afflictions. Do we need to give up these lovely foods? No, sometimes they bring just the perfect level of fresh, sweet flavor and energy we want in a recipe. They can make a dish simply sparkle. But some of us may need to choose them more moderately for health.

With a better understanding, it is easy to choose good quality. Especially when picking through organic produce, don't let appearance blind you in your choices. Organic vegetables and fruit don't always look picture perfect. Those arrow-straight carrots and perfectly shiny apples are the result of chemical additives and waxes. When choosing from naturally grown produce of course, avoid limp, yellow greens, vegetables and fruits with blemishes and bruises or produce with a woody, stringy appearance. Remember that organic produce has not been preserved in any way and will spoil or wilt sooner than nonorganic produce. Simply use common sense and choose the freshest, perkiest vegetables and you will do all right. If your schedule permits, buy fresh produce a couple of times each week, buying just what you will use in a few days. You will lose much less to spoilage that way.

One last point: While I am almost militant in my support of using organic produce, variety in your choices is equally important. So try not to let cost or availability inhibit getting the variety you need. Supplement your organic purchases with commercial produce where necessary to get variety in your diet, ensuring that you and your family get a proper balance of nutrients.

Storing Vegetables

Okay, so you've just returned home from shopping and your counter is brimming with life and color that only fresh vegetables (okay, and fresh flowers) can bring to your life. Now you need to store your vegetables in a way that will support their freshness. I don't recommend washing vegetables before storing them, unless of course you are certain to dry them very well before refrigerating. If they are wet, you are inviting rot. Vegetables store best in cotton or plastic bags; paper sacks sap the moisture from your vegetables very quickly, leaving them wilted and limp and not at all appetizing. Remove all ties and bands from the vegetables, especially greens, so that air can circulate around them. If your kitchen is cool, or you have a cool, dry basement, root vegetables like carrots, rutabaga, turnips, winter squash and even onions do not need to be refrigerated at all. Just keep them dry so they do not develop mold. It just takes a bit of common sense to keep produce fresh for as long as possible.

Cooking Vegetables

Now the real dilemma. You didn't think I would leave you out in the cold to fend for yourself, did you? You have bought wonderful, fresh, organic produce. You have unpacked it and stored it properly. The most frequent question I am asked is, besides steaming and boiling and stir-frying, what is there to do with vegetables? And then there are people who tell me that their vegetable experiences have consisted of overcooked asparagus, mushy, brown broccoli and soggy carrots. And even more tell me that most of this glorious produce that was purchased in a moment of culinary rapture simply rots in the crisper drawer.

Don't let yourself fall into this trap. Just a few basic principles of cooking can open up new avenues of culinary expression. You can develop a style all your own and begin to create delicious vegetable dishes by learning just a few basics and by stocking your pantry with a few staple ingredients to enhance the natural flavors of vegetables.

Your ingredients, including your produce as well as your staples, need not be fancy, but they should always be of the best quality. Stocking your pantry with some good oils—extra-virgin olive oil for cooking and salads; avocado oil for creating buttery taste; light and dark sesame oil for flavor; various vinegars—red wine, umeboshi, brown rice and balsamic; dried vegetables—daikon, lotus root and mushrooms; nuts, seeds and pine nuts; olives and capers; sea salt, natural soy sauce and miso—will enable you to easily enhance the flavor of your cooking.

Vegetable cooking turns each meal into a seasonal celebration, but the main reason we cook vegetables is to render them more digestible, so that, in turn, we can assimilate them completely and benefit fully from their nourishment. Regardless of the techniques used, cooking vegetables softens their tough outer coating of cellulose (a hard-to-digest fiber that protects the food from the elements).

Overcooking and undercooking are the two biggest pitfalls to overcome. Practice and vigilance are the keys to mastering cooking techniques. Vegetables are considered done when a fork easily pierces them or when you taste them and they have achieved the tenderness you like. It's that easy. Cooking times in even the best recipes are only estimates, since everything hinges on the cutting style used as well as the size and freshness of the vegetable.

There are several basic cooking techniques that, once familiar to you, will become the springboards for many delicious dishes. Combining more than one technique to achieve a certain texture in a dish, using oil or water in a sauté, steaming and then baking—all can be used to enhance your cooking.

Boiling and Blanching

If you think of bland, limp, boring vegetables when you think of boiling, think again. Boiling is a quick and efficient method of cooking that produces firm, full-bodied flavors with vibrant colors and leaves most of the nutrients intact. Boiling vegetables also employs a good bit of moisture and, as a result, nourishes the skin, making it soft and pliable.

To properly boil vegetables, use a deep pot with plenty of water. Cook the vegetables in small amounts so as not to lose the boil. (You can also add a pinch of salt to the water; this will help return the water to a boil very quickly. It also helps the vegetable to hold on to nutrients, as salt seals the veggie.). Cooking times will vary, depending on the vegetable, its freshness, cutting style, and size, but what you are looking for is a just-tender vegetable—not mushy, not crunchy, just right.

Blanching is simply a shorter version of boiling and is usually reserved for more delicate vegetables like watercress, red radishes and green onions, and for very thinly sliced vegetables when you want a firmer, crispier texture.

Boiled and blanched vegetables continue to cook after being removed from the boiling water, so to keep them from becoming overcooked, simply plunge them briefly into cold water and drain well or undercook them slightly so that as they finish cooking, they do not become mushy. I prefer the latter. I am of the belief that plunging vegetables into cold water drains away flavor, but that is just me. You may see it in some of my recipes, but I do not use this method as a regular practice.

Steaming

Steamed vegetables cook in the hot steam produced by boiling a small amount of water.

Unlike boiling, the vegetables are cooked on racks above the water. Collapsible stainless-steel racks or bamboo steamers are most commonly used in this cooking style.

Bring the water to a high boil before adding the vegetables and cover the pot tightly while cooking. The best results occur when the vegetables are arranged in a single layer and the rack is not overfilled.

Most vegetables steam very well, retaining their full flavor and vibrant color, but they are less moist than boiled vegetables because they do not come in contact with the water. It is said that they retain more nutrients as a result. Steaming imparts great vitality since the vegetables are cooked over high heat, very quickly, with little moisture.

Stewing and Braising

Braising is slow simmering in a small amount of stock or some other liquid, like oil. Braising is generally employed to cook only one vegetable, whereas stewing usually consists of a combination of several complementary vegetables simmering in their own juices with just a small bit of added liquid to ensure thorough cooking.

Braising and stewing result in incredibly tender, sweet vegetables. The flavor of the vegetables, broth and seasoning blend together as the liquid is reduced, forming a rich sauce. Firm vegetables, especially sweet root vegetables and heartier ground vegetables are very well suited to this style of cooking. Cutting the vegetables into large pieces, bringing them to a boil gently over medium heat, and cooking them slowly over low heat prevents the vegetables from turning to mush as they cook.

This style of cooking creates great strengthening energy for us, especially if the vegetables are arranged in the pot to enhance the blending of all of their energies. Vegetables like carrots, turnips, rutabaga, onions, leeks, cabbage, winter squash, Brussels sprouts, parsnips, daikon, celery and even fennel lend themselves very well to this style of cooking.

Sautéing

The French word for *jump* or *leap* is *sauté*, which perfectly describes what sautéing veggies seem to be doing in the hot skillet as they cook to perfection.

To sauté, heat a small amount of oil in a skillet; the hot oil sears the skin of the vegetable, allowing it to cook, but sealing in valuable nutrients and flavor. Add vegetables gradually to prevent the heat from reducing too much, which would steam the veggies instead of sautéing them, and stir frequently or shake the pan to prevent sticking and burning. You may also sauté with water instead of oil, but you will not achieve the rich, full-bodied flavors that you get when sautéing with oil.

Most vegetables adapt well to this style of cooking, if you remember a few basic tips. To avoid limp results make sure the vegetables are dry before cooking. Cut the vegetables uniformly in thickness to ensure even cooking, keeping in mind that the thinner and more delicate the cut, the quicker the vegetables will cook. Diagonal cutting styles expose more surface area to the heat as well as the seasonings, giving a fuller flavor to the finished product. Begin the process of cooking with the vegetables that require the longest cooking time and try not to overfill the skillet. Sautéing requires room to move the vegetables around for even, thorough cooking. Finally, remove the veggies immediately when cooking is complete to maintain the crispness and vitality of the finished sauté.

Frying

I can hear your horrified gasps already. Frying? All that oil? All that fat? I thought this was about healthy cooking! But that's what I'm referring to here. Remember that if you are eating in a vegetarian manner (even just most of the time), your daily diet is very low in fat compared to the average modern diet. That gives you a bit of extra freedom when it comes to eating a small amount of fried foods. So, while frying isn't a cooking method to be used daily . . . or even several times a week, occasional fried foods add rich, satisfying flavors to meals.

The most common styles of frying are shallow pan-frying and the ever-popular deep-frying. Shallow frying is done by heating a small amount of oil, about ¼ to ½ inch, in a skillet and cooking the vegetables until golden and crispy. Drain well on paper towels to soak up any excess oil.

Deep-frying is a method that paradoxically uses more oil in cooking, but imparts very little oil to the food; that is, if you deep-fry properly. Deep-frying should be done in a deep pot with at least 2 to 3 inches of oil. I usually use light olive or avocado oil because they won't foam as you cook; they have very light flavors and are not volatile under heat. Here's how you do it. Heat the oil over medium heat so that the oil warms slowly and thoroughly. To test the readiness, simply drop a small piece of what you will be cooking into the oil. If it sinks and returns quickly to the top, your oil is hot enough to fry. If that scares you, simply look at the oil. When patterns form in the bottom of the pot, the oil is hot. When the oil is ready, increase the heat to high and drop a few vegetables into the hot oil. Do not overfill the pot, as this will lower the oil temperature too much to fry well. As soon as the vegetables rise to the top of the oil and are golden, remove them from the pot and drain well on paper towels. Deep-fried foods are best when served immediately after frying. In my house, people eat the fried bits as they come out of the pan! I can barely get the food to the dinner table.

If you fry properly, you will notice that when returning the oil to its container, very little is missing. That is the point. Deep-fried foods should not taste oily but should have a rich, satisfying flavor. Understand that proper deep-frying has the food in the oil for only a brief period, not long enough for it to absorb a lot. Also, after deep-frying, filter the oil through paper or cheesecloth, store in a tightly sealed container in the refrigerator and you may reuse it two or three times before discarding it. You know it's time to change the oil when the color turns very dark when you reheat it.

Baking and Roasting

While it may take a bit longer than other methods of cooking, baking or roasting requires no work during the cooking process. And the results—rich, succulent, concentrated flavors that melt in your mouth! Baked vegetables take on a sweetness like no other form of cooking can produce. A little dressing-up at the beginning of cooking results in a delectable finished product.

Winter squash, Brussels sprouts, onions, carrots, parsnips, leeks, celery, cauliflower, zucchini, yellow squash, even asparagus are all perfect candidates for baking and roasting. Their firm texture and thicker skins help to preserve their own inner moisture. To prepare vegetables for the simplest form of baking, simply cut them into medium-size wedges or chunks and place in a casserole. Sprinkle lightly with sea salt or soy sauce to help seal in moisture and bring out the natural sweet taste, add a tiny amount of water to create steam, cover and bake. Most vegetables give the tastiest results when baked at 350F (175C) for 1 to 1½ hours. The slow cooking brings out the natural sweetness in the veggies. You can vary this dish and add richness without the fuss of complicated sauces and gravies, with just a little creativity. Lightly drizzle the vegetables with olive oil before baking, and, for savory flavor, sprinkle with dried or fresh herbs; for sweetness, add a drizzle of rice syrup or honey—this is a most delicious way to seduce people into eating their veggies as well as giving the comforting, warming energy that is created by baking them. This method of cooking creates a calm, centered feeling and helps keep us warm during the crisp days of autumn and the extreme cold weather of winter.

Broiling and Grilling

Most people associate these styles of cooking with meat, poultry and fish, not with vegetables. Well, that thinking is about to change; continue reading. Grain dishes like polenta or pasta, served with a side dish of grilled summer vegetables, and fresh summer salads made up of crisp greens and cool cucumbers with broiled vegetables tossed in are heavenly combinations. Top a whole wheat pizza crust with perfectly grilled or broiled vegetables and a simple sauce to create a pizza that will not miss the cheese. With backyard grills and broilers in every oven, these increasingly popular styles of cooking can be employed any time.

Broiling and grilling consist of cooking vegetables, usually thinly sliced and marinated, over high heat until the outside areas are lightly seared and the insides are tender. These vegetables are even better when the marinade is brushed over them while cooking. And your marinade can be as simple as extra-virgin olive oil with a sprinkling of sea salt and pepper!

Broiling is very quick and at its best when the vegetables are thinly sliced, even into ribbons and then marinated before cooking under high heat, with occasional bastings of marinade. Both cooking styles are very quick and you will need to pay attention so that the vegetables don't burn. The good news is that these cooking styles are usually done just before dinner, when you will be in the kitchen doing last minute things anyhow. You may as well be paying attention to your cooking veggies.

Lots of vegetables lend themselves well to grilling and broiling: summer squash, carrots, zucchini, parsnips, leeks, onions, corn on the cob (still in thin layers of husk), shallots, red onions, red peppers, chiles, tomatoes, asparagus, celery root and green onions are only a few. Most firm, hard vegetables do not take as well to these quick styles of cooking, as they need time over the fire to soften and release their flavors. That said, if winter squash is thinly sliced and you are attentive and patient, you can broil some lovely squash or sweet potato slices as sweet as dessert.

Marinades can (and should) be very simple. Their job is to enhance the vegetables' flavors, not overpower them. A bit of olive oil, vinegar, mustard, garlic, lemon juice, salt or soy sauce, pepper, rice syrup or honey and some herbs are all good choices. Combine ingredients that will support the character of the vegetables you will be cooking.

Pickling

This much-ignored style of preparing vegetables is very simple and yields delicious results. As a chef, I have always delighted in, and used extensively, marinated and pickled fruits and vegetables in my cooking. For me, it is a taste I acquired as a child. My mother would harvest her small vegetable garden at the end of summer, gather up her bounty and prepare pickled fruits and vegetables for use throughout the winter months—pickled tomatoes, peppers, cucumbers and cauliflower filled the jars that lined the shelves in our basement canning room, alongside the lush canned peaches, applesauce, tomato sauce and pickled melon for use in other winter dishes.

As I began my study of macrobiotic and vegetarian cooking, I began to realize that pickles are more than just delightfully tasty; they are also very beneficial to our health. Pickles are reputed to have originated thousands of years ago in the Far East, where ancient cultures developed pickling methods as a way to store vegetables without spoilage.

Pickled foods work as an aid to digesting our food. The fermentation that is part of the pickling process uses bacteria that change the natural sweetness of vegetables and fruits into lactic acid, an enzyme that aids in digestion, strengthening the stomach and intestines. Pickles are also rich sources of vitamins like B and C. Pickles can be simply and quickly prepared and should become an integral part of any healthy diet.

Sea Vegetables

I can almost hear you already. Seaweed? She really expects us to eat seaweed? Well, before you turn the page, let me dispel a few myths. Let's start by not calling it seaweed. I prefer "sea vegetables." "Weed" implies an unwanted plant that has no practical use; neither description applies here.

Since ancient times, sea vegetables have been prized by many cultures. In sixth-century China, sea vegetables were considered delicacies fit for the most honored guests. And in most traditional cultures, sea vegetables were prized for their medicinal value.

Throughout the South Pacific, sea vegetables have a long history of use. Hawaiian royalty cultivated over seventy varieties, while Maori soldiers sustained themselves on a type of nori during long marches through the arid deserts of the Middle East.

Northern and Western Europe also have a long recorded history as well. Ancient Celts and Vikings chewed on dulse during long trips, and nori or laver has been in use since ancient Rome. In fact, laverbread is still sold in markets today.

However, it is the Japanese, with their extensive coastline, who more than any other culture developed the culinary art of cooking sea vegetables. They have raised the art of preparation of sea plants to the highest form. In fact, sea vegetables are "farmed" almost as heavily as land vegetables.

The sea is the beginning of all life. For millions of years, land erosion has enriched the sea with a wealth of all the minerals necessary to support life. Sea plants contain between ten and twenty times the minerals of land vegetables, like calcium, iron, potassium, iodine and magnesium, not to mention the trace minerals so necessary for body functions. What this translates to for us is that we need to consume only small amounts of these nutrition-packed foods to benefit—generally about 5 percent of our daily food intake.

With the environment in the condition it is, just how safe is it to eat sea vegetables? Interestingly, sea plants do not absorb pollutants as fish do. Where pollution levels are high, sea plants simply do not grow. In fact, one of the characteristics of sea vegetables is their ability to remove radioactive and metallic poisons from the body. It seems that alginic acid, which sea vegetables contain in abundance, bind toxins in the body, allowing for easy elimination. High in vitamins A, B (except B_{12}), C, D, E and K, sea vegetables can help the body dissolve fat in and around various organ systems of the body. Sea plants contain chlorophyll, which aids in the production of hemoglobin, strengthening red blood cells.

Sea plants are among the oldest forms of life that exist. These simple foods reproduce by producing spores and have changed very little over hundreds of thousands of years of evolution. In spite of their simple nature, sea plants vary widely in species. Many, though not all, are edible, but there are several species that are commonly used in cooking today. We have at our disposal about twelve varieties varying widely in taste, texture and nutritional value.

Sea vegetables are usually sold packaged in dried form, making them ideal for long-term storage. Because they are dried, sea vegetables require brief soaking before preparation. They expand during soaking, so always soak less than you want to cook. Soaking times will vary with each sea vegetable: A rule of thumb is to simply soak them until they are tender; usually between five and ten minutes is sufficient. When they are tender, discard the soaking water and slice the sea vegetables into bite-size pieces for cooking.

Cooking sea vegetables is just like cooking other vegetables. Some may be eaten directly from the package; some require light cooking; and some need stronger cooking techniques, like sautéing or stewing. Seasoning is an important aspect of cooking sea vegetables. Coming from the ocean, they naturally have a mildly salty taste. As a result, seasoning should be delicate and light, so that the natural flavor of the vegetables comes through, not just salty taste.

In this section, I would like to simply introduce you to sea vegetables, with just a small sampling of the vast amount of recipes that exist. I'll introduce you to the most commonly used sea plants and describe some of the most basic cooking techniques that will result in delicious sea vegetable dishes for you to try.

Baked Brussels Sprouts and Shallots

This crowd-pleaser is succulent, so make a good bit of it. They will come back for seconds every time. A rich and tasty dish like this warms the body and makes us feel nourished and satisfied.

MAKES 4 OR 5 SERVINGS

2 to 3 cups fresh Brussels sprouts, trimmed and left whole
3 or 4 shallots, halved
2 or 3 cloves fresh garlic, finely minced
Sea salt
2 tablespoons extra-virgin olive oil
2 tablespoons balsamic vinegar

Preheat oven to 375F (190C). Cut a shallow cross in the base of each Brussels sprout; this promotes thorough cooking. In a casserole, arrange Brussels sprouts and shallots, avoiding overlap. Sprinkle generously with garlic. Drizzle lightly with sea salt, olive oil and balsamic vinegar. Toss to coat the vegetables. The goal is to cook the vegetables in their own juices, causing them to contract, reduce and secrete their own sweet tastes.

Cover the casserole and bake 45 to 50 minutes. Remove the cover and bake until vegetables lightly brown and any liquid reduces to a thick syrup. Toss gently before serving.

Brussels Sprouts with Ginger-Plum Sauce

A simple yet elegant glazed stew that makes a lovely side dish. Very pretty when complete, it is a unique addition to a holiday meal, but you won't want to restrict yourself to once a year with this one.

MAKES 4 TO 6 SERVINGS

4 to 5 cups fresh Brussels sprouts, trimmed and left whole
1 or 2 red onions, cut into thick wedges
Soy sauce
1 cup spring or filtered water
2 to 3 teaspoons fresh ginger juice (see Note, page 164)
2 teaspoons kuzu or arrowroot, dissolved in 1 tablespoon cold water
2 teaspoons umeboshi or red wine vinegar
2 tablespoons unsweetened plum preserves

Cut a shallow cross in the base of each Brussels sprout. Layer onion and then the sprouts in a heavy pot. Sprinkle lightly with soy sauce. Add water, cover and bring to a slow boil, not a rolling boil, over medium–low heat. Simmer 25 to 30 minutes. Season to taste with soy sauce and add ginger juice. Simmer 5 to 7 minutes. Gently stir in dissolved kuzu and cook, stirring without breaking vegetables, until a thin glaze forms over the vegetables, about 3 minutes. Meanwhile, whisk together vinegar and preserves to loosen. Remove from heat and stir in preserve mixture to coat. Transfer to a bowl and serve warm.

Colorful Homestyle Hashbrowns

Once again, my hard-core macrobiotic readers may need to take a breath when they see me using potatoes, a member of the nightshade family. Some believe that potatoes should not be included in healthy cooking. I am of the belief that one should eat a wide variety of vegetables, so on occasion, have a party and enjoy a potato!

MAKES 4 OR 5 SERVINGS

2 to 3 tablespoons extra-virgin olive oil
1 small red onion, cut into thin half-moon slices
Sea salt
6 or 7 potatoes, preferably a mix of purple, red and Yukon Gold
3 sprigs basil, leaves removed and finely shredded
Cracked black pepper
2 or 3 sprigs flat-leaf parsley, coarsely chopped
Juice of ¼ lemon

Place oil and onion in a deep skillet over medium heat. When the onion begins to sizzle, add a pinch of salt and sauté 2 to 3 minutes.

While the onion sweats, scrub the potatoes; do not peel. Cut into ½-inch cubes. Stir the potatoes into the onion and reduce the heat to low. Fry the potatoes, stirring frequently, until they are crisp on the outside and soft on the inside, 30 to 35 minutes. Stir in shredded basil and salt and pepper to taste. Cook 5 minutes more. Remove from heat, stir in parsley and lemon juice and serve hot.

You Won't Believe It's Not Mashed Potatoes

We all love mashed potatoes (except me; I love them roasted in the oven with olive oil, but I digress . . .), but we hate the calories, refined carbs and fat that come with this ultimate comfort food. Not anymore!

MAKES 3 OR 4 SERVINGS

1 head cauliflower, broken into florets
⅛ cup unsweetened soymilk
3 tablespoons vegetarian buttery spread (like Earth Balance)
Sea salt
Cracked black pepper
Small bunch chives, finely minced

Place cauliflower in a steamer basket above a pot of boiling water. Cook, covered, until fork-tender, about 12 minutes.

Preheat oven to 325F (165C). Lightly oil a 9-inch baking dish and set aside. Transfer cauliflower to a food processor or blender. Add soymilk, the spread and salt and pepper to taste and puree until smooth. Spoon into prepared baking dish and bake, uncovered, about 8 minutes, until bubbly. Fold in chives and serve hot.

Splendid Spanakopita

I love Middle Eastern foods and once I got past my fear of working with phyllo, a whole new culinary world opened up. Trust me, it's just dough, really delicate dough, but worth mastering. And you will love this recipe . . . different, delicious and easy.

MAKES ABOUT 20 SPANAKOPITA

2 tablespoons extra-virgin olive oil, plus extra for brushing
½ small red onion, finely diced
2 cloves fresh garlic, finely minced
Sea salt
15 to 20 cremini mushrooms, brushed free of dirt and coarsely chopped
Scant pinch ground nutmeg
2 sprigs basil, leaves removed and finely shredded
4 cups arugula, rinsed well and coarsely chopped
4 cups Tofu Cheese (page 118), coarsely crumbled
1 (1-pound) package phyllo pastry sheets, thawed in the refrigerator for several hours before use (see Note, page 176)
About 2 cups ground almond meal or whole wheat bread crumbs

Place oil, onion and garlic in a skillet over medium heat. When the onion begins to sizzle, add a pinch of salt and sauté 2 minutes. Stir in mushrooms, a pinch of salt and nutmeg and sauté until mushrooms begin to brown, about 7 minutes. Turn off heat, stir in basil, arugula and Tofu Cheese and season lightly with salt. Transfer to a bowl to cool and set aside.

Preheat oven to 350F (175C) and line a baking sheet with parchment paper.

On a dry, flat work surface, remove the sheets of phyllo, cut them in half lengthwise and lay them flat. Cover the phyllo with a damp towel while you work (so it doesn't stiffen). Using a half sheet at a time, brush phyllo lightly with oil and sprinkle with ground almonds. Lay another half sheet on top, brush with oil and sprinkle with almonds. Lay a third half sheet on top and brush with oil. Place about ¼ cup of the arugula mixture in one corner of the phyllo layers, fold the other corner over the mixture, forming an angular shape. Continue to fold over on an angle, creating a pastry triangle around the arugula. Place on lined baking sheet and repeat until all the filling is used. Brush each triangle lightly with oil and bake until golden brown and crispy, about 20 minutes. Serve hot or at room temperature.

■ **NOTE** Any unused phyllo can be tightly wrapped and kept in the refrigerator for future use. It will keep for several weeks. Do not refreeze.

Guacamole

My husband makes the best guacamole I have ever tasted, truly. Until I was persuaded to taste his version, I was not a big fan, but now I can't get enough. I decided to share it so when you all invite me over, you can make a "guac" I will love! This is the only dish he makes that includes cilantro, one of my favorites.

MAKES 3 OR 4 SERVINGS

2 ripe avocados, halved and seed removed
½ red onion, finely minced
2 serrano chiles, seeded, ribs removed and finely minced
2 tablespoons finely minced fresh cilantro
¼ cup fresh or frozen corn kernels
1 to 2 tablespoons fresh lemon juice
Sea salt
Cracked black pepper
½ ripe tomato, seeded and coarsely chopped

Scoop avocados into a bowl. Using a fork, mash the avocados until smooth. Fold in onion, chiles, cilantro, corn and lemon juice. Mix in salt and pepper to taste. Gently fold in tomato. Chill for at least 1 hour before serving to allow flavors to develop.

Snap Peas with Marinated Mushrooms

Simple, elegant, healthy, delicious, nutrient-rich and designed to relax tension in the shoulders and legs. See? There's more to veggies than meets the eye.

MAKES 4 OR 5 SERVINGS

½ cup extra-virgin olive oil
2 to 3 tablespoons red wine vinegar
1 teaspoon brown rice syrup
1 teaspoon sea salt
½ teaspoon cracked black pepper
4 ounces cremini mushrooms, thinly sliced
1 ounce dried shiitake mushrooms, soaked until soft, thinly sliced
8 ounces sugar snap peas, ends and strings removed, left whole
2 sprigs basil, leaves removed and shredded

Make the marinade for the mushrooms. In a saucepan, combine oil, vinegar, rice syrup, salt and pepper over low heat and cook, stirring, until warmed through, about 3 minutes. Turn off heat and stir in mushrooms. Set aside to marinate for 35 minutes.

Bring a pot of lightly salted water to a boil. Cook snap peas about 2 minutes. Drain well and rinse under cold water to stop cooking.

Make the salad by draining mushrooms, reserving marinade. Toss mushrooms with snap peas and basil. Stir in enough marinade to coat. Serve immediately.

Stuffed Zucchini, Sicilian Style

On my first trip to Sicily, we visited my husband's Aunt Pina. Sicily was magical in every way . . . but the food and the wine were out of sight. And we never ate a meal outside the house! Robert's aunts cooked and cooked and we ate and ate. This was my favorite of the recipes Auntie Pina taught me.

MAKES 4 SERVINGS

2 large zucchini, split lengthwise, flesh scooped out, mashed and reserved
Extra-virgin olive oil
2 cloves fresh garlic, finely minced
1 onion, small dice
Sea salt
Small pinch crushed red pepper flakes
2 stalks celery, cut into small dice
½ cup diced vegan mozzarella cheese alternative
Whole wheat bread crumbs
2 cups Tomato Sauce (page 205)

Preheat oven to 375F (190C). Lightly oil a shallow baking dish that will accommodate the zucchini halves laying side by side and set aside.

Place a small amount of oil, the garlic and onion in a small skillet over medium heat. When the onion begins to sizzle, add a pinch of salt and red pepper flakes and sauté 3 to 4 minutes. In another skillet, place a small amount of oil, celery and mashed zucchini flesh over medium heat. When the vegetables begin to sizzle, add a pinch of salt and sauté about 2 minutes. Stir in sautéed onion and garlic, season to taste and stir to combine. Remove from heat and stir in cheese alternative. Fold in enough bread crumbs to hold the mixture together as a stuffing (as little as ½ cup to as much as 1 cup).

Lay the zucchini halves, cut sides up, in the baking dish. Spoon filling abundantly into each half. Spoon tomato sauce generously over top the stuffed zucchini and bake uncovered until the filling is set, about 30 minutes. Serve hot.

Stir-Fried Veggies with Black Bean Sauce

A simple dish when time is short and you need to get something that looks like dinner on the table fast. Rich, spicy and veggie loaded, serve this dish over brown rice and you have the perfect dinner.

MAKES 4 OR 5 SERVINGS

BLACK BEAN SAUCE
2 tablespoons extra-virgin olive oil
4 tablespoons cooked black turtle beans, mashed with a fork
1 clove fresh garlic, minced
Generous pinch crushed red pepper flakes
½ cup white wine
1 tablespoon soy sauce
2 tablespoons brown rice syrup
2 teaspoons arrowroot

Extra-virgin olive oil
½ red onion, cut into thin half-moon slices
2 cloves fresh garlic, thinly sliced
Sea salt
1 carrot, cut into thin matchstick pieces
1 red bell pepper, roasted over a flame, peeled, seeded and diced (see Note, page 262)
2 small zucchini, cut into thin matchstick pieces
2 yellow summer squash, cut into thin matchstick pieces
6 fresh shiitake mushrooms, stems removed and caps thinly sliced
1 small bunch dark leafy greens (kale, collards, bok choy or a mix), shredded
3 fresh green onions, thinly sliced on the diagonal
3 sprigs basil, leaves shredded

Make the sauce: Heat a wok or heavy skillet over medium-high heat. Add oil, beans, garlic and red pepper flakes and stir-fry 2 minutes. Reduce heat to low and add wine, soy sauce and rice syrup. Cook, stirring, until the mixture heats through. Stir in arrowroot and cook, stirring, until mixture thickens. Set aside.

Heat a wok over medium heat. Add oil, onion, garlic and a pinch of salt and stir-fry 1 minute. Stir in carrot, bell pepper and a pinch of salt and stir-fry 1 minute. Stir in zucchini, yellow squash and a pinch of salt and stir-fry 1 minute. Stir in shiitake mushrooms and a pinch of salt and stir-fry 1 minute. Finally, stir in greens, sprinkle with water (use your fingertips) and stir-fry until greens are bright green and just wilted. Stir in Black Bean Sauce, green onions and basil and stir-fry until the sauce is blended through the vegetables. Transfer to a serving platter and serve immediately.

Veggie Margarita with Fried Chips

I adapted this recipe from a dish I saw being served in Belize. The table next to ours was *eating* their margaritas and having a blast doing it. After a little visit with the chef, I had the recipe . . . a little adapting and I had my version of this tropical party food, without the tequila, but with all of the flavor.

MAKES 2 TO 3 SERVINGS

1 ripe tomato, seeded and cut into small dice
1 small ripe, but firm avocado, seeded, peeled
    and cut into small dice
½ red onion, cut into small dice
Sea salt
Cracked black pepper
3 or 4 sprigs cilantro, finely minced
Fresh lime juice

TORTILLA CHIPS
Avocado oil
4 to 6 soft corn tortillas, sliced into triangles
Sea salt

Place tomato, avocado and onion in separate bowls. Season each to taste with salt and pepper and toss to coat.

Take a margarita glass and layer tomato, cilantro, then avocado, cilantro, then onion, with cilantro on top. Gently pour lime juice (or tequila) over the ingredients, up to the onion. Do not float the ingredients. Set aside to marinate while you fry the chips.

Fry chips: Heat about 3 inches of oil in a wok over medium heat. When oil is hot (you will know because patterns will form at the bottom of pan), fry tortilla pieces in batches until crisp and golden. Drain on paper towels and toss with salt while the chips are hot so the salt sticks.

To serve, set the "margarita" on a plate with chips around the rim.

Whole Stewed Stuffed Artichokes

Artichokes are, hands down, my favorite vegetable. They are sensual, delicious and satisfying like no other. They take me back to my childhood, when my mother cooked them and I ate them with my grandfather. The fact that they're also a rich source of antioxidants is just icing on the cake.

MAKES 4 MAIN-COURSE SERVINGS

2 lemons, halved
4 large artichokes
1 ripe tomato, seeded, fine dice
4 or 5 sprigs parsley, finely minced
2 cloves fresh garlic, finely minced
Sea salt
3 tablespoons extra-virgin olive oil
Dry white wine or spring or filtered water

Squeeze juice of 1 lemon into a large bowl of water, adding lemon halves to the water. Prepare the artichoke by pulling the outer base leaves back until they snap off. Using kitchen scissors, trim the sharp tips of the leaves off the artichoke. Slice off the top third of the artichoke. Using a spoon, scoop out the fibrous choke. Place each artichoke in the lemon water as it is prepared to prevent discoloring.

Combine tomato, parsley and garlic in a small bowl and season to taste with salt. Mix well. Spoon some tomato mixture into each artichoke center.

Stand the artichokes on their bases in a soup pot. Drizzle with olive oil. Pour enough wine or water into the pot to cover one-third of the artichokes. Sprinkle wine lightly with salt. Cover and bring to a boil. Reduce heat to low and cook until the artichokes are tender, about 35 minutes to 1 hour (depending on the size of the artichokes). Transfer to a serving platter and serve hot.

Okra and Edamame with Fingerling Potatoes

I am not a fan of okra . . . the texture is just not high on my list. My husband loves it; I mean, *loves* it. And since I love him, I had to figure out a way to cook okra that he would love and I could live with.

MAKES ABOUT 4 SERVINGS

8 to 10 small fingerling potatoes, unpeeled, halved lengthwise
4 or 5 green onions, thinly sliced on long diagonals
2 large rosemary sprigs, leaves stripped off stems
¼ cup extra-virgin olive oil
Sea salt
Cracked black pepper
6 to 8 (3-inch) okra pods
1 cup shelled edamame
1 cup fresh or frozen corn kernels
Juice of ½ lemon
1 small shallot, finely minced

Preheat oven to 450F (230C). Place potatoes, green onions, rosemary, 2 tablespoons of the oil and a light sprinkle of salt and pepper in a mixing bowl and toss to coat. Transfer to a rimmed baking pan and spread veggies so there is no overlap. Cook, uncovered, 20 minutes. Add okra to roasting pan, mix well to coat

with oil and return to oven to roast about 30 minutes, until okra and potatoes are tender.

While potatoes cook, bring a pot of water to a boil. Add edamame and cook 2 minutes. Remove with a slotted spoon and place in a small bowl. Add a pinch of salt to the water and cook corn 4 minutes. Drain and add to edamame.

Whisk together the remaining oil, lemon juice, shallots and salt and pepper to taste to make a dressing.

Remove vegetables from the oven and toss with corn and edamame and dressing to coat. Transfer to a serving platter and serve warm.

Ratatouille

This classic Mediterranean oven stew is one of my favorites to make when the veggies are in full season . . . summer! I know it means lighting the oven on a hot day, but when you sit down to this glorious, sensual stew, laden with the succulent flavors of the season, you'll thank yourself for the effort.

MAKES ABOUT 4 SERVINGS

3 tablespoons extra-virgin olive oil
3 cloves fresh garlic, finely minced
2 teaspoons dried basil
1 eggplant, cut into ½-inch cubes, soaked in salted water 1 hour and drained well
Sea salt
1 cup extra-firm tofu, finely crumbled
2 teaspoons white miso
2 zucchini, thinly sliced on the diagonal
1 large red onion, sliced into thin rings
2 cups thinly sliced cremini mushrooms
1 red bell pepper, roasted over a flame, peeled, seeded and thinly sliced (see Note, page 262)
2 large, ripe tomatoes, coarsely chopped

Preheat oven to 350F (175C). Oil a 2-quart casserole with 1 tablespoon of the oil and set aside.

Place remaining oil, garlic and basil in a skillet over medium heat. Sauté garlic until lightly browned. Stir in eggplant. Sauté until eggplant is soft, about 10 minutes. Season lightly with salt and sauté 1 minute.

Spread eggplant evenly over the bottom of prepared casserole. Mix crumbled tofu and miso together. Sprinkle a few tablespoons of the tofu mixture over the eggplant. Layer zucchini over the tofu. Sprinkle with a few tablespoons of the tofu mixture. Continue layering in this fashion: onion, tofu mixture, mushrooms, tofu mixture, bell pepper, tofu and finally top with tomatoes.

Bake, uncovered, 45 minutes. Remove from oven and allow to stand 10 minutes before serving.

Portobello Burgers

Burgers, schmurgers! Who needs the saturated fat, cholesterol and heart disease that come with burgers when you can enjoy the same "meaty" texture with this satisfying version of a burger.

MAKES 6 BURGERS

CARAMELIZED ONION TOPPING
Extra-virgin olive oil
2 or 3 cloves fresh garlic, thinly sliced
5 or 6 red onions, thin half moon slices
Sea salt
Mirin or white wine
Generous pinch crushed red pepper flakes
Juice of 1/2 lemon

2 to 3 tablespoons extra-virgin olive oil or
** avocado oil, plus extra for brushing**

1 tablespoon balsamic vinegar
Generous pinch crushed red pepper flakes
Sea salt
6 portobello mushrooms, stems removed,
** gills intact, brushed free of dirt**
6 whole grain burger buns
Ketchup (optional)
Mustard (optional)
6 leaves fresh romaine lettuce
1 to 2 ripe tomatoes, sliced into rings
6 to 8 tablespoons alfalfa sprouts

Make onion topping: Place a small amount of oil, the garlic and onions in a deep skillet over medium heat. When onions begin to sizzle, add a pinch of salt, a generous dash of mirin and red pepper flakes and sauté 3 to 4 minutes. Season lightly with salt and cook, stirring frequently until onions begin to caramelize, as long as 25 minutes. Remove from heat, stir in lemon juice and set aside.

Preheat the grill to hot or warm a lightly oiled grill pan over medium heat. Whisk together olive oil, vinegar, red pepper flakes and a generous pinch of salt. Rub each mushroom thoroughly with the oil mixture and grill on both sides until tender and lightly browned, 5 to 6 minutes each side.

To assemble the burgers, brush one side of each slice of the rolls lightly with oil and grill, oil-side down, until lightly browned, about 2 minutes. Lay the bread slices, grilled side up, on a dry work surface. Spread ketchup and mustard (if using) on each cut side. Lay a lettuce leaf and tomato slice on 6 halves of the rolls. Lay a whole portobello mushroom on top of the lettuce. Mound onion topping on each mushroom and top with sprouts. Place tops of buns on top and serve.

French Fries

I know what you're thinking? French fries, really? Really . . . okay, they're not fried, but they are just as delicious and satisfying, and if you can have all that without all the fat of frying, won't life be great?

MAKES 3 OR 4 SERVINGS

2 Yukon Gold potatoes, peeled
Extra-virgin olive oil
Sea salt

Preheat oven to 450F (225C).

Slice potatoes lengthwise into ½-inch-thick slices. Cut the slices into ½-inch-thick spears (like French fries). Toss them with a generous amount of olive oil to coat the potato pieces. Spread in a rimmed baking sheet, avoiding overlap and bake, uncovered, about 35 minutes, until browned and crisp, stirring occasionally to ensure even browning.

Remove from oven and toss with a light seasoning of salt. Serve immediately.

■ **NOTE** For even healthier fries, substitute sweet potatoes for Yukon Gold potatoes. You increase your intake of antioxidants and carotenoids.

Roasted Squash and Mushrooms

I love the simplicity of this dish. It's so easy, you'll be all smiles as you serve it. And I love the energy of this dish; it relaxes and tones the middle organs. Easy and relaxing . . . sounds like the perfect side dish to me.

MAKES ABOUT 4 SERVINGS

6 tablespoons extra-virgin olive oil
1 teaspoon sea salt
4 cups cubed unpeeled delicata or butternut squash
4 cups mixed mushrooms (cremini, shiitake, oyster), stemmed, halved
Juice of ½ fresh lemon

Preheat oven to 425F (220C). Place oil, salt, squash and mushrooms in a mixing bowl and toss to coat. Spread in a rimmed baking sheet, avoiding overlap. Bake, uncovered, 25 to 35 minutes, until vegetables are tender and liquid from mushrooms has evaporated. Remove from oven and drizzle with lemon juice. Serve hot.

Zucchini Fettuccine with Marinara

A foray into raw cuisine; kind of cool, really. This is the perfect summer entrée . . . whether you embrace raw foods or not.

MAKES 4 OR 5 SERVINGS

1 to 2 pounds plum tomatoes, quartered
1 cup packed fresh basil leaves, plus sprigs for garnish
½ cup dry-packed, sun-dried tomatoes, softened in warm water and chopped
4 tablespoons extra-virgin olive oil
1 teaspoon brown rice syrup
1 shallot, minced
Sea salt
Cracked black pepper
3 zucchini, ends trimmed

1 summer squash, ends trimmed

1 red or orange bell pepper, halved and
seeded

8 ounces vegan mozzarella cheese
alternative, grated

1 cup coarsely chopped hazelnuts

Place tomatoes, basil, sun-dried tomatoes, 3 tablespoons of the oil, rice syrup, shallot and salt and pepper to taste in a food processor and process until mixture resembles a fine salsa.

Using a sharp vegetable peeler, pare zucchini and summer squash on all sides, creating thin ribbons. Discard soft, seeded centers.

Using a sharp knife, slice bell pepper into very thin strips.

Combine squash, zucchini and bell pepper in a mixing bowl. Stir in tomato mixture and adjust seasonings to your taste. Fold in cheese alternative and hazelnuts and stir gently to combine ingredients. Serve garnished with basil sprigs.

Glazed Carrots

This sweet, sticky carrot dish is delicious served as a side dish, especially when the rest of your meal is simple and you'd like to add a little zip to it.

MAKES 4 SERVINGS

Sea salt

2 carrots, cut into small irregular pieces

1 (3-inch) piece kombu, soaked until tender
and sliced thinly

½ teaspoon light sesame oil

2 tablespoons barley malt

2 tablespoons brown rice syrup

Slivered almonds, lightly pan-toasted (see
Note, page 55), for garnish

Bring a large pot of water to a boil with a pinch of sea salt. Add carrots and cook until just tender, about 5 minutes. Remove with a strainer and cook kombu pieces in the same water 5 to 7 minutes. Drain and toss with carrots. Set aside while preparing the glaze.

Bring oil, barley malt, rice syrup and a generous pinch of salt to a boil in a small saucepan over medium heat, cooking until foamy. Stir glaze into carrots and kombu until well coated. Transfer to a serving bowl and garnish generously with almonds.

Savory Roasted Vegetables

This incredibly delicious dish is so simple to make, yet you will be asked for the recipe time and again. Its rich, satisfying taste is balanced nicely with the tang of reduced balsamic vinegar. The combination of vegetables offered here is but one option. Any firm, hearty vegetables will serve nicely, so let your taste guide you.

MAKES 4 TO 6 SERVINGS

1 bay leaf

2 cups button mushrooms, brushed clean and
left whole

2 cups small Brussels sprouts, trimmed and
left whole

2 parsnips, cut into large, irregular chunks

2 leeks, rinsed well and cut into 2-inch pieces

2 cups 1-inch daikon chunks

Soy sauce

Extra-virgin olive oil

Reduced balsamic vinegar (see Note, page
160)

2 teaspoons fresh lemon juice

Preheat oven to 375F (190C). Place bay leaf on the bottom of a shallow baking dish to help tenderize and sweeten the vegetables. Arrange the vegetable pieces on top, avoiding overlap and sprinkle lightly with soy sauce and oil, coating the veggies well. Cover the baking dish and bake about 1 hour, until vegetables are tender. Remove the cover, stir in a light sprinkling of reduced balsamic vinegar and return dish to oven to lightly brown the vegetables and turn any remaining liquid into a syrup. Toss gently with lemon juice and remove bay leaf before serving.

■ **NOTE** To reduce balsamic vinegar, place 1 cup balsamic vinegar in a nonreactive saucepan. Simmer, uncovered, over low heat until volume is reduced to ½ cup. Store, refrigerated, in a tightly sealed glass jar.

The flavor of the vinegar becomes very sweet and concentrated when reduced, so a small amount will go a long way. For instance, a full casserole that will feed 4 people will need only about 2 to 3 tablespoons of reduced vinegar to achieve the full-bodied flavor you are looking for.

Spicy Daikon and Kombu

A spicy-hot side dish that not only is delicious but aids in digestion and helps get stagnant energy moving. Great for kick-starting weight loss and improving your assimilation of food.

MAKES ABOUT 4 SERVINGS

1 (3-inch) piece kombu, soaked until tender and thinly sliced
2 cups ¼-inch rounds daikon
Generous pinch chili powder or shi-chi-mi (an Asian hot pepper condiment)

Spring or filtered water
2 cups packed bitter leafy green vegetables, like mustard greens or watercress, diced
Soy sauce
Juice of 1 orange

Place kombu pieces on the bottom of a deep skillet. Arrange daikon on top. Sprinkle with chili powder and add a small amount of water to just cover bottom of pan. Cover and bring to a boil. Reduce heat and simmer until daikon is just tender, about 5 minutes. Add greens to pan, season very lightly with soy sauce, re-cover and steam until the greens are bright green, about 2 minutes. Remove vegetables from skillet and transfer to a serving bowl. Drizzle with orange juice and toss to mix ingredients.

Watercress with Tangy Tangerine Dressing

This "light as a spring breeze" salad is a wonderful dish to add a bit of freshness to a hearty meal or to simply cool off in hot weather. To keep the dressing on the sweet side, you need more tangerine juice than lemon juice.

MAKES 2 TO 3 SERVINGS

1 bunch fresh watercress, rinsed well and hand shredded
⅔ cup pecan halves, lightly pan-toasted (see Note, page 46)

TANGY TANGERINE DRESSING
Juice from 3 tangerines
Juice of 1 lemon
Pinch sea salt
Pinch cracked black pepper

Generous dash red wine vinegar
¼ cup extra-virgin olive oil

Shred watercress in a medium salad bowl. Add pecans.

Make the dressing: Whisk together all ingredients until combined. Chill watercress and dressing separately, tossing together just before serving.

Vegetable Crepes

Nothing is quite so elegant to serve at a brunch or a light supper as crepes. Impressive to guests and intimidating to most cooks, crepes are a spectacular dish. In reality, they are very easy to make—just give yourself a little practice time to get the hang of them and they will become a standard in your cooking repertoire.

MAKES 4 TO 6 SERVINGS

CREPES
2 cups whole wheat pastry flour, sifted
Pinch sea salt
About 2 cups spring or filtered water

FILLING
1 tablespoon avocado or olive oil
1 onion, finely diced
Sea salt
2 cups button mushrooms, brushed clean and
    thinly sliced
¼ cup white wine
1 to 2 carrots, cut into small dice
2 cups finely shredded cabbage
1 cup thin matchstick pieces yellow summer
    squash

Avocado oil, for cooking crepes
Creamy Mushroom Sauce (page 274),

Roasted Pepper Sauce (page 277),
Parsleyed Nut Sauce (page 276) or other
sauce

Make crepe batter: Sift flour and salt together. Slowly stir in cold water to form a batter similar to pancake batter—thin but not watery. Whisk the batter very well to incorporate air into the crepes to ensure the lightness of the finished product. Set batter aside 15 minutes before proceeding.

Prepare filling while batter rests: Heat oil in a skillet over medium heat. Add onion and a pinch of salt and cook, stirring, until onion is wilted, about 3 minutes. Add mushrooms and a pinch of salt and cook, stirring, until soft, about 5 minutes. Add wine and cook, stirring, until mushrooms absorb liquid. Stir in carrots, cabbage and a pinch of salt and cook, stirring, until cabbage begins to wilt, 5 to 7 minutes. Add yellow squash, season to taste with salt and cook, stirring, until vegetables are soft, 2 to 3 minutes. If any liquid has accumulated in the skillet, simmer until completely absorbed. Transfer filling mixture to a bowl and set aside to cool while cooking the crepes.

Lightly oil a 6- to 8-inch skillet or crepe pan over medium heat. Pour in about ¼ cup of batter and quickly turn the skillet in a circular motion, evenly distributing the batter over the bottom. The crepe should be on the thin side, so adjust the amount of batter as needed. As soon as bubbles appear on the surface of the crepe and it begins to pull away from the pan, turn the finished crepe out of the pan onto a tea towel or parchment paper to cool. Cover with a dampened towel to keep the crepes moist. Do not let the crepes get too cold and stiff before assembling (but if that happens, steam them before proceeding).

Assemble crepes: Place a hearty spoonful of filling on the side of the crepe closest to you.

Roll, jelly-roll style, to form a cylinder, with the closing edge underneath the crepe to hold it closed. Arrange crepes on a platter and serve with a sauce either pooled under each crepe or lightly spooned on top.

Green Beans Vinaigrette

A classic vegetable dish prepared in a deliciously healthful way. Adjust the ingredient amounts in the vinaigrette to achieve the taste you like best. The amounts here are only guidelines to give you a starting point.

MAKES 5 OR 6 SERVINGS

1 pound green beans
Spring or filtered water

VINAIGRETTE
1 tablespoon extra-virgin olive oil
2 cloves fresh garlic, thinly sliced
Juice of 1 lemon
2 to 3 tablespoons prepared stone-ground
   mustard
Sea salt
1 tablespoon brown rice vinegar
1 tablespoon umeboshi vinegar
1 tablespoon brown rice syrup
Generous pinch dried rosemary

Slivered almonds, lightly pan-toasted (see
   Note, page 55), for garnish

Remove bean tips and thinly slice beans on the diagonal, making long, thin slivers. Bring water to a boil in a pot. Add beans and cook until tender and bright green, about 3 minutes. Do not overcook or the dressing will make the beans limp and mushy.

Drain beans and set aside to cool.

Prepare the vinaigrette: Heat olive oil in a small skillet over medium heat. Add garlic and cook until brown, about 3 minutes. Skim garlic from oil and discard. Whisk together lemon juice, mustard, salt to taste, vinegars, rice syrup, rosemary to taste and the garlic-flavored oil. Whisk until well emulsified.

Toss the dressing with the cooked beans and serve warm or chilled, garnished with almonds.

Stuffed Lotus Root

A unique-looking vegetable, with a potatolike taste, lotus root comes equipped with many tubelike chambers ideal for stuffing. Famous in the Far East for its restorative effect on the lungs, lotus root can be used in many ways, but none quite so unique— or as tasty—as this.

MAKES 5 OR 6 SERVINGS

1 large lotus root, cleaned and tips removed
   from either end, exposing tubes
Spring or filtered water
Pinch sea salt

FILLING
2 tablespoons almond butter
2 tablespoons barley miso
Spring or filtered water

Place whole lotus root in a pressure cooker with about ½ inch of water and a pinch of salt. Seal and bring to full pressure. Reduce heat and cook over low heat 7 minutes. Remove from heat and force pressure down according to manufacturer's directions. Remove lotus root to prevent overcooking and set aside to cool while preparing the filling.

To make filling: Mix together almond butter and miso with enough water to create a thick, creamy paste. When the lotus is cool enough to handle, press one end into the filling and turn. Continue pressing and turning while the filling travels upward, eventually filling the tubes completely. When all the chambers are filled, slice the lotus root into thin rounds and serve.

■ **VARIATION** To add a real party flair to this dish, quickly deep-fry the stuffed lotus slices before serving.

Sweet Chinese Cabbage

Pressure-cook a tender Chinese cabbage? Before you have me committed for insanity, hear me out. Quickly pressure-cooking the whole cabbage head brings out its delicate sweetness and creates a warm, strengthening energy without the dish becoming heavy. Try it and see. This dish is so sweet and delicate in taste that no dressings or garnishes are necessary, although some toasted black sesame seeds would be a nice touch.

MAKES 4 TO 6 SERVINGS

1 head Chinese cabbage
Spring or filtered water
Sea salt

Rinse cabbage and leave whole. Do not drain it after rinsing. Place cabbage in a pressure cooker and add ½ inch of water and several pinches of salt. Seal the lid and bring to full pressure. Reduce heat and cook over low heat 5 minutes. Remove from heat and allow pressure to reduce naturally. Remove cabbage and slice into bite-size pieces.

Red and Green Cabbage Medley

This marinated, savory cabbage is a delicious side dish, rounding out any hearty autumn or winter meal. And it is gorgeous!

MAKES 4 TO 6 SERVINGS

2 cups 1-inch pieces green cabbage
2 cups 1-inch pieces red cabbage
Spring or filtered water

MARINADE
3 tablespoons extra-virgin olive oil
3 tablespoons sweet white miso, dissolved in
**   ¼ cup water**
1 tablespoon brown rice syrup
1 tablespoon brown rice vinegar
1 tablespoon umeboshi vinegar

Place each cabbage in its own section in a deep skillet. Add ¼ inch of water and simmer over low heat 4 to 5 minutes, until wilted and just tender. Drain cabbage and transfer to a bowl, mixing well to combine the colors.

Make marinade: Warm oil, dissolved miso and rice syrup in a small saucepan over low heat. Remove pan from heat and stir in vinegars. Toss with hot cabbage and allow to stand 30 minutes before serving. Toss well just prior to serving.

Hearty Sautéed Greens with Ginger

A different take on leafy greens, the pungent, hot taste of ginger makes this a side dish with a kick.

MAKES 3 OR 4 SERVINGS

2 teaspoons avocado oil
6 or 7 slices fresh ginger, cut into fine
     matchsticks
1 bunch leafy greens (kale or collards),
     cleaned and finely sliced
Soy sauce
1 to 2 teaspoons fresh ginger juice (see Note,
     below) (optional)
Dark sesame oil, for finishing

Heat oil in a deep skillet over medium heat. Add ginger and cook 1 to 2 minutes. Add greens and sprinkle lightly with soy sauce. Cook until bright green and tender, but not mushy, 2 to 3 minutes. If a more intense ginger taste is desired, add a small amount of ginger juice at the end of cooking. Transfer to a serving bowl, drizzle lightly with sesame oil to taste and serve immediately.

■ **NOTE** Ginger juice is obtained by finely grating fresh ginger and squeezing the juice from the pulp.

Watercress and Summer Vegetables

This light, colorful summer side dish showcases the peppery taste of watercress against a background of bright, fresh seasonal vegetables. Mixing cooked and raw veggies is not only a wonderful eating experience, but keeps the energy of the dish light and fresh.

MAKES 3 OR 4 SERVINGS

1 to 2 yellow summer squash, cut into thin
     matchsticks
1 to 2 cups fresh corn kernels
4 to 5 red radishes, thinly sliced
1 bunch watercress, rinsed well and hand
     shredded
1 red bell pepper, roasted over a flame,
     peeled, seeded and cut into thin strips (see
     Note, page 262)
Generous pinch sea salt
Generous pinch cracked black pepper
Juice of 1 lemon
3 tablespoons balsamic vinegar
¼ cup extra-virgin olive oil

Bring a pot of water to a boil and separately blanch the summer squash and corn until tender, about 1 minute each. Toss cooked vegetables with radishes, watercress and bell pepper. Season with salt and black pepper. Whisk together lemon juice, vinegar and oil until emulsified. Lightly dress the vegetables just before serving.

Mochi-Stuffed Chinese Cabbage

Soft, creamy and oh, so satisfying, this delicious breakfast dish will help keep you warm on chilly winter mornings.

MAKES 4 OR 5 SERVINGS

4 ounces brown rice mochi, cut into 4 or 5
     (3 × 2 × ½-inch) pieces

4 or 5 large Chinese cabbage leaves, rinsed
and left whole
Spring or filtered water
Sea salt or soy sauce

Wrap a piece of mochi in each cabbage leaf
and arrange, tightly packed, in a skillet. Pour
in ½ inch of water and add a generous pinch
of salt or a little soy sauce. Cover and cook
over medium-low heat until mochi has
melted slightly and cabbage is tender, about 7
minutes. Arrange on a serving platter and
serve immediately.

■ **VARIATION** If any cooking liquid remains,
you can turn it into a delicious sauce by stirring in a small amount of dissolved kuzu or
arrowroot and cooking until the sauce
thickens into a glaze. Spoon over stuffed
cabbage and serve.

Marinated Lotus Root

A quick and delicious pickle that you can prepare
with very little effort. The slightly sweet taste of
mirin makes this a real winner.

MAKES ABOUT 2 SERVINGS

4 or 5 pieces fresh lotus root, cut into paper-
thin slices
Umeboshi vinegar
Spring or filtered water
Mirin

Place lotus slices in a shallow bowl. Completely cover with equal amounts of vinegar,
water and mirin. Allow to stand at room temperature 1 to 2 hours before serving. This
pickle will keep, refrigerated, about 1 week.

Green Rolls

A unique and beautiful way to serve leafy green
vegetables. Chilled, these make a most refreshing
summer snack, although you will find yourself whipping them up year-round as a delicious accompaniment to any meal.

MAKES 4 OR 5 SERVINGS

Spring of filtered water
3 or 4 carrot sticks
7 or 8 leaves Chinese cabbage, rinsed and left
whole
1 bunch collard greens, rinsed and stems
removed
1 bunch watercress, rinsed and left whole
Black sesame seeds, toasted (see Note, page
46), for garnish

Bring a pot of water to a boil and separately boil
each vegetable in the order listed above. Cook
each until just crisp—tender, not too soft, 1 to
3 minutes each. Lay on flat plates to cool.

To assemble the rolls, place 2 or 3 collard
leaves on a bamboo sushi mat or dish towel. Top
with 2 or 3 cabbage leaves, then place a thick
strip of watercress and 1 carrot stick on the
edge closest to you. Roll, jelly-roll style, using
the mat or towel as a guide. When completely
rolled, squeeze gently to remove excess water
and seal the roll. Then slice into 1-inch-thick
rounds, arrange on a serving platter and sprinkle the tops of the rolls with black sesame seeds.

■ **VARIATION** *Nori Rolls with Greens:* Omit
Chinese cabbage leaves. Lay a sheet of nori
on a sushi mat or dry surface. Continue
recipe as above, varying carrot sticks with
Pickled Red Cabbage (page 166). Serve
garnished with a dash of umeboshi paste or
a sprinkle of sesame seeds.

Pickled Red Cabbage

The color of this pickle is almost as delicious as its delicate sweet-and-sour taste.

MAKES 3 OR 4 SERVINGS

1 cup finely shredded red cabbage
About 1 tablespoon umeboshi vinegar
About 1 tablespoon sweet brown rice vinegar
About 1 tablespoon mirin

Place shredded cabbage in a bowl and sprinkle generously with equal amounts of the vinegars and mirin. Place a plate on top with a 5-pound weight on top of that. Press for several hours or up to 24 hours. Just prior to serving, taste the pickle; if too salty, rinse gently and serve. This pickle will keep, refrigerated, for several days.

Sukiyaki Vegetables

In this traditional style of cooking, vegetables are lightly simmered with a delicate vinegar-based glaze—a delicious complement or finishing touch to round out any healthy meal. Use as many or as few vegetables as you desire. This recipe calls for lots of variety, but sukiyaki may be simple as well as abundant.

MAKES ABOUT 4 SERVINGS

1 teaspoon avocado oil
2 or 3 cloves fresh garlic, finely minced
1 leek, rinsed well and thinly sliced
Soy sauce
1 or 2 carrots, cut into thin matchsticks
2 stalks broccoli, cut into small florets, with
    stems peeled and thinly sliced
2 celery stalks, cut into thin diagonal slices

2 to 3 leaves Chinese cabbage, cut into 1-inch
    pieces
4 or 5 fresh snow peas (in season), trimmed
    and left whole
1 cup spring or filtered water
Brown rice vinegar
Umeboshi vinegar
1 to 2 teaspoons kuzu or arrowroot, dissolved
    in 2 tablespoons cold water
1 teaspoon dark sesame oil, for finishing

Heat oil in a wok over medium heat. Add garlic, leek and a dash of soy sauce and cook, stirring, until leek is bright green and softened, 2 to 3 minutes. Add carrots and a dash of soy sauce and cook, stirring, 2 or 3 minutes. Repeat with broccoli, celery, cabbage and snow peas, adding each in the order listed above with a dash of soy sauce; the most delicate are cooked last, so that none of the vegetables overcook. Sprinkle lightly with soy sauce. Add about 1 cup water. Simmer over low heat, covered, until the vegetables are crisp-tender, about 5 minutes. Season to taste with vinegars. Stir in dissolved kuzu and cook, stirring, until liquid is thickened, about 3 minutes. Gently stir in sesame oil for flavor. Transfer to a serving platter and serve warm.

■ **NOTE** Do not cook the vinegars longer than it takes to thicken the glaze, as they will turn quite bitter.

Italian-Style Stuffed Mushrooms

This delicious, traditional Italian dish was adapted for a nondairy, low-fat version; just a few ingredient substitutions and you have a tasty alternative to the original. My mother would be pleased.

MAKES 4 SERVINGS

About 8 large button mushrooms, brushed clean
1 tablespoon extra-virgin olive oil
2 or 3 cloves fresh garlic, finely minced
1 onion, minced
Sea salt
Generous pinch dried basil or 3 or 4 leaves fresh basil, minced
¼ cup minced fresh flat-leaf parsley
Small piece dried hot chile, minced (optional)
About ½ cup fresh whole wheat bread crumbs
Juice of ½ lemon
Spring or filtered water

Remove mushroom stems and mince. Set caps aside.

Heat oil in a skillet over medium heat. Add garlic, onion and a pinch of salt and cook, stirring, until onion is translucent, about 4 minutes. Add herbs, mushroom stems and chile (if using) and mix well. Stir in bread crumbs (the amount will depend on how many and how large the mushrooms are) and cook, stirring, until all ingredients are combined. Season lightly with salt, remove from heat, and stir in lemon juice. The stuffing should have the consistency of a thick paste. Add a small amount of water if stuffing is too dry.

Preheat oven to 350F (175C). Lightly oil a shallow baking dish. Spoon stuffing into each mushroom cap until full and arrange in pre-pared baking dish. Pour ¹⁄₁₆ inch of water into the pan to steam the mushrooms, cover tightly and bake about 20 minutes. Remove cover and return to oven for a few minutes to brown the stuffing. Arrange on a serving platter and serve hot or at room temperature.

Onion Tartlets

A healthy take on a traditional French onion tartlet recipe.

MAKES 4 OR 5 SERVINGS

PASTRY
1 cup whole wheat pastry flour
Pinch of sea salt
Avocado oil
Cold spring water

1 teaspoon avocado oil
2 to 3 medium onions, finely diced
Sea salt
2 teaspoons brown rice syrup

Prepare pastry: Whisk the flour and salt together into a bowl. Slowly add about 3 tablespoons of oil, creating the consistency of wet sand. Slowly add water, by the tablespoon, while stirring with a wooden spoon, until the dough gathers, creating a soft consistency. Gather the dough in a ball and set aside to rest, covered with a damp towel.

Heat oil in a skillet over low heat. Add onions, a light sprinkling of salt and rice syrup and cook until soft, sweet and caramelized, about 1 hour, stirring frequently to avoid sticking.

When the onions are almost done, finish the crusts: Preheat oven to 350F (175C). Lightly oil a 12-cup muffin pan and set aside. On a lightly floured surface, thinly roll out the dough into about a 12 × 9-inch rectangle. Cut the dough into about 3-inch rounds and press each one into a prepared muffin cup. Prick each crust in several places and fill each with cooked onions. Bake about 20 minutes, until the crusts are golden and the filling begins to set.

Cool slightly before carefully removing from the muffin cups. Arrange on a platter and serve warm with a fresh salad and a hearty soup for a light, satisfying supper.

Blanched Cole Slaw in Plum-Mustard Dressing

A different take on the usual mayonnaise-laden cole slaw we have come to expect at barbecues. This zesty version will surprise and delight you—a crisp and delicious summer picnic dish.

MAKES 4 SERVINGS

1 carrot, cut into very fine matchsticks
1 cup finely shredded green cabbage
1 cup finely shredded red cabbage
4 to 6 red radishes, cut into very fine matchsticks
About 2 tablespoons minced fresh flat-leaf parsley

PLUM-MUSTARD DRESSING
2 tablespoons finely minced onion
1 tablespoon umeboshi paste
3 to 4 tablespoons prepared stone-ground mustard
4 ounces tofu, boiled 5 minutes and drained, then finely crumbled
Juice of 1 lemon
1 tablespoon brown rice syrup
Sea salt
Spring or filtered water

Bring a large pot of water to a boil and quickly blanch carrot and cabbages until crisp-tender. Mix vegetables together with radishes and parsley and set aside while preparing the dressing.

Make dressing: Place all dressing ingredients, except water, in a food processor, seasoning lightly with salt. Process until very smooth, adding a little water if needed to achieve a mayonnaiselike consistency. Toss with vegetables and chill thoroughly.

Sweet Glazed Onions

These delicate stuffed onions, filled to capacity with fresh corn and vegetables and then smothered with a sweet-and-spicy glaze, are so delicious. Who says vegetables are boring?

MAKES 4 SERVINGS

4 medium onions
Corn kernels cut from 1 ear of corn or 1 cup frozen corn
½ cup finely diced winter squash
1 carrot, finely diced
About ½ cup fresh whole wheat bread crumbs
Spring or filtered water
2 tablespoons brown rice syrup
3 to 4 tablespoons prepared stone-ground mustard
Generous dash of balsamic vinegar
Sea salt
Extra-virgin olive oil

Preheat oven to 375F (175C). Peel the onions and cut each onion crosswise through the center into 2 equal halves. Remove the centers, leaving a bowl. Dice the centers finely for the filling.

Mix together the diced onion, corn, squash, carrot and enough bread crumbs and water to make a stuffing that holds together. Press the stuffing firmly into each onion bowl and arrange in a shallow baking dish so that onions fit together snugly. Pour ¹⁄₁₆ inch of water into dish.

Whisk together the rice syrup, mustard, vinegar and a generous pinch of salt. Spoon a little mustard sauce over each onion, reserving remaining sauce. Sprinkle each onion lightly with additional bread crumbs and drizzle with olive oil. Cover and bake 20 to 25 minutes. Remove cover, drizzle onions with remaining mustard mixture and a touch more oil and bake about 5 minutes to brown the bread crumbs and glaze the onions. Serve warm.

Winter Greens with Marinated Mushrooms and Walnuts

Although there are several steps in this recipe, the delicious results are worth it. And really, it takes only minutes. Easy and sinfully delicious—don't you just love it?

MAKES ABOUT 4 SERVINGS

2 to 3 tablespoons balsamic vinegar
Pinch sea salt
2 cloves fresh garlic, finely minced
¼ cup extra-virgin olive oil
4 or 5 button mushrooms, brushed clean and quartered
5 to 6 tablespoons walnut pieces
1 bunch hearty greens (kale, collards, broccoli rapini), large stems removed

Whisk together vinegar, salt, garlic and olive oil in a bowl. Add mushrooms and stir to coat. Allow to marinate 1 hour.

Meanwhile, lightly pan-toast the walnuts

over medium heat until fragrant, about 3 minutes. Finely mince and set aside to cool.

Leaving the greens whole, quickly steam them until they are a dark, rich green, about 3 minutes. Slice the greens into bite-size pieces. Just before serving, toss the greens, walnuts, mushrooms and remaining marinade together. Serve immediately.

Chinese-Style Vegetables

No need to send out for Chinese anymore. Now you can create your own Chinese-style feast, smothered in a rich, savory sauce, without the monosodium glutamate, heavy salt and oil—so easy to do.

MAKES 4 OR 5 SERVINGS

2 or 3 dried shiitake mushrooms, soaked until tender in warm water
1 tablespoon avocado oil
2 or 3 cloves fresh garlic, minced
1 onion, cut into thin half-moon slices
Sea salt
1 or 2 carrots, cut into thin matchsticks
2 or 3 celery stalks, cut into thick diagonal slices
1 cup thin matchstick pieces daikon
2 or 3 stalks broccoli, cut into small florets
1 cup cauliflower, cut into small florets
4 or 5 snow peas, trimmed and left whole

CHINESE SAUCE
1 to 2 cups spring or filtered water
Soy sauce
1 to 2 teaspoons kuzu or arrowroot, dissolved in 1⁄4 cup cold water
Generous dash brown rice vinegar

1 teaspoon dark sesame oil, for finishing

Cut mushrooms into thin slices and simmer in soaking water 10 minutes to tenderize them. Set aside.

Heat oil in a skillet or wok over medium heat. Add garlic, onion, and a pinch of salt and cook, stirring, 2 to 3 minutes. Drain and add mushrooms and a pinch of salt and cook, stirring, 3 to 4 minutes. Add carrots and a pinch of salt and cook, stirring, 2 to 3 minutes. Stir in remaining vegetables, except snow peas, and cook, stirring, until all are crisp-tender, about 3 minutes. Add snow peas and sprinkle lightly with water. Cover and steam 2 to 3 minutes, until snow peas are bright green. Remove from heat.

Prepare sauce: Heat water and soy sauce in a saucepan over medium heat. Stir in dissolved kuzu and cook, stirring, until sauce is thick and clear, 3 to 4 minutes. Remove from heat and season with vinegar. Stir well and toss gently with cooked vegetables. Drizzle with sesame oil and serve hot.

Cabbage Wedges with Pumpkin Seed-Shiso Condiment

Lightly steamed cabbage wedges tossed with crunchy pumpkin seed–shiso condiment ignite an explosion of flavors sure to please. Shiso powder and dried shiso leaves are easily obtained by mail order or in Asian or natural foods stores.

MAKES ABOUT 4 SERVINGS

Spring or filtered water
1 head green cabbage, cut into 2-inch-thick wedges

PUMPKIN SEED–SHISO CONDIMENT
1 cup pumpkin seeds, rinsed and well drained
4 to 5 teaspoons shiso powder

Bring ¼ inch of water to a boil in a pot over high heat. Carefully add cabbage wedges and steam over high heat until tender, about 10 minutes. Transfer to a serving bowl.

Prepare condiment: Pan-toast the pumpkin seeds in a skillet over medium heat until golden, fragrant and slightly puffy like pillows, about 5

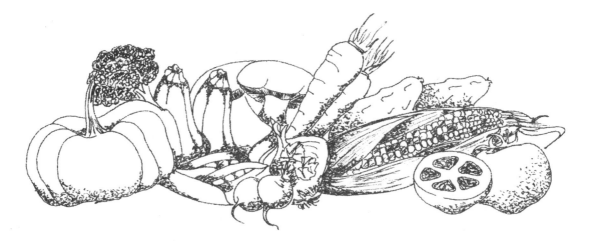

minutes. Pour seeds into a suribachi (grinding bowl) and grind into a coarse meal. Add shiso powder and continue to grind until ingredients are combined and a coarse powder forms. Toss half of condiment gently with cooked cabbage and serve warm. (Reserve remaining condiment to serve with whole grain dishes.)

Lemony Daikon Pickle

This sour-pungent pickle goes quite well with fish or rich-tasting foods, providing a very clean, refreshing taste to balance a heavy meal.

MAKES 4 SERVINGS

1 cup paper-thin half-slices daikon
1 lemon, peeled and cut into paper-thin
half-slices
Umeboshi vinegar

Place daikon and lemon slices in a small bowl and sprinkle lightly with umeboshi vinegar. Toss well. Place a small plate on top of vegetables and top with a weight. Press for 30 minutes. Squeeze excess liquid from vegetables before serving. This pickle will keep, refrigerated, for several days.

Daikon Canapés with Walnut "Chutney"

These simple and delicious canapés combine the clean, peppery flavor of steamed daikon with a rich walnut-miso paste for a unique party appetizer or side dish.

MAKES ABOUT 4 SERVINGS

10 to 12 slices daikon
¼ cup walnut pieces
½ teaspoon barley miso
1 teaspoon avocado oil
1 to 2 green onions, thinly sliced, for garnish

Steam daikon pieces over boiling water until tender, but not too soft, 2 to 3 minutes. Arrange on a serving platter.

Lightly pan-toast the walnuts in a skillet over medium heat until fragrant, about 4 minutes. Process walnuts and miso in a blender or food processor until pureed, slowly adding oil to create a thick, spoonable chutneylike paste. Dot each daikon piece generously with paste and garnish with green onions. Serve at room temperature or chilled.

Wilted Greens with Lemon

A delicious way to serve hearty leafy greens that is commonly seen in Italian cuisine. The zesty tang of fresh lemon juice softens the greens, wilting them and imparting a light citrus essence. But the best part is that the lemon helps make the dish more digestible. Nothing is arbitrary in cooking.

MAKES 4 SERVINGS

1 tablespoon extra-virgin olive oil
2 or 3 cloves fresh garlic, finely minced
1 bunch leafy greens (escarole, broccoli
rapini), cleaned well and sliced into bite-
size pieces
Sea salt
Grated zest and juice of 1 lemon

Heat oil in a skillet over medium heat. Add garlic and cook 1 minute. Add greens and a light seasoning of salt and cook until greens are tender and begin to wilt, about 5 minutes. Stir in lemon zest and cook 1 to 2 minutes. Remove from heat and toss greens with lemon juice. Serve immediately.

Wilted Green Beans with Summer Herbs

This dish is like an ode to summer. It is especially fine cooked a bit ahead of time and chilled before serving.

MAKES 4 OR 5 SERVINGS

1 pound fresh green beans, trimmed
2 tablespoons extra-virgin olive oil
2 tablespoons balsamic vinegar
6 to 8 leaves fresh basil, minced
1 to 2 sprigs rosemary, minced
¼ cup minced fresh flat-leaf parsley
Sea salt
Juice of 1 lemon
Lemon slices or red pepper rings and fresh herb sprigs, for garnish

Preheat oven to 500F (260C). Toss whole beans with oil, vinegar, a sprinkling of herbs and a pinch of salt. Spread on a baking sheet without overlapping beans too much. Oven-roast, uncovered, about 10 minutes, until beans are tender, tossing once or twice during the cooking. Remove from oven, toss with lemon juice and transfer to a serving bowl. Chill before serving. Serve garnished with fresh lemon slices or red pepper rings and fresh herb sprigs.

Braised Leeks with Mushrooms

A rich and savory combination, this tasty dish makes a great appetizer served on crusty whole grain bread. This is a great energizer as well, with the strong upward energy of leeks coupled with the vitality of sautéing.

MAKES 4 OR 5 SERVINGS

¼ cup mirin
¼ cup spring or filtered water
1 teaspoon extra-virgin olive oil
2 or 3 cloves fresh garlic, minced
2 or 3 small leeks, cut lengthwise, rinsed well and thinly sliced
1 portobello mushroom, brushed clean and thinly sliced
Sea salt
Grated zest and juice of 1 orange
Minced fresh flat-leaf parsley, for garnish

Heat mirin, water and oil in a deep skillet over medium heat. Add garlic and leeks and cook, stirring, about 3 minutes. Add mushroom. Cook, stirring, until mushroom is softened, 5 to 7 minutes. Season lightly with salt, cover, and cook over medium heat about 15 minutes. Remove cover and cook until any remaining liquid is absorbed into the dish. Remove from heat and stir in orange zest and juice. Transfer to a serving bowl and serve, garnished with parsley.

Onion "Butter"

This smooth, sweet, vegetable butter has the dairy version beat hands down. Delicious on bread, as a topping for pizza, dolloped on grains, or even tossed with noodles, this spread is a real winner. It takes a long time to prepare but will keep, refrigerated, for about two weeks. Plus, the long cooking time creates a warm, strengthening energy that is hard to beat.

MAKES 5 OR 6 SERVINGS

2 teaspoons avocado oil
10 to 12 sweet onions (Vidalia, Walla Walla or Oh, So Sweet are best), cut into thin half-moon slices
Sea salt
About 2 teaspoons spring or filtered water

Heat oil in a deep, heavy skillet over low heat. Add onions and several pinches of salt to help reduce them quickly. Cook onions until wilted, stirring occasionally, about 20 minutes. Sprinkle lightly with water and cook, covered, over very low heat (use a flame tamer if necessary) at least 5 to 6 hours or as long as 9 hours. (Do not add too much water, just a sprinkle from wet fingers, or the mixture will become runny.) The onions will become very creamy and turn a dark, caramel color.

Remove the cover and allow any remaining liquid to absorb into the dish before stirring. The resulting "butter" should be thick and creamy, not watery.

■ **VARIATION** A quicker version of this spread (although not nearly as sweet) can be made by sautéing the onions as above, then baking them, covered, at 400F (205C) for 1½ to 2 hours, then removing the cover and baking until the onions reduce and become creamy.

"Candied" Onions

Sweet and savory, these oven-roasted onions make a great warming side dish. In our house we heap them on toasted bread or pizza; so yummy! These onions will keep, refrigerated, about 1 week.

MAKES ABOUT 4 SERVINGS

6 to 8 onions, cut into thick wedges
2 or 3 cloves fresh garlic, finely minced
1 tablespoon extra-virgin olive oil
About 2 teaspoons spring or filtered water
Sea salt
Reduced balsamic vinegar (see Note, page 160)
Juice of ¼ lemon

Preheat oven to 375F (190C). Arrange onion wedges snugly in a baking dish and sprinkle with garlic. Drizzle with oil, water, a light sprinkling of salt and a generous drizzle of reduced balsamic vinegar. Cover and bake about 45 minutes. Remove cover and bake about 30 minutes, until onions are very soft. Toss gently with lemon juice, transfer to a serving bowl and serve hot.

Mushroom Pâté

Pâtés are truly lovely, serving as rich spreads, stuffings for vegetable boats or canapés, on bread or crackers or toast points—even dolloped in soups just before serving.

MAKES 4 TO 6 SERVINGS

1 teaspoon avocado oil
4 or 5 shallots, finely minced
2 or 3 cloves fresh garlic, finely minced
Soy sauce
1 pound button mushrooms, brushed clean and finely diced
1 teaspoon fresh ginger juice (see Note, page 164)
Mirin or white wine
2 tablespoons pecans, lightly pan-toasted (see Note, page 46) and minced
Juice of 1 lemon
Sprigs flat-leaf parsley, for garnish

Heat oil in a skillet over medium heat. Add shallots, garlic, and a dash of soy sauce and cook until fragrant, about 3 minutes. Add mushrooms, soy sauce to taste, ginger juice and a splash of mirin and cook, stirring, until mushroom liquid has been reabsorbed into the vegetables, 10 to 15 minutes. Transfer cooked mushroom mixture to a food processor and puree until smooth. Spoon into a bowl and gently fold in pecans and lemon juice. Transfer to a small serving bowl, cover and refrigerate to cool completely before serving. Garnish with parsley sprigs.

Sunchokes Vinaigrette

This delicious sweet-and-sour side salad closely resembles the German version of potato salad.

MAKES 4 TO 6 SERVINGS

1 to 2 pounds sunchokes (Jerusalem artichokes)
3 to 4 tablespoons extra-virgin olive oil
2 tablespoons balsamic vinegar
Pinch sea salt
10 to 12 leaves fresh basil, shredded

Gently scrub sunchokes to clean the skin and boil until just tender, 15 to 20 minutes. Plunge into cold water and cut into bite-size pieces. Whisk together the remaining ingredients, adding salt and basil to taste. Add dressing to sunchokes, toss to combine and chill 1 hour before serving. Toss again just prior to serving.

Autumn Greens in Tangy Vinaigrette

Peppery autumn greens serve best in this recipe. Watercress, endive, radicchio and even romaine lettuce have the strong taste needed to stand up to this unusual, cider-based vinaigrette dressing.

MAKES 4 OR 5 SERVINGS

4 to 5 cups watercress, Belgian endive, radicchio and romaine lettuce
1 shallot, finely minced
2 cloves fresh garlic, finely minced
2 tablespoons apple cider
2 tablespoons sweet brown rice vinegar
¼ cup extra-virgin olive oil
Sea salt

Rinse the greens and drain well. Slice into bite-size pieces and set aside. Whisk together remaining ingredients, seasoning lightly to taste with salt. Toss with greens and allow to marinate 15 to 20 minutes. Toss again just prior to serving. The dressing should have caused a bit of wilting and the flavors will have developed.

Winter Vegetable Pâté

This brightly colored pâté heralds the autumn, showcasing the abundance of the harvest. Its sweet taste and rich texture make it a festive way to serve the strengthening, warming ground vegetables we need to get through the cold winter months.

MAKES ABOUT 4 SERVINGS

Spring or filtered water
1 onion, diced
1 Garnet or other orange sweet potato, cut into 1-inch cubes
1 cup 1-inch cubes butternut squash
Soy sauce
2 to 3 tablespoons sesame tahini
2 teaspoons brown rice syrup

Heat a dry skillet over medium heat. Add about 1 tablespoon water and water-sauté the onion until translucent, about 5 minutes. Add sweet potato, squash, a dash of soy sauce and about ¼ inch of water and bring to a boil. Cover, reduce heat and simmer over low heat until sweet potato and squash are very tender, about 25 minutes. Season lightly with soy sauce and allow to simmer, uncovered, until any remaining liquid has been absorbed.

Transfer vegetables to a food processor; add tahini and rice syrup and process until smooth, thick and creamy, adding water only if the consistency appears too stiff. Transfer to a serv-ing bowl and serve as a spread with crusty, whole grain bread or crackers.

Mushroom-Leek Strudel

This delicate pastry strudel couldn't be easier. Reduced vegetables wrapped in flaky phyllo pastry create a rich, satisfying side course, especially when accompanied by a hearty bean soup and lightly cooked vegetables.

MAKES 4 TO 6 SERVINGS

1 tablespoon extra-virgin olive oil
2 or 3 cloves fresh garlic, finely minced
1 or 2 leeks, cut lengthwise, rinsed well and thinly sliced
2 to 3 cups button mushrooms, brushed clean and thinly sliced
Sea salt
3 phyllo pastry sheets (see Note, page 176)
Avocado oil
Whole wheat bread crumbs

Heat oil in a skillet over medium heat. Add garlic and cook 1 minute. Add leeks and a pinch of salt and cook, stirring, until bright green and just wilted, about 5 minutes. Stir in mushrooms, season lightly with salt and cook until wilted and beginning to reduce, 5 to 7 minutes. Reduce heat to medium-low, cover and cook 20 minutes, stirring frequently. The vegetables will get very soft, becoming rather dark in color. Remove the cover and allow any remaining liquid to be absorbed into the vegetables. Transfer to a bowl and set aside to cool.

Preheat oven to 375F (190C). Line a baking sheet with parchment paper and set aside. Lay a sheet of phyllo pastry on a dry, flat work surface. Brush lightly with oil and sprinkle with bread crumbs. (This makes the pastry flaky and gives the strudel body.) Repeat with remaining phyllo sheets.

Spread the cooled filling along a short side of the layered phyllo pastry. Quickly and gently roll up the strudel, jelly-roll style, turn under the ends and transfer to prepared baking sheet, seam side down. With a sharp knife, make deep slits, marking the slices. Brush lightly with oil. Bake about 30 minutes, until the pastry is golden and flaky.

Remove pastry from oven and allow to cool about 5 minutes before slicing completely through on marked lines. Transfer to a serving platter and serve warm.

■ **NOTE** The best choice for phyllo pastry is the packaged variety, sold in the freezer department at most supermarkets. Before use, thaw in the refrigerator about 6 hours, storing any unused phyllo in the refrigerator or freezer until you need it again. It is very important that you thaw the phyllo in the refrigerator, not at room temperature, to prevent it from getting too soft and sticking together.

Whole wheat phyllo is available at some gourmet and natural foods stores. I prefer to use it when possible.

Winter Veggie and Bean Stew

A hearty vegetable and bean casserole sure to warm you up on cold winter nights.

MAKES 4 OR 5 SERVINGS

1 tablespoon avocado oil
1 onion, cut into large dice
Soy sauce
1 cup large dice winter squash
1 cup large dice white turnips
1 or 2 carrots, cut into large dice
1 or 2 parsnips, cut into large dice
About 2 tablespoons whole wheat pastry flour
1 cup cooked kidney beans, drained
2 to 3 tablespoons prepared stone-ground
    mustard
Fresh ginger juice (see Note, page 164)
Spring or filtered water
2 or 3 stalks broccoli, cut into small florets,
    for garnish

Preheat oven to 375F (175C). Lightly oil a deep casserole and set aside.

176

Heat oil in a skillet over medium heat. Add onion and a dash of soy sauce and cook until wilted. Add squash, turnips, carrots and parsnips and cook, stirring, to combine. Sprinkle lightly with flour and cook, stirring, until flour sticks to vegetable pieces. Season lightly with soy sauce and cook a few minutes more. Set aside.

Mix together kidney beans, mustard, ginger juice and soy sauce to taste in a large bowl. Fold in cooked vegetables. Spoon into prepared casserole and sprinkle lightly with water. Cover and bake 45 minutes, until vegetables are tender and have a stewlike consistency. Remove cover and bake about 10 minutes, until stew begins to firm up a bit; it will not set up, but it will thicken.

While the stew is baking, steam broccoli over boiling water until crisp-tender, 5 minutes. When the casserole is done, remove from oven and arrange broccoli around the edges of the casserole. Serve immediately.

Herb-Scented Vegetable Tart

This elegantly beautiful tart makes a lovely centerpiece on any table. Ideal for a holiday, or any day.

MAKES 6 TO 8 SERVINGS

8 ounces extra-firm tofu
1 onion, minced
2 to 3 fresh garlic cloves, minced
2 tablespoons dried rosemary
¼ cup minced fresh flat-leaf parsley
Sea salt
Spring or filtered water
1 tablespoon extra-virgin olive oil
1 onion, cut into thin half-moon slices
3 or 4 small zucchini, cut into thin matchsticks

2 cups button mushrooms, brushed clean and thinly sliced
4 or 5 phyllo pastry sheets (see Note, page 176)
2 or 3 red bell peppers, roasted over a flame, peeled, seeded and cut into thin strips (see Note, page 262)
4 or 5 fresh basil leaves, finely minced, or 2 tablespoons dried basil
2 to 3 tablespoons slivered almonds, pan-toasted (see Note, page 55), for garnish

Preheat oven to 375F (175C). Line a 15 × 10-inch jelly-roll pan or deep baking sheet with foil, brush lightly with oil and set aside.

In a food processor, process tofu, minced onion, garlic, rosemary, parsley, a little salt and enough water to make a smooth, spreadable paste. Set aside.

Heat oil in a skillet over medium heat. Add sliced onion and a pinch of salt and cook until wilted, about 5 minutes. Add zucchini and a pinch of salt and cook 2 or 3 minutes. Add mushrooms, season lightly with salt and cook about 5 minutes. Simmer, uncovered, until any remaining liquid has been absorbed into the vegetables.

Meanwhile, place a sheet of phyllo pastry in prepared pan so that the edges extend beyond the rims on all sides. Crinkle these edges to form the outer edge of the tart. Brush with oil and add another sheet of pastry. Repeat with remaining pastry sheets, brushing with oil and crinkling the edges of the pastry.

Gently spoon the tofu mixture over the phyllo pastry, spreading evenly. Arrange cooked vegetables over the top of the tofu mixture. Arrange the bell peppers in an attractive pattern on top of the vegetables. Bake, uncovered, about 15 minutes, until the crust is golden brown and flaky. Remove pan from oven and sprinkle the top of the tart with basil and almonds. Serve warm.

Russian Cabbage Pie

The Eastern European version of the French *galette*. Called a "pirog," this free-form pie is filled with savory vegetables and makes a great entrée, set off by a light soup and a crisp salad.

MAKES 6 TO 8 SERVINGS

2 recipes Basic Sourdough Bread (page 282)
Generous pinch dried rosemary
Spring or filtered water
½ head green cabbage, finely shredded
1 tablespoon extra-virgin olive oil, plus extra
   for brushing
3 or 4 cloves fresh garlic, minced
Pinch caraway seed
1 onion, diced
Sea salt
1 or 2 carrots, cut into thin matchsticks

Prepare dough as directed in recipe. Quickly knead in rosemary to distribute it evenly through the dough. Shape into a ball and set aside, covered, while preparing the filling.

Bring a pot of water to a boil and cook cabbage 3 to 4 minutes, until it begins to wilt. Drain and set aside.

Heat 1 tablespoon oil in a skillet over medium heat. Add garlic, caraway seed, onion and a pinch of salt and cook, stirring, until the onion is translucent, 5 minutes. Add carrots and cook, stirring, to combine. Stir in cabbage and season lightly with salt to taste. Drizzle with a little water, cover and cook over medium heat 15 minutes, stirring frequently. Remove from heat and allow to cool to room temperature before proceeding.

Preheat oven to 375F (190C). Line a large baking sheet with parchment, dust with flour and set aside. On a floured surface, roll out half the dough into a 10 × 14-inch rectangle.

Transfer carefully to the prepared baking sheet. Spread cabbage filling over the dough, leaving a 1-inch border all around. Roll out second piece of dough slightly smaller than the first and gently lay on top of the cabbage filling. Seal the pie by pulling up the bottom edges of the pastry, joining with the top dough and crimping to form crust edges. Brush lightly with olive oil. With a sharp knife, cut several vents to allow steam to escape during baking.

Bake on the center oven rack about 40 minutes, until the crust is golden brown and the pie is firm when tapped lightly. Remove from oven and allow to stand 10 minutes before slicing.

Ragout Provençal

Nothing is more welcoming on a biting cold winter day than coming home to a hearty stew: The aroma tantalizes your senses with anticipation of the delicious food that awaits you. This French-inspired ragout enhances the rich flavors of the vegetables with an aromatic blend of herbs.

MAKES 4 OR 5 SERVINGS

1 large onion, cut into medium-thick wedges
3 or 4 ripe tomatoes, quartered
1 cup large chunks turnips
2 cups button mushrooms, brushed clean and
   quartered
2 red bell peppers, roasted over a flame,
   peeled, seeded and cut into large pieces
   (see Note, page 262)
2 medium zucchini, cut into medium chunks
2 to 3 cups cubed butternut squash
3 to 4 celery stalks, cut into ½-inch-thick
   diagonal pieces
8 to 10 black olives, pitted
3 or 4 cloves fresh garlic, minced

Generous pinch *each* dried oregano and basil
About 1 tablespoon extra-virgin olive oil
Sea salt
Mirin or white wine
Spring or filtered water

Preheat oven to 300F (150C). Lightly oil a deep casserole and set aside.

Toss together the vegetables, olives, garlic, oregano and basil and arrange so mixture is evenly distributed in the casserole. Drizzle with oil and season with salt and mirin to taste. Add enough water to barely half-cover ingredients.

Bake, uncovered, about 4 hours, until vegetables are creamy and soft, stirring about every 30 minutes and adding water as needed to keep the casserole moist. Remove dish from oven and serve over grain or noodles for a hearty winter main course.

Savory Cassoulet

Stewed vegetables in a thick gravy make a great centerpiece for a hearty winter meal.

MAKES 4 OR 5 SERVINGS

½ head red cabbage, shredded
1 head cauliflower, cut into medium florets
1 head broccoli, cut into medium florets
2 or 3 tart apples (Granny Smith or other), cut into large dice
1 cup dried cannellini or navy beans, cooked without seasoning until tender
2 or 3 shallots, diced
2 cloves fresh garlic, finely minced
3 cups dark beer, water or stock
About 2 tablespoons caraway seed
Soy sauce
3 to 4 tablespoons whole wheat pastry flour

Preheat oven to 400F (205C). Combine all ingredients, except flour, in a roasting pan, sprinkling lightly with caraway seed and seasoning to taste with soy sauce. Sprinkle the top generously with flour.

Bake, uncovered, 30 minutes. Reduce heat to 300F (150C), cover and bake 2 hours, stirring occasionally. The vegetables will become very tender and the sauce will thicken slightly. Serve hot.

Italian-Style Sautéed Broccoli

My mother had a knack of making the simplest foods taste delicious. She had a way of cooking the broccoli until just bright green and crisp-tender, and laced through it were lightly sautéed mushrooms and tomatoes. It was rich and delicate at the same time. I hope you enjoy this elegant dish as much as I have over the years.

MAKES 4 OR 5 SERVINGS

Spring or filtered water
1 head broccoli, cut into small florets, stems peeled and thinly sliced
1 tablespoon extra-virgin olive oil
2 or 3 cloves fresh garlic, minced
1 onion, diced
Sea salt
4 or 5 button mushrooms, brushed clean and thinly sliced
1 to 2 tomatoes, diced (do not seed or peel)
Cracked black pepper

Bring a large pot of water to a boil over high heat. Add broccoli and cook until bright green but not completely tender, about 3 minutes. Drain well and set aside.

Heat oil in a skillet over medium heat. Add garlic, onion and a pinch of salt and cook, stirring, until onion is wilted and translucent, 5 minutes. Add mushrooms and a pinch of salt and cook, stirring, 2 or 3 minutes. Add tomatoes, season lightly with salt and pepper and stir well. Cover and simmer 10 to 15 minutes. Remove cover and stir in broccoli. Simmer, uncovered, 2 to 3 minutes. Serve hot.

Sweet and Sour Cabbage with Tart Apples

My version of this Eastern European dish is savory with caraway seeds and sweetened lightly with red currant jam—great for autumn or winter.

MAKES ABOUT 4 SERVINGS

Spring or filtered water
½ head red cabbage, shredded
2 tart apples (Granny Smith or other),
  unpeeled, cored and diced
2 teaspoons brown rice syrup
2 tablespoons brown rice vinegar
2 tablespoons red wine vinegar
¼ cup unsweetened red currant or raspberry
  jam
About 2 tablespoons caraway seed

Bring a pot of water to a boil over high heat. Add cabbage and cook until crisp-tender, about 5 minutes. Drain and transfer to a bowl. Toss apples into hot cabbage and set aside.

Whisk together rice syrup, vinegars, jam and caraway seed to taste. Toss with hot cabbage until combined. Allow to stand about 15 minutes so flavors can develop. Serve warm.

Nut-Stuffed Winter Squash

This tantalizing entrée combines sweet squash, savory nutmeats and aromatic spices—a delicious centerpiece dish, especially when served with a light soup, crusty whole grain bread and a crisp, fresh salad.

MAKES 2 SERVINGS

½ cup quinoa
Spring or filtered water
Sea salt
1 acorn squash, halved and seeded
½ cup minced pecans
1 onion, finely diced
About 2 teaspoons light sesame oil
¼ cup minced fresh flat-leaf parsley
Pinch each cinnamon and nutmeg
About ¼ cup fresh whole wheat bread crumbs

Rinse quinoa several times to help remove saponin, which can make the grain taste bitter if not rinsed off. Bring quinoa, 1 cup water and a pinch of salt to a boil in a saucepan over medium heat. Reduce heat and cook, covered, over low heat until quinoa is tender and fluffy and water is completely absorbed, about 25 minutes.

Preheat oven to 350F (175C). Lightly oil a baking dish large enough to hold squash. Cut the bottoms off the acorn squash just enough so that each half sits squarely, cut side up. Arrange the squash halves in prepared baking dish.

Combine cooked quinoa, pecans, onion, a light drizzle of oil, parsley, spices, a little salt and enough bread crumbs to make a stuffing that holds together. Divide stuffing among squash halves, filling them abundantly. (You may have more quinoa filling than you need; serve it as a side dish.)

Add a little water to the baking dish. Cover tightly with foil and bake 1 hour, until the squash pierces easily with a fork. Remove cover and bake about 5 minutes to firm the filling. Serve warm.

■ **VARIATION** Serve with Creamy Mushroom Sauce (page 274) spooned over top just before serving.

Cauliflower in Creamy Caper Sauce

When I lived in Italy, one of my favorite dishes was boiled cauliflower smothered in a creamy caper sauce. I would travel to Venice on weekends just to have lunch! Here's a slightly altered version, with a lighter, but equally delicious sauce.

MAKES ABOUT 4 SERVINGS

Spring or filtered water
1 head cauliflower, cut into bite-size florets

CAPER SAUCE
1 cup soy or rice milk
3 to 4 tablespoons capers, drained well
Extra-virgin olive oil
1 to 2 teaspoons kuzu or arrowroot, dissolved
   in 2 tablespoons cold water
¼ cup minced fresh flat-leaf parsley
Juice of 1 lemon

Bring a pot of water to a boil over high heat. Add cauliflower and cook until just tender, about 5 minutes. Drain and arrange cauliflower on a serving platter.

Prepare the sauce: Combine soy or rice milk, capers and a dash of oil in a small saucepan over low heat. When warmed through, stir in dissolved kuzu and cook, stirring, until the sauce is thick and creamy, about 3 minutes. Remove from heat and stir in parsley. Whisk in lemon juice, spoon over cauliflower and serve warm.

Broccoli with Artichoke Hearts

This brightly colored vegetable dish has a light, fresh taste that goes well with heartier fare.

MAKES 4 SERVINGS

1 head broccoli, cut into small florets
1 tablespoon extra-virgin olive oil
Generous pinch crushed red pepper flakes
2 or 3 cloves fresh garlic, finely minced
Sea salt
1 (6-ounce) jar marinated artichoke hearts,
   drained and halved
Juice of 1 lime

Bring a small amount of water to a boil and steam broccoli until bright green and crisp-tender, 4 or 5 minutes. Drain and set aside.

Heat oil in a skillet over medium heat. Add red pepper flakes, garlic and a pinch of salt. Cook 1 minute. Stir in artichoke hearts, a light seasoning of salt and cook about 3 minutes. Remove from heat and stir in broccoli and lemon juice. Transfer to a serving bowl and serve immediately.

Spicy Mushroom Turnovers

These little treats are a great addition to any autumn party buffet or served as a side dish accompanying a hearty soup and lightly cooked vegetables for a simple but delicious meal.

MAKES 5 OR 6 SERVINGS

1 tablespoon extra-virgin olive oil
3½ cups button mushrooms, brushed clean
   and minced
Sea salt
White wine
½ cup minced green onions
About 2 tablespoons whole wheat pastry flour
¼ teaspoon ground coriander
Scant pinch crushed red pepper flakes
¼ teaspoon ground cumin, or to taste
½ cup firm tofu, crumbled
Spring or filtered water
¼ cup minced fresh flat-leaf parsley
14 phyllo pastry sheets (see Note, page 176)
Extra-virgin olive oil for brushing

Heat oil in a skillet over medium heat. Add mushrooms and a pinch of salt and cook, stirring, about 3 minutes, stirring frequently. Add wine to barely cover the bottom of the skillet and cook, stirring until the mushrooms are tender and have absorbed the liquid. Add green onions and a pinch of salt and cook, stirring, 3 minutes. Slowly sprinkle in flour, stirring until vegetables are coated. Season lightly with salt, coriander, red pepper flakes and cumin.

Process tofu in a food processor with enough water to make a smooth paste. Stir into vegetable mixture, remove from heat and fold in parsley. Set aside.

Preheat oven to 375F (190C). Line a large baking sheet with parchment and set aside. Cut each sheet of phyllo in half, lengthwise. Working with 1 sheet at a time, lightly brush the pastry with oil. Spoon about 1 tablespoon of filling onto one end of the pastry piece and begin folding from the bottom left corner. Fold again from the bottom forming a triangle. Continue folding over and over, wrapping pastry around the filling, creating layers of pastry around the mushroom mixture. Place finished turnovers on prepared baking sheet and repeat the process with the remaining pastry and filling.

Just before placing pastries in the oven, lightly brush the surface of each with olive oil. Bake 25 to 30 minutes, until the pastry is flaky and golden brown. Transfer to a platter and serve warm.

Golden Squash Rings

Acorn squash is one of the most beautiful autumn vegetables. Cut into rings and baked to perfect, delicate sweetness, this side dish is a beautiful homage to the bounty of the harvest.

MAKES 4 TO 6 SERVINGS

About ¼ cup *each* dried whole wheat bread
   crumbs and cornmeal
Pinch sea salt
Generous pinch pumpkin pie spice, or a
   combination of allspice, cinnamon and
   nutmeg
4 to 6 tablespoons brown rice syrup
3 tablespoons amasake
2 teaspoons avocado oil
1 large acorn squash, seeded, cut crosswise
   into ½-inch-thick rings, unpeeled and
   seeds removed
Sprigs flat-leaf parsley, for garnish

Preheat oven to 400F (205C). Line a baking sheet with parchment paper and set aside. Combine bread crumbs and cornmeal with a pinch of salt and pumpkin pie spice in a shallow bowl. Whisk together rice syrup, amasake and oil in another bowl, whisking until smooth. Dip each squash ring into syrup mixture, then coat with cornmeal mixture.

Place each ring on prepared baking sheet. Bake 25 minutes, until squash is tender and coating is crispy. Arrange on a platter and serve garnished with parsley sprigs.

Ume-Radish Pickles

The peppery radishes in this recipe turn a beautiful, rich pink. Keep about 2 weeks in a tightly sealed jar in the refrigerator.

MAKES 3 OR 4 SERVINGS

5 or 6 red radishes, cleaned and left whole
3 umeboshi plums, pitted
Spring or filtered water

Place radishes, plums and enough water to cover in a saucepan over medium heat. Bring to a boil, reduce heat and simmer, uncovered, about 15 minutes, until pale pink and slightly crisp. Remove from heat and allow radishes to stand in the cooking liquid until cooled completely. Transfer radishes and cooking liquid to a jar. Serve pickles whole, halved or thinly sliced.

Summer Zucchini with Italian Lemon Relish

This zesty summer dish is a great way to use up some of those zucchini that seem to take over the entire garden.

MAKES 3 OR 4 SERVINGS

5 or 6 zucchini, cut into ¼-inch-thick diagonal slices
3 or 4 green onions, diced
Grated zest and juice of 1 lemon
¼ cup minced fresh flat-leaf parsley
2 to 3 tablespoons capers, drained, rinsed and minced
Lemon slices, for garnish

Steam zucchini over boiling water until just tender, about 5 minutes. Transfer to a serving platter.

Puree the green onions, lemon zest and juice, parsley and capers together to form a coarse paste. Spoon a small bit of relish over each piece of zucchini and serve garnished with lemon slices.

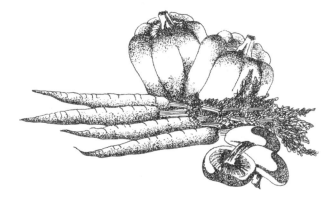

Chestnuts and Greens Medley with Walnuts

Fresh chestnuts can be cooked and peeled ahead of time and kept refrigerated for this recipe. The sweet chestnuts, rich fried tempeh, winter greens and savory walnuts create a symphony of flavors in this hearty mix of leafy greens—a wonderful dish to grace any holiday table.

Makes about 4 servings

8 to 10 ounces fresh chestnuts
Spring or filtered water
2 tablespoons extra-virgin olive oil
4 slices whole grain bread, crusts removed
    and cut into ½-inch cubes
1 or 2 celery stalks, diced
2 or 3 cloves fresh garlic, minced
Sea salt
1 bunch hearty winter greens (kale or
    collards), thinly sliced
Balsamic vinegar
4 ounces tempeh, cut into ¼-inch cubes and
    lightly pan-fried (page 130) until golden
½ cup walnut pieces, pan-toasted (see Note,
    page 46) and coarsely minced

Make a slit in the flat side of each chestnut. Cook in boiling water over high heat 15 minutes. Drain chestnuts, wrap in a towel to keep them warm and set aside 10 minutes. Peel off both the hard outer shell and the inner papery layer. Set chestnuts aside while preparing the rest of the dish.

Heat 1 tablespoon of the oil in a skillet over medium heat. Add bread cubes and cook, stirring constantly, until crispy, a few minutes only. Transfer bread cubes to a bowl. Add remaining oil to the same skillet. Add celery, garlic and a pinch of salt and cook 2 minutes. Add greens,

sprinkle lightly with salt and cook, stirring, until deep green and shiny with oil, about 5 minutes. Remove from heat and stir in a little vinegar to taste. Transfer to a bowl and toss with chestnuts, bread cubes, tempeh and walnuts until ingredients are well incorporated. Arrange on a platter and serve immediately.

Galettes

You may call them pies, tarts or free-form quiches, but you will always call them delicious. These vegetable-filled pastries—galettes—are French in origin and can be filled with any manner of braised vegetables, purees, even vegetable and bean combinations. Their crusts are heartier and their fillings more substantial than pizzas; they are flat and free-form shaped, unlike their more sophisticated tart counterparts. Ragged edges and slightly lopsided shapes create the charm of this peasant fare. (But for those cooks who love symmetry, the dough can be trimmed and shaped to please your eye as well.)

Makes 4 to 6 servings (1 large galette or 4 individual galettes)

½ recipe Basic Sourdough Bread dough
    (page 282)
Filling of choice (recipes follow)
Extra-virgin olive oil

Prepare bread dough as directed. Prepare filling.

Preheat oven to 400F (205C). On a floured baking sheet or baking stone, roll out dough into a 14-inch-round diameter. Spread filling evenly over surface, leaving a 1-inch border. Fold up edges, pinching between your fingers to create pleats, exposing the filling in the center. Brush crust lightly with oil. Bake about 40 minutes, until the dough rises slightly and turns a deep golden brown. Remove from oven and serve hot.

Winter Squash and Tofu Cheese Galette Filling

MAKES ENOUGH FILLING FOR 1 LARGE GALETTE

1 medium winter squash (butternut or buttercup)
Avocado oil
Sea salt
1 onion, diced
Generous pinch dried basil
½ cup Tofu Cheese (page 118), crumbled coarsely

Preheat oven to 375F (175C). Halve the squash and remove the seeds. Lightly brush the cut sides with oil and sprinkle lightly with salt. Arrange in a baking pan. Bake until squash is tender, about 1 hour. Scoop out flesh and mash until smooth.

Heat 1 teaspoon oil in a skillet over low heat. Add the onion and basil and cook, stirring, about 5 minutes. Season lightly with salt and stir into mashed squash. Gently fold in half the Tofu Cheese.

Use mixture to fill galette. Sprinkle the remaining tofu cheese on top of the exposed filling.

Mushroom-Leek Galette Filling

MAKES ENOUGH FILLING FOR 1 LARGE GALETTE

1 tablespoon extra-virgin olive oil
3 or 4 cloves fresh garlic, minced
2 leeks, cut lengthwise, rinsed well and thinly sliced

Generous pinch *each* dried basil and thyme
Sea salt
1½ pounds button mushrooms, brushed clean and thinly sliced
Juice of 1 lemon

Heat oil in a skillet over medium heat. Add garlic, leeks, basil and thyme and a pinch of salt and cook, stirring, 2 to 3 minutes. Add mushrooms and a pinch of salt and cook until they begin to exude liquid and darken in color, stirring frequently. Season lightly with salt, cover and cook over low heat until vegetables are soft, about 15 minutes. Remove from heat and stir in lemon juice. Cool to room temperature before using to fill galette.

Italian Vegetable Galette Filling

MAKES ENOUGH FILLING FOR 1 LARGE GALETTE

1 tablespoon extra-virgin olive oil
2 or 3 cloves fresh garlic, minced
2 or 3 shallots, minced
Sea salt
1 or 2 zucchini, cut into small dice
2 or 3 celery stalks, cut into small dice
1 cup button mushrooms, brushed clean and diced
2 to 3 plum tomatoes, cut into small dice (do not seed or peel)
About 2 tablespoons sweet white miso
Spring or filtered water

Heat oil in a skillet over medium heat. Add garlic, shallots and a pinch of salt and cook, stirring, 2 to 3 minutes. Add zucchini, celery, mushrooms and a pinch of salt and sauté 5 minutes, stirring occasionally. Add tomatoes and a pinch of salt and stir well. Dissolve miso in about ¼ cup warm water and pour over vegetables. Cover and cook over low heat about 15 minutes, until vegetables are soft. Remove cover and allow any remaining liquid to be absorbed. Cool to room temperature before using to fill galette.

Scalloped Vegetables

I remember loving the creamy sauce my mother concocted to create the most delicious scalloped vegetables. When I changed my approach to food, I began experimenting with healthier, low-fat ingredients, still trying to achieve rich, satisfying dishes. Here is one success.

MAKES 4 TO 6 SERVINGS

Spring or filtered water
2 onions, cut into thick wedges
2 cups cauliflower, cut into small florets
½ head green cabbage, cut into ½-inch chunks
2 cups Brussels sprouts, trimmed and halved

WHITE SAUCE
¼ cup Onion Stock (page 75)
2 tablespoons whole wheat pastry flour
1½ cups soy or rice milk
Sea salt

4 ounces brown rice mochi, grated
About ¼ cup fresh whole wheat bread crumbs

Heat ¼ inch water in a skillet over medium heat. Add onions and simmer 2 minutes. Top with other vegetables, cover and lightly steam until crisp-tender, about 5 minutes. Drain well. Transfer to a bowl and set aside while preparing the sauce.

Preheat oven to 350F (175C). Lightly oil a deep casserole and set aside.

To make the sauce: Combine stock and flour in a saucepan over medium heat. Cook until bubbly, stirring. Whisk in milk and simmer until the sauce thickens, about 10 minutes, stirring frequently to prevent scorching. Season lightly with salt and remove from heat.

Layer vegetables and sauce in prepared casserole, finishing with sauce on top. Spread a thin layer of mochi over sauce and top with bread crumbs. Using your fingertips sprinkle mochi with water. Cover loosely and bake about 25 minutes, until mochi melts. Remove cover and return to oven to brown the top. Serve hot.

Tender Spring Vegetables

Nothing heralds the coming of spring quite like fresh, tender vegetables, delicately cooked and tossed with a light chive dressing.

MAKES ABOUT 4 SERVINGS

Spring or filtered water
6 to 8 baby carrots, cut into 2-inch pieces
4 or 5 snow peas, trimmed and left whole
6 to 8 red radishes, halved lengthwise
4 or 5 green onions, cut into 3-inch lengths
3 or 4 small turnips, cut into thin half-moons
1 bunch watercress, trimmed
1 tablespoon extra-virgin olive oil
Sea salt
Grated zest and juice of 1 lemon
Small handful fresh chives, minced

Bring a pot of water to a boil and separately cook each vegetable, in order listed, until crisp-tender, not soft, 1 to 3 minutes each. Plunge each vegetable into cold water to stop the cooking process and preserve its fresh, light energy. Toss together in a bowl.

Heat oil in a skillet over medium heat. Add

all the vegetables, stirring only until coated with oil. Season lightly with salt and remove from heat. Gently stir in lemon zest and juice and chives. Arrange on a platter and serve immediately.

Grilled Summer Squash

Grilling is a most wonderful way to prepare vegetables. Quick and easy, it is an ideal cooking technique for summer, when vegetables are at their peak. Grilling cooks the vegetables over direct heat, one side at a time, browning the outside. The delicious, smoky exterior gives way to a tender and juicy interior. Marinating the vegetables before cooking adds a bit of extra zip.

MAKES 4 TO 6 SERVINGS

2 tablespoons balsamic vinegar
2 teaspoons prepared stone-ground mustard
1 clove fresh garlic, thinly sliced
2 to 3 tablespoons extra-virgin olive oil
Generous pinch sea salt
4 or 5 fresh basil leaves, finely minced
4 or 5 summer squash, cut lengthwise into
    about ¼-inch-thick slices

In a small bowl, whisk together all ingredients except squash. Place squash in a shallow baking dish and spoon marinade over top to cover. Allow to marinate at room temperature about 30 minutes. Remove garlic slices from marinade before grilling.

Preheat grill. Lightly oil grill rack. Arrange squash slices on rack and grill over medium heat until lightly browned on each side, basting occasionally with marinade. (Cooking time may vary, but usually 2 to 5 minutes per side is sufficient.) Arrange on a platter and serve immediately by itself or as part of a salad.

Italian-Style Marinated Carrots

My mother used to make this dish every summer. She usually served them as part of a cold antipasto, but I have discovered that they make a great summer side dish on their own.

MAKES 4 TO 6 SERVINGS

Spring or filtered water
4 or 5 carrots, cut into ½-inch-thick rounds
½ cup umeboshi or red wine vinegar
1 clove fresh garlic, finely minced
¼ cup extra-virgin olive oil
Pinch sea salt
1 sprig fresh rosemary, leaves removed

Bring a small amount of water to a boil over high heat. Add carrots, cover and cook over medium heat until just tender, 10 to 15 minutes. Drain and transfer to a bowl.

Combine remaining ingredients in a small bowl and toss with cooked carrots until well-mixed. Cover and refrigerate several hours. When ready to serve, stir well and allow carrots to stand at room temperature, 30 minutes.

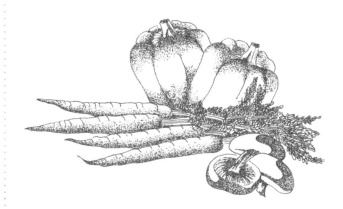

Stuffed Winter Squash

This is a lovely centerpiece dish to serve at holiday feasts or buffets. Along with the basic recipe are several variations on stuffings, each more delicious than the next, so choosing the one you want to make could be the toughest part of the preparation. In each recipe, you will notice the directions call for cooling the stuffing before filling the squash. Placing hot stuffing in a naturally sweet squash can cause it to sour, so take the time to cool it down before proceeding.

MAKES 4 TO 6 SERVINGS

1 large winter squash (buttercup, hokkaido or hubbard)
Light olive or avocado oil
Spring or filtered water
Stuffing of choice (recipes follow)

Preheat oven to 325F (165C). To begin, remove the top of the squash, jack–o'–lantern style, so that you can scoop out the seeds and pulp. Replace the top and lightly oil the outer skin. Place in a baking dish with about ½ inch of water. Bake, uncovered, about 25 minutes. Remove from oven and allow to cool while preparing the stuffing.

To stuff squash, pack stuffing firmly into the opening, until fully stuffed. Replace the squash top and place in a baking dish with a small amount of water. Increase oven temperature to 350F (175C). Cover squash with a foil tent and bake until squash pierces easily with a fork and filling is hot. The exact baking time will vary, depending on the size of the squash, anywhere from 1 to 3 hours.

■ **NOTE** Any filling that doesn't fit in the squash can be baked separately in a casserole for about 35 minutes.

Sourdough Stuffing

MAKES ENOUGH FILLING FOR 1 LARGE WINTER SQUASH

1 large sourdough loaf, crusts removed and cubed
1 tablespoon extra-virgin olive oil
1 clove fresh garlic, minced
1 medium onion, diced
2 cups diced celery
1 cup button mushrooms, brushed clean and diced
1 cup tempeh cubes, pan-fried (page 130) until golden
½ cup pine nuts, lightly pan-toasted (see Note, page 46)
Sea salt
Fresh ginger juice (see Note, page 164)
¼ cup minced fresh flat-leaf parsley
Spring or filtered water

Preheat oven to 300F (150C). Arrange bread cubes on a baking sheet. Bake until bread dries slightly, about 10 minutes.

Meanwhile, heat oil in a skillet over medium heat. Add garlic and onion and cook 2 to 3 minutes. Add celery and mushrooms and cook, stirring, until tender, about 7 minutes. Combine bread cubes, vegetables, tempeh, pine nuts, sea salt to taste, ginger juice to taste and parsley. Slowly add enough water, while mixing, to make a soft stuffing. Allow to cool completely before using.

Bulgur-Pecan Stuffing

MAKES ENOUGH STUFFING FOR 1 LARGE WINTER SQUASH

½ cup currants or raisins
Mirin
Spring or filtered water
1 cup pecans
Sea salt
2½ cups bulgur
1 teaspoon extra-virgin olive oil
1 red onion, diced
2 to 3 celery stalks, diced
Generous pinch dried basil
2 pears (Bosc or other), halved, cored and
    cubed

Preheat oven to 400F (205C). Soak currants in a mixture of half mirin and half water until tender, about 30 minutes. Spread pecans evenly on a baking sheet and toast them lightly in oven, about 8 minutes. Coarsely dice pecans and set aside.

In a medium saucepan, bring 5 cups of water to a boil with a pinch of salt. Stir in bulgur, cover and cook over low heat until all liquid has been absorbed and bulgur is tender, about 15 minutes.

While bulgur cooks, heat oil in a skillet over medium heat. Add onion and a pinch of salt and cook until translucent, 5 minutes. Add celery and a pinch of salt and cook over medium heat until tender, about 10 minutes. Add basil, stir in pears and a pinch of salt and cook 2 to 3 minutes. Transfer mixture to a large bowl and add bulgur and pecans. Drain currants and gently fold into mixture. Allow to cool completely before using.

Mushroom-Rice Stuffing

MAKES ENOUGH STUFFING FOR 1 LARGE WINTER SQUASH

2 to 3 dried shiitake mushrooms
1 to 2 dried porcini mushrooms
Spring or filtered water
2 cups brown basmati rice, rinsed well,
    soaked for at least 1 hour and drained
1 cup wild rice, rinsed well
5½ cups Mushroom Stock (page 75)
Sea salt
Bay leaves
2 cloves fresh garlic, minced
1 onion, diced
2 to 3 celery ribs, diced
1 pound button mushrooms, brushed clean
    and diced
¼ cup minced fresh flat-leaf parsley

Soak dried mushrooms in hot water until tender. Combine both rices and stock, 3 pinches of salt and bay leaves in a pressure cooker over medium heat. Seal and bring to full pressure. Reduce heat to low and cook 25 minutes. Remove from heat and allow to stand, undisturbed for another 25 minutes. Transfer rice to a bowl, discard bay leaves and set aside.

Heat 2 tablespoons water in a skillet over medium heat. Add garlic, onion and a pinch of salt and water-sauté 3 to 4 minutes. Add celery, button mushrooms and a pinch of salt and cook until very soft, about 8 minutes. Drain porcini and shiitake mushrooms, remove stems and dice. Stir into vegetables and simmer 3 to 4 minutes. Add the mushroom mixture to cooked rice, season to taste with salt and mix well. Fold in parsley and allow to cool completely before using.

■ **NOTE** For added richness, sauté in 2 tablespoons extra-virgin olive oil in place of the water-sauté.

Cornbread and Chestnut Stuffing

MAKES ENOUGH STUFFING FOR 1 LARGE WINTER SQUASH

Cornbread with Fresh Corn (page 285), cubed
1 loaf sourdough bread, crusts removed and cubed
1 pound fresh chestnuts
1 tablespoon avocado oil
1 onion, finely minced
Generous pinch dried sage
¼ cup minced fresh flat-leaf parsley
Soy sauce
2 or 3 celery stalks, minced
1 cup firm tofu, cut into tiny cubes and shallow-fried (page 228) until golden
2 cups Vegetable Stock (page 74)

Preheat oven to 300F (175C). Spread bread and cornbread cubes evenly on a baking sheet. Bake 20 to 30 minutes to dry. Set aside.

Make a slit in the flat side of each chestnut. Cook in boiling water over high heat 15 minutes. Drain chestnuts, wrap in a towel to keep them warm and set aside 10 minutes. Peel off both the hard outer shell and the inner papery layer. Set chestnuts aside.

Heat oil in a skillet over medium heat. Add onion, sage, parsley and a dash of soy sauce and cook, stirring, 2 or 3 minutes. Add celery and a dash of soy sauce and cook until tender, about 8 minutes. Season lightly with soy sauce and remove from heat. Stir in chestnuts and fried tofu and transfer to a large bowl.

Add bread cubes and mix well, slowly adding stock, while stirring, until stuffing forms a soft ball. Taste and adjust seasoning. Allow to cool completely before using.

Twice-Stuffed Squash

We love squash. I mean we *really* love squash, to the point that, by the end of winter, the palms of our hands have turned a pale orange. This delightful centerpiece dish can be made with any flavorful winter squash: hokkaido, buttercup, even acorn.

MAKES 2 TO 4 SERVINGS

1 small winter squash (about 2 pounds)
Spring or filtered water
½ teaspoon light olive or avocado oil
1 onion, diced
Sea salt
1 cup firm tofu, crumbled
¼ cup minced fresh flat-leaf parsley
½ cup hazelnuts, pan-toasted (see Note, page 46) and minced
Sprigs flat-leaf parsley, for garnish

Preheat oven to 375F (190C). Lightly oil a baking dish. Halve the squash lengthwise and place, cut sides down (seeds and all), in prepared baking dish. Add a little water and bake about 40 minutes, until you can just pierce the skin with a fork.

Heat oil in a skillet over medium heat. Add the onion and a pinch of salt and cook, stirring, until translucent, 5 minutes. Stir in tofu, sprinkle lightly with salt and cook about 5 minutes. Set aside.

Scoop out the seeds and stringy pulp from the squash halves. Remove the flesh, reserving one half for another use. Place half of the squash flesh and the tofu mixture in a food processor. Season lightly with 1 to 2 pinches of salt. Process until smooth, adding only a little water if needed to produce a creamy texture. Stir in parsley.

Spoon squash mixture into the reserved squash shells and place in a lightly oiled baking dish. Sprinkle with hazelnuts and bake, uncovered, until the top is golden, about 20 minutes. Transfer to a platter and serve hot, garnished with parsley sprigs.

Olive Broccoli

My mother really had a challenge cooking for me as a kid. I hated everything. This was one of her favorites—and one that I would actually eat!

MAKES 4 SERVINGS

1 head broccoli
Spring or filtered water
1 teaspoon extra-virgin olive oil
Red wine vinegar
Grated zest and juice of 1 lemon
1 red bell pepper, roasted over a flame, peeled, seeded and diced (see Note, page 262)
½ cup oil-cured black olives, pitted and minced

Split broccoli lengthwise into spears, trimming off any coarse stems and leaves. Bring a small amount of water to a boil over high heat. Add broccoli and steam until bright green and crisp-tender, about 4 minutes. Drain and transfer to a bowl. Immediately drizzle lightly with oil and vinegar and toss gently. Stir in lemon zest and juice, bell pepper and olives and turn the ingredients gently to combine. Arrange on a platter and serve warm.

Baked Herbed Onions

Baking onions whole and unpeeled helps keep their full-bodied, sweet flavor.

MAKES 5 TO 6 SERVINGS

5 or 6 red or Vidalia onions, unpeeled
3 to 4 fresh basil sprigs, slivered
1 to 2 fresh rosemary sprigs
¼ cup extra-virgin olive oil
2 tablespoons brown rice syrup
1 tablespoon brown rice vinegar
2 tablespoons balsamic vinegar
1 cup Onion Stock (page 75)
Sea salt
Cracked black pepper

Preheat oven to 375F (190C). Lightly oil a baking dish and set aside. Slice the base off each onion, retaining the root, to make a flat surface so the onions stand upright. Make a small slit in the top of each onion and insert some basil and rosemary into each one. Arrange the onions in prepared baking dish.

Whisk together the oil, rice syrup, vinegars, stock and salt and pepper to taste. Pour mixture over the onions and bake 1 to 1½ hours, uncovered, basting occasionally, until the onions are soft when pierced with a knife. Before serving, split the skins and remove; they should pull away very easily. Transfer onions to a platter and serve hot.

Sesame Cabbage

Chinese cabbage is a mild Asian vegetable with a delicate taste and versatile nature. More hearty than lettuce, it can be used in a variety of ways: shredded in slaws, blanched, pressed, sautéed or steamed. In this dish, it is lightly simmered and gently flavored.

MAKES 4 TO 6 SERVINGS

½ cup tan sesame seeds, rinsed and well
    drained
1 cup Vegetable Stock (page 74)
4 or 5 green onions, cut into thin diagonal
    slices
1 small head Chinese cabbage, shredded
1 tablespoon light sesame oil
Pinch crushed red pepper flakes, or to taste
Sea salt
Brown rice vinegar

In a hot, dry skillet, lightly pan-toast the seeds over medium heat until fragrant, about 4 minutes. Place in a bowl and set aside.

Bring the stock to a boil over high heat and boil 3 to 4 minutes to reduce and concentrate the flavors. Add the green onions and cabbage, reduce the heat to medium and cook until vegetables are tender, 3 to 4 minutes. Drizzle with oil and stir in red pepper flakes. Season

lightly with salt and stir well. Remove from heat and stir in vinegar to taste. Toss with sesame seeds and transfer to a serving bowl. Serve hot, or chilled in warm weather.

Braised Onions, Shallots and Leeks

Love onions? Then this recipe is for you.

MAKES 4 TO 6 SERVINGS

1 tablespoon extra-virgin olive oil
3 red onions, cut into thick wedges
3 Vidalia (or yellow) onions, cut into thick
    wedges
Sea salt
4 or 5 shallots, halved
3 leeks, cut lengthwise, rinsed well and sliced
    into 2-inch lengths
Spring or filtered water
Fresh basil, minced, or dried basil
Juice of 1 lime
Reduced balsamic vinegar (see Note, page
    160)

Heat oil in a deep skillet over low heat. Add onions and a pinch of salt and cook, stirring, until they begin to soften, about 10 minutes. Add shallots and a pinch of salt and cook, stirring, 4 to 5 minutes. Add leeks and a pinch of salt and cook, stirring, until bright green and tender, 5 minutes. Add a little water and a sprinkling of basil. Cover and cook over medium heat until tender, about 30 minutes. Season lightly with salt and simmer until any remaining liquid has been absorbed. Remove from heat and stir in lime juice and vinegar to taste. Transfer to a platter and serve.

Chestnuts and Brussels Sprouts

When I lived in Italy and the winter arrived, the cold air brought with it an abundance of fresh chestnuts or *castagne*. And we used them in everything, from desserts to stuffings to snacks. In this dish, the sweet taste and chewy texture of the chestnuts harmonize beautifully with the crisp, fresh taste of Brussels sprouts.

MAKES 4 TO 6 SERVINGS

12 to 15 fresh chestnuts
Spring or filtered water
1 tablespoon extra-virgin olive oil
2 cloves fresh garlic, minced
2 pounds Brussels sprouts, trimmed
Sea salt
2 cups Vegetable Stock (page 74)
Grated zest and juice of 1 lemon

Make a slit in the flat side of each chestnut. Cook in boiling water over high heat 15 minutes. Drain chestnuts, wrap in a towel to keep them warm and set aside 10 minutes. Peel off both the hard outer shell and the inner papery layer. Set chestnuts aside.

Heat oil in a deep skillet over medium heat. Add garlic and cook 1 to 2 minutes. Add Brussels sprouts and a generous pinch of salt and cook, stirring to combine. Add chestnuts and stock, cover and simmer over low heat until Brussels sprouts are just tender, 10 to 12 minutes. Season lightly with salt and simmer 3 to 4 minutes. Remove from heat and drain well if any liquid remains. Stir in lemon zest and juice and transfer to a serving bowl. Serve warm.

■ **NOTE:** If fresh chestnuts are unavailable, you may use canned or frozen ones.

Ginger-Glazed Acorn Squash

The sweet and spicy glaze makes this side dish better than dessert!

MAKES 4 SERVINGS

2 acorn squash, halved lengthwise and seeds removed
Spring or filtered water
3 tablespoons avocado oil
3 tablespoons brown rice syrup
2 teaspoons fresh ginger juice (see Note, page 164)
Dash grated nutmeg
Dash ground cinnamon
Sea salt
5 tablespoons unsweetened or fruit-sweetened apricot preserves

Preheat oven to 350F (175C). Lightly oil a baking dish. Place squash halves, cut sides down, in prepared baking dish. Add a little water and bake about 20 minutes.

Whisk together oil, rice syrup, ginger juice, spices, a generous pinch of salt and preserves. Remove squash from the oven and turn cut sides up. Brush insides of squash with syrup mixture and spoon the remaining mixture equally into each hollow. Cover loosely with foil or oiled parchment paper and return squash to the oven. Bake until tender, about 35 minutes. Arrange on a platter and serve hot.

Parrot Fritters

No, no, I'm not suggesting you sauté Polly when she wants a cracker. It's just a name that I gave to these fritters made of parsnips and carrots. The creamy, sweet taste of the vegetables is complemented deliciously by the crispy outer coating achieved by pan-frying—a great starter dish or party food.

MAKES 4 TO 6 SERVINGS

3 carrots, cut into 2-inch pieces
3 parsnips, cut into 2-inch pieces
Spring or filtered water
Sea salt
Pinch baking powder
About ¼ cup whole wheat pastry flour
½ cup coarsely minced walnut pieces
¼ cup minced fresh flat-leaf parsley
About ½ cup yellow cornmeal
Avocado oil, for frying
Sprigs flat-leaf parsley, for garnish

Place carrots, parsnips and a small amount of water in a saucepan over medium heat and bring to a boil. Cover, reduce heat and simmer until tender, about 25 minutes. Drain and spoon vegetables into a food processor. Season lightly with salt and add baking powder. Process, slowly adding flour, until mixture begins to firm up. Transfer to a bowl and fold in walnuts and parsley.

With moist hands, shape batter into 2-inch ovals or discs. Pour cornmeal into a bowl and coat each fritter with cornmeal, covering the entire surface.

Heat about ½ inch of oil in a deep skillet over medium heat. Fry several fritters at a time until golden, about 3 minutes per side. Do not overfill the skillet as it will reduce the temperature of the oil, resulting in oily fritters, not crispy treats. Drain well on paper towels before arranging on a serving platter. Serve garnished with parsley sprigs.

Ray's Brussels Sprouts and Corn

One of my greatest inspirations is sharing recipes and seeing how people interpret and make them their own. I gave this simple vegetable stew recipe to a good friend. The only change he made was to add bay leaves during the cooking. The result was fabulous.

MAKES 4 TO 6 SERVINGS

2 red onions, cut into thick wedges
2 pounds Brussels sprouts, trimmed and left whole
2 ears of corn, cut into 1½-inch rounds
Spring or filtered water
2 to 3 bay leaves
Sea salt

In a heavy pot, layer onions, Brussels sprouts and corn rounds. Add about $\frac{1}{16}$ inch of water and bring to a boil over medium heat. Add bay leaves. Reduce heat, cover and simmer over low heat 15 minutes. Season lightly with salt and simmer 10 minutes. Remove the lid and allow any remaining liquid to be absorbed. Remove bay leaves and discard. Transfer vegetables to a bowl and serve warm.

Parsnip Slaw

A unique take on cole slaw. Served warm, this sweet side dish has become a standard on my Thanksgiving table.

MAKES 4 SERVINGS

Spring or filtered water
5 to 6 parsnips, cut into thin matchsticks
1 red onion, cut into thin half-moon slices
¼ cup minced fresh flat-leaf parsley
1 recipe Tofu Mayo (page 272)

Bring a pot of water to a boil, add parsnips and boil until crisp-tender, 2 to 3 minutes. Remove from pot with a strainer, drain and place in a bowl. In same water, quickly blanch onion, about 30 seconds, and add to parsnips. Toss vegetables with parsley and Tofu Mayo and serve warm.

Christmas Parsnips

This wonder dish came to be when I had to create a quick and colorful dish for a fund-raiser televised by our local public broadcasting station affiliate. The task was quick-and-easy holiday cooking. I think you'll agree this dish fits the category.

MAKES 4 SERVINGS

1 tablespoon extra-virgin olive oil
2 or 3 cloves fresh garlic, minced
1 cup fresh cranberries, sorted and rinsed
Sea salt
2 cups thin matchstick pieces parsnips
3 or 4 green onions, cut into 1-inch pieces
½ cup fresh orange juice
1 to 2 teaspoons kuzu or arrowroot, dissolved in 3 tablespoons cold water

Heat oil in a wok or skillet over medium heat. Add garlic and cook 1 minute. Add cranberries and a pinch of salt and cook until cranberries begin to pop. Add parsnips and a pinch of salt and cook until parsnips are just tender, about 4 minutes. Stir in green onions, season to taste with salt and cook 1 minute. Stir in orange juice and dissolved kuzu and cook until a thin glaze forms over the vegetables, about 3 minutes. Transfer to a platter and serve hot.

Nori Condiment

Delicious as an accompaniment for whole grains.

MAKES 3 TO 4 SERVINGS

7 or 8 sheets nori
Spring or filtered water
Soy sauce

Shred nori into small pieces and place in a small saucepan. Add enough water to just cover and season lightly with soy sauce. Bring to a boil over low heat and cook, uncovered, until all liquid has been absorbed and the nori has become very creamy, about 20 minutes. Transfer to a small bowl and serve warm or at room temperature.

Fresh Daikon and Kombu in Orange Sauce

A refreshingly clean-tasting dish.

MAKES 3 OR 4 SERVINGS

Spring or filtered water
1 (6-inch) piece kombu, soaked about 5
    minutes or until tender and cut into thin
    pieces
1 medium daikon, cut into ½-inch rounds

ORANGE SAUCE
Juice and grated zest of 1 orange
1 teaspoon fresh lemon juice
1 teaspoon balsamic vinegar
½ teaspoon sea salt
1 teaspoon brown rice syrup

Bring about 1 inch of water to a boil in a small saucepan. Add kombu and cook over low heat, about 10 minutes. Remove with a strainer and cook daikon in the same water until just tender, about 10 minutes. Drain and combine with kombu. Arrange on a serving platter.

Make sauce: Whisk together all sauce ingredients in a small bowl and spoon over the hot daikon and kombu. Allow to marinate 15 to 20 minutes. Chill completely before serving.

Carrot and Kombu Rolls

A lovely combination of flavors presented in a unique and beautiful way. Use small to medium carrots for this recipe.

MAKES 4 SERVINGS

4 (8-inch) pieces kombu, soaked about 5
    minutes or until tender
12 (3-inch) carrot pieces
Spring or filtered water
Soy sauce

Cut 3 pieces of kombu into 2-inch pieces, reserving the fourth piece. Wrap each piece of kombu around a carrot piece. Cut the remaining piece of kombu in half and into thin strips. Tie each strip around a carrot, holding the wrapped kombu in place with a knot.

Place the carrots in a pot and add enough water to half-cover. Bring to a boil over medium heat, cover and simmer over low heat about 40 minutes. Season lightly with soy sauce and simmer 7 to 10 minutes. Transfer to a platter and serve warm.

Wakame Casserole

This casserole resembles a quiche with its light texture and rich taste.

MAKES 4 TO 6 SERVINGS

1 teaspoon dark sesame oil
1 cup diced onion
1 pound tofu, crumbled
½ cup toasted sesame tahini
2 cups wakame, soaked 5 minutes and diced
Soy sauce
Black sesame seeds, for garnish

Heat oil in a skillet over medium heat. Add onion and cook, stirring, until translucent, 2 to 3 minutes. Set aside.

Preheat oven to 350F (175C). Lightly oil a casserole and set aside. Process tofu and tahini in a food processor until smooth. Transfer to a bowl and mix in onion, wakame and soy sauce to taste. Spread evenly in prepared casserole and sprinkle generously with sesame seeds. Cover and bake 35 minutes. Remove cover and bake until the top browns and the casserole sets, 10 to 15 minutes. Serve hot.

Marinated Wakame and Vegetables

A quick and easy vegetable dish with a zesty marinated taste.

MAKES 4 TO 6 SERVINGS

Spring or filtered water
½ cup thin matchstick pieces carrot
1 head cauliflower, cut into small florets
4 or 5 snow peas, trimmed and left whole
½ cup wakame, soaked 3 minutes, drained and diced

MARINADE
Juice of 1 lime
¼ cup brown rice vinegar
1 teaspoon soy sauce
1 tablespoon balsamic vinegar
Spring or filtered water

Bring a pot of water to a boil. Separately cook each vegetable until crisp-tender: carrots about 30 seconds, cauliflower about 3 minutes and snow peas about 30 seconds. Drain well and mix with diced wakame.

Make marinade: Mix together all ingredients, adding only 1 or 2 tablespoons water to gentle the flavor of the marinade but not make it watery.

Toss the vegetables with the marinade and allow to stand about 30 minutes to allow the flavors to develop. Toss gently again just before serving.

Dulse with Corn and Broccoli

A colorful and delicious summer sea vegetable dish.

MAKES ABOUT 4 SERVINGS

Spring or filtered water
Corn kernels, cut from 3 ears fresh corn
2 stalks broccoli, cut into florets, with stems peeled and diced
1 cup dulse, rinsed, set aside to soften and diced
1 green onion, cut into thin diagonal slices
1 teaspoon brown rice vinegar
1 teaspoon balsamic vinegar
1 teaspoon soy sauce

Bring a pot of water to a boil and separately cook the corn about 30 seconds, broccoli stems and broccoli flowerets about 2 minutes, until crisp-tender. Toss with dulse and green onion. Drizzle with vinegars and soy sauce and toss gently to incorporate all ingredients. Adjust seasoning to your taste, but take care not to make the dish too salty. Remember, dulse is a sea plant and is naturally salty. Transfer to a bowl and serve warm or, in hot weather, chilled.

Jim's Hiziki Strudel

Cooking for people who are not necessarily attracted to sea vegetables can be quite a challenge. A friend of mine came up with this dish and, so far, no one has been able to resist the rich sautéed vegetables and hiziki wrapped in a flaky pastry crust.

MAKES 6 TO 8 SERVINGS

2 teaspoons light sesame oil
1 cup hiziki, soaked until tender (about 10
**   minutes), and drained**
1 to 2 teaspoons mirin
Spring or filtered water
1 onion, cut into half-moon slices
1 cup thin matchstick pieces carrot
Soy sauce

STRUDEL DOUGH
1 cup whole wheat pastry flour
½ cup semolina flour
Pinch sea salt
¼ cup avocado oil
About 2 tablespoons spring or filtered water

Tan sesame seeds

Heat sesame oil in a skillet over medium heat. Add hiziki and cook, stirring, about 4 minutes. Add mirin and enough water to half-cover and simmer over low heat 20 minutes. Add onion and carrot, season lightly with soy sauce, cover and simmer 10 minutes. Remove the cover and allow to cook until any remaining liquid has been absorbed. Transfer to a bowl and set aside to cool while preparing the strudel dough.

Make the dough: Sift together flours and salt into a bowl. Stir in oil with a fork until crumbly. Slowly add enough water so dough just holds together. Gather into a ball and knead 2 to 3 minutes.

Preheat oven to 350F (175C). Line a baking sheet with parchment paper and set aside. Roll out dough between sheets of waxed paper into a thin rectangle. Remove 1 sheet of paper and spread hiziki filling over pastry, leaving about 1 inch of dough exposed all around. Roll, jelly-roll style, using paper to help roll, and seal the ends of the strudel with a fork. Gently transfer to prepared baking sheet. Cut several slits in the top of the strudel so it will not split during baking. Sprinkle with sesame seeds.

Bake about 35 minutes, until golden and the strudel sounds hollow when tapped. Cool about 10 minutes before slicing. Cut into 1-inch-thick slices, arrange on a platter and serve warm.

Vinegared Hiziki

A small amount of this zesty strong dish will go a long way.

MAKES 4 SERVINGS

½ cup hiziki, soaked 10 minutes
Spring or filtered water
Soy sauce
2 teaspoons mirin
½ red bell pepper, roasted over a flame,
**   peeled, seeded and diced (see Note, page**
**   262)**
1 cup diced watercress
2 tablespoons brown rice vinegar
Juice of 1 lemon

Place hiziki in a saucepan with enough water to half-cover, season lightly with soy sauce and mirin and bring to a boil. Reduce heat and simmer, uncovered, 5 minutes. Cover and cook

30 minutes more. Add bell pepper, cover and simmer 5 minutes. Remove cover and cook away any remaining liquid. Remove pan from heat. Toss watercress into the hot hiziki to wilt, and stir in vinegar and lemon juice. Transfer to a bowl and serve warm.

Arame Sauté

A quick and delicious dish chock-full of lightly cooked vegetables, accented with arame.

MAKES 2 OR 3 SERVINGS

½ cup arame
Spring or filtered water
Soy sauce
1 teaspoon mirin
1 teaspoon dark sesame oil
2 or 3 shallots, diced
1 clove fresh garlic, thinly sliced
2 cups button mushrooms, brushed clean and thinly sliced

1 cup thin matchstick pieces carrots
2 or 3 stalks broccoli, cut into florets and stems peeled and diced
2 tablespoons sunflower seeds, lightly pan-toasted (See Note, page 46)

Rinse arame well and set aside. It will soften in a few minutes without soaking.

Place arame in a small saucepan with enough water to half-cover. Bring to a boil, cover and cook over low heat 15 minutes. Season lightly with soy sauce and mirin and cook until all liquid has been absorbed.

Heat oil in a skillet over medium heat. Add shallots, garlic and a splash of soy sauce and cook, stirring, until translucent, 5 minutes. Add mushrooms and a splash of soy sauce and cook, stirring, until wilted. Add carrots and a splash of soy sauce and cook, stirring, 1 to 2 minutes. Finally, stir in broccoli and season very lightly with soy sauce. Cover and cook over low heat until broccoli is bright green and crisp-tender, about 4 minutes. Stir in arame and sunflower seeds. Transfer to a bowl and serve warm.

Pastabilities

THERE IS NOTHING on earth I would rather eat than a bowl of pasta, truly . . . not chocolate or any gourmet indulgence. Growing up in an Italian household, pasta was a staple of our diet. I can remember my mother asking what we would like for dinner and all of us piping up "macaroni" (it hadn't yet been dubbed "pasta" and yuppiefied for mainstream acceptance). As I grew, and my love affair with cooking developed, I began experimenting with macaroni and sauces from every cookbook, magazine, booklet and olive oil label I could get my hands on. Later, as I traveled around the Mediterranean, I came across the most amazing chefs creating a wide variety of pasta dishes—delicious combinations of simple, fresh ingredients resulting in stunning sauces and accompaniments to this remarkable food.

Pasta is undeniably the most popular food in our diet today. Even our insane obsession with high-protein diets couldn't take pasta down! Surrounded by folklore and stereotypical images, it is nonetheless true that pasta is a serious and very important food. It is an extraordinary dietary staple that has remained a constant throughout culinary history and has achieved worldwide popularity.

Today, thanks to our increasing knowledge of calories, excess fat intake and the newly rediscovered sensibility of eating carbohydrates (thank goodness!), pasta has become, once again, the victorious queen of the table. Simple to prepare and completely delicious, pasta is being touted as a central food in today's new low-fat, low-cholesterol diet. And easy? With today's hectic pace, it is nice to know that there is a healthful and delicious food choice that can become the centerpiece dish in everything from a quick weekday supper to an elegant dinner party designed to impress.

Pasta seems to have threaded its way through just about every culture recorded, but I will concentrate on the use of noodles in Asian and Italian cuisine, because these are the cultures that use pasta on a grand scale, elevating their preparation to an art form. Frankly, these are the ones I am the most experienced with and love the most, and since it *is* my book . . .

While I will include recipes for making pasta from scratch, the purpose of these recipes is to show you how to use ready-made, good-quality macaroni. I will admit that although I love to make noodles from scratch on occasion, my schedule usually doesn't allow me the luxury too often. And with all the great pasta products available to us today, you can have great quality anytime. Let me tell you, though, pasta-making is a great art and a wonderful way to relax in your kitchen when you have spare time. And nothing tastes quite like it. Give it a go one day, just for fun.

Pasta is a general term for a wide variety of noodle shapes on the market today. Traditionally, pasta was made simply of wheat flour, water and salt. As modern people craved richer and richer foods, chefs created pastas made with eggs and even cheese, unnecessary ingredients for delicious pastas. I recommend that you read labels and make your choices. Most pasta is composed of durum or semolina flour, a hard wheat. This particular grain gives the pasta a lovely texture and light flavor with a light yellow color, typical of Italian macaroni. Asian pastas are composed of everything from whole wheat flour to buckwheat flour. Domestic pastas are made from wheat, rice, corn and even more exotic grains, like quinoa and amaranth, to accommodate dietary restrictions with regard to wheat. I have to say, though, some of them are quite nice and worth experimenting with.

In addition, of course, there are tons of organic pastas, traditionally made and gloriously delicious. Like everything else I prepare, I always want the best-quality ingredients available to me and will choose the organic every single time I can. Oh, before you even think it, the price for organic is only slightly higher than the commercial brands, so there are no excuses for not serving the very best.

So in this section, let's talk pasta—types, shapes and styles as well as sauces and methods of cooking. Pasta loves sauce, everything from oil and garlic to rich savory gravies. With so many ways to enjoy pasta today—salads, appetizers, main courses and side dishes—you can eat it from morning till night. (Okay, maybe that would be excessive.) An impressive array of creative recipes awaits you—colorful dishes made with the finest-quality pastas and combined with fresh vegetables, herbs and spices, light dressings and rich sauces. Use these recipes as a stepping-stone to creating your own pasta repertoire.

Cooking Tips

A few tips on cooking pasta before we begin. Al dente means "chewy" ("to the tooth," to be exact); pasta should still retain some body after cooking. It should be firm, but not undercooked, and certainly not mushy. There is a reason Italians are so obsessed with al dente pasta. Ever notice that Italians eat pasta all the time and very few of them are struggling with extra pounds the way we do? It's all in the cooking, silly. Italians know that al dente pasta is not an "insulin trigger," so that a small portion of macaroni will suffice, with no need to eat more and more and more. Slightly undercooking noodles ensures that your blood sugars stay level and you are satisfied with a human-sized portion and don't end up eating a meat platter of macaroni.

To achieve real al dente-style pasta, simply cook the noodles for about a minute less than the package directions indicate. Test for doneness by tasting a piece. Al dente is achieved when the pasta is soft, but resists your bite ever so slightly. You may also test by removing a noodle from the water and cutting it with your fingernail. If the noodle is cooked through and cuts easily, with no white, uncooked center, the pasta is ready to drain. And there is always the method of throwing pasta against the wall. If it sticks, it's done. Kind of a drag when cleanup time rolls around, though.

Also, remember to cook pasta in a large pot with lots of water so it can cook thoroughly and evenly without sticking together. Salting the water helps the pasta to retain its firmness, so I do it all the time. It also returns the water to a boil quicker than unsalted water and, some say, prevents the noodles from becoming too soft and mushy. And adding a drizzle of olive oil to the water before cooking your pasta helps to prevent sticking.

To Rinse or Not to Rinse . . . Italy Versus Japan

Rinsing helps remove excess starch from the pasta and prevents the noodles from clumping together in one large lump. When you rinse pasta, use an ample-sized colander with plenty of room for the noodles to be moved. Rinse until no warmth remains to ensure that they will not stick. If you want the noodles to be hot when you serve them, simply plunge them into hot water just before serving time. This method is great when making pasta salads or when you want to serve the sauce ladled over the pasta and not incorporated throughout the dish. However, most Italian cooks, me included, will tell you that rinsing pasta is unnecessary (some even say it is rude); that unrinsed pasta holds the sauce better, which is true. In this case, cook the pasta, drain, immediately toss it with the desired sauce and serve. I never rinse . . . with one exception: Japanese noodles. My experience has been that they are a bit more salty than other noodles and rinsing helps remove some of that excess salt from their surface.

Gnocchi

I thought that I invented this gnocchi recipe. I was so excited that I called an Italian friend to break this groundbreaking culinary news. Much to my dismay, he informed me that chefs in northern Italy have been making gnocchi with rice for many years; that, in fact, gnocchi made with potatoes is a relatively recent development. So much for my invention. Oh, well, they are truly delicious anyway, so enjoy.

MAKES 4 TO 6 SERVINGS

½ cup white rice
1 cup plus ¼ cup spring or filtered water
1½ cups semolina flour
1 cup unbleached white flour
Sea salt
Extra-virgin olive oil

Cook rice in 1 cup water over low heat until soft, about 30 minutes. Puree cooked rice in a food processor until creamy. Combine with flours and a pinch of sea salt, mixing until a stiff dough forms, slowly adding remaining water if necessary. Knead dough about 10 minutes until flexible, ear-lobe consistency. Coat a fork or gnocchi comb with flour. Pull off a 2-inch ball of dough, and roll, by hand, on a floured surface, into a long, thin cylinder, about ¼ inch thick. Cut crosswise into bite-size pieces of dough and push the fork or comb along the piece so that a roll forms with ridges. Place each gnocchi on a floured baking sheet while preparing the rest of the pasta.

You may either cook the pasta immediately or allow them to dry for a few days, on the baking sheet, covered lightly with a cloth. Store dried gnocchi in an airtight container until cooked.

To cook gnocchi, bring a large amount of water to a boil with a pinch of sea salt and a dash of olive oil. Drop in gnocchi and stir.

When they rise to the top of the pot, taste one. Continue to cook until the tenderness you desire is achieved. They should be chewy, but not hard or undercooked or mushy.

Cauliflower Sauce

This simple sauce is deliciously reminiscent of conventional white sauces, without the dairy fat and high caloric content.

MAKES 4 TO 6 SERVINGS

1 tablespoon extra-virgin olive oil

2 cloves fresh garlic, sliced

Several leaves fresh basil, minced, or generous pinch dried basil

½ cup diced onion

1 head cauliflower, cut into small florets and stem diced

Rice or soy milk

Sea salt

1 recipe Gnocchi (opposite) or other pasta, cooked

¼ cup minced fresh flat-leaf parsley

Heat oil in a skillet over medium heat. Add garlic and cook until lightly browned. Take care not to burn it or the oil will turn bitter. Remove garlic from oil and discard. Add basil and onion and cook, stirring, until translucent, about 5 minutes. Add cauliflower and stir well. Add enough milk to just half-cover ingredients, season lightly with salt and cover. Reduce heat and simmer, uncovered, until cauliflower is soft, 10 to 15 minutes. Puree until smooth, adding water if necessary to achieve a creamy sauce. Toss with hot gnocchi and parsley and serve immediately.

Squash Gnocchi with Basil Oil

Okay, this is a bit of work. I will admit that. But these are so sensual, so delicious, so worth the work, you'll find yourself making them more than you ever thought.

MAKES 8 TO 10 SERVINGS, ABOUT 1 POUND OF DOUGH

PASTA DOUGH

1 to 2 cups semolina flour

1 cup cooked white rice, pureed until smooth

1 teaspoon sea salt

2 tablespoons extra-virgin olive oil

1 cup pureed cooked butternut squash or canned pumpkin

Spring or filtered water

BASIL OIL

¼ cup extra-virgin olive oil

2 cloves fresh garlic, thinly sliced

Pinch crushed red pepper flakes

Pinch sea salt

6 to 8 leaves fresh basil, left whole

Fresh basil sprigs, for garnish

Make the pasta: Sift flour onto a dry work surface. Make a well in the center of flour and add rice, salt, oil and squash. Mix gradually, kneading into a smooth, soft dough by drawing a small amount of flour in from the edges as you knead. Add more flour if the dough seems too sticky or more water if it feels too dry. In both cases, add small amounts very slowly so as not to jeopardize the quality of the dough. Continue kneading until dough is a soft, workable ball, about 10 minutes. Set aside 10 minutes to rest.

Flour a fork. Pinch off 1-inch pieces of dough and roll into balls between your fingers. Run the pasta ball on the fork to create ridges. Transfer to a parchment paper-lined baking sheet that has been sprinkled with semolina. Repeat until you have made the desired amount of gnocchi. (The balance of the dough can be frozen up to 1 month.)

Bring a pot of water to a boil, with a pinch of salt and a drizzle of olive oil. Cook the gnocchi until just tender, about 2 minutes. The gnocchi will sink to the bottom of the pot. When they rise, they're done. Drain, but do not rinse.

While the pasta cooks, make the oil: Place all ingredients in a saucepan over low heat and cook 3 to 4 minutes to develop the flavors. Strain the oil and toss with cooked gnocchi. Garnish with fresh basil sprigs and serve immediately.

Mac and Cheese

Nothing says comfort food quite like mac and cheese, but now that you have committed to a vegan way of eating, is that comfort gone forever? Not hardly. And you don't have to resort to using only sauces made with nutritional yeast, either. My version is yummy, creamy and as close to the real thing as I have tasted, if I do say so myself.

MAKES ABOUT 6 SERVINGS

8 ounces elbow or small shell pasta
4 tablespoons vegetarian buttery spread (like Earth Balance)
4 tablespoons whole wheat pastry flour
Sea salt
Cracked black pepper
2 cups unsweetened soymilk
1 cup shredded vegan sharp cheese alternatives
Whole wheat bread crumbs

Bring a large pot of water to a boil with a pinch of salt and cook pasta until it is about 80 percent done. Drain well.

While the pasta cooks, prepare the sauce: Melt the spread in a saucepan over medium-low heat. Whisk flour into the melted spread and cook, stirring until smooth and bubbly. Stir in a generous pinch of salt and pepper. Slowly whisk in soymilk and cook, whisking, until thickened, 3 to 4 minutes. Stir in cheese alternative and continue to cook until melted.

Preheat oven to 350F (175C) and lightly oil an 8 × 10 baking dish. Alternate layers of cheese sauce and cooked macaroni in prepared baking dish, ending with sauce on the top. Sprinkle generously with bread crumbs and bake 20 to 25 minutes, until hot and bubbly.

On Top of Spaghetti

Spaghetti and meatballs were such a part of my life as a kid that I could not imagine giving them up when I changed my life. Turns out, I didn't have to . . .

MAKES 4 OR 5 SERVINGS

1 recipe Tomato Sauce (opposite)

MEATLESS BALLS

1 cup crumbled soy ground "meat" (such as Gimme Lean!)

⅓ cup finely minced red onion

½ to ⅔ cup fresh bread crumbs

1 teaspoon finely minced fresh basil

½ teaspoon dried oregano

½ teaspoon garlic powder

½ teaspoon sea salt

½ teaspoon cracked black pepper

¼ cup tomato paste

1 pound whole wheat spaghetti

Preheat oven to 375F (190C). Oil a baking sheet and set aside.

Prepare balls: Combine all ingredients well and form into balls. Place on prepared baking sheet and bake 20 minutes, turning once, halfway through cooking.

Meanwhile, bring a pot of water to a boil. Add a drizzle of oil and a pinch of salt. Cook spaghetti until just tender to the bite, about 10 minutes. Drain well; do not rinse.

Mix balls gently into some of the sauce. Toss spaghetti with sauce to coat and serve with balls on top.

Rich, Tasty, Creamy, Yummy Lasagna

I am not much for fake foods, designed to fool us into eating healthy, but sometimes, they can work. And while different than their conventional versions, they can be delicious and satisfying and familiar ways to help us transition to healthier choices. This lasagna is fabulous, tofu or not. I make my sauce from scratch, but feel free to use a jarred or canned one to make life easier.

Makes 10 to 12 servings

TOMATO SAUCE

Extra-virgin olive oil

1 small onion, finely diced

3 or 4 cloves fresh garlic, finely minced

Sea salt

Generous pinch dried oregano

1 (6-ounce) can tomato paste

Spring or filtered water

2 (28-ounce) cans diced tomatoes, undrained

1 carrot, left whole

2 bay leaves

3 to 4 sprigs basil, leaves removed

Cracked black pepper

1 pound uncooked eggless lasagna noodles

1 pound extra-firm tofu

3 sprigs basil, leaves removed and minced

3 tablespoons extra-virgin olive oil

Sea salt

1 (8-ounce) package vegan mozzarella cheese alternative, grated

Prepare the tomato sauce: Place a small amount of oil, onion and garlic in a soup pot over medium heat. When the onion begins to sizzle, add a pinch of salt and oregano and sauté 2 to 3 minutes. Add tomato paste, 2 cans of water (tomato paste can) and stir until smooth. Add tomatoes with juice, a light seasoning of salt, carrot and bay leaves. Bring to a boil, reduce heat to low and cook, covered, 45 minutes, stirring occasionally. Remove carrot and bay leaves; season to taste with salt and pepper; stir in basil and cook, uncovered, 15 minutes more.

While the sauce cooks, bring a pot of water to a boil and cook lasagna noodles until about 80 percent done, 8 to 9 minutes. Drain and rinse noodles and place them back in the pasta cooking pot, submerged in cold water.

Preheat oven to 400F (205C).

Coarsely crumble tofu into a mixing bowl and mix in basil, oil and salt to taste. Mix well with your hands to create a ricotta–cheeselike texture.

Assemble lasagna: Spoon a thin layer of sauce over the bottom of a 13 × 9-inch baking dish. Lay noodles flat on top of the sauce to cover the bottom of the dish. Cover with one-third of the tofu mixture, a sprinkling of cheese alternative, sauce to cover and another layer of noodles. Cover with another one-third of the tofu mixture, a sprinkling of cheese alternative, sauce to cover and another layer of noodles. Create one more layer with remaining tofu, a sprinkling of cheese alternative and noodles to cover. Spoon sauce generously over top of lasagna and sprinkle with cheese alternative to cover, allowing sauce to peek through. Cover tightly with foil and bake 30 minutes. Remove cover and bake 25 minutes, until the edges have browned lightly. Remove from oven and allow to stand 15 minutes before cutting into wedges.

Almost-Traditional Pad Thai

Thai food is one of my true pleasures in life. I love the spicy flavors, which lift my energy and enliven my taste buds, and I love the creative use of vegetables and tofu. This is my version of a classic Thai dish. I hope you like it.

MAKES ABOUT 4 SERVINGS

8 ounces rice noodles

1 tablespoon peanut oil

3 cloves fresh garlic, finely minced

2 red bell peppers, roasted over a flame, peeled, seeded and thinly sliced into ribbons (see Note, page 262)

2 large, ripe tomatoes, diced (do not seed or peel)

4 ounces snow peas, trimmed

8 ounces extra-firm tofu, cut into ¼-inch-thick spears

Soy sauce

Scant pinch chili powder

Juice of 1 lime

2 to 3 tablespoons finely minced fresh cilantro

¼ cup cashews, lightly pan-toasted (see Note, page 46), coarsely chopped

3 or 4 green onions, thinly sliced on the diagonal

1 cup fresh mung bean sprouts

Bring a large pot of water to a boil and cook noodles until just tender, about 4 minutes. Drain well and set aside.

In a wok or deep skillet, heat oil over medium heat. Stir in garlic and bell peppers and stir-fry 3 minutes. Stir in tomatoes, snow peas and tofu, season lightly with soy sauce and chili powder and stir-fry until vegetables are tender, about 4 minutes. Add lime juice and bring dish to a low simmer. Cook, stirring frequently, 3 minutes. Stir in cooked noodles and cilantro. Transfer to a serving platter and sprinkle with cashews, green onions and bean sprouts. Serve immediately.

Soba and Slaw Salad with Peanut Dressing

I was making lunch for my staff one day when I came up with this one. I opened the fridge and realized that I needed to go food shopping . . . now! But I had to come up with a meal in thirty minutes, so I pulled together what I had and thanked heaven that I keep my pantry well-stocked all the time.

MAKES ABOUT 4 SERVINGS

Spring or filtered water
6 ounces soba noodles
2 cups shredded red cabbage
1 cup shredded green cabbage
1 cup grated carrots

PEANUT DRESSING
3 tablespoons soy sauce
2 tablespoons brown rice vinegar
1 tablespoon avocado oil
3 cloves fresh garlic, finely minced
3 tablespoons creamy peanut butter
2 teaspoons Thai chili paste
2 tablespoons unsweetened soymilk

2 to 3 tablespoons dry roasted peanuts, coarsely chopped
2 to 3 fresh green onions, thinly sliced on the diagonal

Bring a pot of water to a boil and cook soba until just tender to the bite, about 10 minutes. Drain and rinse very well. Transfer to a mixing bowl. Mix in cabbage and carrots and set aside.

Make dressing: Combine all ingredients, except soymilk, in a saucepan over medium-low heat. Slowly whisk in soymilk. Cook, stirring constantly, until the sauce is smooth and well blended, about 3 minutes. Gently mix sauce into noodles and vegetables. Transfer to a serving platter and sprinkle with peanuts and green onions.

Chap Che with Fried Tofu

A Thai classic, turned vegetarian. Usually made with beef, my version is high in flavor and nutrients and low in saturated fats and other less-than-healthy ingredients.

MAKES 4 SERVINGS

FRIED TOFU
5 to 6 tablespoons avocado oil
2 to 3 tablespoons brown rice syrup
Generous pinch chili powder
2 to 3 tablespoons soy sauce
8 (¼-inch-thick) slices extra-firm tofu

6 ounces very thin bean thread noodles
½ cup soy sauce
3 tablespoons sesame oil
3 tablespoons brown rice syrup
2 cloves fresh garlic, minced
1 tablespoon avocado oil
1 red onion, cut into thin half-moon slices
2 carrots, fine matchstick pieces
1 to 2 cups button mushrooms, brushed free of dirt and thinly sliced
3 cups baby spinach or arugula

Fry tofu: Mix oil, rice syrup, chili powder and soy sauce together in a skillet over medium heat. Lay tofu slices in hot oil mixture and fry until golden, about 2 minutes. Turn and fry until golden on the other side, about 1 minute. Transfer to a plate and set aside.

Soak noodles in a bowl of warm water until softened, about 10 minutes. Drain in a colander. Bring a pot of water to a boil, add noodles, and cook 2 minutes. Drain well and rinse under cool water until cooled through.

Whisk together soy sauce, sesame oil, rice syrup and garlic. Set aside.

Heat avocado oil in a deep skillet over medium heat. Add onion and sauté 1 minute. Stir in carrots and sauté 2 minutes. Stir in mushrooms and sauté 3 minutes. Finally stir in spinach and sauté just until tender, about 30 seconds. Stir in noodles and soy sauce mixture and cook, uncovered, until liquid is absorbed, 3 to 4 minutes.

Transfer cooked noodle mixture to a shallow platter and arrange tofu slices on top. Serve immediately.

Cold Noodles with Tempeh

My favorite part of eating out at a Chinese restaurant is the cold noodle dishes. I love the sauces, the flavors and the chilled noodles themselves. But since I can't eat out every night, I had to come up with my own version.

MAKES 4 OR 5 SERVINGS

8 ounces firm tofu, boiled for 5 minutes, drained
⅓ cup sesame tahini
Juice of 1 lemon
1 teaspoon brown rice syrup

Soy sauce
Spring or filtered water
8 ounces udon noodles, cooked

FRIED TEMPEH
6 tablespoons avocado oil
2 tablespoons soy sauce
8 ounces tempeh, sliced into 1-inch triangles

½ bunch parsley, minced

In a blender, place tofu, tahini, lemon juice, rice syrup and soy sauce to taste and puree until smooth. Slowly add water and keep pureeing to create desired texture, remembering that a thicker sauce will stick to the noodles better. Toss with noodles until well-coated. Cover tightly with plastic and chill thoroughly.

While the noodles chill, fry the tempeh: Heat oil and soy sauce in a skillet over medium heat. Lay tempeh in pan and fry until golden on one side, about 2 minutes. Carefully turn tempeh and fry on the other side until golden, about 2 minutes.

To serve, toss noodles with parsley (this also loosens the sauce) and arrange on a shallow platter. Arrange tempeh on top and serve immediately.

Soba Noodles with Ginger and Green Onions

This noodle dish, quickly sautéed with ginger and garlic, makes a delicious supper served with lightly cooked green vegetables and a soup.

MAKES 2 TO 3 SERVINGS

1 (8-ounce) package soba noodles
1 tablespoon light sesame oil

2 cloves fresh garlic, minced

2 or 3 dried shiitake mushrooms, soaked until tender and sliced

1 to 2 teaspoons freshly grated fresh ginger and juice (page 164)

4 or 5 green onions, thinly sliced

1 teaspoon mirin

Soy sauce

¼ cup tan sesame seeds, pan-toasted (see Note, page 46)

¼ cup minced fresh flat-leaf parsley or mint

Sprigs flat-leaf parsley or mint, for garnish

Cook noodles as directed on the package until tender, 8 to 10 minutes. Drain, rinse well and set aside.

Heat oil in a skillet over medium heat. Add garlic and cook, stirring, until fragrant, about 2 minutes. Add mushrooms and cook, stirring, 3 to 4 minutes. Add grated ginger and juice to taste, green onions, mirin, a light seasoning of soy sauce and sesame seeds and cook, stirring, 2 to 3 minutes. Toss mixture with noodles and stir in parsley. Serve in individual noodle bowls garnished with parsley sprigs.

Capellini with Olives and Walnuts

This recipe combines the mild-mannered character of pasta with the rich, pungent flavors of olives, capers and garlic, all beautifully enhanced by nutmeats.

Makes 2 or 3 servings

1 tablespoon extra-virgin olive oil

2 or 3 cloves fresh garlic, minced

1 red onion, cut into thin half-moon slices

Sea salt

2 to 3 tablespoons capers, drained and lightly rinsed

½ cup walnut pieces, pan-toasted (see Note, page 46)

Spring or filtered water

1 (8-ounce) package capellini

10 to 12 pitted green olives, minced

¼ cup minced fresh flat-leaf parsley

2 ripe tomatoes, coarsely chopped

Heat oil in a skillet over medium heat. Add garlic, onion and a pinch of salt and cook, stirring, until fragrant, about 2 minutes. Add capers and cook, stirring, 3 to 4 minutes. Add walnut pieces and a small amount of water. Check flavor and add a light seasoning of salt, if needed. Cover and simmer 7 to 8 minutes over medium-low heat. Puree the sauce in a food processor until walnuts are about half broken. The sauce should be coarse, not smooth.

While the sauce simmers, cook pasta according to package directions until al dente. Drain pasta; do not rinse. Toss immediately with the hot sauce, olives, parsley and tomatoes and serve.

Chinese Noodle Salad

A quick and easy salad, jam-packed with fresh, crisply cooked vegetables and a spicy, sweet and sour sauce.

MAKES 2 TO 3 SERVINGS

Spring or filtered water
¼ cup diced carrot
10 to 12 snow peas, cut into thin matchsticks
¼ cup thin matchstick pieces daikon
2 or 3 green onions, cut into thin diagonal
    pieces
3 or 4 slices fresh ginger, cut into thin
    matchsticks

MARINADE
½ cup fresh orange juice
2 tablespoons fresh ginger juice (see Note,
    page 164)
1 teaspoon sweet rice vinegar
¼ teaspoon soy sauce
1 teaspoon dark sesame oil
Generous dash of umeboshi or red wine
    vinegar

1 (8-ounce) package thin lo mein noodles or
    somen, cooked until just tender
½ cup roasted peanuts
Orange zest strips
2 tablespoons minced fresh cilantro or mint
    (optional)

Bring a pot of water to a boil. Cook the carrot, snow peas and daikon separately in that order, in boiling water until crisp–tender, 1 to 3 minutes each. Drain well and transfer to a bowl. Add green onions and ginger and set aside.

Prepare the marinade: Mix all ingredients together in a small bowl. Pour over the vegetable mixture. Allow to marinate 30 minutes.

Toss the noodles with the marinated vegetables and marinade, peanuts, orange zest and cilantro (if using). Chill before serving.

Linguine with Summer Vegetables in Orange Sauce

I lived in Florida for several years and fell completely in love with the flavor of fresh orange juice in cooking. This unique pasta dish, tossed with fresh vegetables and dressed in a surprisingly sweet orange oil, is ideal in the summer months.

MAKES 2 OR 3 SERVINGS

Spring or filtered water
1 cup fresh green peas
Corn kernels cut from 2 ears of corn
1 (8-ounce) package linguine
1 tablespoon avocado oil
¼ cup minced onion
Sea salt
½ red bell pepper, roasted over a flame,
    peeled, seeded and thinly sliced (see Note,
    page 262)
Generous splash mirin
Grated zest and juice of 1 orange
2 or 3 fresh chives, minced

Bring a large pot of water to a boil and add the peas and corn kernels. Bring back to a boil and remove vegetables with a slotted spoon. Return water to a boil and cook linguine according to package directions until just tender to the bite.

While linguine cooks, heat oil in a deep skillet over medium heat. Add onion and a pinch of salt and cook, stirring, until onion is wilted, about 3 minutes. Add bell pepper and a pinch of salt and cook, stirring, 3 to 4 minutes.

Sprinkle with mirin and add orange zest and juice. Cover and simmer 1 to 2 minutes; take care not to overcook, as the juice can change from sweet to bitter.

Drain linguine; do not rinse. Stir linguine into skillet along with peas and corn. Toss with chives, transfer to a bowl and serve warm.

Penne with Broccoli and Raisins

This recipe is a different take on pasta with oil and garlic, which is quite common in Italy. The delicately sweet taste of the raisins gives this dish a unique little surprise with every bite.

MAKES 2 TO 3 SERVINGS

¼ cup raisins
Spring or filtered water
¼ cup extra-virgin olive oil
2 or 3 cloves fresh garlic, minced
1 large onion, minced
Sea salt
½ cup pine nuts or walnuts
8 ounces penne
1 head broccoli, cut into small florets and
   stems cut into fine matchsticks
Fresh flat-leaf parsley or basil, minced

Plump the raisins by soaking them in warm water to cover 10 minutes and drain.

Heat the oil in a skillet over medium heat. Add the garlic, onion and a pinch of salt and cook, stirring occasionally, until the onion is translucent, about 3 minutes. Add pine nuts and sprinkle lightly with salt. Cover, reduce heat and simmer while pasta cooks.

Meanwhile, bring a large pan of water to a boil and cook pasta 4 to 5 minutes. Add broc-

coli to the pot and cook until pasta is just tender to the bite and broccoli is bright green. Drain well; do not rinse. Toss pasta and broccoli with onion mixture and raisins and serve garnished with parsley.

Cialsons with Leafy Green Pesto

Cialson is the Sicilian name for ravioli. This recipe is part of my husband's rich Sicilian heritage. My version eliminates a few undesirable ingredients but retains the classic spicy, herb-scented flavor. I especially love to serve these pasta pockets filled with aromatic pesto lightly dressed with a light olive oil sauce.

MAKES ABOUT 4 SERVINGS

1 recipe Basic Pasta Dough (page 233)
¼ cup whole wheat bread crumbs
2 tablespoons spring or filtered water, plus
   extra for cooking pasta
1 small bunch kale, boiled until deep green,
   then finely minced
Generous pinch cinnamon
Generous pinch nutmeg
1 teaspoon dried rosemary
1 tablespoon minced fresh flat-leaf parsley
¼ cup extra-virgin olive oil
2 cloves fresh garlic, minced
1 onion, minced
Sea salt
Sprigs flat-leaf parsley, for garnish

Prepare dough. Cover and set aside.

Place bread crumbs in a bowl and add water, mixing until water is absorbed and bread crumbs are soft. Combine cooked greens with bread crumbs, cinnamon, nutmeg, rosemary and parsley.

On a floured surface, thinly roll out dough. Using a round cutter or a glass, cut out 3-inch circles, using as much of the dough surface as possible. Place about 1 teaspoon of kale mixture on each circle, brush edges of pasta round with water to seal, fold in half and seal edges with a fork.

Bring a large pot of water to a boil and cook *cialsons* 3 to 5 minutes or until just tender to the bite. They should be chewy and not too soft. They will rise to the top of the boiling water when they are done.

Heat olive oil in a skillet over medium heat. Add garlic, onion and a pinch of salt and cook until garlic is fragrant, about 2 minutes. Drain *cialsons*; do not rinse. Toss immediately with garlic mixture. Garnish with parsley sprigs.

■ **VARIATION** Substitute 1 recipe Fresh Basil Pesto (page 278) for the kale filling above.

Spaghetti with Walnut Sauce

The rich taste of walnuts is nicely balanced by the peppery taste of the bitter greens, which interestingly, also serve to aid the body in digesting the rich sauce.

MAKES 4 OR 5 SERVINGS

Spring or filtered water
1 bunch dandelion, broccoli rapini or arugula
16 ounces spaghetti
1 cup walnut pieces, blanched
2 to 3 cloves fresh garlic, minced
8 to 10 leaves fresh basil, plus extra for garnish
3 tablespoons white miso
2 to 3 teaspoons extra-virgin olive oil

1 cup rice milk
Sea salt
1 teaspoon kuzu or arrowroot, dissolved in 3 tablespoons cold water

Bring a large pot of water to a boil. Add greens and boil until bright green, about 5 minutes. Remove with a strainer, cool and mince; set aside. Return water to a boil and cook pasta in same water until tender to the bite while preparing sauce.

Process walnuts, garlic, basil, miso, olive oil, rice milk and a pinch of salt in a food processor until coarsely pureed. Transfer puree to a saucepan and cook, stirring, over low heat until hot. This helps render the ingredients more digestible as well as develops the flavors. Stir in dissolved kuzu and cook, stirring, until creamy and thickened, 3 to 4 minutes.

Drain pasta; do not rinse. Toss immediately with sauce and cooked greens and serve garnished with fresh basil.

Fettuccine Alfredo

This classic dish has been called a "heart attack on a plate" by nutritionists. This version gets its rich flavor from pine nuts, without the high fat and calorie contents.

MAKES 2 TO 3 SERVINGS

1 cup pine nuts
1 tablespoon sweet white miso
2 cloves fresh garlic, minced
2 teaspoons fresh lemon juice
1 teaspoon brown rice syrup
¼ cup extra-virgin olive oil
Spring or filtered water
1 (8-ounce) package fettuccine, cooked
2 or 3 sprigs basil, for garnish

Place nuts, miso and garlic in a food processor. With motor running, slowly add all the liquid ingredients, except water, and process until blended. Add water in small amounts to adjust the consistency, keeping the sauce fairly thick. Transfer to a saucepan and cook, stirring, over low heat just enough to cook the miso and oil but not enough to turn the lemon juice bitter, about 1 minute.

Cook fettuccine according to package directions just until tender to the bite. Drain fettuccine; do not rinse. Toss immediately with sauce and serve garnished with basil.

Linguine with Hazelnuts

Hazelnuts play a large role in Italian cooking. Their slightly sweet taste has helped create many a delicious sauce or condiment. People have said that I should buy stock in a hazelnut farm to cut my expenses. I think that may be a hint of some kind.

Makes 4 to 6 servings

1 head garlic, unpeeled
¼ cup plus 2 teaspoons extra-virgin olive oil
Sea salt
1 cup hazelnuts
1 pound whole wheat or semolina linguine
1 onion, diced
¼ cup minced fresh flat-leaf parsley
¼ cup reduced balsamic vinegar (see Note, page 160)
Sprigs flat-leaf parsley, for garnish

Preheat oven to 350F (175C). Slice the top (about ¼ inch) off the garlic head and place in a small ovenproof dish. Sprinkle lightly with 2 teaspoons oil and 1 or 2 pinches of salt. Cover and bake about 1 hour, until soft. Remove garlic from oven, leaving oven on, and allow to

cool enough so it can be handled. Squeeze the garlic pulp from each clove and mash thoroughly.

Spread hazelnuts on a baking sheet and roast in the oven until fragrant, about 15 minutes. Transfer to a paper sack and seal for 10 minutes. Roll roasted nuts in a towel to remove most of the thin outer skins. (They will not all come off.) Grind the nuts in a food processor or nut chopper into a coarse meal and set aside.

Cook linguine according to package directions until just tender to the bite.

While the linguine cooks, heat the remaining ¼ cup olive oil, roasted garlic pulp, onion and a generous pinch of salt over low heat until heated through; this will develop the flavors and render the oil and onion more digestible. Remove from heat and stir in parsley, reduced vinegar and most of the hazelnuts, reserving a few for garnish.

Drain linguine; do not rinse. Toss sauce with the hot linguine and transfer to a serving platter. Garnish with remaining nuts and parsley sprigs. Serve hot.

Angel Hair with Bell Peppers

The smoky taste of roasted red bell peppers is nicely offset by the crisp, fresh taste of snow peas. Sparklingly beautiful colors make this dish a terrific centerpiece for any meal.

MAKES 4 TO 6 SERVINGS

1 tablespoon avocado oil
2 or 3 shallots, diced
Sea salt
Small piece of dried hot chile, diced
2 red bell peppers, roasted over a flame, peeled, seeded and cut into thin strips (see Note, page 262)
1 green bell pepper, roasted over a flame, peeled, seeded and cut into thin strips (see Note, page 262)
15 to 20 snow peas, trimmed
Spring or filtered water
16 ounces angel hair pasta
10 or 12 leaves fresh basil
Red bell pepper rings or parsley sprigs, for garnish

Heat oil in a skillet over medium heat. Add shallots and a pinch of salt and cook until shallot is translucent, about 5 minutes. Add chile, bell peppers and a pinch of salt and cook, stirring, 2 to 3 minutes. Add snow peas and cook, stirring, until crisp-tender, about 2 minutes. Set aside.

Bring a large pot of water to a boil and cook pasta according to package directions until just tender to the bite. Drain pasta, reserving 1 cup cooking water; do not rinse. Return pasta and reserved water to the pot. Add the cooked vegetables and basil and salt to taste. Toss well and transfer to a platter. Serve immediately garnished with red pepper rings.

Noodle Sushi

This is a great dish. I mean it. Making maki rolls is easy. Your tool investment involves an inexpensive (about $.99—I told you it was inexpensive!) bamboo mat, available at most natural and Asian food stores, as well as kitchen shops. There's a trick to this dish that makes it a snap to make: The noodles are tied into bundles. You'll have to trust me on the filling. It may sound strange, but it is a wonderful study in contrasting tastes. Try it and see.

MAKES 4 OR 5 SERVINGS

1 (8-ounce) package soba noodles
3 sheets toasted nori
Peanut butter
Dill pickles, cut lengthwise into spears
Pickled ginger, for garnish

Cut several pieces of cotton string about 4 inches long. Remove noodles from the package and tie them into small bundles with several pieces of string, about 1 inch from the ends of each bundle.

Bring a large pot of water to a boil and cook noodle bundles until just tender to the bite. Gently drain, and rinse, without pulling bunches apart. Lay out a cotton towel and gently spread the noodle bunches flat on the towel. By bundling them, you eliminate the time it would take to straighten all the noodles out after cooking. With a sharp knife, trim away the short tied ends of the bunches and discard, because those parts did not cook thoroughly. Wrap the noodles carefully in the towel to absorb any excess water.

Next, lay a sheet of nori on the bamboo mat, shiny side against the mat. Place one-third of noodles flat against the nori, leaving 1 inch of nori exposed on the side away from you. Spread a thin line of peanut butter along the noodles on the edge close to you. Place pickle spears on top of the peanut butter to cover the length of the noodles. Using the mat as a guide, roll the nori around the noodles and filling, jelly-roll style, gently pressing as you roll. Wet the edge of the nori with moist fingers to seal the roll and press gently. With a sharp knife, slice the nori roll into 1-inch pieces and arrange on a serving platter, cut side up, and repeat with remaining noodles, filling and nori. Serve garnished with pickled ginger.

Curried Lentils and Udon

Lentils are easy to cook because they do not require soaking and cook relatively quickly, in about forty-five minutes. Combined with curried, sautéed veggies, this dish is infused with flavor. I love to serve it as a hearty stew in cold weather, complemented by some lightly cooked green vegetables or a crisp salad on the side.

MAKES 3 TO 4 SERVINGS

1 (1-inch) piece kombu or 1 bay leaf
1 cup green or brown lentils, rinsed and drained
3 cups Onion Stock (page 75) or spring or filtered water
Sea salt
1 tablespoon extra-virgin olive oil
2 medium red onions, cut into thin rings
2 teaspoons curry powder, briefly pan-toasted to bring out flavor
1 cup fresh or frozen green peas
16 ounces whole wheat or rice udon
2 to 3 green onions, cut into thin diagonal slices, for garnish

Place kombu in a pot, top with lentils and add stock. Bring to a boil and cook, uncovered, 10

minutes. Reduce heat, cover and cook until tender, 40 to 45 minutes. Season to taste with salt and simmer 5 minutes. Set aside, retaining any cooking liquid that remains.

Heat olive oil in a skillet over medium heat. Add onions and a pinch of salt and cook, stirring, until onions are translucent and slightly browned, 10 to 12 minutes. Sprinkle in curry powder, stirring to coat the onions, and cook about 5 minutes. Add lentils and a small amount of their cooking liquid and simmer, uncovered, 5 to 7 minutes. The mixture will thicken slightly. Stir in peas and simmer 1 to 2 minutes.

While sauce is cooking, cook udon according to package directions until tender to the bite. Drain and rinse.

Place udon noodles in individual serving bowls. Top generously with lentil sauce and serve garnished with green onions.

Chilled Soba Noodles

A summer dish in traditional Japanese cooking, it serves us just as well in warm weather. Refreshingly chilled and served with spicy condiments and a rich dipping sauce, this simple noodle dish is appealing for lunch or dinner. I round out this meal with steamed vegetables or a fresh salad.

MAKES 2 TO 3 SERVINGS

Spring or filtered water
1 (8-ounce) package soba noodles

DIPPING SAUCE
2 cups Onion Stock (page 75)
½ teaspoon soy sauce
2 teaspoons brown rice syrup
2 tablespoons fresh ginger juice (see Note, page 164)
1 tablespoon brown rice vinegar

Condiments: thinly sliced green onions, fresh wasabi or hot chiles and very thin strips of nori

Bring a large pot of water to a boil and add noodles. Return the water to a boil and add 1 cup cold water. Return the water to a boil and add 1 cup cold water. Return the water to a boil for a third time. The noodles should be done. Drain and rinse well and drain again. Chill cooked noodles completely before serving. If they stick together, run cold water over them and drain well just prior to serving.

Prepare dipping sauce: Season stock with soy sauce and simmer over low heat. Stir in the rice syrup and ginger juice and warm 3 to 4 minutes. Remove from heat and stir in vinegar. Pour dipping sauce into small individual bowls. Place chilled noodles in individual serving bowls as well.

This dish is traditionally served accompanied by a condiment tray. After each person dips noodles into the sauce, they eat them garnished with an item or two from the condiment tray.

Pasta Primavera

Usually, this very traditional Italian dish is served smothered in a heavy cream sauce complemented by lightly cooked vegetables. My version creates a rich, white sauce without dairy, using slowly cooked onions to give the sauce a sweet, smoky flavor. Tossed with freshly cooked, crisp vegetables, it is a taste sensation.

MAKES 4 OR 5 SERVINGS

1 tablespoon extra-virgin olive oil
4 cloves fresh garlic, minced
1 red onion, diced
Up to 5 tablespoons whole wheat pastry flour
Sea salt
2 cups rice or soy milk
½ cup green beans, rinsed and cut into 1-inch pieces
½ cup thin half-moon slices yellow summer squash
1 medium carrot, cut into thin matchsticks
2 stalks broccoli, cut into small florets, with stems trimmed and sliced
16 ounces fettuccine
Sprigs flat-leaf parsley, for garnish

Heat oil in a skillet over low heat. Add garlic and cook until fragrant, about 2 minutes. Add onion and a pinch of salt and cook, stirring, until onion is wilted and lightly browned, about 10 minutes. Slowly stir in flour to coat the onion and season lightly with salt. Slowly whisk in milk, stirring constantly to avoid lumps. Cook, stirring frequently, until the sauce thickens, about 5 minutes.

While the sauce is cooking, bring a large pan of water to a boil and separately cook each vegetable until crisp-tender: 2 to 3 minutes for the green beans; 1 to 2 minutes for summer squash; 1 to 2 minutes for the carrot; and 2 to 3 minutes for broccoli. Drain each vegetable using a slotted spoon and toss them together. Set aside.

Return the water to a boil. Cook the fettuccine in the vegetable cooking water until just tender to the bite, about 8 minutes. Drain well; do not rinse. Toss the hot fettuccine with the cooked vegetables and white sauce until all ingredients are combined. Serve immediately, garnished with parsley sprigs.

Pesto-Filled Ravioli

This very rich-tasting dish is at its best when served in a simple sauce of warmed olive oil and minced fresh parsley—a bit of effort, but worth it for a special occasion.

MAKES ABOUT 4 SERVINGS

RAVIOLI DOUGH
2 cups semolina flour
½ cup unbleached white flour
Pinch sea salt
About 1 cup cold water

PESTO FILLING
1 cup pumpkin seeds, lightly pan-toasted (see Note, page 46)
2 to 3 teaspoons sweet white miso
½ cup extra-virgin olive oil
2 cloves fresh garlic, minced
1 cup tightly packed flat-leaf parsley, coarsely minced
2 teaspoons red wine vinegar
½ teaspoon brown rice syrup

Extra-virgin olive oil and minced parsley or seasoned broth, warmed, to serve

Prepare the dough: Combine the flours and salt thoroughly in a bowl. Slowly add water, mixing until a spongy dough forms. Knead on a lightly floured surface until the dough takes on a silky, firm texture, about 20 minutes. Wrap the dough in a damp cotton towel and allow to rest 30 minutes before proceeding.

Make the filling: Process all filling ingredients together in a food processor until a thick, smooth paste forms. Adjust seasoning to taste. Do not add any extra water. This paste needs to be very thick to work as a filling in ravioli that will be boiled.

On a floured surface, roll the dough as thinly as possible. Cut into 4-inch squares. Place 1 teaspoon of filling on one corner of a dough square and fold into a triangle shape. Brush edges of dough square with water and seal with fingers, crimping the edges or use a fork to seal the ravioli to create a decorative edge. Repeat until dough and filling are used up.

Bring a large pot of water to a boil and cook ravioli until tender; the time will depend on the thickness of your dough and size of your ravioli. The ravioli will rise to the surface of the cooking water when they are done and should be chewy, but not doughy or sticky. Drain ravioli, rinse gently and serve tossed lightly with warm olive oil and parsley mixture. These ravioli are also delicious served in a lightly seasoned broth.

Tofu-Noodle Bake

This hearty casserole is an easy one-dish meal. I usually round out dinner with a fresh salad or lightly steamed vegetables. With all the rich flavors in the casserole, you really don't need much else.

MAKES 4 TO 6 SERVINGS

8 ounces firm tofu, crumbled
1 teaspoon white miso
1 teaspoon umeboshi paste
3 tablespoons toasted sesame tahini
1 teaspoon brown rice syrup
½ teaspoon soy sauce
4 to 6 tablespoons spring or filtered water
2 cups cooked small noodles (elbows, shells, bows, spirals)
2 shallots, diced
1 carrot, diced
1 stalk broccoli (including stem), diced
1 (4-ounce) package brown rice mochi, very thinly sliced

Preheat oven to 400F (205C). Lightly oil a casserole and set aside. In a food processor, process tofu, miso, umeboshi paste, tahini, rice syrup and soy sauce with enough water to make a creamy, spoonable paste.

Toss noodles and vegetables together and gently fold in sauce. Spoon noodle mixture into prepared casserole, spreading evenly. Cover the top of the noodles with mochi and sprinkle very lightly with water, so the mochi will melt. Make a loose foil tent over the casserole, without touching the mochi, as it will stick. Bake about 40 minutes, until mochi has melted. If mochi has not melted, sprinkle with a little more water and return to the oven for about 5 minutes.

When the mochi has completely melted, remove the cover and return casserole to the oven to brown the top, about 5 minutes. Serve hot.

Crispy Chinese Noodles and Vegetables

A delicious tradition that you can serve at home, too.

MAKES 4 TO 6 SERVINGS

Spring or filtered water
16 ounces udon noodles
2 tablespoons dark sesame oil
½ leek, cut lengthwise, rinsed well and thinly sliced
Sea salt
1 carrot, cut into small ½-inch chunks
1 cup small ½-inch chunks daikon
2 stalks broccoli, cut into small florets and stems peeled and diced
1 cup 1-inch pieces seitan
Soy sauce
1 to 2 teaspoons fresh ginger juice (see Note, page 164)
1 tablespoon kuzu or arrowroot, dissolved in 2 tablespoons cold water
Grated zest and juice of 1 lemon
Green onions, sliced, or parsley sprigs, for garnish

Bring a large pot of water to a boil and add noodles. Return the water to a boil and add 1 cup cold water. Return the water to a boil and add 1 cup cold water. Return the water to a boil for a third time. The noodles should be done. Drain and rinse well and drain again.

Heat 1 tablespoon of the oil in a skillet over medium heat. Add noodles and cook, tossing, until they are coated with oil. Cook until the edges of some noodles get crispy. Transfer to a serving platter and cover loosely while preparing the vegetables.

Heat remaining oil in the same skillet. Add the leek and a pinch of salt and cook 2 minutes. Add carrot, daikon, broccoli stems and another pinch of salt and cook 3 to 4 minutes, stirring frequently. Add seitan and broccoli florets and season lightly with soy sauce and ginger juice to taste. Add about ⅛ inch of water and cook until vegetables are crisp-tender, 3 to 5 minutes. Stir in dissolved kuzu and cook, stirring, until a thin glaze forms over vegetables, about 3 minutes. Remove from heat and stir in lemon zest and juice. Spoon mixture over fried noodles and serve immediately, garnished with green onions.

Spaghetti Pancakes

My mom used to make these from leftover spaghetti, fresh vegetables, ricotta and mozzarella cheese. We thought they were the greatest thing. I have made a few changes in the recipe, like using mochi instead of cheese, but the essence of this dish remains intact. I hope your kids enjoy it as much as we did . . . and still do as grown-up kids . . .

MAKES 4 OR 5 SERVINGS

1 to 2 tablespoons avocado oil
1 small onion, diced
Sea salt
½ red bell pepper, roasted over a flame, peeled, seeded and diced (see Note, page 262)
½ cup button mushrooms, brushed clean and diced
1 small carrot, diced
8 ounces firm tofu
1 green onion, diced

Umeboshi vinegar
Spring or filtered water
1 (4-ounce) package brown rice mochi, grated
6 to 8 ounces leftover whole wheat spaghetti

Heat 1 teaspoon of the oil in a skillet over medium heat. Add onion and a pinch of salt and cook, stirring, until translucent, about 5 minutes. Add bell pepper, mushrooms and a pinch of salt and cook until mushrooms are wilted, about 5 minutes. Add carrot, season lightly with salt and cook, stirring, until carrot is crisp-tender, about 4 minutes. Set aside.

Crumble tofu into a food processor or blender. Add green onion and a dash of umeboshi vinegar. Process, slowly adding a small amount of water, until a coarse consistency, somewhat like ricotta cheese. Set aside.

To make the pancakes, heat remaining oil in a skillet over medium heat. Place about 4 tablespoons of mochi in the center of the skillet, forming a small circle. Top with a small bit of spaghetti, cooked vegetables, and tofu mixture. Cover with another 4 tablespoons of mochi. Fry on one side until crispy and golden brown and then turn the pancake over and cook the other side. Remove to a serving platter and repeat until ingredients are used up. Serve immediately.

219

White Lasagna

This is a nice, rich and elegant version of lasagna, laced through with lots of veggies to make a great entrée.

MAKES 4 TO 6 SERVINGS

2 recipes Béchamel Sauce (page 274)
3 tablespoons toasted sesame tahini
Soy sauce
Spring or filtered water
6 to 8 ounces whole wheat lasagna noodles, cooked until almost done
1 onion, cut lengthwise into thin slices
1 cup button mushrooms, brushed clean and thinly sliced
2 or 3 stalks broccoli, cut into tiny flowerets
1 (4-ounce) package brown rice mochi, very thinly sliced

Preheat oven to 400F (205C). Lightly oil a 13 X 9-inch baking dish and set aside. Combine the sauce with the tahini and season lightly with soy sauce. You may need to thin it slightly with water to maintain the slightly loose, creamy consistency desired.

Spread a thin layer of sauce over the bottom of the baking dish and add a single layer of noodles, taking care to completely cover the bottom of the dish. Top the noodles with a generous layer of sauce and then one-third of the vegetables, evenly distributed over the sauce. Arrange a few slices of mochi over the vegetables. Repeat until all ingredients are used up, making sure to end with noodles, then mochi on the top. Sprinkle lightly with water so the mochi will melt and cover loosely with foil, making a tent over the baking dish. Bake 35 minutes, until mochi melts.

Remove cover and return dish to oven to brown the top, about 5 minutes. Allow the lasagna to stand about 15 minutes before cutting to allow the ingredients to firm up a bit.

Mochi Spaghetti Pancakes

I learned this recipe from Wendy Esko, a fine whole foods cook and instructor. A unique take on pasta, these crispy, rich pancakes are always a hit at my table.

MAKES 5 OR 6 SERVINGS

2 tablespoons avocado oil
1 onion, diced
Sea salt
1½ cups button mushrooms, brushed clean and thinly sliced
1 carrot, coarsely grated
Soy sauce
1½ pounds brown rice mochi, coarsely grated
6 ounces spaghetti, cooked, drained and rinsed well
½ cup Tofu "Cream Cheese" (page 117)
½ cup black olives, pitted and sliced into thin rounds

Heat 2 teaspoons of the oil in a skillet over medium heat. Add onion and a pinch of salt and cook, stirring, 2 minutes. Add mushrooms, carrot and a pinch of salt and cook, stirring, 2 to 3 minutes, stirring occasionally. Season lightly with soy sauce and cook 2 minutes or until vegetables are tender. Set aside.

Heat remaining oil in a fresh skillet or on a griddle and tilt to distribute evenly over the pan's surface. Place about 4 tablespoons grated mochi in the center of the skillet and press with back of spoon to form a 4-inch round. Place a small handful of cooked spaghetti on top. Evenly spread about 3 tablespoons cooked vegetables over spaghetti and top with a tablespoon of tofu cream and a few olive slices. Sprinkle another 3 tablespoons grated mochi over top. Cover pan and cook over medium-low heat about 5 minutes. Gently flip the pancake and cook another 5 minutes. Both sides of the pancake should be golden and crisp. (If not brown, turn the heat up to high and cook until browned.) Transfer to a serving platter. Repeat process until all ingredients are used up, making 5 or 6 pancakes. Serve immediately.

Macro Chow Mein

A traditional crowd pleaser, this version has lots of fresh veggies served over homemade, crunchy chow mein noodles.

MAKES 4 SERVINGS

Avocado oil, for deep-frying
8 ounces whole wheat spaghetti, cooked and
    drained
1 (1-inch) piece kombu
Spring or filtered water
1 onion, cut into half-moon slices
1 carrot, cut into thick matchsticks
2 celery stalks, cut into thick diagonal slices
1 cup button mushrooms, brushed clean and
    thickly sliced
1 cup sliced water chestnuts, drained well
10 to 12 snow peas, trimmed, left whole
1 cup shredded Chinese cabbage
8 ounces firm tofu, cubed
Soy sauce
1 tablespoon kuzu or arrowroot, dissolved in
    ¼ cup cold water
Green onion, sliced, for garnish

Heat about 3 inches of oil in a deep pot over medium heat. Add small batches of the spaghetti and deep-fry until golden brown and crispy. Drain well and set aside.

In a medium saucepan, place kombu and about 2 inches of water. Simmer the kombu 5 minutes and remove. Add onion, carrot, celery, mushrooms and water chestnuts to the pot and cook over low heat until just tender, about 5 minutes. Add snow peas, Chinese cabbage and tofu, season lightly with soy sauce and simmer until cabbage is wilted, about 5 minutes. Stir in dissolved kuzu, and cook, stirring, until a thin glaze forms over vegetables, about 3 minutes.

Arrange fried spaghetti on a serving platter and spoon vegetables and sauce over top. Serve immediately, garnished with green onions.

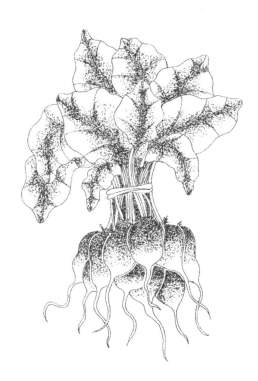

Pasta with Tofu Cheese and Mushrooms

The original version of this recipe uses crumbled feta cheese. My nondairy version substitutes tofu cheese—a rich, cheeselike product lightly fermented in miso. The result is so much like the real thing (not to mention easy to make), you won't even miss the feta.

MAKES 4 SERVINGS

1 tablespoon extra-virgin olive oil
1 or 2 cloves fresh garlic, finely minced
1 cup button mushrooms, brushed clean and thinly sliced
Sea salt
1 bunch watercress
1 pound small pasta (spirals, rotini, twists), cooked al dente and drained
1 recipe Fresh Basil Pesto (page 278)
4 ounces Tofu Cheese (page 118), crumbled coarsely
1 ripe tomato, finely diced, for garnish

Heat olive oil in a skillet over medium heat. Add garlic, mushrooms and a pinch of salt and cook, stirring, until mushrooms are wilted, about 5 minutes. Set aside.

Bring a pot of water to a boil, blanch watercress for about 30 seconds, then plunge into cold water to stop the cooking process. Cut into small pieces and mix with mushrooms.

Toss together pasta, pesto and vegetables. Gently fold in the tofu cheese just before serving. Arrange in a bowl and serve warm, garnished with tomato.

Fettuccine with Broccoli

This is a colorful, full-bodied pasta entrée sure to please even the fussiest eaters. It combines the smoky taste of roasted peppers with pungent olives, all nicely offset by fresh, crisp broccoli.

MAKES 2 OR 3 SERVINGS

1 tablespoon extra-virgin olive oil
2 cloves fresh garlic, minced

10 to 12 oil-cured black olives, pitted and halved

1 red bell pepper, roasted over a flame, peeled, seeded and cut into thin strips (see Note, page 262)

1 green bell pepper, roasted over a flame, peeled, seeded and cut into thin strips (see Note, page 262)

Sea salt

Grated zest and juice of 1 orange

Balsamic vinegar

8 ounces fettuccine

2 stalks broccoli, cut into small florets

¼ cup minced fresh flat-leaf parsley

Sprigs flat-leaf parsley, for garnish

Heat oil in a skillet over medium heat. Add the garlic and cook until fragrant, about 2 minutes. Add olives and cook 1 to 2 minutes. Add bell peppers, season lightly with salt and cook, stirring, 3 to 4 minutes. Stir in orange zest and juice and simmer 2 to 3 minutes. Remove from heat and sprinkle lightly with balsamic vinegar. Set aside.

Bring a large pot of water to a boil, add fettuccine and cook 3 to 4 minutes. Add broccoli and cook until broccoli is bright green and fettuccine is just tender to the bite, about 5 minutes more. Drain pasta and broccoli and immediately toss with olive-and-bell-pepper mixture. Gently fold in minced parsley and arrange on a platter. Serve warm, garnished with parsley sprigs.

Linguine Rustica

A fresh vegetable sauce creates a kaleidoscope of colors and a symphony of tastes—the perfect topping for pasta. This makes a great meal rounded out with crusty whole grain bread and a fresh salad.

MAKES 2 OR 3 SERVINGS

Spring or filtered water

8 ounces linguine

1 teaspoon extra-virgin olive oil

3 cloves fresh garlic, minced

3 to 4 shiitake mushrooms, thinly sliced

1 small leek, cut lengthwise, rinsed well and thinly sliced

Sea salt

2 carrots, diced

2 small zucchini, diced

1½ cups Mushroom Stock (page 75)

2 teaspoons kuzu or arrowroot, dissolved in 2 to 3 tablespoons cold water

10 to 12 leaves fresh basil, minced, or generous pinch dried basil

½ cup walnuts, lightly pan-toasted (see Note, page 46)

2 to 3 sprigs flat-leaf parsley, minced

Sprigs basil, for garnish

Bring a large pot of water to a boil. Add linguine and cook according to package directions until just tender to the bite.

While linguine is cooking, heat olive oil in a skillet over medium heat. Add garlic and cook, stirring, until fragrant, about 2 minutes. Add mushrooms, leek and a pinch of salt and cook until mushrooms are wilted. Stir in carrots and zucchini and a pinch of salt. Gently add stock and bring to a boil. Reduce heat and simmer, uncovered, until vegetables are tender, about 5 minutes. Stir in dissolved kuzu and cook, stirring, until the sauce thickens slightly and is clear, about 3 minutes.

Drain linguine; do not rinse. Stir linguine into the vegetables and season lightly with salt. Stir in basil, walnuts and parsley and simmer 1 to 2 minutes before transferring to a pasta platter. Serve immediately, garnished with basil sprigs.

Fusilli with Basil and Kale

This fun-shaped pasta with long, spiraling curls makes a festive dish. Dotted with vegetables and tossed in a garlicky sauce, Roman style, this recipe is a real attention grabber.

MAKES 4 SERVINGS

Spring or filtered water
1 pound fusilli
2 teaspoons extra-virgin olive oil
7 or 8 cloves fresh garlic, minced
3 or 4 shallots, minced
Sea salt
½ cup dry-packed, sun-dried tomatoes,
  soaked until tender and diced
1 cup Vegetable Stock (page 74)
1 bunch kale, finely diced
2 teaspoons kuzu or arrowroot, dissolved in 2
  to 3 tablespoons cold water
12 to 18 fresh basil leaves, minced, or
  generous pinch of dried basil
Basil leaves, for garnish

Bring a large pot of water to a boil and add fusilli. Cook until just tender to the bite, 8 to 10 minutes.

While fusilli cooks, heat olive oil in a deep skillet over medium heat. Add garlic and cook 1 to 2 minutes. Add shallots and a pinch of salt and cook, stirring, until shallots are translucent. Stir in sun-dried tomatoes and season lightly with salt. Add stock and simmer until tomatoes are soft, 6 to 8 minutes. Add kale and a light seasoning of salt and cook until kale is wilted and turns a deep green, about 8 minutes. Stir in dissolved kuzu and cook, stirring, until a thin sauce forms, about 3 minutes.

Drain fusilli; do not rinse. Add fusilli and sauce to pasta cooking pot and stir until fusilli is well-coated with sauce. Gently fold in basil.

Transfer fusilli to a pasta bowl and serve immediately, garnished with fresh basil leaves.

Udon with Ginger-Scented Vegetables

This pasta dish is inspired by one of the many cookbooks I have turned to for inspiration over the years. The original dish is from cookbook author Faye Levy; like most other recipes I have adapted, it has evolved and changed over time and, frankly, never comes out exactly the same way twice.

MAKES 2 OR 3 SERVINGS

Sprint or filtered water
8 ounces udon noodles
3 tablespoons dark sesame oil
2 cloves fresh garlic, minced
4 or 5 green onions, cut into thin diagonal
  slices
1 carrot, cut into long, thin sticks
Sea salt
1 cup finely shredded Chinese cabbage
1 tablespoon finely minced fresh ginger
10 to 12 snow peas, tips and strings removed,
  left whole
Soy sauce

Bring a large pot of water to a boil and cook noodles until just tender to the bite, 10 to 12 minutes. Rinse noodles well and drain. Set aside.

Heat sesame oil in a wok over medium heat. Add garlic and green onions and sauté 1 to 2 minutes. Add carrot and a pinch of salt and sauté 1 to 2 minutes. Stir in cabbage and a pinch of salt and cook until wilted, about 5 minutes. Add ginger and cook 3 to 4 minutes. Add snow peas and season to taste with soy sauce. Cook until snow peas are bright green and crisp-tender, about 3 minutes. Quickly toss in udon noodles and stir until ingredients are combined. Serve immediately.

Capellini in Creamy Mushroom Sauce

More delicate, milder sauces are perfect for capellini. Its thin strands easily absorb more gentle flavors. In this dish, mushrooms are simmered in a savory broth with soy or rice milk to create a creamy sauce.

MAKES 2 OR 3 SERVINGS

1 teaspoon avocado oil
1 onion, diced
Sea salt
2 cups button mushrooms, brushed clean and thinly sliced
1 portobello mushroom, thinly sliced
1½ cups Mushroom Stock (page 75)
½ cup soy or rice milk
Spring or filtered water
8 ounces capellini
Fresh chives, minced

Heat oil in a medium saucepan over medium heat. Add the onion and a pinch of salt and cook, stirring, until onion is translucent, about 3 minutes. Add button mushrooms and a pinch of salt and cook, stirring, until mushrooms are wilted. Add portobello mushroom and a pinch of salt and cook, stirring, 2 to 3 minutes. Add stock and milk, season lightly with salt and bring to a boil. Reduce heat and cook, uncovered, about 30 minutes or until the mushrooms are very soft and the sauce is flavorful and thickens slightly.

While the sauce is cooking, bring a large pot of water to a boil and cook the capellini according to package directions until just tender to the bite. Drain; do not rinse. Toss pasta immediately with the mushroom sauce and stir in chives. Transfer to a pasta bowl and serve immediately.

Fettuccine with Pecans

This dish was a challenge to put on paper; you can use just about any vegetables and herbs, and even the nuts can vary. This is my favorite combination, but try this dish with yours.

MAKES 2 OR 3 SERVINGS

Spring or filtered water
8 ounces fettuccine
2 tablespoons avocado oil
⅔ cup pecans, coarsely minced
2 cloves fresh garlic, minced
2 or 3 shallots, diced
Sea salt
1 red bell pepper, roasted over a flame, peeled, seeded, and cut into small strips (see Note, page 262)
1 yellow summer squash, cut into thin matchsticks
4 or 5 Brussels sprouts, thinly sliced
1 parsnip, cut into thin matchsticks
Green onions, cut into thin diagonal slices

Bring a large pot of water to a boil and cook fettuccine according to package directions until just tender to the bite. Drain, rinse well and set aside.

Heat 1 tablespoon of the oil in a skillet over medium heat. Add pecans and cook until lightly browned, about 3 minutes. Remove with a slotted spoon; set aside.

In the same skillet, heat the remaining oil. Add garlic, shallots and a pinch of salt and cook 2 minutes. Add bell pepper, summer squash and a pinch of salt and cook 2 to 3 minutes. Stir in Brussels sprouts, parsnip, a pinch of salt and ⅛ inch of water. Simmer vegetables, uncovered, until tender, about 5 minutes. Season lightly with salt and simmer another 5 to 10 minutes. The cooking liquid should be absorbed.

Toss cooked fettuccine with vegetables, pecans and green onions. Transfer to a pasta platter and serve immediately.

Baked Tempura Noodles

This very traditional dish is a real treat. It's not a complicated recipe, but there are several steps involved. Take heart; the finished dish is so rich and satisfying, that you'll completely forget the work as you sit back, completely sated.

MAKES 4 OR 5 SERVINGS

TEMPURA BATTER
1 cup whole wheat pastry flour
Pinch sea salt
1 tablespoon powdered kuzu or arrowroot
About ¾ cup dark beer or sparkling water

Avocado or soy oil, for deep-frying
1 onion, cut into thin wedges
2 carrots, cut into thin diagonal slices
4 or 5 button mushrooms, brushed clean and
 halved
1 burdock root, cut into thin diagonal slices
1 parsnip, cut into thin diagonal slices
8 ounces udon noodles, cooked, rinsed and
 drained
1 to 1½ cups Vegetable Stock (page 74) or
 spring or filtered water

Make the batter: Combine flour, salt and kuzu in a bowl. Slowly stir in beer until a thin, pancakelike batter forms. The batter should not be too thin. Set aside at room temperature 30 minutes before using.

Heat about 3 inches of oil in a deep pot over medium heat. Coat vegetable pieces in batter, letting excess drip off, and add to oil. Increase heat to high. Deep-fry, in small batches, until golden brown and crispy. Do not fry too many pieces at one time or the oil temperature will cool and the vegetables will be oily instead of crispy. Drain the vegetables on paper towels. Repeat until all the vegetables are cooked.

Preheat oven to 350F (175C). Lightly oil a deep casserole. Layer noodles and vegetables alternately in casserole until ingredients are used up, ending with vegetables on top. Pour stock over the casserole, cover and bake 1 hour. Remove the cover and return to the oven 5 to 10 minutes to set up the casserole. Serve immediately.

Spicy Peanut Noodles

This is a wonderful pasta dish flavored with peanuts and lemon. And, it's incredibly easy—you'll have dinner ready in the time it takes to cook the noodles.

MAKES 2 OR 3 SERVINGS

Sprint or filtered water
8 ounces udon noodles
½ cup unsweetened peanut butter
1 teaspoon brown rice syrup
Soy sauce
Grated zest and juice of 1 lemon
2 teaspoons fresh ginger juice (see Note,
 page 164)

¼ cup minced, boiled peanuts
Green onions, cut into thin diagonal slices,
　　for garnish

Bring a large pot of water to a boil and add udon. Return water to a boil and add 1 cup cold water. Return water to a boil and add another 1 cup cold water. Return water to a boil a third time. When the water boils the third time, the noodles are done. Drain and rinse well. Set aside.

Process peanut butter, rice syrup, soy sauce to taste, lemon zest and juice, ginger juice and peanuts in a blender or food processor until smooth. For a thinner sauce, add a small amount of water, but don't make it too runny. If it is too thin it won't stick to the noodles as well. Toss cooked udon with sauce and serve garnished with green onions.

Fusilli with Mushrooms, Asparagus and Sun-Dried Tomatoes

A curly pasta is ideal for a dish like this one because it stands up well to the vegetables and traps the creamy, rich sauce in all its little nooks and crevices.

MAKES 4 SERVINGS

2 tablespoons extra-virgin olive oil
2 to 3 cloves fresh garlic, minced
2 to 3 cups mixed wild mushrooms (cremini,
　　shiitake or button), brushed clean, and
　　thinly sliced
10 to 12 asparagus spears, cut into 1-inch
　　pieces
4 ounces dry-packed, sun-dried tomatoes,
　　thinly sliced

Sea salt
¼ cup mirin
4 ounces silken tofu
½ cup rice milk
¼ cup minced fresh flat-leaf parsley
Sprint or filtered water
1 pound fusilli

Heat oil in a deep skillet over medium heat. Add garlic and sauté about 1 minute. Add mushrooms, asparagus, sun-dried tomatoes and a pinch of salt. Cook until vegetables are tender and most of the liquid has evaporated, about 10 minutes. Add mirin and boil until reduced by half, about 3 minutes.

Whisk tofu and rice milk with parsley until blended. Stir mixture into skillet, season lightly with salt and simmer until liquid is reduced to sauce consistency, about 8 minutes.

While the sauce simmers, bring a pot of water to a boil. Add fusilli and cook according to package directions just until tender to the bite. Drain well; do not rinse. Transfer to a large bowl. Spoon sauce over pasta and toss to coat.

Noodles with Basil, Fresh Mint and Peanuts

Inspired by Vietnamese cuisine, I have changed this recipe slightly, using basil in place of the traditional cilantro. My dear husband refuses to eat anything remotely associated with cilantro, so I have learned to cook without it (except in guacamole, where he loves it. Go figure . . .).

MAKES 2 OR 3 SERVINGS

¼ cup brown rice vinegar
¼ teaspoon soy sauce
1 tablespoon brown rice syrup
1 small onion, cut into thin rings
1 cucumber, peeled, seeded and sliced into
     paper-thin rounds, then halved
Spring or filtered water
8 ounces somen noodles
Avocado or soy oil, for frying
4 ounces firm tofu, cut into ½-inch cubes
Juice of 1 fresh lime
2 tablespoons light sesame oil
½ teaspoon crushed red pepper flakes
⅓ cup tightly packed fresh mint leaves,
     minced
⅓ cup loosely packed fresh basil leaves,
     minced
4 green onions, cut into thin diagonal slices
3 fresh plum tomatoes, seeded and diced
3 to 4 tablespoons boiled peanuts

Whisk vinegar, soy sauce and rice syrup together in a bowl. Add onion rings and cucumber and toss to coat well. Set aside to marinate at least 30 minutes or up to 4 hours, stirring occasionally.

Bring a pot of water to a boil. Add noodles and cook according to package directions until tender. Drain and rinse under cold water. Drain well. Set aside.

Heat about ½ inch oil in a skillet over medium heat. Quickly shallow-fry the tofu cubes until golden brown. Drain on paper towels and set aside.

Whisk together the lime juice, sesame oil and pepper flakes. Stir in mint and basil. Combine noodles with tofu cubes, lime juice mixture, onion rings and cucumber with marinade, green onions and tomatoes. Toss gently to combine ingredients. Sprinkle with peanuts and serve.

Fettuccine with Seitan and Sugar Snap Peas

A lovely, fresh pasta dish that says summer, this simple-to-prepare, one-dish meal is nicely complemented by a crisp summer salad.

MAKES 2 OR 3 SERVINGS

Spring or filtered water
10 to 12 ounces sugar snap peas, trimmed,
     left whole
1 or 2 carrots, cut into thin matchstick pieces
8 ounces fettuccine
2 tablespoons extra-virgin olive oil
1 pound seitan, cut into ½-inch pieces
¼ cup minced fresh flat-leaf parsley
1 to 2 tablespoons whole wheat pastry flour
1 cup Vegetable Stock (page 74)
¼ cup mirin
Sea salt
3 or 4 green onions, cut into thin diagonal
     slices
Generous pinch sweet paprika
Lemon wedges

Bring a small pot of water to a boil and boil snap peas 1 minute. Remove with a strainer and rinse under cold water. Add carrots to water, cook 30 seconds and drain. Mix with peas. Set aside.

Bring a large pot of water to a boil and cook fettuccine according to package directions just until tender.

While the fettuccine cooks, heat oil in a deep skillet over medium heat. Add seitan and cook until golden brown, about 2 minutes, turning as needed. Transfer to a plate, cover loosely and set aside.

In the same skillet, stir in parsley and flour and cook 30 seconds. Stir in stock and mirin and season lightly with salt. Simmer until sauce thickens, stirring constantly, about 2 minutes. Add peas and carrots and simmer 1 minute, stirring constantly.

Drain fettuccine; do not rinse. Arrange on a serving platter. Spoon sauce over fettuccine and top with seitan pieces. Sprinkle with green onions and paprika and serve with lemon wedges.

Capellini with Chile Sauce

A Mexican dish, *sopa seca* (dry soup), is served the same way Italians serve a pasta course. This version makes a great side dish, first course or complete lunch entrée. The lime slices are a must when serving, as they cool the fire of the chiles, and help the body assimilate the oil.

MAKES 2 OR 3 SMALL SERVINGS

4 fresh ancho chiles, stems, seeds and veins removed and minced
Spring or filtered water
2 to 3 cups Vegetable Stock (page 74) or spring or filtered water
Generous pinch cumin
2 cloves fresh garlic, minced
Sea salt
¼ cup extra-virgin olive oil
4 ounces capellini (packaged in nests)
1 to 2 limes, quartered

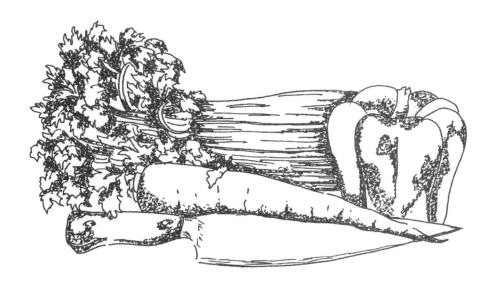

Place chiles in a saucepan with enough water to just cover and simmer 5 minutes. Remove from heat and allow to soak 5 minutes. Drain and set aside.

Pour ¼ cup of the stock into a blender or food processor and add cumin and garlic. Puree into a smooth paste. Season lightly with salt, add 1 cup of stock and the chiles and process until pureed, adding more stock, if needed, to thin the sauce.

Heat oil in a large saucepan over medium heat. Add capellini nests and fry, keeping nests intact, until golden, turning as needed to brown evenly. Drain off any excess oil.

Add sauce to the capellini and simmer over low heat about 3 minutes, stirring occasionally to prevent sticking. Cover and simmer until pasta is tender, 6 to 8 minutes. Transfer to a serving bowl and serve with lime quarters.

Penne with Vegetable Sauce

This traditional dish of sun-washed Apulia, Italy, is reflective of the fertile region, which makes up the heel of Italy's boot. Apulia's abundant produce finds its way beautifully into a wide variety of pasta dishes.

MAKES 2 OR 3 SERVINGS

2 tablespoons extra-virgin olive oil
1 onion, diced
2 or 3 cloves fresh garlic, minced
Sea salt
1 red bell pepper, roasted over a flame, seeded, peeled, and diced (see Note, page 262)
2 or 3 small zucchini, cut into ¼-inch pieces
2 or 3 yellow summer squash, cut into ¼-inch pieces
4 ounces dry-packed, sun-dried tomatoes,

soaked 10 to 15 minutes in warm water, then drained and diced
½ cup spring or filtered water, plus extra for cooking pasta
8 ounces penne
10 to 12 leaves fresh basil, shredded
2 ripe tomatoes, diced (do not seed or peel)
Sprigs basil, for garnish

Heat oil in a deep skillet over medium heat. Add onion, garlic and a pinch of salt and cook until quite soft, 10 minutes. Add bell pepper, zucchini and summer squash, season lightly with salt and cook until the vegetables begin to soften, about 3 minutes. Add sun-dried tomatoes and water, adjust salt to taste, cover skillet and reduce heat to simmer, cooking until the vegetables are soft and a sauce begins to form, about 10 minutes, adding water as needed to achieve a saucelike consistency.

While the sauce cooks, bring a large pot of water to a boil and cook penne according to package directions just until tender. Drain; do not rinse. Toss pasta immediately with sauce and basil and diced tomatoes. Serve immediately, garnished with basil sprigs.

Tagliatelle with Green Beans

Another gem from Apulia. In this unique pasta dish the fresh green beans are simmered a long time so that they become soft. That way, you can twirl them on your fork along with the pasta.

MAKES 2 OR 3 SERVINGS

1 tablespoon extra-virgin olive oil
4 cloves fresh garlic, minced
1 red onion, cut lengthwise into thin slices

Generous pinch crushed red pepper flakes
5 or 6 plum tomatoes, peeled and diced
1 pound long, thin green beans, trimmed and
    left whole
½ cup Vegetable Stock (page 74)
Sea salt
Spring or filtered water
8 ounces tagliatelle or linguine
Sprigs flat-leaf parsley, for garnish

Heat oil in a large saucepan over medium heat. Add garlic and sauté about 1 minute. Add onion, red pepper flakes and tomatoes and cook 2 minutes. Add beans, stock and a light seasoning of salt. Cover pan and reduce heat until mixture just simmers. Cook until the beans are very tender, about 1 hour, stirring occasionally and adding water as needed. Stir frequently near the end of cooking to prevent scorching.

Bring a large pot of water to a boil and cook tagliatelle according to package directions just until tender. Drain, reserving ¼ cup cooking water; do not rinse. Return the pasta to the pot. Add the sauce and the pasta water to help sauce coat the noodles. Toss well and transfer to a serving bowl. Serve immediately, garnished with parsley sprigs.

Orecchiette with Seitan and Broccoli Rapini

The sharp flavor of the rapini is best preserved, along with its vitamins, if you steam it. It is also a lovely complement to the rich taste of the seitan.

MAKES 4 SERVINGS

Spring or filtered water
2 pounds broccoli rapini, rinsed well and
    drained

2 tablespoons plus ¼ cup extra-virgin olive oil
1 onion, cut lengthwise into thin slices
Sea salt
1 pound seitan, coarsely minced
3 or 4 cloves fresh garlic, minced
Generous pinch crushed red pepper flakes
1 pound orecchiette
Sprigs flat-leaf parsley, for garnish

Add about 1 inch of water to a large pot and bring to a rolling boil over high heat. Add rapini, cover the pot and steam until bright green, about 1 minute. Drain and set aside.

Heat 2 tablespoons olive oil in a skillet over medium heat. Add onion and a pinch of salt and sauté until onion is translucent, 3 to 4 minutes. Add the seitan and cook over low heat, stirring frequently, until browned, about 10 minutes. Stir in garlic and red pepper flakes and season lightly with salt. Cook until garlic has softened, about 3 minutes.

Slice rapini into small pieces and stir into skillet. Add ⅛ inch of water, cover and cook over low heat 3 to 4 minutes.

While the sauce is cooking, bring a large pot of water to a boil, add orecchiette and cook until just tender to the bite. Drain orecchiette; do not rinse. Transfer pasta to a serving bowl and toss with rapini sauce and the remaining ¼ cup olive oil. Serve immediately, garnished with parsley sprigs.

Penne with Cauliflower and Golden Raisins

Sautéed cauliflower with capers, golden raisins and pine nuts is a classic southern Italian combination. Tossed with penne, the sweet and pungent flavors are simply exquisite.

MAKES 4 SERVINGS

½ cup golden raisins
¼ cup mirin or white wine
½ cup pine nuts
Spring or filtered water
1 head cauliflower, cut into small florets
¼ cup extra-virgin olive oil
3 to 4 tablespoons capers, drained and lightly
   rinsed
Generous pinch crushed red pepper flakes
Sea salt
1 pound penne
¼ cup minced fresh flat-leaf parsley

Combine the raisins and mirin in a small bowl and soak 20 minutes.

Pan-toast the pine nuts in a hot, dry skillet over medium-low heat, stirring constantly, until slightly golden and fragrant, about 4 minutes. Set aside.

Bring a pot of water to a boil. Add cauliflower and cook until tender, about 5 minutes. Remove cauliflower with a strainer and return water to a boil for penne.

Heat oil in a skillet over medium heat. Add capers and sauté 1 minute. Add cauliflower and sauté until just beginning to brown, about 3 minutes. Stir in the pine nuts, raisins with mirin and red pepper flakes. Season to taste with salt. Reduce heat to low and simmer until the liquid is almost gone.

Cook penne in boiling water until just tender to the bite. Drain well, reserving about ¼ cup cooking water; do not rinse. Transfer penne to a bowl. Toss with cauliflower sauce, cooking water and parsley. Serve immediately.

Fettuccine with Leeks and Butternut Squash

This is a great winter pasta entrée. Wide fettuccine is ideal for holding the hearty, creamy squash sauce. Served with lightly cooked greens and crusty bread, this dish is the stuff of dreams.

MAKES 4 OR 5 SERVINGS

2 tablespoons extra-virgin olive oil
2 or 3 medium leeks, cut lengthwise, rinsed
   well and thinly sliced
Sea salt
1 medium butternut squash, halved, seeded,
   peeled and diced
¼ cup Vegetable Stock (page 74) or spring or
   filtered water
1 cup rice or soy milk
Spring or filtered water
1 pound fettuccine
1 teaspoon kuzu or arrowroot, dissolved in ¼
   cup cold water
¼ cup minced fresh flat-leaf parsley

Heat oil in a skillet over medium heat. Add leeks and a pinch of salt and sauté until wilted, about 5 minutes. Add squash and a pinch of salt and cook, stirring frequently, 5 to 6 minutes. Add stock and milk and season lightly with salt. Cover, reduce heat to low and cook until squash is quite soft, about 10 minutes, stirring occasionally.

While sauce is cooking, bring a large pot of water to a boil. Add fettuccine and cook just until tender to the bite, about 10 minutes.

While fettuccine cooks, transfer squash and leek mixture to a food processor and puree until smooth. Return to skillet and simmer over low heat 2 to 3 minutes. Stir in dissolved kuzu and cook, stirring, until mixture thickens, about 3 minutes.

Drain fettuccine; do not rinse. Toss with sauce and minced parsley and serve immediately.

Tricolor Spirals with Red Onion and Radicchio

A traditional dish from my mother's native Naples, it literally bursts with a symphony of flavors. A great starter dish or main course.

MAKES 4 OR 5 SERVINGS

¼ cup extra-virgin olive oil
2 large red onions, cut lengthwise into thin slices
3 to 4 tablespoons capers, drained and lightly rinsed
10 to 12 oil-cured black olives, pitted and minced
½ cup mirin or white wine
1 large head radicchio, shredded
Sea salt
Spring or filtered water
1 pound tricolor pasta spirals
Sprigs flat-leaf parsley, for garnish

Heat oil in a deep skillet over low heat. Add onions and cook, stirring frequently, until soft and just beginning to brown, about 30 minutes.

Add capers and olives to onion mixture and cook, stirring, 4 minutes. Add mirin and cook until liquid is almost gone, 4 to 5 minutes. Add radicchio, season lightly with salt and cook, stirring constantly, until it turns a dark burgundy color, 3 to 4 minutes.

Bring a large pot of water to a boil. Add pasta and cook just until tender to the bite,

about 10 minutes. Drain, reserving about ½ cup cooking liquid; do not rinse. Return pasta to the empty pot and toss with sauce and pasta cooking water. Transfer to a bowl and serve garnished with parsley sprigs.

Basic Pasta Dough

Here is a basic pasta dough for those days when you want to be adventurous in the kitchen.

MAKES 4 SERVINGS OF FRESH PASTA

1 cup whole wheat pastry flour or durum wheat flour
2 cups semolina flour
Pinch sea salt
About 1 cup cold water

Combine flours and salt thoroughly. Slowly add water to form a spongy dough. On a lightly floured surface, knead the dough for about 20 minutes, until it becomes silky and smooth. To determine whether the dough has been kneaded enough, pinch some between your fingers; it should have the same consistency as your ear lobe. Wrap the dough in a damp towel and allow to stand for 30 minutes before using.

■ **VARIATION** To make buckwheat soba noodles, substitute buckwheat flour for the pastry or semolina flour.

Sensational Salads

THROUGHOUT THE WORLD, salads stand as a symbol of freshness and lightness. Salads make me appreciate the endless variety of foods available to us in the vegetable kingdom.

To the whole foods cook, salads are so much more than a plate of raw, limp lettuce, tomato and cucumber slices with a couple of radish slivers thrown in for flair, and drenched with a heavy dressing. Salad preparation is another way of living and eating in harmony with our surroundings. A wide range of cooking techniques and ingredients make salads a limitless culinary adventure.

John Evelyn, a seventeenth-century horticulturist, noted that a successful salad depended largely on the proper balance of ingredients. In Japan the success of *sunomono* and *aemono*, the traditional equivalents of salads, whose names translate to "vinegared" and "dressed," place the focus on composition, harmony and balance.

Until modern times salads were never limited to servings of raw vegetables. The word salad derives from the Latin *herba salata*, meaning "salted greens," which is exactly what composed the original forms of salads. In traditional cuisine, the edible parts of green herbs and plants were tossed only with salt. It was intuitively known that processing raw vegetables with salt or vinegar was a way to create balance: The contracting energy of salt draws moisture from the expanded nature of raw vegetables, making them softer and easier to digest.

In warmer cultures like Greece and Italy, tradition shows us that salads were dressed with salt, plus oil and vinegar. The addition of these ingredients serves to balance the salt as well as lubricate the plant fibers, making them much more digestible. An added plus from the use of vinegar is the natural fermentation it causes in vegetables, again, a digestive aid.

Remember too, that human beings cannot digest cellulose, the tough outer fiber that protects plants. So we invented methods of cooking, pickling and fermenting to break down foods for easier digestion. That's not to say that raw is not a valid way to eat, but you have to *do* something to the raw ingredients to make the nutrients biologically available to our digestive systems.

It's interesting how we, as a culture, have moved from traditional salads to the consumption of more raw foods. In terms of energy, raw vegetables have an expanded energy and a cooling effect on the body. This type of energy can help balance the contracting, heat-producing effects of meat, cheese, egg and poultry consumption. So the rise in popularity of raw foods can be directly linked to the increased intake of animal foods that we have seen in modern times. It is nature's way of attempting to restore balance under extreme conditions.

In whole foods cooking, salads resemble their traditional predecessors. I use a wide variety of cooked, marinated, pickled and raw ingredients to compose salads. I serve them, year-round, in various forms, as a means of adding light and fresh energy to my meals.

I use just about anything to make a base for a salad. In this section, I would like to introduce you to a wide cross section of my favorites, including whole grain salads, pasta salads, vegetable salads, bean and bean-product salads, sea vegetable salads (oh, be daring!) and the ever-glorious fruit salads. As the years have progressed, I find myself enjoying the light energy of raw foods more and more, in concert with my many cooked dishes, so I have been experimenting with that a lot. You'll see that in this section.

Cooking methods for salads encompass just about anything in addition to and including . . . not cooking. Typical salads from my kitchen might be boiled, blanched, pressure-cooked (yes, you read right, pressure-cooked), steamed, pressed, pickled, deep-fried, roasted, grilled and sautéed. Using one or combining several of these techniques, combined with fresh ingredients, has resulted in some wonderfully unique and satisfying salad dishes on our table.

VEGETABLE SALADS

Tossed Salad with Smoky Cashews

Yummy is the only word I can think of when someone says "cashews." Sure, they are rich in good fats and protein and nutrients, but I can never get past *yummy*.

MAKES ABOUT 4 SERVINGS

SMOKY CASHEWS
1 cup raw cashews
2 tablespoons finely minced fresh rosemary
1 teaspoon smoked hot paprika
2 tablespoons maple syrup granules
2 teaspoons sea salt
1 tablespoon avocado oil

1 small cucumber, diced
2 cups cherry tomatoes, halved
3 Belgian endive, shredded
1 small radicchio, shredded
1 cup fine matchsticks jicama
¼ cup avocado oil
Juice of 1 lemon
2 teaspoons brown rice syrup
Sea salt
Cracked black pepper

Preheat oven to 350F (175C). Spread cashews in a single layer on a rimmed baking sheet. Toast in oven, stirring once or twice, about 10 minutes, until golden. While hot, toss cashews with remaining ingredients to coat. Cashews can be served warm or at room temperature.

For salad, combine cucumber, tomatoes, endive, radicchio and jicama in a mixing bowl.

Whisk together remaining ingredients, seasoning to taste with salt and pepper. Toss vegetables with enough dressing to coat and fold in cashews. Serve immediately.

Chopped Salad with Ginger-Miso Dressing

I love this salad . . . it's loaded with lots of fresh, seasonal vegetables and smothered in a miso dressing, which is not only delicious, but will help me digest the raw ingredients more efficiently. I love nature.

MAKES ABOUT 5 SERVINGS

1 cup cherry tomatoes, halved
1 cup diced cucumber (do not peel or seed)
¾ cup shredded butternut squash or carrot
1 cup diagonally sliced snow peas
3 or 4 fresh green onions, thinly sliced on the
**   diagonal**

GINGER-MISO DRESSING
2 tablespoons brown rice vinegar
2 tablespoons sweet white miso
1 tablespoon shelled hempseeds or sesame
**   seeds**
1 tablespoon extra-virgin olive oil
1 teaspoon brown rice syrup
1 teaspoon Dijon mustard
Spring or filtered water

Several leaves butter or red lettuce

Combine tomatoes, cucumbers, squash, snow peas and green onions in a mixing bowl.

Make dressing: Whisk together all ingredients, slowly adding water to make a smooth dress-

ing, but do not thin too much or it will not stick to the veggies. Toss salad and dressing together to coat.

Arrange lettuce leaves on a platter and mound salad on top.

Escarole and Collard Green Salad with Pomegranate Vinaigrette

This is a gorgeous salad and perfect for the holiday season, when we may be indulging just a little more than we should. It is so pretty that no one will realize how healthy it is, but you can rest easy knowing that you are giving your loved ones the gift of health at your holiday feast.

MAKES 4 TO 6 SERVINGS

POMEGRANATE VINAIGRETTE
¾ cup pomegranate juice
1 tablespoon grated tangerine zest
2 tablespoons brown rice syrup
¾ cup extra-virgin olive oil
2 to 3 tablespoons balsamic vinegar
⅔ teaspoon sea salt
Generous pinch ground cinnamon

1 head escarole, rinsed very well, hand-
**   shredded**
3 or 4 collard leaves, rinsed well, stems
**   trimmed, blanched, shredded**
3 or 4 Belgian endive, halved lengthwise,
**   sliced into thin slivers**
Seeds from 2 pomegranates (when in season)
½ cup pecan pieces, pan-toasted (see Note,
**   page 46), coarsely chopped**

Make vinaigrette: Place pomegranate juice, tangerine zest and brown rice syrup in a small saucepan over medium heat. Cook until reduced to ¼ cup, about 5 minutes. Transfer to a mixing bowl. Whisk in oil, vinegar, salt and cinnamon. Set aside.

Place greens in a mixing bowl. Spoon dressing over greens and toss to coat. Transfer salad to a platter and sprinkle with pomegranate seeds and pecans.

Parsley-Cucumber Salad

Salads don't come easier than this one. Simply cut the vegetables, blanch the greens and toss with dressing for a dish that is so refreshing, it'll become a regular on your summer dinner table.

MAKES ABOUT 4 SERVINGS

7 or 8 leaves leafy greens, such as kale, collards or Chinese cabbage
Spring or filtered water
1 cucumber, thinly sliced into rounds, then cut into halves
1 recipe Lemon-Parsley Dressing (page 271)

Use one or more types of greens and cook in a pot of boiling water until bright green and just tender, about 3 minutes. Drain and cool in iced water to stop the cooking process. Drain well and cut into bite-size pieces. Toss the cooked greens and cucumber with the dressing. Chill several hours before serving.

Spinach Salad with Mango and Candied Peanuts

Once again, I can hear all my macrobiotic friends saying that I have lost my mind. Spinach? Isn't that on the no-no list of macro foods? Well, rather than live by lists, I tend to look at nutrients and what value a veggie can bring to my health. But if you just can't eat spinach, make this salad with baby arugula.

MAKES 4 SERVINGS

CANDIED PEANUTS
⅓ cup maple syrup granules
6 tablespoons extra-virgin olive oil
3 tablespoons balsamic vinegar
1 cup raw peanuts

6 to 8 ounces baby spinach, rinsed very well
1 ripe large mango, peeled, pitted and thinly sliced
Sea salt
Cracked black pepper

Lightly oil a sheet of aluminum foil and set aside.

Combine maple syrup granules, 1 tablespoon of the oil and 1 tablespoon of the vinegar in a skillet over medium heat. Cook, stirring until a syrup develops, about 3 minutes. Stir in peanuts and cook, stirring constantly, until peanuts are coated with syrup and toasted, about 7 minutes. Spread nuts on oiled foil and using a fork, separate them so they do not stick together. Set aside to allow the coating to harden, 25 to 30 minutes.

Prepare salad: Combine spinach, mango slices and cooled peanuts in a mixing bowl and toss gently with remaining oil and vinegar and salt and pepper to taste.

Marinated Root Vegetable Salad

This is a simple yet elegant winter salad. It has a robust taste, so I usually serve it in small amounts as a side dish on a bed of Belgian endive. The white miso imparts a distinctly "cheesy" taste, which is nicely complemented by the sweet mirin.

MAKES 4 OR 5 SERVINGS

⅓ cup *each* thin matchsticks carrot, daikon, rutabaga and turnip
2 teaspoons white miso
2 teaspoons avocado oil
1 teaspoon mirin
1 teaspoon soy sauce
2 tablespoons spring or filtered water
2 small Belgian endive, shredded

Place vegetables in a medium bowl. Mix miso, oil, mirin, soy sauce and water until smooth, pour mixture over vegetables and toss. Marinate at room temperature at least 30 to 45 minutes before serving, tossing occasionally while marinating. Serve on a bed of Belgian endive.

Vegetable Aspic

Aspics are an unusual way to serve chilled vegetables. Cut into squares and served on a bed of lightly dressed wild greens, aspics are a unique approach to serving salads. This recipe is a particularly pretty version.

MAKES 5 OR 6 SERVINGS

½ cup *each* corn kernels, diced carrot, diced celery and tiny cauliflower florets

4 cups Vegetable Stock (page 74)
5 to 6 tablespoons agar-agar flakes
Soy sauce
4 or 5 cups torn salad greens, like arugula
Lemon-Parsley Dressing (page 271)

Cook corn, carrot, celery and cauliflower separately in the order listed by adding to boiling water, bringing back to a boil, removing with a slotted spoon, then cooling in iced water. Drain vegetables well and mix together in a shallow 1½-quart casserole.

Place stock and agar-agar in a pan over medium-low heat and cook, uncovered, until flakes dissolve, about 10 minutes, stirring occasionally. Season lightly with soy sauce and simmer 7 minutes more.

Pour hot liquid over vegetables and allow to stand in a cool place until just beginning to gel, about 30 minutes. Chill thoroughly before cutting into squares. Serve on a bed of greens drizzled with Lemon-Parsley Dressing.

French Carrot Salad

This recipe was given to me by one of my dearest friends, Liliane Papin, a delightfully creative French cook. The naturally sweet salad is deliciously balanced by the delicate tart flavors of vinegar and lemon.

MAKES 3 TO 4 SERVINGS

2 cups grated carrots
3 tablespoons umeboshi vinegar
2 tablespoons extra-virgin olive oil
Juice of 1 lemon

Toss the carrots with the vinegar, oil and lemon juice. Allow to marinate at least 30 minutes in the refrigerator before serving. Toss occasionally while marinating to be sure the flavors blend evenly. Serve chilled or at room temperature.

Warm Salad with Cranberry Dressing

The unique dressing makes this salad truly deluxe. I love to serve this as the final course at my holiday feasts.

MAKES 4 SERVINGS

Several leaves *each* bok choy, kale and
   collards
½ bunch watercress

CRANBERRY DRESSING
2 cups fresh cranberries, picked over and
   rinsed
Grated zest and juice of 1 orange
2 or 3 tablespoons brown rice syrup
2 tablespoons extra-virgin olive oil
Sea salt
1 teaspoon ground ginger
⅛ cup umeboshi vinegar

¼ cup pecans, minced and pan-toasted (see
   Note, page 46)

Lightly steam the greens separately in the order listed until bright green and just tender. Cut into bite-size pieces; place in a bowl and toss together. Set aside while preparing the dressing.

Prepare the dressing: Place cranberries, orange zest and juice and rice syrup in a food processor and pulse until finely minced. Combine olive oil, a pinch of salt and ginger in a small saucepan over low heat and warm. Stir in cran-

berry mixture and simmer until warmed through, 5 to 7 minutes. Remove from heat and stir in vinegar. Toss with cooked greens just before serving. Top with pecans.

Yellow Squash Salad

Bright colors blend wonderfully with the delicate flavors of these tender summer vegetables. I love to serve this salad at weekend brunches simply because of its cheery colors.

MAKES 5 OR 6 SERVINGS

1 to 2 tablespoons extra-virgin olive oil
1 pint cherry tomatoes, quartered
2 or 3 yellow summer squash, cut into about
   ½-inch cubes
2 or 3 fresh green onions, cut into ½-inch
   lengths
2 very small cucumbers, preferably Kirby, cut
   into ½-inch pieces
1 to 2 tablespoons balsamic vinegar
1 tablespoon brown rice vinegar
Sea salt
Juice of 1 lemon
Juice of 1 lime
Several fresh basil leaves, shredded
2 cups baby arugula, chilled

Heat olive oil in a skillet over medium heat. Add tomatoes, yellow squash and green onions and cook, stirring, until just tender, about 3 minutes. Stir in cucumbers and cook, stirring, 1 minute more. Transfer to a bowl.

Prepare the dressing: Whisk together vinegars, salt to taste, lemon juice, lime juice and basil. Pour dressing over vegetables, toss gently and mound on top of a bed of arugula. This salad is best served warm, with the arugula nicely chilled.

Roasted Zucchini Salad

By the end of the summer, the zucchini that has taken over the garden has been used in just about every way I can imagine, everything from soups to breads to quiches to muffins to stir-fries. You get the picture. This warm salad is a real end-of-summer treat.

MAKES 4 OR 5 SERVINGS

¼ cup pine nuts or walnuts
2 or 3 fresh zucchini, cut into ½-inch sticks
2 or 3 yellow summer squash, cut into ½-inch
    sticks
About 2 tablespoons extra-virgin olive oil
Sea salt
About 1 teaspoon dried basil
Juice of 1 lemon
2 or 3 tablespoons balsamic vinegar
1 bunch watercress or dandelion, rinsed well
    and diced

In a dry skillet, toast pine nuts over medium-low until lightly browned and fragrant, about 5 minutes, stirring. Set aside.

Preheat oven to 375F (190C). Lightly oil a baking sheet and set aside. In a medium bowl, toss the zucchini and summer squash with a small amount of oil and a sprinkling of salt and basil. Spread evenly on prepared baking sheet and roast, uncovered, 15 to 20 minutes, until lightly browned. Set aside to cool slightly.

Whisk together the lemon juice and balsamic vinegar, pour over cooked squash and nuts and toss. Serve warm over watercress.

New Potato Salad

A summer classic, with a twist. Not potato salad as we, in America know it; this is potato salad, Italian style . . . no heavy mayo here, just richly flavored with olive oil and herbs. You won't miss the deli.

MAKES 8 TO 10 SERVINGS

Spring or filtered water
2 pounds new potatoes, unpeeled, cut into ½-
    inch cubes
Sea salt
1 small red onion, finely diced
3 to 4 tablespoons capers, drained (do not
    rinse)
3 or 4 ripe tomatoes, diced (do not peel or seed)

DRESSING
⅔ cup extra-virgin olive oil
3 or 4 shallots, finely diced
¼ cup balsamic vinegar
Juice of ½ lemon
2 teaspoons brown rice syrup
3 or 4 sprigs flat-leaf parsley, finely minced
2 or 3 stalks fresh basil, leaves removed and
    finely diced
Sea salt

1 or 2 basil sprigs, for garnish

Bring a large pot of water to a boil. Add potatoes and a pinch of salt and cook until just tender, 12 to 15 minutes. Drain and transfer to a mixing bowl. Mix in onion and capers. Gently fold in tomatoes. Set aside.

Prepare dressing: Place oil and shallots in a small saucepan and cook over low heat 3 to 4 minutes to soften shallots. Remove from heat and whisk in remaining ingredients, seasoning with salt to taste—remember the salty flavors of the capers. Allow dressing to cool about 3 minutes before gently tossing it with the potatoes. Serve warm, garnished with basil sprig(s).

It's All Greek to Me Salad

Everyone thinks that choosing salad as a meal is the healthy option. Well, in many cases, salads can have as many calories and as much saturated fat as any burger and fries combo. In my version of this classic, I've cut the fat and calories. And the flavor? Well, you decide.

MAKES 3 TO 4 SERVINGS

DRESSING
⅓ cup extra-virgin olive oil
1 tablespoon fresh lemon juice
2 cloves fresh garlic, finely minced
Generous pinch dried basil
2 tablespoons sweet white miso
1 tablespoon red wine vinegar
1 teaspoon brown rice syrup
Sea salt
Cracked black pepper

1 large head romaine lettuce
10 to 12 cherry tomatoes, halved
1 medium cucumber, cut into fine matchstick pieces
1 small red onion, cut into very thin half-moon slices
½ pound Tofu Cheese (page 118), coarsely crumbled
10 to 12 oil-cured black olives, pitted and halved

Prepare the dressing: Whisk together all ingredients, adding salt and pepper to taste. Chill completely to develop flavors.

Hand-shred lettuce into bite-size pieces and combine with remaining ingredients. Just before serving, toss salad with dressing and serve immediately.

Hail Caesar Salad

This Mexican salad classic—yes, Mexican, you read right—is one of my favorite salads when I want a little more heartiness in a salad meal. With no eggs, anchovies or cheese, you may be wondering how I achieve the same satisfaction. You'll just have to try it and see for yourself.

MAKES 3 OR 4 SERVINGS

DRESSING
8 ounces silken tofu
2 tablespoons stone-ground mustard
1 teaspoon brown rice syrup
½ sheet toasted sushi nori, finely shredded
2 cloves fresh garlic, finely minced
Juice of 1 lemon
Extra-virgin olive oil
Sea salt

1 head romaine lettuce
3 to 4 slices whole grain bread, cubed, baked or pan-fried into croutons

Prepare dressing: Place all dressing ingredients, except oil, in a food processor or blender, seasoning with salt to taste. Puree until smooth, slowly adding enough oil to achieve the consistency you want for the dressing. You want it to be smooth and thick.

Toss lettuce and croutons with dressing and serve immediately.

Beet and Avocado Salad

Sweet, nutrient-rich beets meet avocados for a pairing as perfect as Romeo and Juliet without the tragedy. The fennel and arugula add complementary flavors and aid in digestion to create a salad made in heaven.

MAKES 3 OR 4 SERVINGS

3 or 4 medium beets
⅔ cup extra-virgin olive oil
Juice of 1 lemon
Sea salt
Cracked black pepper
1 firm, but ripe avocado, peeled, pitted and
    cubed
1 small fennel bulb, thinly sliced
½ very thinly sliced red onion
1 cup baby arugula

Preheat oven to 400F (205C). Wet a sheet of parchment paper and wring out excess water. Lay a double-thick sheet of foil on a work surface with parchment paper on top. Lay beets on paper and wrap foil and parchment tightly around beets. Bake 1 to 1½ hours, until tender. Cool slightly before opening foil. When the beets have cooled enough to handle, peel and cut into 1-inch cubes.

Whisk oil, lemon juice, salt and pepper to taste in a bowl until combined. Transfer 2 tablespoons of the dressing to a small bowl and stir in avocado.

Toss beets, fennel, onion and arugula with the remaining dressing and arrange on a platter. Mound avocado on top of the salad and serve.

Spicy Cole Slaw

A trendy twist on a classic dish for any picnic, tailgate party, barbecue, buffet, after-school snack, lunch, brunch, with a burger . . . you get the idea.

MAKES 4 TO 6 SERVINGS

1 small head green cabbage, finely shredded
2 cups fresh or frozen corn kernels
3 red bell peppers, roasted over a flame,
    peeled, seeded and coarsely chopped (see
    Note, page 262)
¾ cup coarsely chopped fresh cilantro
1 cup red wine vinegar
⅓ cup extra-virgin olive oil
1 tablespoon ground cumin
1 jalapeño chile, finely chopped (seeds left in
    for hotter flavor)
Sea salt

Combine cabbage, corn, bell peppers and cilantro in a mixing bowl. Whisk together vinegar, oil, cumin, chile and salt to taste. Toss with vegetables to coat. Chill completely before serving to allow flavors to develop.

Avocado and Corn Relish on Radicchio Salad

There is something about the combination of avocado with grain and bitter greens that is just irresistible. Maybe it's the fact that together, they are perfect for digestion; maybe it's because the ingredients are all so nutrient-dense. Oh, I remember . . . it's the glorious flavors!

MAKES 3 TO 5 SERVINGS

¾ cup avocado or extra-virgin olive oil
2 cloves fresh garlic, minced
½ red onion, diced
4 cups fresh or frozen corn kernels
Sea salt
Cracked black pepper
Ground cinnamon
2 avocados, peeled, seeded and cut into ¼-inch cubes
1 red bell pepper, roasted over a flame, peeled, seeded and diced (see Note, page 262)
4 poblano chiles, roasted over a flame, peeled, seeded and diced (see Note, page 262)
4 to 6 green onions, thinly sliced on the diagonal
Juice of 1 lemon
Several leaves of radicchio

Heat ½ cup of the oil in a large skillet over medium heat and sauté garlic and onion 1 to 2 minutes. Stir in corn and salt and pepper to taste and a pinch of cinnamon and sauté 5 minutes. Set aside to cool in skillet.

Stir avocados, bell pepper, chiles and green onions gently into corn mixture with lemon juice and remaining oil. Transfer to a bowl and set aside for 30 minutes before serving to allow flavors to develop.

To serve, arrange whole leaves of radicchio on a platter and mound relish on top.

Gazpacho Salad

I discovered this recipe in my favorite food magazine, *Food and Wine*. I must tell you that I have had great fun over the years adapting recipes from this publication. Some adaptations have been major overhauls and some, like this one, have only needed a bit of tinkering here and there.

MAKES 4 TO 6 SERVINGS

TOMATO VINAIGRETTE
2 or 3 tomatoes, peeled
½ red onion, diced
2 or 3 cloves fresh garlic, minced
¼ cup extra-virgin olive oil
Sea salt
6 tablespoons balsamic vinegar
3 tablespoons umeboshi vinegar

6 cups diced whole grain sourdough bread, crusts removed
2 or 3 ripe tomatoes, diced
1 cucumber, peeled, seeded and diced
1 red bell pepper, roasted over a flame, peeled, seeded and diced (see Note, page 262)
3 or 4 green onions, diced
2 tablespoons minced fresh flat-leaf parsley

Prepare vinaigrette: Puree tomatoes, onion and garlic in a blender or food processor. In a small saucepan, warm oil with a generous pinch of salt. Whisk in the vinegars and mix with the tomato puree.

In a medium bowl, toss the bread with half the vinaigrette and marinate about 30 minutes. Just before serving, mix together the vegetables,

parsley, marinated bread and remaining vinaigrette. Serve immediately.

Red and Green Cabbage Salad

A simple marinated salad that is delicious served
warm or chilled. The easy miso marinade is complemented by the nutty flavor of the caraway seeds.

MAKES 4 TO 6 SERVINGS

Spring or filtered water
½ head green cabbage, finely shredded
¼ head red cabbage, finely shredded
About 2 tablespoons caraway seed

MARINADE
3 tablespoons light sesame oil
3 tablespoons spring or filtered water
3 tablespoons white miso
2 teaspoons brown rice vinegar
2 tablespoons brown rice syrup

Bring a pot of water to a rolling boil. Add
green cabbage and cook until just tender, about
3 minutes. Remove with a slotted spoon and
place in a bowl. Add red cabbage to boiling
water and cook until just tender, about 3 minutes. Drain, add to green cabbage and toss with
caraway seed.

To make the marinade: Whisk together all
ingredients until blended. Toss with warm cabbage and allow to marinate, tossing occasionally, about 15 minutes before serving.

Italian Antipasto

Antipasto is one of the most delightful parts of an
Italian feast. Simple or complex, these salads can
be the starter for your meal or the meal itself! When
I was in Italy, I learned that the only constraints on
composing a great antipasto were the limits of your
imagination. This is one of my favorite variations.

MAKES 4 TO 6 SERVINGS

MARINADE
2 teaspoons red wine vinegar
Juice of 1 lemon
2 teaspoons balsamic vinegar
1 tablespoon mirin or honey
3 tablespoons extra-virgin olive oil
½ cup spring or filtered water
Pinch *each* dried basil and rosemary
2 cloves fresh garlic, finely minced
1 teaspoon dry mustard
Sea salt

2 teaspoons extra-virgin olive oil
1 red onion, cut into thin rings
1 carrot, cut into thin matchsticks
1 cup thin matchsticks rutabaga
1 small turnip, cut into thin matchsticks
2 or 3 celery stalks, thinly sliced
1 cup button mushrooms, brushed clean and
    quartered
1 red bell pepper, roasted over a flame,
    peeled, seeded and sliced into thin strips
    (see Note, page 262)
Lettuce leaves
About ¼ cup black olives, pitted and left whole
Whole wheat crackers or toast points

Make the marinade: Whisk together all ingredients, seasoning lightly with sea salt. Set aside.
Heat olive oil in a skillet over medium heat.

Add onion and cook, stirring, until limp, 2 to 3 minutes. Add carrot, rutabaga and turnip and cook, stirring, 2 to 3 minutes. Add remaining vegetables and cook, stirring, until tender, 4 to 5 minutes more. Stir in marinade and simmer, uncovered, until liquid is mostly absorbed, about 10 minutes. Remove from heat and allow to cool completely before serving. Arrange on a serving platter over a bed of crisp lettuce. Garnish with olives. Serve accompanied by crackers.

Marinated Vegetable and Tofu Salad

Similar to antipasto, this marinated salad combines fresh crisp vegetables with lightly sautéed tofu cubes—a salad version of East meets West. This salad takes several hours to make, so it is probably best to put it together the day before you will be serving it.

MAKES 4 SERVINGS

MARINADE
½ **cup barley malt**
½ **cup brown rice syrup**
¼ **cup spring or filtered water**
¼ **cup dark sesame oil**
2 **cloves fresh garlic, finely minced**
Generous dash soy sauce

1 **carrot, cut into thin matchsticks**
1 **onion, cut in half through stem end, then thinly sliced crosswise**
½ **red bell pepper, cut into thin strips**
½ **yellow bell pepper, cut into thin strips**
1 **or 2 zucchini, cut into thin matchsticks**
1 **(1-pound) brick extra-firm tofu**
3 **or 4 tablespoons light sesame oil**
1 **clove fresh garlic, minced**
Soy sauce

Make marinade: Combine all ingredients in a small saucepan over low heat and heat 3 to 4 minutes, until warmed through.

Toss marinade with carrot, onion, bell peppers and zucchini. Cover and refrigerate about 4 hours, tossing occasionally.

Cut tofu into 16 cubes and pat with paper towels to absorb excess water. Heat sesame oil in a deep skillet over medium heat. Add garlic and cook 2 minutes. Add tofu and cook until golden on all sides, turning carefully. Sprinkle lightly with soy sauce and cook 2 to 3 minutes more.

Stir tofu into vegetables and marinate 3 to 4 hours more in the refrigerator, tossing occasionally. Serve chilled.

Composed Salad Plate

This is a classic salad plate that will conjure up images of warm summer days in an outdoor French cafe.

MAKES 4 SERVINGS

HERB DRESSING

2 tablespoons prepared mustard
2 tablespoons balsamic vinegar
2 or 3 tablespoons extra-virgin olive oil
2 cloves fresh garlic, finely minced
¼ cup minced fresh flat-leaf parsley
¼ cup minced fresh chervil
Pinch dried basil
Sea salt

Spring or filtered water
½ pound green beans, trimmed and cut into 1-inch pieces
3 or 4 whole red radishes
1 red onion, cut in half through stem end, then thinly sliced crosswise
1 small bunch watercress, rinsed and left whole
1 cup cooked cannellini or white navy beans, drained
Several black olives, pitted and left whole

Prepare dressing: Whisk together all ingredients, seasoning with just a pinch of salt.

Bring water to a boil in a pot over high heat. Add green beans and cook 1 to 2 minutes. Remove with a slotted spoon, drain and set aside. Add radishes and boil, whole, 2 to 3 minutes. Remove with a slotted spoon, drain and set aside. Add onion and boil 30 seconds. Remove with a slotted spoon, drain and set aside. Hand-shred watercress and set aside.

Divide vegetables among individual salad plates, arranging the vegetables in an attractive design. I like to make a bed with watercress, then arrange the onion, cannellini beans and green beans in the center and top the salad with several radishes and olives. Just before serving, drizzle the salads with the dressing and serve immediately.

Bitter Greens Salad

Bitter greens go very well with a sweet-tasting dressing. For this particular combination of flavors, I have found that a raspberry-based dressing creates a delicious and satisfying final course.

MAKES 4 SERVINGS

LEMON DRESSING

1 tablespoon soy sauce
3 to 4 tablespoons avocado oil
2 tablespoons balsamic vinegar
Grated zest and juice of 1 lemon
1 to 2 tablespoons brown rice syrup
Pinch sea salt
1 cup fresh or thawed frozen raspberries

4 cups bitter greens (a combination of arugula, watercress, endive and radicchio)
¼ cup walnut pieces, lightly pan-toasted (see Note, page 46)

Make dressing: Whisk together all ingredients, except the berries, and chill completely.

Rinse the greens very well and pat dry. Tear greens into bite-size pieces. (Do not slice, as the greens can take on an unpleasant flavor.) Arrange room-temperature greens on chilled plates. Stir raspberries into dressing and drizzle over greens. Garnish with nuts and serve immediately.

Mesclun Salad

A very nice spring salad. Mesclun is a term used to describe a combined assortment of tender baby lettuces and bitter greens, like arugula and radicchio. In this case, a sweet, citrus-laced vinaigrette completes the dish.

MAKES 4 SERVINGS

ORANGE VINAIGRETTE
Juice of 2 oranges
¼ cup balsamic vinegar
2 tablespoons umeboshi vinegar
½ cup extra-virgin olive oil
Several fresh chives, minced
2 to 3 teaspoons prepared mustard
Pinch ground ginger
Sea salt

4 cups mesclun mix, rinsed well and drained
10 to 12 cherry tomatoes

Make vinaigrette: Whisk together all ingredients, seasoning lightly with salt to taste. Set aside.

Tear larger greens into bite-size pieces and, just before serving, toss gently with tomatoes and dressing. Divide among individual plates and serve immediately.

Grilled Vegetable and Green Salad

This is a great dish; the smoky flavors of grilled vegetables complement the fresh, earthy tastes of spring greens. I like to use watercress or arugula in this recipe because of their distinct peppery taste. Serve this up with warm, crusty whole grain bread for a delicious, light repast.

MAKES 4 SERVINGS

LEMON-MISO DRESSING
2 tablespoons balsamic vinegar
Grated zest and juice of 1 lemon
1 tablespoon sweet white miso
Generous pinch sea salt
¼ cup extra-virgin olive oil
Pinch dried basil
Sea salt

1 red onion, cut into thick wedges
1 or 2 zucchini, cut into ¼-inch-thick diagonal slices
1 or 2 parsnips, cut into ¼-inch-thick diagonal slices
1 or 2 celery stalks, cut into 2-inch-thick pieces
1 red bell pepper, cut into thick strips
1 bunch watercress, large stems removed
1 cup cooked chickpeas, drained
2 tablespoons pine nuts, toasted (see Note, page 46)

Preheat grill or broiler.
Make dressing: Whisk together all ingredients, seasoning lightly with salt to taste.

Toss all the vegetables, except watercress, with dressing. Arrange vegetables on grill and cook, turning, until tender, about 5 minutes per side. Toss cooked vegetables with chickpeas so dressing coats the beans.

Arrange the watercress around the edges of individual salad plates and heap the grilled vegetables and chickpeas in the center. Sprinkle with pine nuts and serve.

Elegant Boiled Salad

There really isn't a more delightful complement to a hearty meal than a medley of simple boiled vegetables, not drenched in dressing or sauce, just nobly and beautifully served *au naturelle*. Sound boring to you? Trust me on this one. Served as part of a more complicated meal, this simple medley of fresh, lightly cooked vegetables will shine.

MAKES ABOUT 4 SERVINGS

1 carrot, cut into thin rounds
1 cup finely shredded green cabbage
1 or 2 yellow summer squash, halved
    lengthwise, then cut into thin slices
2 cups cauliflower florets
1 bunch hearty leafy greens
    (kale, collards or bok choy)
1 cup thin matchsticks daikon
1 red onion, cut in half through stem end, then
    thinly sliced crosswise

Cook carrot, cabbage, summer squash, cauliflower, greens, daikon and onion separately in the order listed by adding to boiling water, bringing back to a boil, removing with a slotted spoon, then cooling in iced water. When you get to the greens, boil them whole and then cut into bite-size pieces after cooling. When all the vegetables are prepared, simply toss together and serve warm or chilled.

Grilled Vidalia Onion Salad

There is nothing sweeter (in my opinion, anyway) on earth than grilled Vidalia onions. This cooking technique really brings out their naturally sweet taste. Marinated in a light balsamic vinaigrette, this salad is a real treat.

MAKES 4 SERVINGS

2 tablespoons extra-virgin olive oil
Juice of 1 lemon
Pinch dried basil or several fresh basil leaves,
    minced
2 cloves fresh garlic, finely minced
2 or 3 tablespoons balsamic vinegar
2 teaspoons umeboshi vinegar
2 large Vidalia onions, cut into ⅛-inch-thick
    slices
Green or red leaf lettuce

Preheat grill or broiler. Mix together oil, lemon juice, basil, garlic and vinegars in a small bowl. Brush onion slices on both sides with oil mixture and grill until lightly browned on both sides and limp, 3 to 4 minutes per side. Arrange lettuce leaves on a serving platter and top with grilled onion rings. Serve immediately.

Italian Onion Antipasto

I am never really sure whether to serve this as a side dish or a warm salad. I lean toward salad, because smaller portions are better.

MAKES 4 SERVINGS

4 large onions, peeled and ends removed
4 cloves fresh garlic, peeled
4 pinches dried thyme
Extra-virgin olive oil
Sea salt
Spring or filtered water
4 to 6 leaves romaine or red leaf lettuce

Preheat oven to 375F (190C). Lightly oil a shallow casserole.

Stand the onions on their root ends in pre-pared casserole. Press a clove of garlic and a pinch of thyme into the center of each onion. Drizzle with a little olive oil and sprinkle lightly with salt. Add just enough water to cover the bottom of the casserole, cover and bake 40 minutes. Remove cover and return casserole to oven for about 10 minutes, until onions are tender. Remove onions from casse-role, slice into thick wedges and serve hot wedges on lettuce.

Artichoke and Olive Salad

This salad has incredible flavor. I use jars of mari-nated artichoke hearts, which I lightly broil to give the dish a delicate, smoky flavor.

MAKES 4 TO 6 SERVINGS

2 (14-ounce) jars marinated artichoke hearts
Extra-virgin olive oil
Generous pinch dried basil
1 cup green olives, pitted and coarsely
    chopped
About ¼ cup minced fresh flat-leaf parsley
¼ cup pine nuts, lightly pan-toasted (see
    Note, page 46)
Balsamic vinegar
Several radicchio leaves

Preheat oven to 375F (190C) or preheat broiler. Lightly oil a baking sheet and set aside.

Drain and halve artichoke hearts. Arrange artichokes in a single layer on prepared sheet. Drizzle with a little olive oil and sprinkle with basil. Bake or broil until lightly browned. Remove from oven and cool. Toss with olives, parsley, pine nuts and a light drizzle of balsamic vinegar. Serve warm or chilled on a bed of radicchio.

Broccoli-Cauliflower Terrine

This is a beautiful dish. I adapted the recipe from conventional terrines and created a rich, creamy version minus the heavy cream.

MAKES 6 SERVINGS

½ head cauliflower, diced
2 cups spring or filtered water
Sea salt
4 tablespoons agar-agar flakes
½ red bell pepper, roasted over a flame, peeled,
    seeded and diced (see Note, page 262)
Umeboshi vinegar
Several button mushrooms, brushed clean
    and left whole
2 or 3 stalks broccoli, diced
½ cup soy or rice milk
3 to 4 cups salad greens

Place cauliflower, 1 cup of the water, a pinch of salt and 2 tablespoons of the agar-agar in a saucepan over medium-low heat. Bring to a boil and simmer until cauliflower is tender and agar-agar has dissolved, 10 to 12 minutes. Process in a food processor or blender until pureed. Transfer mixture to a small bowl and fold in bell pepper and a light seasoning of umeboshi vinegar.

Lightly oil an 8 × 4-inch loaf pan. Press plastic wrap into the pan and lightly oil plastic wrap. Spoon cauliflower mixture into the pan and spread evenly. Take the whole mushrooms and slice off 2 sides of the caps, so that each mushroom has 2 flat sides. Press mushrooms vertically into cauliflower mixture, with flat sides touching. Allow mixture to begin to firm up while preparing the broccoli portion of the terrine.

Place broccoli, remaining 1 cup water, remaining 2 tablespoons agar-agar, a pinch of salt and milk in a saucepan over medium-low heat. Bring to a boil and simmer until broccoli is tender and agar-agar has dissolved, 10 to 12 minutes. Process in a food processor or blender until pureed. Cool to about room temperature before spooning mixture gently over the almost-set cauliflower mixture, spreading evenly.

Cover the terrine tightly with plastic wrap and chill 2 to 3 hours, until firmly set. Gently turn the terrine out onto a platter and cut into 6 thick slices. Each slice will show a rich green layer on top of the creamy, white bottom with a cross section of a whole mushroom appearing in the middle. Serve chilled over a bed of delicate greens.

Walnut-Watercress Salad

A lovely and simple side salad to be served warm or chilled, with a smooth creamy dressing.

MAKES 2 OR 3 SERVINGS

1 bunch watercress, rinsed well and patted dry
2 tablespoons walnut pieces, lightly pan-toasted (see Note, page 46)
1 recipe Sour Tofu Dressing (page 270)

Hand-shred watercress into bite-size pieces and toss with toasted nuts.

To serve, toss watercress with dressing and serve immediately. Don't dress the salad too early; the heavy texture of the creamy dressing can really destroy the delicate nature of the watercress.

BEAN SALADS

Navy Bean Salad

Serve this dish as a starter or side dish. It is especially memorable served with warm whole grain bread and a light soup for a quick and easy summer dinner.

MAKES 4 OR 5 SERVINGS

1 (1-inch) piece kombu or 1 bay leaf
1 cup dried navy beans, sorted and rinsed
3 cups spring or filtered water
Sea salt
¼ cup *each* fresh corn kernels, diced carrot, thinly sliced green onion and diced cucumber
1 recipe Green Sauce (page 275)
Sprigs flat-leaf parsley, for garnish

Place kombu or bay leaf on the bottom of a pot and top with beans and water. Bring to a boil, uncovered, and boil 10 minutes. Reduce heat, cover and cook until beans are tender, 40 to 45 minutes. Season lightly with salt and cook 5 to 7 minutes more. Drain and cool.

Drop corn and carrot into salted boiling water and quickly blanch. Drain and toss with green onion and cucumber in a large bowl. Remove bay leaf (if used), toss beans, vegetables and a generous amount of Green Sauce together. Serve garnished with parsley sprigs.

■ **VARIATION** This dish is also delicious if you puree the beans before adding the veggies, creating a most wonderful and unique pâté, dotted with vegetables. Serve in a pool of Green Sauce with toast points.

Italian Bean and Tomato Salad

With interesting ingredients, salads can become much more than plates of raw lettuce. This hearty salad, accompanied by warm, crusty bread, makes a summer meal all on its own.

MAKES 4 SERVINGS

About 3 cups shredded green leaf lettuce
4 or 5 cherry tomatoes, quartered
2 celery stalks, diced
1 carrot, shredded
1 cup cooked cannellini beans, drained
2 tablespoons balsamic vinegar
Sea salt
Generous pinches dried oregano and basil
2 tablespoons extra-virgin olive oil

Gently combine lettuce, tomatoes, celery, carrot and beans in a medium bowl. Whisk together vinegar, salt to taste, herbs and oil in a small bowl. Toss dressing with salad. Serve at room temperature or chilled.

Kissimmee Orange-Chickpea Salad

I must confess: This recipe was originally designed to be a chicken salad, but the ingredients screamed "chickpeas!" to me. What do you think?

MAKES 4 TO 6 SERVINGS

1 (1-inch) piece kombu or 1 bay leaf
1 cup chickpeas, rinsed and sorted
3 cups Vegetable Stock (page 74) or spring or filtered water
2 oranges
2 or 3 celery stalks, cut into thin diagonal pieces
3 or 4 fresh green onions, cut into very thin diagonal pieces
Several leaves fresh basil, minced
¾ cup slivered almonds
Grated zest and juice of 1 lemon
1 tablespoon brown rice syrup
2 tablespoons prepared mustard
1 cup Tofu Mayo (page 272)
Sea salt
2 to 3 cups shredded mesclun mix or other tender greens

Place kombu or bay leaf in a heavy pot, top with chickpeas and stock and boil, uncovered, over high heat 10 minutes. Cover, reduce heat and cook until beans are tender, about 1 hour. Drain, discard bay leaf (if used) and set chickpeas aside.

Peel the oranges and with a sharp knife, removing all the bitter white pith surrounding the flesh of the fruit. Separate the segments and cut into small pieces. Set aside.

Mix together the chickpeas, celery, green onions, basil, almonds and orange segments. Whisk together the lemon zest and juice, rice syrup, mustard, Tofu Mayo and a generous pinch of salt. Toss dressing gently with the salad and serve on a bed of greens, chilled or at room temperature.

■ **NOTE** You can use canned organic chickpeas to save time when making this salad. Just be sure to rinse them very well, as the water can give the beans a stale taste.

Black Bean Salad

A very versatile salad. I love serving it chilled at a summer lunch or warm as the centerpiece dish of a hearty autumn or winter meal. Dressed lightly with a zesty citrus vinaigrette, this dish is a real crowd pleaser.

MAKES 4 SERVINGS

1 (1-inch) piece kombu or 1 bay leaf
1 cup dried black turtle beans, sorted and
    rinsed
3 cups spring or filtered water
1 red bell pepper, roasted over a flame, peeled,
    seeded and diced (see Note, page 262)
2 or 3 celery stalks, diced
1 red onion, diced

¼ cup minced fresh flat-leaf parsley
Grated zest of 1 lemon

DRESSING
⅓ cup extra-virgin olive oil
Sea salt
2 teaspoons umeboshi vinegar
3 tablespoons balsamic vinegar
2 teaspoons brown rice syrup
2 cloves fresh garlic, minced
Juice of 1 lemon
Juice of 1 orange
Several leaves of escarole, rinsed well

Place kombu or bay leaf in a pot, top with beans and water and boil, uncovered, over high heat about 10 minutes. Cover, reduce heat and simmer over low heat until beans are tender, about 45 minutes. Drain, discard bay leaf (if used) and transfer beans to a medium bowl. Stir in bell pepper, celery, onion, parsley and lemon zest.

Make dressing: Warm oil and salt to taste over low heat 3 to 4 minutes. In a small bowl, whisk together all the dressing ingredients and gently toss with the salad. Serve warm or chilled on a bed of escarole.

■ **NOTE** You may use canned organic black beans to save time in this recipe. Just be sure to rinse them very well, as the water in the can will give the beans a stale taste.

Chickenless Salad

This amazing salad has fooled some of the biggest chicken salad fans. It has all the ingredients that make a great chicken salad, except the bird! This salad is great on a bed of fresh, crisp greens or served as a hearty sandwich.

MAKES 4 SERVINGS

1 (1-pound) brick extra-firm tofu
Soy sauce
Spring or filtered water
3 celery stalks, diced
1 small red onion, diced
1 red bell pepper, roasted over a flame, peeled,
    seeded and diced (see Note, page 262)
½ teaspoon *each* basil, sage, rosemary and
    oregano
2 teaspoons sweet paprika
1 to 1½ cups Tofu Mayo (page 272)

Preheat oven to 400F (205C). Lightly oil a baking sheet and set aside.

Cut tofu into ¼-inch-thick slices. Place slices in a shallow dish and cover with a mixture that is 1 part soy sauce to 4 parts water. Allow tofu to marinate 10 minutes. Place tofu slices on prepared baking sheet and bake 30 to 35 minutes, until deep golden brown and crispy on the outside.

Remove tofu slices from oven and allow to cool until you can handle them. Shred the tofu slices with a sharp knife, creating irregular, angular pieces similar to shredded chicken. Mix with vegetables, herbs, paprika and Tofu Mayo until ingredients are coated. Chill thoroughly before serving.

■ **VARIATION** Broil tofu for a few minutes rather than baking it. You may also use prepared baked tofu (as well as vegan mayo), which you can purchase in any natural foodstore.

Basil–White Bean Salad

Crusty whole grain bread and freshly cooked vegetables are the ideal companions for this pesto-dressed bean salad.

MAKES 4 OR 5 SERVINGS

1 (1-inch) piece kombu or 1 bay leaf
1 cup dried cannellini beans, sorted and rinsed
3 cups spring or filtered water
1 bunch watercress, blanched until bright
    green
2 or 3 celery stalks, diced
1 red bell pepper, roasted over a flame, peeled,
    seeded and diced (see Note, page 262)

PESTO
½ cup Tofu Mayo (page 272)
2 cloves fresh garlic, minced
1 cup loosely packed fresh basil leaves
1 teaspoon white miso
¼ cup pine nuts or walnuts
1 tablespoon umeboshi vinegar
1 teaspoon brown rice syrup

Place kombu or bay leaf in a pot, top with beans and water and boil, uncovered, over high heat about 10 minutes. Cover, reduce heat and simmer over low heat until beans are tender, about 45 minutes. Do not season. Remove bay leaf (if used). Dice watercress and toss together with beans, celery and bell pepper. Cover and refrigerate until needed.

Meanwhile make pesto: Combine all ingredients in a food processor and process until smooth. Transfer to a small bowl, cover and chill completely.

About 1 hour before serving, whisk pesto to loosen and toss gently into the salad. Transfer to a serving bowl, cover and chill about 30 minutes before serving.

■ **VARIATION** I must tell you that I also like to serve this salad warm. Lightly warm the dressing and toss it with freshly cooked beans just before serving. The choice is yours!

Tuscan Bean Salad

Any recipe that uses rosemary reminds me of my time in the hills of Tuscany. The aromatic flavor of this herb scented more foods than I can even remember. I especially love it mixed with delicate white beans and fresh vegetables to create this refreshing summer centerpiece dish.

MAKES 4 SERVINGS

ROSEMARY DRESSING
¼ cup extra-virgin olive oil
Sea salt
2 to 3 tablespoons balsamic vinegar
Juice of 1 lemon
¼ cup minced fresh rosemary

2 or 3 cloves fresh garlic, peeled
2 cups cooked cannellini beans, drained
1 small red onion, finely diced
2 or 3 red radishes, diced
1 cucumber, seeded and diced

Make dressing: In a small saucepan, gently warm the oil and salt to taste. Remove pan from heat and whisk in the vinegar, lemon juice and rosemary. Set aside.

Take the whole garlic cloves and gently rub them around the interior of the salad bowl. This will give you the essence of the garlic with only a hint of flavor, without competing with the strong rosemary infusion. Discard garlic cloves.

Place the beans and vegetables in the salad bowl and toss well with the dressing. Cover tightly and refrigerate several hours before serving, allowing the flavors to fully develop.

Peppery Chickpea Salad

One of the most popular and versatile beans, chickpeas are always favorite salad ingredients, since they stand up well in both hot and cold dishes. My only caution is to remember to cook chickpeas very well, so that they are tender but firm, not crunchy. This salad draws upon a lot of Mediterranean foods: It's laden with peppers, olives and marinated artichoke hearts, lightly dressed in a garlic vinaigrette.

MAKES 4 SERVINGS

2 cups cooked chickpeas, drained
1 *each* yellow, red and green bell peppers,
    roasted over a flame, peeled, seeded and
    diced (see Note, page 262)
1 small red onion, finely diced
10 to 12 oil-cured black olives, pitted and
    coarsely diced
1 (14-ounce) jar marinated artichoke hearts,
    drained and quartered
2 celery stalks, diced
Lightly steamed greens, like kale

GARLIC VINAIGRETTE
¼ cup extra-virgin olive oil
3 or 4 cloves fresh garlic, minced
3 to 4 tablespoons balsamic vinegar
Grated zest and juice of 1 lemon
Sea salt

Toss together all the salad ingredients in a large bowl and set aside.

Make vinaigrette: Heat oil in a small skillet over medium heat. Add garlic and cook about 1 minute. This infuses the oil with garlic flavor, while mellowing the sometimes sharp taste. Remove from heat and whisk in remaining ingredients. Toss with the salad and serve warm over a bed of steamed greens.

Tempeh Salad

Now, before you continue, I have to explain that when I was a kid my idea of fish was tuna salad or the crunchy outer coating of frozen fish sticks. As a grown-up finicky eater, I still don't like (or eat) fish, but remembered the taste of tuna salad. This is my vegetarian version of that type of creamy, sandwich-filler salad.

MAKES 2 OR 3 SERVINGS

1 (8-ounce) package tempeh, steamed 10 minutes and cooled to room temperature
¼ cup *each* diced carrot, red onion and celery
2 or 3 tablespoons organic sweet relish (from a natural foods store)
Generous pinch dried dill weed
Tofu Mayo (page 272)

Crumble tempeh into a coarse meal. Toss with vegetables, relish, dill and Tofu Mayo to form a creamy salad. Serve chilled over a bed of lettuce or in your favorite sandwich.

■ **VARIATION** Some people like to toss in some powdered kelp to create an authentic tuna-salad taste in this recipe. If you would like the veggies to be more tender, blanch them before using them in the recipe. You may also use one of the ready-made varieties of vegan mayo in place of making your own from scratch.

Split-Pea Pâté

A pâté, this time featuring split peas, that is truly spectacular and amazingly easy to make.

MAKES 4 TO 6 SERVINGS

1 cup split peas, sorted and rinsed
1 (1-inch) piece wakame, soaked briefly until tender and diced
3 cups spring or filtered water
Soy sauce
2 cups whole wheat elbow noodles, cooked, rinsed and drained
¼ cup *each* fresh corn kernels, diced carrot, diced onion and diced celery
Umeboshi vinegar
2 to 3 cups baby arugula

Combine peas, wakame and water in a pot and bring to a boil. Boil, uncovered, several minutes or until the foam that forms dissipates. Cover and cook over low heat until creamy, about 1 hour.

Oil a shallow 1½-quart casserole and set aside.

Season peas lightly with soy sauce and cook several minutes more. Turn off heat and stir in noodles, vegetables and a light sprinkling of umeboshi vinegar. Pour into prepared casserole and refrigerate until set. Slice into squares and serve on a bed of baby arugula.

GRAIN SALADS

Brown Rice Salad

This is a refreshing way to serve brown rice in warm weather. The light citrus-scented dressing flavors the salad in the most tantalizing way.

MAKES 4 OR 5 SERVINGS

¼ cup *each* corn kernels, green peas, diced carrot and diced celery
Small handful watercress sprigs
Pinch sea salt
3 tablespoons brown rice vinegar
3 tablespoons umeboshi or red wine vinegar
½ cup fresh orange juice
Grated zest of 1 orange
Juice of 1 lemon
1 tablespoon balsamic vinegar (optional)
2 cups cooked long-grain brown rice

Cook corn, peas, carrot, celery and watercress separately in the order listed by adding to boiling water, bringing back to a boil, removing with a slotted spoon then cooling in iced water. Drain vegetables well and mix together in a bowl. Toss vegetables with salt and remaining ingredients, except rice, to taste. Allow to marinate 30 minutes. Toss vegetables with rice just before serving or the rice will be soggy.

■ **VARIATION** You may substitute any cooked whole grain or pasta for the brown rice in this recipe, and you may use any combination of vinegars and lemon juice.

Quinoa and Roasted Veggie Salad

A meal in itself, I was inspired by a fine Southwestern restaurant with this recipe. A few tweaks to their dish, and I had an easy-to-assemble salad that makes a great potluck dish—among other things!

MAKES 4 OR 5 SERVINGS

1 cup quinoa, rinsed well and drained
2 cups Vegetable Stock (page 74), or spring or filtered water
Pinch sea salt
Light sesame oil
8 slices fresh ginger, cut into matchstick pieces
2 or 3 shallots, minced
1 teaspoon *each* dried marjoram and thyme
1 carrot, diced
2 or 3 celery stalks, diced
Juice of 1 lemon
2 or 3 medium zucchini, cut into thin diagonal slices
2 or 3 parsnips, cut into thin diagonal slices
1 red onion, cut in half-moon pieces
2 red bell peppers, cut into thin strips
Several cherry tomatoes, halved
Soy sauce

Combine quinoa and stock in a saucepan and bring to a boil. Add salt, cover and cook over low heat until all the stock has been absorbed, about 25 minutes. Fluff with a fork, transfer to a medium bowl and set aside.

Heat 1 teaspoon sesame oil in a skillet over medium heat. Add ginger, shallots and herbs and cook, stirring, until shallots are translucent. Add carrot and celery and cook, stirring, until vegetables are just tender, 3 to 4 minutes. Remove from heat and stir in lemon juice. Mix into the quinoa and set aside.

Preheat oven to 400F (205C) and lightly oil a baking pan or shallow casserole. Arrange remaining vegetables in the pan and lightly drizzle with sesame oil and soy sauce. Toss well to coat. Roast, uncovered, until vegetables are tender and lightly browned, 20 to 25 minutes.

To serve, arrange a layer of roasted vegetables on individual plates and top with a generous scoop of quinoa salad. Serve warm.

Curried Rice Salad

A tropical twist on rice salad: aromatic basmati rice laced with shredded coconut and vegetables, scented with curry and complemented by the heady flavors of fruit—a wonderful warm salad.

MAKES 4 SERVINGS

1 cup unsweetened shredded coconut
½ cup cashews
1 tablespoon avocado oil
2 cloves fresh garlic, minced
1 onion, diced
1 tablespoon curry powder
½ teaspoon ground ginger
1 cup brown basmati rice, rinsed
2 cups spring or filtered water
Pinch sea salt
2 celery stalks, diced
½ cup dried currants
1 Granny Smith apple, cored and diced
3 or 4 green onions, diced
1 recipe Sweet Mustard Vinaigrette (page 272)

Preheat oven to 350F (175C). Spread coconut on a baking sheet. Lightly toast in oven until golden, about 3 minutes. Arrange cashews in a baking pan. Lightly toast in oven until lightly browned, about 5 minutes. Set coconut and cashews aside to cool.

Heat oil in a deep skillet over medium heat. Add garlic and onion and cook about 3 minutes. Stir in curry powder and ginger and cook, stirring, 2 minutes more. Stir in the rice. Slowly stir in water and bring to a boil. Add salt, cover and cook over low heat 20 minutes. Add celery, currants and apple to rice. Do not stir. Cover and cook over low heat until all liquid has been absorbed, about 20 minutes.

Remove from heat and stir in cashews and green onions. Just before serving, stir in coconut and Sweet Mustard Vinaigrette. Serve warm.

Italian Rice Salad

In Italian cuisine, rice is served almost as often as pasta. In some regions, it is even more important. This recipe was a favorite during the hot summer months I spent in Tuscany, when cooking a lot wasn't a high priority. We served this hot or cold as a satisfying lunch dish.

MAKES 4 SERVINGS

1 tablespoon prepared Dijon mustard
2 tablespoons balsamic vinegar
1 teaspoon brown rice syrup
Sea salt
¼ cup extra-virgin olive oil
Juice of 1 lemon
3 cups cooked long-grain brown or white rice
1 red bell pepper, roasted over a flame, peeled, seeded and cut into thin strips (see Note, page 262)
3 or 4 green onions, cut into thin diagonal slices
¼ cup capers, drained and rinsed well
½ to ⅔ cup oil-cured black olives, pitted and coarsely diced
2 or 3 cloves fresh garlic, peeled
¼ cup minced fresh flat-leaf parsley

Whisk together mustard, vinegar, syrup, a light seasoning of salt and olive oil in a small saucepan. Warm over low heat 3 to 4 minutes. Remove from heat and set aside to cool. Whisk in lemon juice.

Mix together rice, bell pepper, onions, capers and olives in a large bowl. Add oil mixture and toss to combine. Rub the garlic cloves all around the interior of a salad bowl and discard. Transfer rice salad to the serving bowl and mix in parsley just before serving. Serve warm or chilled.

Wild Rice Salad

The rich colors of wild rice create a pretty contrast against the delicate white of polished rice. For this salad, it's okay to cook the rices ahead of time, but I usually toss everything together just before serving because white rice is so soft, it can get mushy if mixed in too soon.

MAKES 4 SERVINGS

½ cup wild rice
¾ cup short-grain white rice
2 cups spring or filtered water
Pinch sea salt
Avocado oil, for deep-frying
8 ounces extra-firm tofu, drained and cubed

2 tart apples, like Granny Smith, unpeeled, cored and diced
½ cup unfiltered, unsweetened apple juice
Juice of 1 orange
Dash of umeboshi vinegar
Generous pinch dried tarragon
1 bunch watercress
3 or 4 green onions, cut into thin diagonal slices
2 celery stalks, diced
¼ cup pecans, lightly pan-toasted (see Note, page 46) and finely chopped

Rinse wild rice and white rice well to remove excess starch and any dust that has gathered. Place rinsed grains and water in a deep saucepan and bring to a boil, uncovered. Add salt, cover and simmer over low heat until wild rice is tender and all liquid has been absorbed, 35 to 40 minutes. Stir gently to loosen grains and transfer to a bowl to cool.

Heat oil in a deep skillet to 375F (190C). Add tofu and deep-fry until golden and crispy, 3 to 4 minutes.

Whisk together the apples, apple juice and orange juice, vinegar and tarragon.

Hand-shred watercress into small pieces and form a ring around the edge of a serving platter. Toss together the rice, green onions, celery, tofu and apple mixture. Mound salad in the center of the platter and sprinkle with pecans. Serve at room temperature.

Brown Rice and Black Bean Salad

Inspired by Spanish cuisine, this salad seems to be at its best when made the day before, allowing the flavors plenty of time to fully develop. And what a delicious way to use up leftover cooked rice!

MAKES 5 OR 6 SERVINGS

1 tablespoon extra-virgin olive oil
2 cloves fresh garlic, minced
1 onion, minced
Generous pinch cumin
1 or 2 green chiles, seeded and minced
Sea salt
1½ cups cooked black turtle beans, cooked
    without seasoning, drained
Grated zest and juice of 1 orange
Brown rice vinegar
2 to 3 cups cooked medium-grain brown rice
¼ cup slivered almonds, lightly pan-toasted
    (see Note, page 55)
¼ cup minced fresh flat-leaf parsley
Orange slices and sprigs flat-leaf parsley, for
    garnish

Heat olive oil in a skillet over medium heat. Add garlic and onion and cook, stirring, 2 to 3 minutes. Stir in cumin, chiles and a pinch of salt and cook, stirring, 3 to 4 minutes. Add beans, season to taste with salt and cook, stirring, 3 to 4 minutes, just long enough for ingredients to combine thoroughly. Remove from heat and stir in orange zest and juice and rice vinegar to taste.

Combine bean mixture, rice, almonds and parsley and press firmly into a lightly oiled bowl or mold. Chill about 1 hour. Invert salad onto a serving platter just before serving and garnish with orange slices and parsley sprigs.

PASTA SALADS

Couscous Salad

Combined with chickpeas and vegetables and lightly dressed, this salad makes a deliciously satisfying one-dish meal.

MAKES 5 OR 6 SERVINGS

6 cups spring or filtered water
Pinch sea salt
3 cups couscous
2 or 3 green onions, thinly sliced
2 or 3 red radishes, thinly sliced, slices cut in
    half
½ cup cooked chickpeas, drained
2 celery stalks, thinly sliced
2 tablespoons minced fresh flat-leaf parsley
1 recipe Istanbul Sauce (page 276)

Bring water and salt to a boil in a large saucepan over medium heat. Add couscous, turn off heat and allow to stand, undisturbed, 10 minutes. Fluff with a fork before proceeding with the recipe.

For a slightly milder taste, drop green onions and radishes into boiling water 30 seconds, drain, cool in iced water and drain before adding to other ingredients.

Toss all ingredients with sauce and serve.

■ **VARIATION** Bulgur may be substituted for the couscous in this recipe.

Pesto Noodle Salad

Traditional basil pesto has always been one of my favorite ways to dress pasta. Served chilled as a summer salad, it is hands-down the greatest. When I changed my diet, eliminating animal foods, I took great pains to create a healthy version that was as delicious as the pesto I was used to making. I think I did it. What do you think?

MAKES 6 SERVINGS

1 pound whole wheat noodles, like penne or
    fettucine
½ cup extra-virgin olive oil
2 tablespoons white miso
½ cup pine nuts or walnuts, lightly pan-
    toasted (see Note, page 46), plus extra for
    garnish
1 cup lightly packed fresh basil leaves
2 tablespoons umeboshi vinegar
1 teaspoon brown rice syrup
1 or 2 cloves fresh garlic, minced
Spring or filtered water
2 stalks broccoli, cut into tiny flowerets and
    steamed until bright green

Cook noodles according to package directions. Drain and rinse well so that noodles do not stick together. Rinse until no warmth remains when you run your hands through the noodles. Set aside and prepare the pesto.

Place oil and miso in a small saucepan over low heat and warm through for a few minutes. Warming makes these ingredients more digestible. Cool slightly before combining oil mixture, pine nuts, basil, vinegar, rice syrup and garlic in a food processor or blender and process until smooth. Gradually add a small bit of water to make a thick creamy sauce, if needed.

Toss the noodles and broccoli together and chill thoroughly. Separately chill the pesto.

When ready to serve, toss together the noodles, broccoli and pesto with some pine nuts for garnish. Serve chilled.

■ **VARIATION** This dish is also delicious served warm.

Asian Noodle Salad with Cashews

A zesty, marinated salad with plenty of color and crunch.

MAKES 2 OR 3 SERVINGS

8 ounces whole wheat udon noodles
Spring or filtered water
2 to 3 cups shredded Chinese cabbage or bok
    choy
1 yellow summer squash, cut into matchsticks
1 zucchini, cut into matchsticks
½ cup matchstick pieces daikon
1 carrot, cut into matchsticks
3 or 4 green onions, cut into thin diagonal
    slices

MARINADE
2 tablespoons dark sesame oil
2 tablespoons soy sauce
Juice of 1 orange
2 tablespoons sweet brown rice vinegar
2 teaspoons mirin
1 clove fresh garlic, minced
Pinch ground ginger
3 to 4 tablespoons black sesame seeds,
    lightly pan-toasted (see Note, page 46) and
    partially crushed

¼ cup cashews, lightly pan-toasted (see Note,
    page 46)

Cook noodles in a large pot of salted boiling water, drain, rinse well and set aside. Combine cabbage, summer squash, zucchini, daikon, carrot and green onions in a large bowl.

Make marinade: Warm oil and soy sauce gently in a small saucepan over low heat 3 to 4 minutes. Whisk remaining marinade ingredients into oil mixture and pour over the vegetables. Allow to marinate 30 minutes, tossing occasionally.

Just before serving, toss marinated vegetables and any remaining marinade with noodles. Stir in cashews and serve at room temperature or chilled.

Warm Pasta Salad with Tofu Cheese

This hearty salad is a great one-dish meal: satisfying pasta smothered in a creamy mushroom sauce and tossed with fresh greens and crumbly, pickled Tofu Cheese.

MAKES 6 SERVINGS

1 pound rotini, rigatoni, spirals or other pasta
Spring or filtered water
2 cups Mushroom Stock (page 75)
1 small leek, sliced lengthwise, rinsed well and diced
2 cups button mushrooms, brushed clean and thinly sliced
Sea salt
3 or 4 leaves escarole, diced
Generous pinch dried rosemary
2 teaspoons kuzu or arrowroot, dissolved in ¼ cup cold water
1 cup crumbled Tofu Cheese (page 118)

Cook pasta in a large pot of boiling water until just tender, drain, rinse and set aside.

Bring 1 cup of the stock and leek to a boil in a saucepan and simmer 2 minutes. Add remaining stock, mushrooms and a light seasoning of salt and cook, covered, over low heat until mushrooms are tender, 5 to 10 minutes. Add escarole, rosemary and dissolved kuzu and cook, stirring constantly, until sauce thickens slightly, about 3 minutes.

To serve, arrange pasta on a platter or in a bowl. Gently stir Tofu Cheese into sauce and spoon over top of pasta. Serve immediately.

Noodle Watercress Salad

This is an elegant side salad, and makes a great summer lunch or centerpiece dish for a summer brunch buffet. I like to serve this chilled, and dress it just prior to serving so that the dressing stays smooth and creamy. That way, the ingredients don't get gummy, as can happen when a pasta salad is dressed too far in advance.

MAKES 2 OR 3 SERVINGS

1 red bell pepper, roasted over a flame, peeled, seeded and cut into strips (see Note, page 262)
1 cucumber, halved lengthwise, then sliced crosswise
1 or 2 celery stalks, cut into thin diagonal slices
1 or 2 green onions, cut into thin diagonal slices
Spring or filtered water
1 bunch watercress
8 ounces small shell pasta, cooked, rinsed and drained
1 recipe Creamy Sesame Dressing (page 271)
Several red bell pepper rings, for garnish

Toss bell pepper with cucumber, celery and green onion in a bowl and set aside.

Bring a saucepan of water to a boil. Add watercress and cook about 30 seconds. Plunge into iced water to stop the cooking process, drain and cut into bite-size pieces. Toss with other vegetables.

In separate bowls, chill the pasta, vegetables and dressing. Just before serving, gently toss all ingredients together, arrange on a platter or in a bowl and serve immediately, garnished with bell pepper rings.

■ **NOTE** Roast bell peppers or fresh chiles by placing over an open gas flame or under a broiler and charring outer skin. Transfer to a paper sack, seal tightly and allow to steam several minutes. Then simply rub the skin away gently with your fingers, removing all the black pieces. Halve the bell peppers, remove the seeds and slice into strips or dice, according to recipe directions.

Herald-of-Spring Salad

Nothing says spring quite like a lightly dressed pasta salad dotted with fresh, tender vegetables, in this case, lightly grilled and blanched.

MAKES 3 TO 4 SERVINGS

1 yellow squash, cut into thin diagonal
   slices
1 zucchini, cut into thin diagonal slices
1 red onion, cut into thin half-moon slices
1 tablespoon extra-virgin olive oil
Sea salt
Spring or filtered water
1 carrot, cut into thin matchsticks
1 cup fresh green peas
3 or 4 Brussels sprouts, quartered
1 cup matchstick pieces daikon

8 ounces whole wheat udon noodles, cooked,
   drained and rinsed
1 recipe Green Goddess Dressing (page 270)

Preheat grill or broiler. Brush squash, zucchini and onion with oil, sprinkle lightly with salt and grill until tender and lightly browned, about 5 minutes. Set aside.

Bring water to a boil in a pot over high heat. Add carrot and cook 1 minute. Remove with a slotted spoon and cool in iced water. Drain and set aside. Add peas and boil 30 seconds. Remove with a slotted spoon and cool in iced water. Drain and set aside. Add Brussels sprouts and boil 2 to 3 minutes. Remove with a slotted spoon and cool in iced water. Drain and set aside. Finally, add daikon to boiling water and cook 1 minute. Drain and cool in iced water. Drain and set aside.

Just before serving, arrange grilled vegetables around a serving platter. Toss blanched vegetables and pasta with dressing and mound in the center of the platter. Serve immediately.

SEA VEGETABLE SALADS

Sea Palm Salad

A beautiful and delicious salad that really showcases the delicate flavor of sea palm, nicely complemented by a light vinaigrette-type dressing.

MAKES 4 SERVINGS

1 cup dried sea palm, soaked and sliced into
   bite-size pieces
Spring or filtered water
Soy sauce
1 cup fresh or frozen corn kernels

1 carrot, diced
½ red onion, diced
½ red bell pepper, roasted over a flame,
peeled, seeded and diced (see Note,
opposite)
1 recipe Italian Dressing (page 271)

Dice sea palm and place in a small saucepan with water to half cover. Sprinkle with soy sauce and bring to a boil. Reduce heat, cover and simmer until tender, about 35 minutes. Remove lid and allow any remaining cooking liquid to cook away.

Cook corn, carrot and onion separately in the order listed by adding to boiling water, bringing back to a boil, removing with a slotted spoon, then cooling in iced water. Drain vegetables well and mix together in a bowl with bell pepper. Toss cooked sea palm and cooked vegetables with Italian Dressing and marinate 30 minutes, allowing the flavors to fully develop. Serve at room temperature or slightly warm.

Hiziki Ribbon Salad

A strong-tasting salad, nicely balanced with tender vegetables and a light citrus dressing. I serve this one in small amounts as a complementary dish to round out a meal.

MAKES 3 TO 4 SERVINGS

1 cup dried hiziki, rinsed well and soaked
until tender, about 10 minutes
Spring or filtered water
Soy sauce
1 tablespoon mirin
3 or 4 red radishes, thinly sliced
Umeboshi vinegar

1 cup fresh green beans, French cut
1 yellow summer squash, cut into
matchsticks
Juice of 1 lemon

Place hiziki in a small saucepan with just enough water to cover, a dash of soy sauce, and mirin. Simmer, uncovered, until tender, about 25 minutes. If water evaporates too quickly, add a bit more and reduce heat so hiziki can cook thoroughly. Cooking uncovered gentles hiziki's strong flavor and brings out its natural sweetness.

While the hiziki is cooking, place radish slices in a small bowl and cover with umeboshi vinegar. Allow to marinate 15 minutes. Bring a small pan of water to a boil and separately boil green beans and squash until just tender, about 10 minutes for beans and 3 to 4 minutes for squash. Cool in iced water, drain and set aside.

When hiziki is tender and cooking liquid has completely evaporated, remove from heat. Allow to cool to room temperature before stirring in marinated radishes, vegetables and lemon juice. Serve chilled or at room temperature.

Cucumber-Dulse Salad

Simple to make and very refreshing, this salad is a must for hot, sticky days. Packed with potassium, dulse is an ideal supplement to your diet during the summer months.

MAKES 4 TO 6 SERVINGS

2 cucumbers, peeled, seeded and cut into
**   very thin slices**
Umeboshi vinegar
1 cup dulse
Juice of 1 lemon
Juice and grated zest of 1 orange
¼ cup sunflower seeds, lightly pan-toasted
**   (see Note, page 46)**

Place cucumbers in a small bowl and sprinkle generously with umeboshi vinegar. Rub between your fingers to coat with vinegar and allow to marinate 1 hour.

Rinse and dice dulse. Toss with lemon and orange juices and allow to marinate 1 hour.

Just before serving, squeeze excess liquid from cucumber slices and toss with dulse, orange zest and sunflower seeds. Serve chilled or at room temperature.

FRUIT SALADS

Fire and Ice Melon Salad

This is a refreshing summer salad of sweet, tender melon and fiery picante sauce.

MAKES 4 SERVINGS

1 cup honeydew melon balls
1 cup cantaloupe balls

1 cup watermelon balls
2 teaspoons medium-hot picante sauce
1 tablespoon brown rice syrup
Juice of 1 lime
Pinch sea salt
Lettuce

Combine melon balls in a bowl. Whisk together the picante sauce, rice syrup, lime juice and salt. Toss gently with melons and serve on a bed of crisp lettuce. Serve at room temperature or nicely chilled.

Tomato, Mango and Cumin Salad

I had never thought to combine tomatoes with cumin until I thought I was reaching for my dried basil and sprinkled cumin on my tomatoes instead. The good news? The flavor was amazing. I know I am not the first to combine these ingredients, but now that I have discovered it, I love it!

MAKES ABOUT 4 SERVINGS

2 cups cherry tomatoes, halved
1 cucumber, thinly sliced on the diagonal (do
**   not peel or seed)**
1 ripe mango, peeled, seeded and thinly sliced
1 small bunch flat-leaf parsley, leaves
**   removed from stems**
¼ cup extra-virgin olive oil
Grated zest of 1 lemon
2 tablespoons fresh lemon juice
2 teaspoons Suzanne's Specialties Raspberry
**   Rice Nectar or rice syrup simmered with ½**
**   cup frozen raspberries, 5 minutes**
½ teaspoon ground cumin
Sea salt
Cracked black pepper

Combine tomatoes, cucumber, mango and parsley in a mixing bowl.

Make the dressing by whisking together oil, lemon zest, lemon juice, rice nectar, cumin, salt and pepper to taste.

Toss salad with dressing to coat and serve.

Watermelon Salad with Serrano Vinaigrette

Summer and salads go together like love and marriage, but did you know that even salads are seasonal? Try this perfectly summery salad to keep you cool and relaxed on the hottest days.

MAKES 4 SERVINGS

1 cup extra-virgin olive oil
2 tablespoons fresh lime juice
2 tablespoons champagne vinegar
1 or 2 shallots, finely minced
1 (2-inch) fresh serrano chile, finely minced
1 tablespoon finely minced fresh basil
Sea salt
2 cups cherry tomatoes, halved
4 cups fresh baby arugula
4 cups 1-inch watermelon cubes, seeds removed, chilled

Whisk together oil, lime juice, vinegar, shallots, chile, basil and salt to taste. Set aside for at least 1 hour, to allow flavors to develop.

Mix together tomatoes and arugula and toss with just enough dressing to coat the leaves. Divide evenly among 4 salad plates. Mound watermelon on top of salads and drizzle with additional dressing to taste.

Winter Pear Salad

A crunchy salad with a symphony of flavors. I like to serve this salad with the dressing lightly warmed. It adds a nice bit of freshness to the usual heartier fare that makes up winter cooking.

MAKES 4 OR 5 SERVINGS

1 bunch watercress
2 cups shredded radicchio
6 Bosc or Bartlett pears, cored and thinly sliced
1 cup crumbled Tofu Cheese (page 118)
1 cup walnut pieces, lightly pan-toasted (see Note, page 46)
1 cup pecan pieces, lightly pan-toasted (see Note, page 46)
1 cup raspberries, preferably fresh (frozen will work)
¼ cup minced fresh flat-leaf parsley

DRESSING
¼ cup balsamic vinegar
¼ cup extra-virgin olive oil
3 tablespoons unfiltered, unsweetened apple juice
Pinch of sea salt
½ teaspoon ground ginger

Hand-shred watercress and toss with radicchio and arrange on a large salad platter. Arrange pear slices decoratively in fan shapes over the greens and sprinkle with Tofu Cheese, nuts, raspberries and parsley.

*Make dressing:*Whisk together all ingredients in a small saucepan and gently warm over low heat. Just before serving, drizzle over pear salad. Serve at room temperature with warm dressing.

Marinated Strawberry Salad

A wonderfully unique way to serve fresh strawberries. The delicate taste of the sweetened vinegar dressing enhances the natural flavor of the berries but doesn't overpower their natural delicious taste.

MAKES 3 TO 4 SERVINGS

**1 quart fresh strawberries, hulled but left
    whole**
½ cup balsamic vinegar
Juice of 1 lemon
2 tablespoons brown rice syrup or honey

Arrange berries in a bowl. Whisk together vinegar, lemon juice and rice syrup in a small bowl. Toss gently with berries and allow to stand 15 to 30 minutes before serving at room temperature or chilled.

Fruit and Radish Slaw

A perfect side dish for winter, when produce is at its most scarce. This sweet, fresh-tasting salad combines a variety of ingredients for a most delicious result.

MAKES 4 SERVINGS

¼ cup sunflower seeds
2 to 3 cups shredded Chinese cabbage
1 carrot, cut into matchsticks
3 or 4 red radishes, cut into thin half-moons
½ cup raisins or dried currants
1 tart apple, cored and diced
2 tablespoons sweet brown rice vinegar
2 teaspoons brown rice syrup

Sea salt
Grated zest and juice of 1 orange
Juice of 1 lemon

Lightly toast the sunflower seeds in a small, dry skillet over medium heat until golden and fragrant, about 5 minutes, stirring. Set aside.

Bring a pot of water to a boil over high heat. Add cabbage and cook 1 to 2 minutes. Remove with a slotted spoon and cool in iced water. Drain and set aside. Add carrot and boil 1 minute. Remove with a slotted spoon and cool in iced water. Drain and set aside. Finally, add radishes and boil 10 seconds. Drain and cool in iced water. Drain and set aside.

Toss sunflower seeds, vegetables, raisins and apple together. Whisk vinegar, rice syrup, a pinch of salt, orange zest and juice and lemon juice together. Gently toss dressing with salad and serve warm.

Radicchio and Apple Salad

The creamy poppy seed dressing is a nice addition to this hearty, autumn salad. I like to serve this when apples are at their peak; use only crisp, fresh fruit.

MAKES 4 SERVINGS

**1 large Granny Smith apple, cored and cut
    into thin slices**
**1 large Golden Delicious apple, cored and cut
    into thin slices**
**1 large Red Delicious apple, cored and cut
    into thin slices**
2 teaspoons fresh lemon juice
2 teaspoons spring or filtered water
3 or 4 large radicchio leaves, shredded

CREAMY POPPY SEED DRESSING
4 ounces silken tofu
½ teaspoon poppy seeds
Juice of 1 lemon
2 teaspoons brown rice syrup
Dash umeboshi or red wine vinegar
2 tablespoons spring or filtered water
Sea salt

**½ cup pecan pieces, lightly pan-toasted (see
 Note, page 46)**

Working quickly so the apples do not discolor, toss the slices in lemon juice and water. Arrange radicchio on a salad platter. Decoratively arrange apple slices on top.

Make dressing: Bring a small pot of water to a boil over medium heat. Add tofu and cook 5 minutes. Drain well. Transfer tofu to a food processor or blender, and add poppy seeds, lemon juice, rice syrup and vinegar. Adjust seasoning to taste and puree until smooth. Add a small amount of water and salt to taste to make a spoonable dressing.

Spoon dressing over apples and radicchio and sprinkle with pecan pieces just before serving. Serve at room temperature.

Fruit and Veggie Platter with Citrus Dressing

A crunchy, refreshing summer treat of a salad, with exotic jicama as the featured ingredient. Tossed with a zippy citrus dressing, it's a sure bet to cool down hot summer days.

MAKES ABOUT 4 SERVINGS

**1 tart apple (such as Granny Smith), cored
 and thinly sliced**

1 teaspoon fresh lemon juice
1 to 2 cups matchstick pieces jicama
**½ red bell pepper, roasted over a flame,
 peeled, seeded and cut into thin strips (see
 Note, page 262)**
3 oranges, peeled and thinly sliced
1 small cucumber, peeled and thinly sliced

CITRUS DRESSING
½ cup fresh orange juice
Juice of 1 lime
Juice of 1 lemon
¼ cup minced fresh flat-leaf parsley
1 tablespoon extra-virgin olive oil
Grated zest of 1 orange
Sea salt

Toss apple slices in lemon juice to prevent discoloration. Arrange apple, jicama, bell pepper, oranges and cucumber attractively on a platter.

Make dressing: Whisk together all ingredients in a small bowl, adding salt to taste, and spoon over vegetables. Allow to marinate 15 to 20 minutes before serving.

Apricot-Almond Salad

A unique combination of colors, flavors and textures compose this creamy salad. Serve this dish when you want your meal to have a distinctive flair.

MAKES 4 SERVINGS

4 ounces silken tofu
1 clove fresh garlic, minced
¼ teaspoon sea salt
Spring or filtered water
1 cup dried apricots, soaked in warm water until soft, about 30 minutes
1 red onion, diced
½ red bell pepper, roasted over a flame, peeled, seeded and diced (see Note, page 262)
2 celery stalks, diced
Generous pinch of dried basil
¼ to ½ cup slivered almonds, lightly pan-toasted (see Note, page 55)
Romaine lettuce leaves

Bring a small pot of water to a boil over medium heat. Add tofu and cook 5 minutes. Drain well.

Transfer tofu to a food processor or blender. Add garlic and salt and process until smooth, adding a small amount of water to achieve a creamy dressing. Spoon into a small bowl and allow to stand 15 minutes.

Dice apricots and gently fold into tofu dressing. Toss with onion, bell pepper, celery, basil and almonds. Serve on a bed of crisp lettuce leaves.

American Fruit and Red Onion Salad

This salad capitalizes on America's love of fruit. But I balance it with the peppery taste of red onions, all lightly marinated—a unique take on fruit salad.

MAKES 3 TO 4 SERVINGS

1 bunch kale or collards, lightly steamed
1 red onion, cut into thin rings
2 oranges, peeled and cut into thin rings
10 to 12 fresh strawberries, thinly sliced
½ cup fresh blueberries

DRESSING
1 tablespoon umeboshi vinegar
2 tablespoons balsamic vinegar
1 teaspoon brown rice syrup
Dash soy sauce
2 tablespoons avocado oil

Arrange steamed greens on a serving platter, top with onion rings, then with oranges. Arrange strawberries and blueberries over onion and oranges.

Make dressing: Whisk together all ingredients in a small bowl and drizzle over salad. Allow to marinate 30 minutes to 1 hour before serving.

Sassy Sauces and Dressings

THERE IS NOTHING more basic to the preparation of a fine dish than the dressing or sauce that may accompany it. This section includes a wide selection of foundation sauces that I employ regularly, plus traditional and more contemporary approaches to sauces and dressings. It is my sincere hope that these ideas will inspire your own experimentation with creating your own sauces and dressings.

Sometimes a sauce can be the savior of an otherwise pedestrian meal. I can't tell you how many times I have relied on a spectacular dressing to add sparkle to a simple meal of grains and vegetables. A sauce or dressing can make the difference between a ho-hum dinner and one that impresses everyone at the table.

All the ideas herein stand on their own. I do not provide many suggestions for uses with these recipes. I leave it to you, the chef, to determine which sauce or dressing goes best on pasta, vegetables, grains, beans, sea vegetables or fruit. Mix and match; experiment and determine what combinations work best for you.

When making your own sauces, anything goes, but, personally, I don't enjoy a whole bunch of conflicting flavors in my recipes. I prefer a predominant taste that is supported by complementary ingredients. I like sauces and dressings that are easy to put together, without

a lot of time-consuming steps and procedures.

The only other tip I will give you is this: Look at your recipe to determine when to dress or sauce the dish. A light salad will wilt and turn limp if dressed too soon with heavy vinaigrette. However, sometimes you want a soft, wilted salad lightly tossed with a citrus-based dressing. And sometimes you want the flavors to develop all together, in which case you add the dressing well before serving. And then there are the times when a dish is cooked in a sauce or sauced late in the recipe. Look at the dish you are making and decide what texture and taste you want for the final product and follow that lead.

Here are some of my favorite dressing and sauce recipes. I hope you enjoy them and that they help you to create some of your own delicious signature recipes. And when all else fails, do what my mother did: Whisk together extra-virgin olive oil, lemon juice, salt and pepper. You can never go wrong!

Creamy Tofu Dressing

MAKES ABOUT 1 CUP

4 ounces silken tofu
½ small onion, grated
2 tablespoons toasted sesame tahini
2 teaspoons balsamic vinegar
Dash soy sauce
Juice of 1 orange
Spring or filtered water (optional)

Bring a small pot of water to a boil over medium heat. Add tofu and cook 5 minutes. Drain well.

Transfer tofu to a food processor or blender. Add remaining ingredients, except water, and puree until smooth and creamy. For a thinner dressing, slowly add a small amount of water until desired consistency is achieved.

■ **VARIATION** Sour Tofu Dressing: Replace orange juice with juice of 1 lemon. Add 2 tablespoons brown rice vinegar to remaining ingredients.

Green Goddess Dressing

MAKES ABOUT ¾ CUP

4 ounces tofu
¼ cup brown rice vinegar
Sea salt
Small handful fresh flat-leaf parsley, minced
3 or 4 green onions, minced
Spring or filtered water (optional)

Bring a small pot of water to a boil over medium heat. Add tofu and cook 5 minutes. Drain well.

Transfer tofu to a food processor or blender. Add remaining ingredients, except water, with salt to taste and puree until smooth. Add a small amount of water to make a thinner dressing.

French Dressing

MAKES ABOUT 1 CUP

½ cup extra-virgin olive oil
½ cup spring or filtered water
2 tablespoons minced fresh flat-leaf parsley
½ teaspoon *each* dried basil, oregano and dill
Pinch sea salt

Warm oil gently in a small saucepan over low heat 3 to 4 minutes. Place all ingredients in a glass jar, seal tightly and shake well.

■ **NOTE** Warming the olive oil makes it more digestible.

French Vinaigrette

MAKES ABOUT 1 CUP

½ cup extra-virgin olive oil
1 clove fresh garlic, finely minced
¼ cup balsamic vinegar
Juice of 1 lemon
1 shallot, grated
1 teaspoon stone-ground mustard
Pinch sea salt
Generous pinch finely minced fresh chives

Warm oil and garlic gently in a small saucepan over low heat 3 to 4 minutes. Add remaining ingredients and whisk together until combined.

Italian Dressing

MAKES ABOUT ½ CUP

1 clove fresh garlic, peeled
¼ cup extra-virgin olive oil
Sea salt
1 onion, grated
2 umeboshi plums, pitted
2 to 3 tablespoons balsamic vinegar
Dried basil or rosemary, to taste

Rub garlic on the bottom of a suribachi (grinding bowl). Warm olive oil and a generous pinch of salt in a small saucepan over low heat 3 to 4 minutes. Combine oil mixture and remaining ingredients in a grinding bowl and grind until smooth.

■ **VARIATION** If a grinding bowl isn't available, use a mortar and pestle or a food processor.

Lemon-Parsley Dressing

MAKES ABOUT 1 CUP

¼ cup avocado oil
Juice of 1 lemon
½ cup fresh orange juice
¼ cup minced fresh flat-leaf parsley
Dash soy sauce
2 tablespoons sweet rice vinegar
Spring or filtered water

Combine all ingredients in a blender and puree until smooth, using only as much water as is needed to make a thin but not runny dressing.

Poppy Seed Dressing

MAKES ABOUT ¾ CUP

¼ cup light sesame oil
2 to 3 teaspoons poppy seeds
2 cloves fresh garlic, minced
2 tablespoons brown rice vinegar
2 tablespoons umeboshi vinegar
1 tablespoon stone-ground mustard
1 teaspoon brown rice syrup
Grated zest and juice of 1 orange

Warm oil gently in a small saucepan over low heat 3 to 4 minutes. Combine oil and remaining ingredients in a bowl and whisk together until blended.

Creamy Sesame Dressing

MAKES ABOUT 1 CUP

4 tablespoons toasted sesame tahini
½ onion, finely minced
2 umeboshi plums, pitted
Dash soy sauce
Juice of 1 lemon
2 teaspoons brown rice syrup
About ¾ cup spring or filtered water

Combine all ingredients in a blender and puree until smooth, slowly adding water to achieve a creamy consistency.

Sesame Soy Dressing

MAKES ABOUT ¾ CUP

1 to 2 tablespoons tan sesame seeds, rinsed
    and drained well
½ cup spring or filtered water
2 tablespoons brown rice vinegar
2 teaspoons brown rice syrup
Generous dash soy sauce
1 teaspoon dark sesame oil
2 cloves fresh garlic, minced
1 teaspoon ground ginger

Dry-roast seeds in a small skillet over medium heat until slightly puffy and fragrant, 2 to 3 minutes.

Simmer remaining ingredients in a small saucepan over low heat 4 to 5 minutes to help flavors develop. Remove from heat and stir in seeds. Serve warm or at room temperature.

Sweet Mustard Vinaigrette

MAKES ABOUT 1 CUP

¼ cup extra-virgin olive oil
Sea salt
2 tablespoons balsamic vinegar
Juice of 1 lemon
1 tablespoon brown rice syrup
2 tablespoons prepared stone-ground
    mustard
1 to 2 cloves fresh garlic, minced

Warm oil and a light seasoning of salt gently in a small saucepan over low heat 3 to 4 minutes.

Whisk oil mixture with remaining ingredients until blended.

Tofu Mayo

MAKES ABOUT 1¼ CUPS

8 ounces firm tofu
2 to 3 tablespoons stone-ground mustard, or
    to taste
2 to 3 teaspoons umeboshi vinegar, or to taste
1 tablespoon brown rice syrup
Sea salt
Juice of 1 lemon
3 to 4 tablespoons avocado oil

Bring a small pot of water to a boil over medium heat. Add tofu and cook 5 minutes. Drain well.

Transfer tofu to a food processor or blender. Add remaining ingredients and puree until smooth and creamy.

Tangy Citrus Dressing

MAKES ABOUT 1 CUP

¼ cup extra-virgin olive oil
Sea salt
2 tablespoons mirin
Juice of 1 lemon
Grated zest and juice of 1 orange
1 shallot, grated
¼ red bell pepper, roasted over a flame,
    peeled, seeded and finely minced (see
    Note, page 262)
3 tablespoons balsamic vinegar
½ teaspoon ground ginger

Warm oil and a generous pinch of salt gently in a small saucepan over low heat 3 to 4 minutes. Whisk together all ingredients until blended.

Tangy Plum-Mustard Dressing

MAKES ABOUT ½ CUP

1 onion, grated
1 tablespoon umeboshi paste
2 tablespoons stone-ground mustard
3 tablespoons dark sesame oil
2 teaspoons brown rice syrup
Spring or filtered water

Combine all ingredients in a blender and puree until smooth, slowly adding water until desired consistency is achieved.

Thousand Island Dressing

MAKES ABOUT 2 CUPS

8 ounces firm tofu
2 tablespoons minced fresh flat-leaf parsley
½ cup black olives, pitted and minced
½ onion, grated
2 celery stalks, finely minced
2 tablespoons natural pickle relish
Generous pinch dill weed
Juice of 1 orange
2 teaspoons brown rice syrup
Generous pinch sea salt
Spring or filtered water

Bring a small pot of water to a boil over medium heat. Add tofu and cook 5 minutes. Drain well.

Transfer tofu to a food processor or blender. Add remaining ingredients and puree until smooth, slowly adding water until desired consistency is achieved.

Umeboshi Vinaigrette

MAKES ABOUT 1 CUP

1 teaspoon light sesame oil
1 onion, diced
3 umeboshi plums, pitted
Juice of 1 lemon
Generous dash umeboshi vinegar
2 tablespoons sesame tahini
Spring or filtered water

Heat oil in a skillet over medium heat. Add onion and cook, stirring, until softened, about 3 minutes. Transfer onion to a food processor or blender. Add remaining ingredients and puree until smooth, slowly adding water until desired consistency is achieved.

Walnut-Raspberry Vinaigrette

MAKES ABOUT 1½ CUPS

1 cup walnut pieces
¼ cup extra-virgin olive oil
1 teaspoon sea salt
3 to 4 tablespoons umeboshi vinegar
3 tablespoons unsweetened raspberry jam
1 tablespoon brown rice syrup

Lightly dry-toast nut pieces in a skillet over medium heat until fragrant, about 3 minutes. Coarsely mince and set aside.

Warm oil and salt gently in a small saucepan over low heat 3 to 4 minutes. Whisk together all ingredients until combined.

Béchamel Sauce

MAKES ABOUT 2 CUPS

9 tablespoons extra-virgin olive oil
2 or 3 cloves fresh garlic, minced
3 or 4 shallots, minced, or 2 tablespoons
   minced onion
¼ cup whole wheat pastry flour
Pinch sea salt
1 to 2 cups spring or filtered water

Heat olive oil in a skillet over medium heat. Add garlic and shallots and cook, stirring, 2 to 3 minutes. Stir in flour and salt and cook, stirring, until vegetables are coated and a paste begins to form. Add water slowly, while stirring, to avoid lumping. Cook over low heat, stirring constantly, until a thick creamy sauce forms, about 5 minutes.

Brown Sauce

MAKES ABOUT 2 CUPS

1 teaspoon avocado oil
1 onion, minced
Sea salt
1 carrot, diced
1 to 2 cups thinly sliced mushrooms, brushed
   free of dirt

2 tablespoons whole wheat pastry flour
1½ cups Vegetable Stock (page 74)
1 tablespoon unsweetened apple butter
Soy sauce

Heat avocado oil in a skillet over medium heat. Add onion and a pinch of sea salt and cook, stirring, 2 to 3 minutes. Add carrot and mushrooms with another pinch of salt and cook until vegetables turn brown and caramelize, stirring frequently, 10 to 15 minutes. Stir in flour, then slowly add stock while continuing to stir. Stir in apple butter and simmer 20 minutes, stirring frequently. Add a dash of soy sauce and simmer a few minutes more.

California Sauce

MAKES ABOUT 1 CUP

¼ cup avocado oil
Dash soy sauce
1 cup fresh orange juice
3 or 4 cloves fresh garlic, minced
¼ cup minced fresh flat-leaf parsley
Juice of 1 lemon

Warm oil and soy sauce gently in a small saucepan over low heat 3 to 4 minutes. Whisk together all ingredients until combined.

Creamy Mushroom Sauce

MAKES ABOUT 2 CUPS

1 teaspoon extra-virgin olive oil
2 or 3 shallots, minced

4 to 5 dried shiitake mushrooms, soaked 10
    minutes, drained and thinly sliced
1 cup button mushrooms, brushed clean and
    thinly sliced
2 cups Mushroom Stock (page 75)
Sea salt
1½ tablespoons kuzu or arrowroot, dissolved
    in 3 tablespoons cold water

Heat oil in a small saucepan over medium heat. Add shallots and cook until translucent. Add shiitake mushrooms and cook 1 minute. Add button mushrooms and cook, stirring, until they begin to release their juices, 5 to 7 minutes. Add stock and bring to a boil. Cover and simmer over low heat 10 minutes. Season lightly with salt and simmer 5 minutes more. Stir in dissolved kuzu and cook, stirring, until sauce thickens slightly and is clear, about 3 minutes.

Raspberry Barbecue Sauce

MAKES ABOUT 1¼ CUPS

¼ cup raspberry vinegar
2 tablespoons avocado oil
1 tablespoon minced fresh mint leaves
4 ounces silken tofu
½ cup unsweetened raspberry jam
Pinch sea salt

Whisk together vinegar, oil and mint. Set aside.

Bring a small pot of water to a boil and cook tofu 5 minutes. Drain well.

Transfer tofu to a food processor or blender. Add vinegar mixture and remaining ingredients and puree until smooth. Refrigerate until ready to use.

Green Sauce

MAKES ABOUT 1 CUP

¼ cup avocado oil
2 umeboshi plums, pitted, or 2 to 3
    tablespoons umeboshi paste
1 bunch green onions, diced
1 bunch fresh flat-leaf parsley, minced
Soy sauce
Spring or filtered water

Warm oil gently in a small saucepan over low heat 3 to 4 minutes. Transfer oil to a food processor or blender. Add plums, green onions, parsley and a dash of soy sauce and process until smooth, slowly adding water to achieve desired consistency.

I Can't Believe It's Not Cheese Sauce

MAKES ABOUT 2½ CUPS

2 tablespoons sweet white miso
2 cups spring or filtered water
¼ cup sesame tahini
2 cloves fresh garlic, minced
Juice of 1 lemon

Dissolve miso in water in a small saucepan over low heat. Add tahini and garlic and warm through. Remove from heat and stir in lemon juice.

Istanbul Sauce

MAKES ABOUT 1¼ CUPS

1 cup sesame tahini
2 tablespoons umeboshi paste
1 onion, grated
Dash soy sauce
1 to 2 teaspoons fresh ginger juice (see Note,
**   page 164)**
Juice of 1 lemon
Spring or filtered water

Combine all ingredients through lemon juice in a blender or food processor and process until smooth, slowly adding water until desired consistency is achieved.

Lemon-Miso Sauce

MAKES ABOUT 1 CUP

1½ tablespoons sweet white miso
½ teaspoon soy sauce
1 cup spring or filtered water
Grated zest and juice of 1 lemon
1 tablespoon sesame butter

Warm miso, soy sauce and water in a small saucepan over low heat 3 to 4 minutes. Whisk in remaining ingredients until smooth and creamy.

Garlic, Mushroom and Leek Sauce

MAKES ABOUT 2 CUPS

½ teaspoon extra-virgin olive oil
4 to 5 cloves fresh garlic, thinly sliced
1 leek, sliced lengthwise and rinsed well and
**   thinly sliced**
Sea salt
2 cups button mushrooms, brushed clean and
**   thinly sliced**
2 teaspoons white miso, dissolved in ¼ cup
**   water**

Heat olive oil in a skillet over medium heat. Add garlic and cook until dark brown, stirring. Remove garlic from oil and discard. Add leek and a pinch of salt and cook, stirring, until bright green. Add mushrooms and a pinch of salt and cook until tender, about 5 minutes. Add dissolved miso, cover and simmer 4 to 5 minutes.

■ **VARIATION** Some freshly squeezed ginger juice (see Note, page 164) is a nice addition to this sauce.

Parsleyed Nut Sauce

MAKES ABOUT 2 CUPS

1 tablespoon light sesame oil
3 or 4 green onions, finely diced
1 teaspoon grated fresh ginger and juice (see
**   Note, page 164)**
¼ cup minced fresh flat-leaf parsley
1 cup walnut pieces, lightly pan-toasted (see
**   Note, page 46)**

1 cup spring or filtered water
Soy sauce
1 teaspoon kuzu or arrowroot, dissolved in 3
    tablespoons cold water

Heat oil in a saucepan over medium heat. Add green onions, ginger and parsley and cook 2 minutes. Add nuts and cook 2 minutes more. Add water and warm through. Season lightly with soy sauce. Stir in dissolved kuzu and cook, stirring, until sauce thickens and is clear, about 3 minutes.

Roasted Pepper Sauce

MAKES ABOUT 2 CUPS

1 cup Vegetable Stock (page 74)
1 tablespoon extra-virgin olive oil
1 onion, diced
2 or 3 cloves fresh garlic, minced
1 carrot, diced
2 celery stalks, diced
4 or 5 red bell peppers, roasted over a flame,
    peeled, seeded and diced (see Note, page
    262)
Generous pinch dried basil
Sea salt

In a deep skillet, bring stock and oil to a boil. Add onion and garlic and simmer over low heat 2 minutes. Add carrot and celery and simmer, covered, 5 to 7 minutes more.

Add bell peppers to skillet along with basil and a light seasoning of salt. Simmer 5 to 7 minutes more or until all vegetables are tender. Transfer mixture to a food processor and pulse a few times to create a slightly chunky sauce.

Roasted Garlic Sauce

MAKES ABOUT 1 CUP

4 heads garlic
3 tablespoons avocado oil
1 shallot, minced
¼ cup mirin or white wine
¼ cup spring or filtered water
2 tablespoons brown rice vinegar
¼ cup soy or rice milk
Sea salt

Preheat oven to 350F (175C). Keep garlic heads whole, but remove outer layers of skin. Place in a small baking dish, drizzle lightly with 1 tablespoon of the oil and bake about 1 hour, until cloves are very soft. Allow to cool until you can easily handle the cloves. Separate garlic cloves and squeeze soft pulp into a small saucepan. Add shallot, mirin, water and vinegar. Simmer over low heat until liquid evaporates, about 15 minutes. Add milk and remaining oil and simmer again until sauce is slightly reduced, about 10 minute more. Season with salt.

Black Olive Pesto

MAKES ABOUT 1 CUP

¼ cup extra-virgin olive oil
10 to 12 oil-cured black olives, pitted
1 teaspoon brown rice syrup
1 cup walnut pieces, lightly pan-toasted (see
    Note, page 46)
2 tablespoons umeboshi vinegar

Warm oil in a small saucepan over low heat 3 to 4 minutes. Transfer oil to a food processor or blender. Add olives, rice syrup, walnuts and vinegar and process until smooth. Slowly add water to achieve a thinner consistency, if desired.

■ **NOTE** When making pestos, I usually keep the mixture in a sealed glass jar in the refrigerator. I add water to thin only to the portion I will be using in a particular recipe. A strong, salty pesto like this one will keep in the refrigerator for about 2 weeks. More delicate pestos made with fresh herbs will not keep quite as long.

Fresh Basil Pesto

MAKES ABOUT 1½ CUPS

¼ cup extra-virgin olive oil
1 cup loosely packed fresh basil leaves
1 cup pine nuts or walnuts, lightly pan-
    toasted (see Note, page 46)
2 cloves fresh garlic, minced
2 tablespoons white miso
2 teaspoons umeboshi vinegar
1 teaspoon brown rice syrup
Spring or filtered water

Warm oil in a small saucepan over low heat 3 to 4 minutes. Transfer oil to a food processor or blender. Add basil, nuts, garlic, miso, vinegar and syrup and process until smooth, adding just enough water to achieve desired consistency. Be careful when adding water; pestos are best when slightly thicker and creamier.

Nori Pesto

MAKES ABOUT ½ CUP

1 teaspoon dark sesame oil
1 onion, diced
¼ teaspoon hot chili powder
6 or 7 sheets nori, shredded
Soy sauce
Spring or filtered water

Heat oil in a saucepan over medium heat. Add onion and chili powder and cook until translucent, about 5 minutes. Add nori, a dash of soy sauce and enough water to cover. Bring to a boil, reduce heat and cook, uncovered, until all liquid has been absorbed and pesto is creamy, about 20 minutes. You may need to add a bit of water midway through cooking if water evaporates too soon. This is a strong pesto; use sparingly.

Apricot Sauce

MAKES ABOUT 2 CUPS

1 cup apricot halves, dried or fresh
¼ cup brown rice syrup
2 cups spring or filtered water
Pinch sea salt
2 teaspoons kuzu or arrowroot, dissolved in 3
    tablespoons cold water

If using dried apricots, soak them in warm water 1 hour before making sauce; drain before using. Combine apricots, rice syrup, water and salt in a saucepan over medium heat and bring to a boil. Reduce heat, cover and cook, stirring occasionally, until fruit is soft, about 30 minutes.

Stir in dissolved kuzu and cook, stirring, until sauce thickens, about 3 minutes.

Mixed Berry Sauce

MAKES ABOUT 1 CUP

2 cups unfiltered, unsweetened apple juice or spring or filtered water
Pinch sea salt
¼ cup fresh strawberries, quartered
¼ cup fresh blueberries
¼ cup fresh raspberries
¼ cup fresh cherries, pitted and halved
1 tablespoon kuzu or arrowroot, dissolved in 4 tablespoons cold water
Dash pure vanilla extract

Bring juice and salt to a boil in a saucepan over medium heat. Stir in fruit and simmer over low heat until fruit softens, 5 to 7 minutes. Stir in dissolved kuzu and cook, stirring, until mixture thickens slightly, about 3 minutes. Remove from heat and whisk in vanilla.

Ginger-Kiwi Sauce

MAKES ABOUT 1 CUP

1 kiwifruit, peeled and diced
1 tablespoon brown rice vinegar
Juice of 1 lime
2 teaspoons brown rice syrup
5 or 6 slices fresh ginger, cut into matchstick pieces
Juice of 1 orange
Pinch sea salt

Combine kiwifruit with vinegar and lime juice. Lightly mash and set aside.

Simmer rice syrup, ginger, orange juice and salt in a small saucepan over low heat 10 minutes, or until mixture reduces to half of the original amount. Strain out ginger pieces. Combine with kiwi mixture and mix well.

Mango-Chile Salsa

MAKES ABOUT 2 CUPS

1 mango, peeled, seeded and diced
1 jalapeño chile, seeded and minced
1 tablespoon minced fresh mint
¼ red onion, grated
Generous pinch *each* cumin, chili powder and sea salt
2 to 3 tablespoons sweet rice vinegar
1 tablespoon extra-virgin olive oil

Mix all ingredients together in a saucepan. Warm gently over low heat 4 to 5 minutes to release flavors.

Breads of Life

IS THERE ANYTHING more wonderful in the entire world than fresh bread? One of my favorite lunches is crusty, warm bread with a hot bowl of soup and a fresh salad. I remember traveling around Europe, mostly broke, existing on simple meals of bread (some of the best I have ever tasted), soup and fresh vegetables, and being quite content, I might add. It's a winning combination for me to this day.

Bread has always symbolized life to me. Bread baking teaches us about success and failure, perseverance and patience. There is no better feeling than the satisfaction we get as golden, crusty loaves, kneaded by our hands, are pulled from the oven.

Baking bread keeps you humble. We all begin with the same simple ingredients—flour, water and leavening. We all perform the same ritual tasks of baking—mixing, kneading, forming, baking to perfection (hopefully). Bread dough is uncompromising and unpredictable. Whether we realize it or not, we must submit to the influences of our environment: heat, cold, drafts, oven temperature.

Growing up in the home of a great bread baker, I could not help but be influenced by my mother's love for this food. She baked every Saturday morning, always enough bread for the family for the week. While most kids my age were out and about, I was hanging out with my mother, soaking up everything she knew. And my education continues to this day with my husband, Robert, who is the bread master in our house. Many are the nights when he emerges from the kitchen, his hands and forearms dusted with flour from lovingly forming a loaf of bread.

As a child, I never remember buying a loaf of bread at a market. And who would want to when the kitchen always held at least two fragrant, crusty loaves for us to feast on? My mother's example gave me the confidence I now possess in the kitchen. She taught me not to be afraid of anything connected to the preparation of good food. She introduced me to the joys of fragrant loaves of raisin bread baking in the warmth of the oven. She taught me to bake with personality. Master the basics, she would say, and then create loaves of bread; don't just bake them. Bread making is a symbol that we possess the ability to nourish not only ourselves, but those we love. My mother used to say that you could always tell homemade loaves of bread because they looked as though they were baked by someone who cared.

Ingredients

First, I use only organic, mostly whole grain flour for my bread. These flours produce hearty, nutty loaves with rich, golden interiors and crunchy crusts. I value the nutritive benefits of whole grain flours, since they retain most of their germ and bran.

I usually leaven with sourdough starter, although I like to create other naturally leavened breads with cooked sour grain. I also use commercial yeasts, but not so much as sourdough . . . not because they don't produce lovely loaves of bread, but because yeast can produce too much expansion in the intestinal tract, weakening our ability to assimilate food.

Creating your own sourdough starter is easy, and the best part is that starter keeps indefinitely with refrigeration and a bit of attention. And since sourdough is a natural leavening agent, you can omit yeast . . . or combine the two for any bread recipe. The result will be a nicely leavened loaf. Just bear in mind that rising times for sourdough are longer than for yeasted loaves: Sourdough needs six to eight hours, while yeast can do its thing in as little as one to two hours.

Baking Tips

So what's the first rule of bread baking? Take a deep breath and relax. It's not difficult to bake a great loaf of bread. It takes some practice, but you're not splitting the atom, you're baking! Over time, you develop an intuitive sense

about it. The more you let this sense develop, the better and better your breads will be.

Kneading bread is an art form in itself. Knead too long and bread can become tough; too little, and it won't rise properly. Relax, though; you'll get the hang of it in just a couple of loaves. You'll know—really—when the loaf has been kneaded enough. In the beginning, let the recipes guide you until intuition takes over.

Shaping loaves can include anything from traditional loaf and baguette pans, rising baskets, clay pots or free-form loaves shaped by hand and baked on oven stones. Free-form loaves are my personal favorite because they allow for creativity. Knotting, braiding, making wreath breads, stuffed breads or nests of bread—well, you get the idea.

So here we go. I'd like to begin this section with a recipe for sourdough starter and then proceed to some bread recipes that have graced my table, some since I was just a kid learning how to bake in my mother's kitchen.

Basic Sourdough Starter

A starter is simply a leavening agent. A true sourdough starter is made by encouraging the development and growth of wild yeast and benign bacteria in a flour and water atmosphere. It is, in fact, these bacteria that create the acids that sour the starter and create the leavening.

You can make this starter with unbleached white flour or whole wheat flour. The white starter will create a lighter loaf and whole wheat will create a hearty, stronger flavor. Keep in mind, however, that any flour can be used to create starters—rye, rice, corn.

The biggest problem people run into with sourdough starter is keeping the starter alive. A little bit of attention will result in your starter lasting a lifetime, literally. Every ten to fourteen days, you will need to "feed" or freshen the starter to maintain it.

Use only filtered or spring water when creating your starter because tap water can contain chemicals, which can inhibit the activity of the wild yeasts. If your starter develops a brownish liquid on the surface, simply stir it in. If mold appears on the surface, gently scrape it off and freshen the starter with flour and water before using it again. If, however, your starter turns pink, develops an unpleasant sour odor (instead of a fragrant, slightly sour aroma) or doesn't bubble when placed in a warm place for forty-eight hours, you need to throw it out and begin again. Sorry . . .

MAKES ABOUT 4 CUPS OF STARTER

2 cups whole wheat or unbleached white flour
3 cups warm spring or filtered water

You will need a crock or container (glass or stoneware is best) that leaves enough room for the starter to double.

Mix the flour and water together well and allow to stand, loosely covered, in a warm place 2 to 5 days. The time will depend partially on the temperature. When you notice that the starter is bubbly and slightly sour-smelling, stir well, cover and refrigerate.

At least once a month, although every other week is best, feed the starter by stirring together one part starter, one part water and 1 to 2 cups flour and allow it to stand in a warm place 12 to 24 hours before returning it to the refrigerator. If you are not baking bread each week, you will find yourself accumulating starter. What we do in our house, is discard some of the starter (or pass it on to friends with instructions on "feeding") before freshening it, so that we don't end up with a refrigerator filled with jars of sourdough starter. When you freshen your starter, wait 2 to 3 days before

using it, so that your breads will have a more delicate flavor.

■ **NOTE** Some bakers like to begin their sourdough starter by soaking dried organic fruit, like raisins, in the water that will be used for the starter, since the sugars present in these fruits will encourage the growth of the wild yeasts needed. Fresh grapes can also be used. If you choose to begin your starter with fruit, it is important to use organic quality, as they do not have any pesticides or fungicides present on their skins.

Basic Sourdough Bread

From this basic loaf, you can create anything—not only different shapes, of course, but also different loaves. Varying the flour, adding nuts or dried fruits, herbs and spices, garlic and oil or olives are just some of the ways you can create variety.

MAKES 2 LOAVES

1¼ cups Basic Sourdough Starter (page 281), stirred before measuring
2¾ cups warm spring or filtered water (about 110F, 45C)
4 to 5 cups whole wheat flour
2 cups semolina flour
1 to 2 teaspoons sea salt

Lightly oil a bowl and set aside. Combine the starter and water in a large bowl. Mix flours together. Add 4 cups of the flour, 1 cup at a time, stirring each one in thoroughly. Add salt and 2 cups of the flour mixture, stirring well, to make a moderately stiff dough.

Turn the dough out onto a floured surface and knead about 10 minutes, adding flour as needed to form a smooth, elastic dough. Place dough in a prepared bowl, turning to coat with oil. Cover tightly with plastic wrap and allow to stand at room temperature 10 to 12 hours.

The dough will be slightly sticky after rising. Turn onto a floured surface and knead briefly, 3 to 5 minutes. Divide into 2 equal pieces.

To create a basic loaf shape, simply take 1 piece of dough and stretch it between your hands until it is about a foot long. Fold each end toward the middle, pressing the ends into the center so that they stick. The dough should be roughly rectangular in shape. Starting with the closest corners of the rectangle, roll them to the center. Continue rolling, forcing the outside to the center until you end up with a loaf resembling a fat football. Find the outside seam and pinch it to seal the loaf. Finally, roll the loaf back and forth on your work surface to smooth, taper and refine your loaf shape. Repeat with remaining dough, creating 2 loaves.

Place loaves on a floured surface (a peel or baking sheet is ideal), cover with a damp kitchen towel and allow to rise at room temperature 2 to 3 hours, until the loaves double in size.

Preheat oven to 450F (230C). Place a shallow pan of water on the lowest rack. Transfer the loaves to a floured baking pan or stone. (If using a stone, remember to heat it in the oven 30 minutes before transferring the bread to it.) With a sharp knife, score each loaf ¼ inch deep, down the center, along the length of the loaf. Brush each loaf with water and bake 15 minutes. Using a spray bottle, mist the oven with water every 5 minutes during this 15-minute period. This extra effort will result in those delicious outer crusts that we all hold near to our hearts.

At the end of 15 minutes, remove the pan of water, brush the loaves with water and reduce the oven temperature to 375F (190C). Return the bread to the oven and bake about 40 minutes, until the loaves sound hollow when tapped on the bottom. Transfer to a rack and cool.

Variations

- **SESAME LOAVES** Follow the basic recipe, substituting 2 tablespoons dark sesame oil and 2 tablespoons light sesame oil for 4 tablespoons of the water in the bread. Just before baking, brush the loaves with sesame oil and sprinkle generously with sesame seeds.

- **POPPY SEED BREAD** Follow the basic recipe, sprinkling the loaves generously with poppy seeds just before baking.

- **LEMON-HERB BREAD** Follow the basic recipe, kneading in grated zest of 1 lemon with a generous pinch each of dried oregano, basil and thyme. Follow your instincts with the amount of herbs to add, using just pinches of each; you don't want the taste to overpower the bread or become bitter.

- **ROSEMARY-OLIVE BREAD** Follow the basic recipe, substituting 3 tablespoons extra-virgin olive oil for 3 tablespoons of water and kneading in 1 to 2 tablespoons dried or fresh, chopped rosemary along with 16 black olives that have been pitted and minced.

- **GARLIC-TOMATO BREAD** Make garlic oil by sautéing 2 cloves finely minced garlic in ¼ cup extra-virgin olive oil until deep, golden brown, about 3 minutes. Remove garlic and allow oil to cool before using in bread. Follow the basic recipe, substituting ¼ cup garlic oil for ¼ cup water in the recipe. Knead in about ⅓ cup finely minced oil-packed sun-dried tomatoes. (Drain tomatoes well before using.)

■ **OATMEAL RAISIN BREAD** Follow the basic recipe, substituting 1½ cups rolled oats for 1½ cups flour. Knead in 2 cups raisins and a generous pinch of cinnamon.

Rye 'n' Raisin Rolls

These lovely little rolls are a wonderful combination of flavors: The hearty, earthy taste of rye is nicely complemented by the delicate sweetness of raisins.

MAKES 24 ROLLS

**1 cup Basic Sourdough Starter (page 281),
stirred before measuring**
3 cups spring or filtered water
4 to 5 cups whole wheat flour
2½ cups rye flour
2 cups raisins
1 to 2 teaspoons sea salt
Cornmeal, for dusting

Lightly oil a bowl and set aside. Combine the starter and water in a large bowl. Add 2½ cups of the whole wheat flour and 1¼ cups of the rye flour, 1 cup at a time, stirring in each one thoroughly. Stir in raisins and salt. Stir in remaining rye flour and enough whole wheat flour, again 1 cup at a time, to make a moderately stiff dough. Turn out onto a floured work surface and knead about 8 minutes or until smooth but still slightly sticky. Place dough in prepared bowl and turn to coat with oil. Cover with plastic wrap and allow to rise at room temperature about 3 hours, until doubled in size.

Return the dough to the work surface and knead briefly, about 3 minutes. Divide the dough in half and roll each half into a log, 3 inches in diameter. Cut each log into 12 equal pieces. Roll each piece firmly on the work surface until a round ball forms.

Place the rolls about 2 inches apart on a cornmeal-dusted baking sheet. Cover with a damp kitchen towel and allow to rise until doubled in size, about 45 minutes.

Preheat oven with a baking stone or tiles to 450F (230C) for 30 minutes. Quickly and carefully transfer the rolls to the stone and bake 15 minutes, misting the oven with water every 5 minutes.

Reduce the oven temperature to 375F (190C) and continue baking an additional 15 minutes, until rolls are deep brown and crusty. They should sound hollow when tapped on the bottom. Transfer to a rack and cool.

■ **VARIATION** If a baking stone is not available, bake on an oiled baking sheet.

Juicy Apple Rolls

These sweet little gems are a delight to serve at a brunch or with tea.

MAKES 9 ROLLS

½ recipe Basic Sourdough Bread (page 282)

FILLING
4 tart apples (Granny Smith or other)
1 teaspoon avocado or light olive oil
1 tablespoon maple syrup granules
Pinch ground cinnamon

Prepare the dough through the first rising. When the dough is almost ready, prepare the filling. Preheat oven to 450F (230C).

Prepare the filling: Halve and core the apples and slice them into 1-inch pieces. Toss the apples with oil, maple granules and cinnamon. Spread evenly on a baking sheet and bake until just tender, about 10 minutes. Set aside to cool and reduce oven temperature to 400F (205C).

Prepare the rolls by turning dough out onto a floured work surface and kneading briefly, about 3 minutes. Roll dough into a log, about 4 inches in diameter. Cut into 9 equal pieces. Roll each piece of dough around on the work surface to smooth the edges. With a rolling pin, roll each piece into an oval, about 7 × 5 inches.

Place a scant ½ cup filling in the center of each piece. Beginning with the long side, roll the dough into a cylinder, leaving the short sides open. Place the rolls, seam side down, on a floured surface, cover with a damp kitchen towel and allow to rise at room temperature until doubled in size, about 40 minutes.

Preheat a baking stone in the oven 30 minutes. Just before baking, make 4 to 5 crosswise slits in the tops of the rolls. Transfer rolls to the baking stone and bake 20 to 25 minutes, until they are golden brown. Transfer to a rack and cool.

■ **VARIATION** If a baking stone is not available, bake on an oiled baking sheet.

Focaccia

An Italian tradition, focaccia is fat pizza—or flat bread—with just about any topping you can think of to pile on top.

MAKES 1 FOCACCIA

½ **recipe Basic Sourdough Bread (page 282)**

TOPPING SUGGESTIONS
Sautéed broccoli rabe with carrots, onions and garlic
Sautéed garlic and onions in olive oil
Sautéed broccoli and onions with

mushrooms, tomatoes and basil or rosemary

Follow basic recipe through the first rising. Lightly oil a 13 × 9-inch baking pan and set aside. Turn out dough onto a floured work surface and knead briefly, about 3 minutes. Flatten slightly and press into prepared pan, filling the pan as best you can. Cover with a damp kitchen towel and allow to rise at room temperature until doubled in thickness, about 40 minutes.

Preheat oven to 450F. Prepare any variety of topping for the focaccia and cool to room temperature before using. Using your fingertips, create dimples in the surface of the dough and spread topping evenly over surface. Bake 15 to 20 minutes, until golden brown.

Cornbread with Fresh Corn

Nothing goes with soup or a hearty bean stew like moist cornbread. This recipe is an adaptation of my mother's family favorite.

MAKES 6 TO 8 SERVINGS

1½ **cups whole wheat pastry flour**
1 **cup yellow cornmeal**
2 to 3 **teaspoons baking powder**
½ **teaspoon sea salt**
¼ **cup avocado or light olive oil**
2 **tablespoons brown rice syrup**
½ **cup soy, almond or rice milk**
½ to 1 **cup spring or filtered water**
½ **cup fresh corn**

Preheat oven to 350F (175C). Lightly oil and flour a 9-inch-square baking dish and set aside. Sift together the flour, cornmeal, baking powder and salt into a bowl. In another bowl, whisk together oil, rice syrup, milk and ½ cup water. Stir into dry ingredients until just blended. Add more water if needed to create a velvety, spoonable batter. Gently fold in corn kernels. Spoon batter into prepared pan and bake 35 to 40 minutes, until golden at the edges and the center springs back to the touch.

Rice Kayu Bread

This is a moist, dense loaf that is not baked. You heard me right. This bread is pressure-cooked or steamed (although you can bake it as well) to create its unique character. The rice for this bread should be cooked to a creamy porridge consistency, by using five parts water to one part grain.

MAKES 1 LOAF

2 cups soft-cooked brown rice, at room temperature
2 cups whole wheat flour, plus additional for kneading
1 teaspoon sea salt

Combine rice with flour and salt in a bowl. With a wooden spoon, mix the dough as thoroughly as possible before taking over the mixing process with your hands. It will be sticky at this point. Turn the dough onto a floured work surface and begin kneading, adding flour as necessary to create a smooth, elastic dough.

Shape the loaf by placing the dough in the center of a floured work surface and flattening it into a round. Work the dough by turning the edges under toward the center, creating a ball. Be sure to work all the air out of the center when folding. Place the dough in an oiled and floured glass or stoneware container (twice the size of the bread) that will fit comfortably into your pressure cooker. Cover with a damp towel and place in a warm area to rise 6 to 8 hours.

Place container, uncovered, in a pressure cooker with 1 inch of water surrounding the container. Seal the pressure cooker, bring to full pressure and cook bread over low heat 1 hour. Remove pot from heat and allow pressure to reduce naturally.

Carefully remove bread from pressure cooker and allow to cool slightly before turning out of container. It will come out easiest while still warm, so don't let the bread cool completely. Wrap bread in a damp towel and allow to stand for about 1 hour before serving.

Sour Grain Bread

MAKES 1 LOAF

Any whole grain will make delicious sour grain breads. Again, these loaves will have a more dense, cakelike texture. We use everything from rice to millet, rye, rice with onions, millet with squash and rice with raisins, to name a few.

After the grain is cooked, sour it by leaving it at room temperature, lightly covered in a glass bowl, 2 to 3 days. It should have a pleasantly sour aroma when ready. Then, stir in about 1 tablespoon miso and allow the grain to stand one more day. It will begin to bubble lightly and should smell slightly sour. It is then ready to use in bread.

Follow directions as for the Rice Kayu Bread (opposite) in proportions and preparation. The difference between the two is in the slightly stronger taste, and because the grains are lightly fermented in these breads, the loaves are a bit lighter and less dense.

When I bake these loaves, I form the loaves as you would any other, kneading 10 minutes, shaping and placing the loaf in an oiled and floured loaf pan. Allow to rise, covered with a damp towel, 6 to 8 hours in a warm place.

Preheat oven to 250F (120C). Bake loaf 30 minutes. Increase oven temperature to 350F (175C) and bake another 1 to 1¼ hours, until the loaf is firm. Remove from pan immediately. Wrap loaf in a damp towel and let rest for about 1 hour before serving.

Fisherman's Bread

Legend has it that Italian sailors took this long-lasting bread on their voyages. I don't know about that; I originally discovered this incredible bread, flavored with anise, pine nuts, raisins and dried fruits, in Genoa. With a few ingredient changes, voilà!— it is a healthy feast.

MAKES 2 LOAVES

2 cups whole wheat pastry flour
⅓ cup maple syrup granules
1 tablespoon anise seed
2 teaspoons baking powder
¼ teaspoon sea salt
1 cup golden raisins
¼ cup diced dried apricots
¼ cup diced dried apple
2 tablespoons pine nuts, lightly pan-toasted
   (see Note, page 46)
3 to 4 tablespoons grated orange zest
¼ cup soy or rice milk
⅛ cup mirin
2 tablespoons avocado oil
⅛ to ¼ cup spring or filtered water

Preheat oven to 375F (190C). Lightly oil a baking sheet and set aside.

Combine flour, maple granules, anise seed, baking powder and salt. Add fruits, pine nuts and orange zest and mix well.

Whisk together milk, mirin, oil and water. Stir liquids into flour mixture until well-blended and a dough begins to form.

Turn dough out onto a lightly floured surface and knead until smooth, about 2 minutes, the dough will still be slightly sticky. Divide dough in half and shape each half into a flat 6 × 4-inch oval or round. Place loaves, side by side, on prepared baking sheet. Bake 30 to 35 minutes, until golden brown. Transfer to a cooling rack.

Herb-Scented Biscuits

These flaky, tender biscuits are so easy to make, it's almost silly. You will love the results—the only problem you will have is making enough.

MAKES 12 TO 16 BISCUITS

2½ cups whole wheat pastry flour
2 teaspoons baking powder
¼ teaspoon sea salt
1 tablespoon dried rosemary or basil
4 tablespoons vegetarian buttery spread (like
   Earth Balance), chilled
⅔ cup soy or rice milk
About 2 tablespoons extra-virgin olive oil

Preheat oven to 350F (175C). Lightly oil a baking sheet and set aside.

In a food processor, combine flour, baking powder, salt, rosemary and spread. Pulse until mixture resembles the texture of coarse cornmeal. Add milk and process until a dough ball forms. Immediately turn off food processor; do not overprocess, or dough will break down. Gather dough into your hands and turn out onto a lightly floured surface.

Roll out dough to a 14 × 12-inch rectangle. Dough will be about ⅛ inch thick. Trim edges evenly. Lightly brush surface of dough with oil. Roll, jelly-roll style, forming a long cylinder. With a sharp knife, slice cylinder into 1-inch-thick rounds. Place, cut side up, on prepared baking sheet. Brush each biscuit with a little oil, if desired.

Bake 20 to 25 minutes on the center rack of the oven, until slightly golden and springy to the touch. Serve warm.

Sticky Cinnamon Rolls

In less than two hours, you can serve up these rolls, jam-packed with raisins, fragrant with cinnamon and dripping with caramel glaze—perfect brunch treats.

MAKES 12 STICKY BUNS

3½ to 4 cups whole wheat pastry flour, plus
    extra for kneading
1 package quick-rising dried yeast
½ teaspoon sea salt
½ cup soy or rice milk
5 tablespoons brown rice syrup
3 tablespoons avocado oil, plus extra for
    brushing
Spring or filtered water
¾ cup maple syrup granules
½ cup coarsely minced pecans
2 teaspoons ground cinnamon
½ cup raisins

In a large bowl, mix 2 cups of the flour, yeast and salt. Set aside. In a saucepan, combine milk, 2 tablespoons of the rice syrup, 2 tablespoons of the oil and ¾ cup water. Stir over low heat until very warm.

Add the warm liquid to the dry ingredients and stir until smooth. Stir in remaining flour, ½ cup at a time, until the dough is moderately stiff. Turn the dough out onto a lightly floured work surface and knead, gradually incorporating more flour as necessary to prevent sticking, until the dough is smooth and elastic, about 10 minutes.

Place dough in a large, lightly oiled bowl, turning several times to coat with oil. Cover tightly with plastic wrap and let rise in a warm place 30 minutes.

Lightly oil a 13 × 9-inch baking dish. Sprinkle evenly with ½ cup of the maple granules and the pecans. Drizzle with the remaining 3 tablespoons rice syrup and 1 tablespoon oil. In a small bowl, combine cinnamon and remaining ¼ cup maple granules.

Gently punch down dough and turn onto a lightly floured work surface. Pat and roll the dough into a 15 × 12-inch rectangle. Brush lightly with oil. Sprinkle evenly with cinnamon mixture and scatter surface with raisins.

Beginning at a short end, roll the dough, jelly-roll style, into a tight log. Pinch the long edge to seal. With a sharp knife, cut the roll into 12 slices. Place the slices, cut side up, about 1 inch apart, in the prepared baking dish. Cover with plastic wrap and set aside in a warm place to rise about 20 minutes.

Preheat oven to 375F (190C). Bake the sticky buns 25 to 30 minutes, until golden brown. Remove from oven and allow to cool about 30 seconds, then invert onto a tray. Allow to cool a few minutes before serving.

Pecan-Orange Scones

Packed with golden raisins and topped with sticky, rich pecans, these orange-scented, crumbly scones are a most welcome sight on any breakfast table.

MAKES 8 SCONES

½ cup golden raisins
¼ cup fresh orange juice
3 cups whole wheat pastry flour

5 tablespoons maple syrup granules

1 tablespoon baking powder

⅛ teaspoon sea salt

8 tablespoons vegetarian buttery spread (like
Earth Balance), chilled

Zest of 1 orange

1 teaspoon umeboshi vinegar

About ⅔ cup soy or rice milk

½ cup brown rice syrup

¼ cup pecans, coarsely minced

Preheat oven to 400F (205C). Line a baking sheet with parchment paper, place inside another baking sheet to prevent scorching and set aside.

Soak the raisins in orange juice to soften and plump.

Sift together the dry ingredients into a bowl. Add the spread in small pieces and cut into the dry ingredients with a pastry blender, fork or 2 knives until mixture resembles coarse cornmeal. Add raisins and orange juice. Stir the zest and umeboshi vinegar into the milk and add to dry ingredients. Stir until the dough is thoroughly moistened and comes together, adding more liquid if needed, but do not overmix.

Turn the dough out onto a floured work surface and gently form into a round. Slice into 8 wedges, form the wedges into rounds and place on the lined baking sheet, about 1 inch apart. Bake until scones are slightly browned, about 20 minutes.

Remove scones from oven. Heat rice syrup in a small saucepan over high heat until it foams. Stir in pecan pieces. Quickly spoon syrup mixture over each scone. Serve warm.

Oat-Raisin Scones

These hearty scones get just a touch of lightness from a hint of orange zest. Hot from the oven, there is nothing quite like one of these with a cup of tea and lots of strawberry jam.

MAKES 8 SCONES

½ cup raisins

5 tablespoons fresh orange juice

1½ cups whole wheat pastry flour

2 teaspoons baking powder

¼ teaspoon sea salt

4 tablespoons vegetarian buttery spread (like
Earth Balance), chilled

¼ cup brown rice syrup

1½ cups rolled oats

Grated zest of 2 oranges

1 teaspoon umeboshi vinegar

½ cup soy or rice milk

Preheat oven to 375F (190C). Line a baking sheet with parchment paper, place inside another baking sheet to prevent scorching and set aside.

Soak the raisins in the orange juice to soften and plump.

Mix the dry ingredients together in a bowl. Cut the spread and the rice syrup into the dry ingredients with a pastry blender, fork or 2 knives until mixture resembles coarse cornmeal. Add oats, raisins and juice, mixing to incorporate the ingredients evenly. Add the orange zest and umeboshi vinegar to the milk and stir into dry ingredients, mixing just until the dough is thoroughly moistened and comes together. Do not overmix.

Turn the dough out onto a floured work surface and gently form into a round about 8 inches in diameter and 1 inch thick. Slice the dough into 8 wedges, shape them into rounds and place on the lined baking sheet about 1 inch apart.

Bake 20 to 25 minutes, until scones are puffy and light golden brown.

Pecan Tea Biscuits

Light, tender and flaky—it's hard to beat the delectable goodness of a biscuit . . . and without all the eggs and milk.

MAKES ABOUT 16 BISCUITS

2 cups whole wheat pastry flour
5 tablespoons maple syrup granules
2 teaspoons baking powder
¼ teaspoon sea salt
¼ cup vegetarian buttery spread (like Earth Balance), chilled
¾ cup soy or rice milk
½ cup pecans, lightly pan-toasted (see Note, page 46) and coarsely minced
½ teaspoon ground cinnamon

Preheat oven to 425F (220C). Lightly oil a baking sheet and set aside.

Sift together the flour, 3 tablespoons of the maple granules, baking powder and salt into a bowl. Cut the spread into the dry ingredients with a pastry blender, fork or 2 knives until mixture resembles coarse cornmeal. Add soy or rice milk and mix just until dough is thoroughly moistened and comes together. Fold in pecans.

Gather biscuit dough into a soft ball and turn it out onto a lightly floured work surface. Knead about 30 seconds, just to form the dough. With a floured rolling pin, roll the dough into a ½-inch-thick round. Dip a biscuit cutter or a glass in flour. Cut dough into rounds by pushing the cutter straight down into the dough without twisting the cutter, as the biscuits may not be as light. Place biscuits on prepared baking sheet about 1 inch apart.

Combine remaining 2 tablespoons maple granules and cinnamon in a small bowl and sprinkle generously over the biscuit tops. Bake 10 to 12 minutes, until light golden brown.

Onion Biscuits

Nothing complements a hearty bowl of soup quite like a light, flaky biscuit. Adding onions to the batter adds a sweetness you just have to taste for yourself.

MAKES ABOUT 12 BISCUITS

1 tablespoon avocado or light olive oil
¼ cup finely minced onion
Sea salt
1½ cups whole wheat pastry flour
1½ teaspoons baking powder
⅛ teaspoon ground nutmeg
¼ cup vegetarian buttery spread (like Earth Balance), chilled
½ cup soy or rice milk

In a small skillet, heat oil over medium heat. Add the onion and a pinch of salt and cook, stirring, until tender and translucent, about 5 minutes; do not brown. Set aside.

Preheat oven to 425F (220C). Lightly oil a baking sheet and set aside. Combine flour, baking powder, nutmeg and a generous pinch of salt in a bowl. Cut the spread into the dry ingredients with a pastry blender, fork or 2 knives until mixture resembles coarse cornmeal. Add onion and milk and mix just until dough is thoroughly moistened and comes together.

Turn dough out onto a lightly floured work surface and knead gently about 30 seconds. Roll the dough into a ½-inch-thick round. Dip a biscuit cutter or a glass in flour. Cut dough into rounds by pushing the cutter straight down into the dough without twisting the cutter, as the biscuits may not be as light. Place biscuits on prepared baking sheet about 1 inch apart.

Bake 12 to 15 minutes, until light golden brown.

Mincemeat Coffee Ring

For mincemeat lovers only! This moist coffee bread, laced through with fragrant mincemeat (my version, of course), is a snap to make and partners beautifully with hot tea on Christmas (or any other) morning.

MAKES 1 (9-INCH) RING; 10 TO 12 SERVINGS

2 cups whole wheat pastry flour
1 tablespoon baking powder
¼ teaspoon sea salt
¾ cup brown rice syrup
¼ cup avocado oil
½ cup rice or soy milk
¾ cup No-Meat Mincemeat (page 314)
1 cup brown rice syrup
2 teaspoons fresh lemon juice

Preheat oven to 350F (175C). Lightly oil and flour a 9-inch ring pan and set aside.

Sift together flour, baking powder and salt into a bowl. Combine rice syrup, oil, milk and mincemeat in another bowl. Add wet mixture to dry ingredients and mix until the ingredients are just combined. It will be a dense batter. Spoon the mixture evenly into the prepared baking pan, filling it not more than two-thirds full.

Bake 30 to 35 minutes, until the bread springs back to the touch. Cool in pan 10 minutes before turning out onto a plate. Place the plate over the cake pan and invert so the bread can drop onto the plate.

While the coffee ring is warm, heat rice syrup over high heat until it foams. Remove from heat and stir in lemon juice. Quickly spoon hot syrup over bread and allow to stand 10 minutes or so before slicing.

Squash Bread

All the goodness of pumpkin pie wrapped up in this moist, slightly sweet snack bread.

MAKES 1 LOAF

2 cups cubed winter squash or pumpkin
Pinch sea salt
Spring or filtered water
2 to 3 cups whole wheat pastry flour
2 teaspoons baking powder
¼ teaspoon sea salt
½ teaspoon ground ginger
¼ teaspoon ground cloves
¼ teaspoon ground cinnamon
⅓ cup soy or rice milk
¼ cup avocado oil
½ cup brown rice syrup
½ cup coarsely minced walnut pieces

Place squash and salt in a heavy saucepan with ⅛ inch of water. Cover and bring to a boil. Reduce heat to low and cook until squash is quite soft, about 20 minutes. Transfer to a food processor and process until smooth. Set aside.

Preheat oven to 350F (175C). Lightly oil and flour a 9 × 5-inch loaf pan and set aside.

Sift together flour, baking powder, salt and spices into a bowl. Combine squash with milk, oil and rice syrup. Stir squash mixture into dry ingredients, mixing just until blended to make a thick, spoonable batter. Fold in walnuts and spoon into prepared pan.

Bake 50 to 55 minutes, until the top of loaf springs back to the touch. Cool in pan 10 minutes before removing loaf from pan and cooling on a wire rack.

■ **VARIATION** Use 1 cup canned organic pumpkin instead of fresh winter squash or pumpkin.

Cranberry-Almond Bread

The tart sweetness of cranberries perfectly complements the nutty crunch of toasted almonds in this gorgeous loaf, streaked with the rich, red color of the berries. Served warm from the oven, with a hot cup of tea, this bread warms any autumn afternoon.

MAKES 1 LOAF

¾ cup whole almonds
2 cups whole wheat pastry flour
2 teaspoons baking powder
¼ teaspoon sea salt
¼ teaspoon ground cinnamon
¼ cup avocado oil
¾ cup maple syrup granules
1 teaspoon almond extract
¾ cup soy or rice milk
2 cups fresh cranberries, sorted, rinsed and
   towel-dried

Preheat oven to 350F (175C). Lightly oil and flour a 9 × 5-inch loaf pan and set aside.

In a hot, dry skillet, lightly pan-toast the almonds over medium heat until fragrant and lightly browned, 5 to 7 minutes. Coarsely mince the almonds by hand or in a nut grinder. Set aside.

Sift together flour, baking powder, salt and cinnamon into a bowl. Whisk together oil, maple granules, almond extract and milk. Stir into dry ingredients, mixing just until blended. Gently fold in the cranberries and almonds. Spoon the batter evenly into the prepared loaf pan.

Bake 55 to 60 minutes, until the top of loaf is golden brown and springs back to the touch or a wooden pick inserted in the center comes out clean. Cool in pan 10 minutes before removing loaf from the pan and cooling on a wire rack.

Lemon-Nut Bread

A not-too-sweet snack bread that serves well in a variety of ways—accompanied by fresh fruit slices, smothered in fruit or nut spreads or my favorite, cut into thin slices and lightly toasted, with a cup of tea.

MAKES 1 LOAF

2½ cups whole wheat pastry flour
2 to 3 teaspoons baking powder
¼ teaspoon sea salt
¾ cup rice or soy milk
¼ cup avocado oil
½ cup brown rice syrup
2 teaspoons grated lemon zest
2 to 3 teaspoons fresh lemon juice
½ cup coarsely minced walnut pieces

Preheat oven to 350F (175C). Lightly oil and flour a 9 × 5-inch loaf pan and set aside.

Sift together flour, baking powder and salt into a bowl. Whisk milk into oil and rice syrup in another bowl. Add lemon zest and juice. Stir into flour mixture and mix until smooth. Fold in nuts. Spoon batter evenly into prepared pan.

Bake 50 to 60 minutes, until the top of loaf springs back to the touch and loaf is golden brown. Cool in pan 10 minutes before removing loaf from pan and cooling on a wire rack.

Olive-Nut Bread

Olives put a unique twist on this nut bread, creating a savory loaf that beautifully complements any soup, stew or pasta meal.

MAKES 1 LOAF

2½ cups whole wheat pastry flour
1 tablespoon baking powder

¼ teaspoon sea salt

1 cup soy or rice milk

¼ cup extra-virgin olive oil

2 teaspoons brown rice syrup

½ cup oil-cured ripe olives, pitted and halved

1 cup coarsely minced walnut pieces

Preheat oven to 350F (175C). Lightly oil and flour a 9 x 5-inch loaf pan and set aside.

Sift together flour, baking powder and salt into a bowl. Whisk milk into oil and rice syrup in another bowl. Stir into flour mixture and mix until just moistened. Fold in olives and nuts. Spoon batter evenly into prepared pan.

Bake 45 to 50 minutes, until loaf is golden and top springs back to the touch. Cool in pan 10 minutes before removing loaf from the pan and cooling on a wire rack. Serve sliced in thin pieces.

Glazed Orange Bread

Orange marmalade is the star of the show in this loaf, where it flavors both the bread and the glaze—a real showstopper.

MAKES 1 LOAF

3 cups whole wheat pastry flour

1 tablespoon baking powder

½ teaspoon sea salt

1½ cups unsweetened orange marmalade

¾ cup fresh orange juice

¼ cup avocado oil

1 cup sunflower seeds, lightly pan-toasted (see Note, page 46)

¼ cup brown rice syrup

Preheat oven to 350F (175C). Lightly oil and flour a 9 X 5-inch loaf pan and set aside.

Sift together flour, baking powder and salt into a bowl. Reserve ½ cup marmalade for the glaze. Combine the remaining marmalade with orange juice and oil in another bowl. Stir into flour mixture, stirring until just moistened. Fold in the sunflower seeds. Spoon batter evenly into prepared pan.

Bake 55 to 60 minutes, until loaf is golden brown and top springs back to the touch. Cool in pan 10 minutes before removing loaf from the pan and cooling on a wire rack.

Heat reserved marmalade and rice syrup over high heat until foamy. Immediately spoon over loaf.

Pancakes

Just like their conventional counterparts, these tender griddlecakes are a great main dish on those lazy weekend mornings when you don't have to rush off and can linger over a leisurely breakfast. Served with any number of conventional or other toppings, these pancakes get their richness from my version of buttermilk—rice or soy milk with just a touch of vinegar to achieve the desired sour taste and necessary leavening.

MAKES ABOUT 12 PANCAKES

1 tablespoon avocado oil, plus extra for cooking

1 cup soy or rice milk, mixed with 1 teaspoon umeboshi vinegar

¾ to 1 cup whole wheat pastry flour

¼ teaspoon sea salt

2 teaspoons baking powder

Heat oil in a small saucepan over medium heat. Transfer to a heatproof bowl and quickly whisk in the milk. Combine dry ingredients in a bowl. Stir milk mixture into dry ingredients and mix until the batter is just moistened and a bit lumpy.

Heat a skillet or griddle over medium heat. Coat with a little oil. Spoon ¼ cupful of batter onto the hot griddle for each pancake. Cook until bubbles pop through the top of the pancakes, 2 to 3 minutes. Turn the pancakes and cook until lightly browned and cooked through, about 1 minute.

■ **VARIATIONS** For an even lighter pancake, use plain amasake in place of the soy or rice milk. Mix the batter the night before you plan to use it and allow it to stand, loosely covered, in a draft-free place until morning. The fermented nature of the amasake will introduce just a bit more leavening to the batter.

■ **BUCKWHEAT PANCAKES** Substitute ¼ cup buckwheat flour for ¼ cup of the pastry flour.

Iowa Corncakes

These sunny yellow griddlecakes have just the right blend of cornmeal and flour. Lovely for a summer brunch topped with a mound of seasonal fruit or fruit sauce.

MAKES ABOUT 12 PANCAKES

1½ cups whole wheat pastry flour
½ cup yellow cornmeal
2 to 3 tablespoons maple syrup granules
½ teaspoon sea salt
2 teaspoons baking powder
1½ cups amasake or soy or rice milk
**2 tablespoons avocado oil, plus extra for
   cooking**

Combine dry ingredients in a bowl. Whisk together wet ingredients in another bowl. Stir into dry ingredients and mix until the batter is just moistened and a bit lumpy.

Heat a skillet or griddle over medium heat. Coat with a little oil. Spoon batter by ¼ cupfuls onto hot griddle. Cook over medium heat until bubbles pop through the top of the pancakes, about 3 minutes. Turn and cook until the pancakes are golden and cooked through, about 1 minute.

Mochi Waffles

These breakfast beauties couldn't be easier to make. Slice the mochi, cook and voilà—puffy, light waffles that make a most delicious, quick breakfast treat. Okay, so this is not really bread, but they are really yummy!

MAKES 4 OR 5 WAFFLES

1 (8-ounce) package brown rice mochi

Heat a nonstick Belgian waffle iron.

While the iron warms, slice the mochi into ⅛-inch-thick strips. When the iron is hot, lay the strips, loosely touching, in the waffle iron. You will need to press firmly to close the iron. Cook waffles 1 minute for softer waffles, up to 2 minutes for crispier ones. Remove waffle from iron, top with your favorite sauce and enjoy.

Svelte French Toast

The best lazy Sunday morning breakfasts are long, leisurely and oh, so cozy. And they should have French toast on the menu, but all those eggs and all that sugar (and nearly eight hundred calories for three slices!) leaves you feeling bloated and lethargic, not relaxed and contented. Well, it's back on the menu now . . .

MAKES 2 SERVINGS

½ **pound silken tofu**
¼ **cup almond milk (or soymilk, but almond is so nice)**
1 teaspoon pure vanilla extract
Generous pinch ground cinnamon
Sea salt
¼ **cup spring or filtered water**
2 tablespoons avocado oil
4 slices whole grain bread
1 cup brown rice syrup
1 cup fresh fruit, diced, or if using berries, halved or left whole

Place tofu, almond milk, vanilla, cinnamon, a pinch of salt and water in a blender and puree until smooth, the consistency of beaten eggs.

Heat a skillet or griddle pan over medium heat with avocado oil. Dredge bread in tofu mixture on both sides and lay on griddle pan. Cook until browned on both sides, turning once, about 2 minutes per side.

While the toast cooks, make the syrup: Place rice syrup, a pinch of salt and fruit in a saucepan over medium-low heat and cook until fruit is soft and syrup is runny, about 5 minutes.

Plate 2 slices of French toast on each plate and ladle syrup over top.

■ **NOTE** If you can't get past using tofu in this recipe, replace it with 2 ripe bananas and proceed with the recipe as stated above.

Waffles

I love waffles on a relaxed Sunday morning when we have time to linger over a leisurely brunch after my husband gets home from a run and me from training at the gym. Nothing does it for us quite like these babies, smothered with a lovely fruit sauce.

MAKES 6 TO 8 WAFFLES

1½ **cups whole wheat pastry flour**
½ **cup semolina flour**
2 teaspoons baking powder
1 teaspoon baking soda
½ **teaspoon sea salt**
1 teaspoon ground cinnamon
¼ **teaspoon ground allspice**
¼ **teaspoon ground nutmeg**
1 cup unfiltered, unsweetened apple juice
¾ **cup soymilk**
⅓ **cup unsweetened applesauce**
2 tablespoons avocado or olive oil
4 tablespoons brown rice syrup
1 teaspoon pure vanilla extract

SAUCE
2 red pears or Granny Smith apples, halved, cored and diced
½ **cup brown rice syrup**
Grated zest of ½ **lemon**
Pinch sea salt

Lightly oil a waffle iron, even if it's a nonstick. Preheat waffle iron.

Whisk together flours, baking powder and soda, salt and spices. Whisk together juice, soymilk, applesauce, oil, syrup and vanilla until well combined. Mix juice mixture into the dry ingredients until a thick batter forms. Cover and set aside while preparing the sauce.

Make sauce: Place all ingredients in a small saucepan over medium heat and bring to a boil. Reduce heat and cook, stirring occasionally, until fruit is quite soft. Keep sauce on very low heat while preparing the waffles.

Spoon batter into waffle iron, filling completely. Close the iron and cook until the waffles rise a bit, are browned and release from the iron. Transfer cooked waffles to a parchment-lined baking sheet and hold them in the oven while cooking the remaining batter, so everything is warm when you serve.

To serve, place waffles on plates and spoon sauce over top.

Tomato Pie

No, I don't mean the English muffin, pop-them-in-the-microwave pizzas. I am talking real pizza here, a real tomato pie. No, it's not smothered in cheese, but you can always add a vegan mozzarella cheese alternative to create that one. This is authentic Italian pizza, just like my mamma used to make.

MAKES 1 LARGE PIZZA

1 package active dry yeast
2 cups warm spring or filtered water
3 tablespoons extra-virgin olive oil, plus extra for drizzling
2 teaspoons sea salt
2½ cups semolina flour
2½ cups whole wheat flour

1 recipe Tomato Sauce (page 205)

In a large bowl, dissolve yeast in ½ cup of the warm water. Let stand until foamy, 5 minutes. Stir in remaining warm water, oil and salt. Using a wooden spoon, slowly stir in semolina flour. Slowly stir in whole wheat flour to form a soft, moist dough (which makes a crispy crust). Turn out dough onto a lightly floured surface and knead to a smooth elastic dough, 10 to 15 minutes. Add flour as needed for kneading, but not too much or the dough will become dry. Transfer dough to a lightly oiled bowl and oil the surface of the dough to prevent a crust from forming. Cover tightly with plastic wrap and set in a warm place to rise until doubled in size, about 2 hours.

While dough rises, prepare the tomato sauce or simply heat through if already made.

Preheat oven to 450F (230C). Lightly flour a round baking stone and preheat 30 minutes or lightly oil a pizza pan. Punch down dough and, on a lightly floured surface, roll out to the size of the stone or pan. Transfer dough to the prepared stone and spread sauce over the crust, leaving about 1 inch around the rim. Drizzle with oil and bake for about 30 minutes, until the crust is golden brown. Remove from oven and allow to cool about 10 minutes (if you can) before slicing.

Stew-Stuffed Loaf

One last recipe idea for bread. This has become Robert's and my favorite way to eat bread.

Robert makes a loaf of one of his delicious breads. My job is to create a thick, hearty vegetable or chunky vegetable and bean stew. I slice off the top of the loaf and hollow out the interior. (Save all that bread for sopping up the sauce.) Next, I ladle a bit of the sauce from the stew onto a serving platter and place the loaf on top. Then, I fill the loaf to capacity with hot stew and serve. We both then break off bits of the bread for scooping stew into individual soup bowls and feast.

Great Dessert Classics

I LOVE DESSERT. There, I've said it, openly admitted my love for that food that we have been indoctrinated by society to deny ourselves—or to eat in the closet. So where does dessert fit into a healthy eating plan? Or, more honestly, does it fit in at all?

You can summarize most people's attitudes on healthful eating with an old cliché: We want to have our cake and eat it, too. We also want to pare fat, cholesterol and excess calories from our diets, but we don't want to give up the pleasure of great-tasting foods. Very few of us can imagine doing without wonderful desserts. While it might make sense to some, from a health viewpoint only the most determined among us can adhere to such a severe regime of eliminating sweets altogether. The real question is, why should we? Life is meant to be enjoyed, not grimly endured. And I am here to tell you that you can enjoy great-tasting food and desserts and great health at the same time.

I grew up in a family of great chefs, especially in the dessert department. My relatives seemed to have this ongoing, good-natured competition to see who could create the sweetest, richest, most decadent—and beautiful—temptation. It was from these incredible cooks that I cultivated a love of combinations like chocolate, hazelnuts and raspberries; flaky tortes bursting with rum cream puddings; fudgy brownies smothered in tangy orange sauce; and cherry-topped cheesecake—all common fare among these culinary wizards. I mastered each recipe, each technique, each little tip and trick, developing my skills so that I eventually began to create signature dessert specialties of my very own.

When my health crisis altered my lifestyle, and my approach to and understanding of food completely changed, the thought of being able to enjoy truly luxurious desserts seemed to be a dream just out of my reach. Oh, I tried, believe me. Tofu cheesecakes that were about as creamy as sand, whole grain cakes and cookies that looked and tasted like hockey pucks, muffins that served double duty as doorstops—you've tried them, too. Dry, unsatisfying, unappealing desserts that tasted terrible but were reportedly good for us: low in fat, high in fiber, low in sugar and cholesterol—and extremely low in taste. After years of failed attempts, I had had enough. I decided that if I was able to make delicious desserts before, I could do it again. So I pulled out all the old rules, tips, wives' tales, techniques and tricks, and gave it a go.

My one rule on dessert creation was that if it didn't look and taste really wonderful, it wasn't worth eating—and certainly wasn't worth all the work to make it. I set out on a quest to create desserts that tasted as irresistible as they looked, without compromising the principles by which I live my life.

Okay, I really have two rules. The second one is simple: Dessert isn't medicine. It is to be enjoyed on occasion, not prescribed. Dessert is an indulgence, not a daily staple. Most important, dessert is to be savored; it shouldn't create more anxiety in our lives.

When it comes to dessert creation, I am as unwilling to compromise on health as I am unwilling to compromise on taste and appeal. In the case of sweet treats, *healthy* and *satisfying* seem to be mutually exclusive terms. So how do we create enjoyable, healthful desserts? How do we bake light, moist cakes and muffins; flaky pie crusts and pastries; rich, chewy cookies? How do we avoid creating those whole foods desserts that have the taste and texture of . . . well . . . healthy desserts?

My years of cooking naturally and creating all manner of recipes have taught me that the key is to make healthful desserts seem like indulgences, so that we'll be satisfied and not bypass them for the binge food that will compromise our health. It is possible to balance the demands of healthy foods with the sensual pleasure of eating. We can eat well without giving up one of our most precious indulgences—dessert.

However, is it possible to achieve full, rich flavor; moist, tender crumb; and satisfying sweet taste without eggs, cream, milk and sugar? Yes,

with careful attention and a bit of skill. It's all about technique and intuition. It is learning, through experimentation and practice, how ingredients react together. For example, conventional cakes are light, moist and springy to the touch due to the combination of eggs, white flour, milk and sugar as well as intense whipping during the mixing process (which imparts air into the batter for that familiar light texture). Whole grain-based cakes will never, never yield exactly that light, airy texture—no way, never, no how. So forget it. With that in mind, you can create a similar end product— a light, moist cake that has full-bodied taste and texture.

The most important thing to remember when creating desserts is that they are an indulgence—and should taste like one, even if they contain nutritionally superior ingredients. A bit of oil for butteriness, nuts for rich taste, sweetener for satisfaction. All of these minor ingredient indulgences will create the illusion of lush flavor and result in desserts that you will enjoy for a lifetime, not the kind of treats that only desperate dieters would eat.

Baking Tips

Assemble all the ingredients you will be needing before you begin to bake. Preheat your oven and prepare your cake pans as well. This will allow you to work quickly. You want to mix the batter and get it in the oven; you don't want it sitting for several minutes while you prepare your pans and heat your oven. This can result in heavy cakes that will not rise well because whole grain flour loves moisture, and leaving the batter sitting for several minutes will cause it to saturate itself.

When mixing ingredients, use pastry knives, forks, spoons—anything but your hands.

Remember, whole grains love moisture, and the oil from your skin is no exception. It can create a tough, spongy dough. Handle the dough only when necessary, or as a recipe directs. Don't knead dough unless the recipe requires it; and when it does, don't over- or underknead. Inexperienced bakers would do well to follow recipes to the letter until they master certain techniques and develop a "feel" for the doughs and batters they are working with. Whenever I asked my mother how she knew a batter was right (she rarely used recipes), she would say that it "felt right." It has taken me years of trial and error, but I now know what she meant. With practice, you too can develop a "feel" for baking. And, lucky for you, there are currently so many resources available to aid you in whole grain baking that you can bypass years of practice if you can follow a recipe.

Flour

I use mostly whole wheat pastry flour when baking cakes, cookies, pie crusts, pastries, muffins, tortes, cupcakes or other baked treats. A softer, finer grind of flour than regular whole wheat flour (which is great for breads), it results in a lighter end product. I very rarely use white flour, bleached or unbleached, in my baking. It is highly refined and compromised, nutritionally deficient and really tough on the digestive tract. Sometimes though, I combine whole wheat pastry flour with semolina flour to achieve a lighter texture and lovely golden color.

As a good chef, I should tell you to always sift flour before mixing with other ingredients to create air in the batter. But I studied with a French pastry chef who said it was a waste of time. He whisked the dry ingredients to put air in the batter and I confess, I have adopted his

method and my results are just fine, thanks. So sift if you like, or whisk.

Mix dry and wet ingredients separately and then simply fold them together until blended. This trick helps you avoid overmixing, which will most assuredly remove air from the batter, leaving you with heavy, tough dough. Also, remember that whole grain loves moisture, so overmixing will cause the flour to saturate itself. So much for a light, springy cake!

Fats

To create moist textures in your pastries, you need to introduce some kind of fat or fat substitute. Conventional baked goods rely on milk, cream, eggs, butter, margarine or artificial fat additives. Since I choose not to cook with any of those foods, I needed to find viable alternatives. My past experience (and that of many other whole foods chefs) showed corn oil to be the clear winner. Imparting a buttery flavor, corn oil created a tender crumb and flavorful pastry every time. But then GMO (genetically modified organisms) foods happened and there wasn't a company that could guarantee that their oil did not contain any of this corn. So while canola and safflower oils, with their mild flavors, were candidates for the job, I did not like them so much that I would make them my first choice. So I needed to find a new baking oil. I was reading one day and came across a recipe that used olive oil as the fat. After I stopped scrunching my nose in distaste, it occurred to me that there was some sense to this. And when I pulled out my mother's old recipe box and discovered that she had used olive oil in everything from cakes to cannoli shells, I decided to give it a try. And the results have been just yummy. You can use either extra-virgin (higher in antioxidants, but more expensive) or light olive oil. Since then I have added avocado oil to my baking repertoire because I love how buttery it is, so now you have a choice. Both yield pastries with a rich buttery flavor and a moist crumb.

However, when adapting recipes from solid fats to oil, you will need to adjust liquid volume. Simply cut back equally on other liquids to accommodate the liquid of the oil, but you will see more of that in the following recipes.

And for those of you who wish to eliminate fat altogether in your baking, I have found that applesauce or pureed, poached pears work nicely to create a moist cake. Be careful with that one, though. Other liquids in the recipe will need to be seriously adjusted to accommodate the liquid in the fruit. For instance, in an average cake recipe, I will use one cup of applesauce plus my liquid sweetener and no other fluids to achieve a proper batter. So play with this one a bit. Many low-fat bakers advocate the use of prune puree in place of oil or fat. That works well in some recipes, but you must remember that pureed prunes will impart a strong taste and dark color to your recipe, so I personally reserve it for heartier items, like spice cakes, fruit cakes or carrot cakes.

Adding citrus zest to a recipe is one of the best ways I have found to add flavor to desserts that may be lacking because of diminished fat content. The zest is the colored part of the outer skin of lemons, oranges and other citrus fruits. Citrus zest adds a delicate, sour flavor to fruit compotes, sauces, cakes, pastries and puddings. Since zest only has a mild sweet zing to it, you can pretty much use it as you desire.

Egg Substitutes

Eggs are used in desserts for two reasons: to leaven and/or to bind. With that in mind, elim-inating them can create leaden pastries and cakes—not good. Have no worries. There are a couple of alternatives to eggs in dessert-making. For leavening, you may add 1 teaspoon of baking powder for every egg in the recipe. (You want to look for nonaluminum baking powder when purchasing. The products are clearly marked.) However, you can also whip together, in a blender, equal parts of flax seeds and boiled apple juice, using 1 teaspoon of this mixture for every egg. This leavening is a bit less predictable, so your results may vary. The final and most unpredictable leavener I have used is oatmeal cream. Simply cook oatmeal and spoon the "cream" off the top before stirring. Allow the cream to ferment lightly for a day before using as a leavening agent. My own results with this one have been spotty, but it is worth a try, particularly in pastries like scones, where hearty texture is a good thing.

In recipes where eggs act as binders, I have simply substituted one teaspoon kuzu or arrowroot for each egg and have been quite successful. For custards or flan, a combination of agar-agar flakes and kuzu has proved most satisfying in providing a firm, creamy pudding. Usually a teaspoon of each—kuzu and agar-agar—is enough to yield the firmest, creamiest custards.

Nuts

Nuts are a wonderful addition to healthful desserts for many reasons. Their fat content gives desserts a rich, distinctive flavor and their texture adds an interestingly appealing crunch. To get the best flavor from nuts, simply roast them lightly before use—the lower the oven temperature, the more flavorful the nuts. For instance, I roast pecans at 275F (135C) for about 20 minutes to bring forth their delicate flavor. Roasting at too high a temperature will result in bitter taste. Pan-roasting nuts yields a more delicate flavor and is the method I prefer on most occasions. Nuts can also be pan-toasted in a dry skillet over medium to medium-low heat; see Note, page 46.

Sweeteners

Now the real issue—sweeteners. Even after all these years, the best-quality sweeteners I have found are grain based. Brown rice syrup ... and in some recipes, barley malt are the sweeteners I choose most of the time. The beauty of grain sweeteners is that they are primarily made from complex sugars, not simple sugars, so they are released into the blood a bit more slowly, providing fuel for the body instead of the rush and crash we get from simple sugars. They are also not all that refined a product; they are simply whole grains, inoculated with a fermenting agent and then cooked until they reduce to a syrup.

Rice syrup yields a delicate sweetness with no aftertaste, which is very satisfying. It is the perfect sweetener for most cakes, pastries, cookies and puddings. Barley malt has a stronger taste, much like molasses, so I reserve its use for desserts that complement its flavor, like spice cakes, carrot cakes and squash custards.

I use honey, maple syrup or fruit sweeteners less often because they are simple sugars and also because they have such a strong, sweet taste. However, these are great sweeteners to use if grain sweeteners are unavailable or if you are making the transition from conventional, sugary desserts to healthier treats and are not used to the more delicate flavors of rice syrup. Honey is also rich in antioxidants and is an inverted sugar, meaning that it digests in the body more slowly than other simple sugars, making it a very viable choice as a healthy sweetener.

There are some new players in the field of healthy sweeteners, even though most of them come from ancient sources, so let's talk about them as well. Stevia, a naturally sweet plant, has its leaves concentrated into powders or liquids and is enjoying a good reputation in natural cooking. Billed as one hundred times sweeter than sugar, the flavor is exactly that, intensely sweet. If you choose to bake with it, it will require some experimenting to find the flavor you want. While there is no bad news about stevia, it is too strong for my taste.

Agave syrup is made from cactus plants and can be a lovely sweetener as well. If you decide to use this one, be sure you are using the least refined one you can find. The darker the color, the better the quality.

And then there is xylitol, a granulated sweetener most commonly made from birch bark. Intensely sweet, you can use much less than you would of its equivalent in regular sugar to achieve a very sweet cake, cookie or pastry. Like stevia, it is too strong for me, but there is good news about this sweetener. The only downside is the price: At this writing, it is quite expensive. I am happy with rice syrup, so I see no reason to switch. If you decide to give xylitol a try, be sure to purchase the organic version made from birch bark only.

When using grain sweeteners, remember that they are liquid, so you will need to adjust your recipes to accommodate them. In adapting, I have found that substituting ½ cup of rice syrup for every 1 cup of sugar in a recipe yields a lovely sweet pastry.

So bake with passion, abandon and a sense of comfort with these new ingredients, and your desserts will be the hit of the party every time!

Apricot Pastries

These delicate crescent cookies are a real treat to serve. I love putting a tray out at the close of an autumn brunch or just about any time some friends and I get together for tea.

MAKES 16 PASTRIES

2 cups whole wheat pastry flour
Generous pinch sea salt
3 tablespoons olive or avocado oil
¼ cup spring or filtered water
¾ cup unsweetened or fruit-sweetened
  apricot preserves
½ cup coarsely chopped walnuts
½ cup raisins
1 teaspoon ground cinnamon

Preheat oven to 350F (175C). Line a baking sheet with parchment paper and set aside. Whisk flour and salt together in a large bowl. Add oil and water and stir with a wooden spoon to evenly distribute liquid throughout the flour. Mold dough into 2 balls, adding a small amount of water if dough feels too dry. Dough should be stiff but flexible. Don't over-handle or knead; just gather it into 2 balls.

Roll 1 ball of dough between waxed paper to form a 9-inch circle. Remove top sheet of paper. Spread entire circle with half of the preserves, nuts, raisins and cinnamon. Cut circle into 8 pie-shaped wedges. From the widest end of each wedge, roll each piece of dough into a crescent shape, pressing the point into the pastry to seal.

Place each pastry on prepared baking sheet, about 1 inch apart. Repeat the process with the other ball of dough.

Bake 12 to 15 minutes, until browned. Immediately remove from baking sheet with a spatula and cool on a wire rack.

■ **VARIATION** While the pastries are still hot, it is a nice touch to glaze them. Heat 3 to 4 tablespoons rice syrup over high heat until it foams and pour, while still hot, over pastries. Allow to set about 30 minutes before serving.

■ **NOTE** The preserves may run out of the pastry during baking, so remove the pastries immediately from the baking sheet after baking or they will stick to the paper, making removal difficult and breakage of the pastries assured.

Surefire Basic White Cake

This completely whole grain cake really is a winner. Bake it just once and you will see that desserts can be delicious without compromising your food choices. I also use this great vanilla cake as the base recipe for all my other cakes, building and changing ingredients for each recipe.

MAKES 1 CAKE

2½ cups whole wheat pastry flour
2 to 3 teaspoons baking powder
⅛ teaspoon sea salt
¼ cup avocado oil
½ cup brown rice syrup
1 teaspoon pure vanilla extract
½ cup spring or filtered water
½ to ⅔ cup soy or rice milk

Preheat oven to 350F (175C). Lightly oil and flour a 9-inch round cake pan or loaf pan and set aside.

Whisk together flour, baking powder and salt in a bowl. Whisk oil, rice syrup, vanilla, water and ½ cup milk together in another bowl. Stir the liquid mixture into the flour mixture, mixing until smooth; do not overmix.

The batter should be thick and spoonable, not runny. Add more milk if needed. Spoon into prepared pan.

Bake on center rack 40 to 45 minutes, until a wooden pick inserted in center comes out clean and cake springs back to the touch; do not open the oven door until cake has baked 20 minutes or the cake may sink.

Cool cake in pan 10 minutes before turning out of pan and cooling on a wire rack.

■ **NOTE** Work carefully with baked cake, realizing that cakes, especially whole grain-based versions, are delicate.

Lemon Torte with Blackberry Sauce

This sweet and tangy torte is a real crowd pleaser. And the cook gets to take big bows for a beauty of a dessert. Only you and I will know how easy it is to make. The sauce can be used in lots of other ways: it goes great over a fresh fruit salad or spooned over your favorite frozen dessert.

MAKES ABOUT 10 SERVINGS

1 recipe Surefire Basic White Cake (page 302)
2 teaspoons grated lemon zest
Juice of 1 lemon
¾ cup unsweetened or fruit-sweetened apricot preserves
¼ cup amasake
2 tablespoons kuzu or arrowroot, dissolved in ¼ cup cold water

BLACKBERRY SAUCE
3 cups unsweetened frozen blackberries
¼ cup brown rice syrup
1 tablespoon kuzu or arrowroot, dissolved in

⅓ cup cold water
2 teaspoons fresh lemon juice

Preheat oven to 325F (175C). Lightly oil a jelly-roll pan or deep baking sheet and set aside.

Make cake batter, adding lemon zest and juice. Spoon batter into pan. Bake 25 to 30 minutes, until center of cake springs back to the touch. Cool in pan 10 minutes before turning out of pan and cooling on a wire rack. Vertically cut cake into 3 equal pieces.

Heat apricot preserves and amasake in a saucepan over medium heat. Stir in dissolved kuzu and cook, stirring, until mixture thickens, 3 minutes. Allow to cool, stirring occasionally so filling doesn't set. Place one of the pieces of cake on a plate and top with filling. Repeat with another cake layer and filling, ending with a thin layer of filling on top. Set aside while preparing the Blackberry Sauce.

Make sauce: Heat berries and rice syrup in a saucepan over medium heat. Stir in dissolved kuzu, and cook, stirring, until thickened, 3 minutes. Stir in lemon juice and remove from heat. Press mixture through a fine strainer to remove seeds. Chill 1 hour.

To serve the torte, pool a small amount of sauce on individual serving plates and place a slice of lemon torte directly on top.

Pear Charlotte

Minus the heavy cream and sugar, this delicious version of a charlotte really showcases the delicate flavors of ripe, succulent pears.

MAKES 6 TO 8 SERVINGS

PASTRY DOUGH
1½ cups whole wheat pastry flour
¼ teaspoon sea salt
Scant ¼ cup avocado oil
¼ cup cold soymilk or cold water (see Note below)

6 to 7 ripe pears, peeled, cored and thinly sliced
1 tablespoon fresh lemon juice, combined with 1½ cups spring or filtered water
¼ teaspoon minced fresh ginger
½ cup brown rice syrup
3 tablespoons kuzu or arrowroot, dissolved in ¼ cup cold water
1 teaspoon avocado oil
⅓ cup unsweetened or fruit-sweetened apricot preserves, strained
1 tablespoon almonds, pan-toasted (see Note, page 55) and minced

Preheat oven to 375F (190C). Lightly oil a 9-inch tart pan and set aside.

Prepare pastry: Mix flour, salt and oil thoroughly, using a fork to blend ingredients. Slowly add soymilk and stir to form a stiff but flexible dough. Gather into a ball and knead 1 to 2 minutes. Roll out thinly between sheets of waxed paper to a 10-inch circle. Lay over prepared tart pan, pressing it into the pan without stretching the dough.

Prick pastry all over with a fork. Cover with foil, firmly smoothing over pastry and then folding foil over pan edges so pastry is com-

pletely encased. Bake 14 minutes. Remove foil and return to oven 6 minutes or until light brown. Set aside.

Meanwhile, stir pear slices in lemon water to prevent discoloring. Reserve several slices for garnish. Combine pears with ginger and rice syrup in a saucepan and simmer over low heat until a chunky puree forms, 15 to 20 minutes, stirring frequently. Stir in dissolved kuzu and oil, and cook, stirring, until mixture thickens, about 3 minutes.

Spread mixture evenly over baked pastry. Arrange reserved sliced pears on top and bake 30 minutes. Remove from oven. Heat apricot preserves over high heat until foamy. Strain and spoon over top of the tart. Allow to stand until cooled before slicing. Sprinkle with almonds before serving.

■ **NOTE** Soy milk makes a much "cakier" pastry than water.

Fruit and Custard Tart

This unusual crust contains rolled oats and almonds instead of flour.

MAKES 6 TO 8 SERVINGS

OAT AND NUT CRUST
1 cup rolled oats
½ cup whole almonds
¼ cup avocado oil
¼ cup brown rice syrup

FILLING
1 cup amasake
2 teaspoons kuzu or arrowroot dissolved in ¼ cup cold water
1 teaspoon pure vanilla extract
3 to 4 cups fresh fruit: sliced strawberries;

halved grapes; sliced peaches, pears or apples (tossed with 1 teaspoon lemon juice to prevent discoloring); blueberries and/or raspberries

GLAZE
¼ cup unsweetened or fruit-sweetened apricot preserves
½ cup brown rice syrup
¼ cup spring or filtered water
1 teaspoon agar-agar flakes

Preheat oven to 350F (175C).

Prepare crust: Process oats and almonds in a food processor into a fine meal. Add oil and rice syrup and process to a stiff dough. With wet hands, press oat mixture firmly into a pie pan. Bake 15 minutes, until set. Set aside.

Prepare filling: Heat amasake over medium heat. Stir in dissolved kuzu and cook, stirring, until mixture thickens, about 3 minutes. Remove from heat and stir in vanilla. Spoon amasake mixture into pie shell. While still soft and warm, arrange fresh fruit in an attractive pattern, covering the amasake completely.

Prepare glaze: Heat preserves, rice syrup, water and agar-agar over low heat, stirring constantly, until agar-agar dissolves, about 10 minutes. The mixture will thicken slightly. Brush or spoon mixture over fruit while very hot. Allow tart to set up about 1 hour before serving.

■ **NOTE** Pouring the hot glaze over the fruit cooks it just enough to make it slightly tender and brings out the sweetness.

Blackberry Trifle

An impressive, and delicious, dessert that showcases berries when they are at their peak.

MAKES 10 TO 12 SERVINGS

1 recipe Surefire Basic White Cake (page 302), baked in a 9-inch-square pan
1 recipe Blackberry Sauce (page 303)
2 recipes Almond Custard (page 306)
2 cups mixed fresh soft fruit: sliced strawberries, halved grapes, whole blueberries or raspberries, thinly sliced peaches
1½ cups slivered almonds, pan-toasted (see Note, page 55)

Cool cake completely. Cut into 1-inch cubes and set aside.

Using a trifle dish or deep clear glass bowl, begin assembling the trifle by drizzling about one-third of the sauce over the bottom. Arrange half of the cake cubes in a layer, patting them down into the sauce. Spread about one-fourth of the custard over the cake and arrange half of the fruit on top of the custard, pressing some pieces against the glass sides so they show.

Spread half of the remaining custard over the fruit. Sprinkle lightly with slivered almonds. Add another one-third of the sauce, then the remaining cake, pressing down slightly. Place the remaining fruit on top of the cake. Top with the last of the custard. Cover the top of the custard well with almonds. Using a spoon, create a ring of sauce around the edge of the bowl. Chill 1 hour, covered, or up to a full day before serving.

Tarte Tatin

I love breaking traditions and making new ones. Here is another delicious, offbeat approach to a very classic dessert.

MAKES 8 TO 10 SERVINGS

4 Granny Smith apples, peeled, quartered and cored
2 tablespoons fresh lemon juice, combined with 2 cups water
½ cup brown rice syrup
1 tablespoon avocado oil
Pinch sea salt
1 recipe Surefire Basic White Cake (page 302)

Preheat oven to 375F (175C). Stir apples in lemon water to prevent discoloration. Drain fruit well in a colander and set aside.

Combine rice syrup, oil and salt in a skillet that can be transferred to the oven. (Cast iron works well.) Stir apples into rice-syrup mixture, taking care to coat the fruit well. Spread mixture evenly over skillet surface. Place over medium heat and warm through. Fruit will begin to release juice. Cook 20 minutes, stirring occasionally. Fruit should become caramelized and pierce easily with a fork. Increase heat if needed so that mixture bubbles vigorously or juices will not brown—but take care not to burn. Remove from heat and allow to cool slightly. Arrange the cooked apple slices attractively in a ring in the same skillet.

Prepare cake batter and immediately spoon over cooked fruit, spreading lightly to evenly coat the surface, but try to not disturb fruit.

Bake on the center rack in oven for 30 to 35 minutes. Cake should be nicely browned and a wooden pick inserted in center of cake should come out clean. Remove from oven and allow to cool 4 to 5 minutes. Run a sharp knife around rim of skillet to loosen cake. Center a serving plate over skillet and invert cake onto the plate. If any fruit pieces or juices remain in the skillet, spoon over the top of cake. If fruit is not sufficiently browned, place cake briefly under the broiler until just browned. Do not burn. Let cake stand 5 minutes before slicing.

Almond-Custard Cake Roll

This recipe is a bit tricky and requires some degree of skill in handling whole grain cakes. But don't be intimidated. It is so beautiful and delicious, it is worth the care and practice to get it right.

MAKES 8 TO 10 SERVINGS

1 recipe Surefire Basic White Cake (page 302)
Flour, for dusting

ALMOND CUSTARD
2 cups amasake
Pinch sea salt
2 tablespoons kuzu or arrowroot, dissolved in ¼ cup cold water
1 teaspoon almond extract

1 cup slivered almonds, pan-toasted (see Note, page 55)

Preheat oven to 350F (175C). Line a jelly-roll pan with parchment paper, allowing it to hang slightly over the edges of the pan. Lightly oil the paper.

Prepare cake batter. Turn batter into prepared pan and spread evenly over the surface. Bake on the center rack 7 to 10 minutes. Cake should spring back to the touch. Remove from oven, drape a damp cloth towel over cake and set aside 5 minutes. Remove towel and run a knife around edges of cake to loosen cake and paper from pan.

Very lightly dust a long sheet of waxed paper with flour. Lift cake and paper from pan and lay, top side down, on waxed paper. Gently peel off paper. Trim off any dry edges of cake. Cover with a fresh sheet of waxed paper. Let stand 5 to 7 minutes, cake should still be warm.

Turn cake over so original top is facing up. Carefully and firmly roll up cake and paper to form an evenly thick log. Secure in waxed paper by folding or twisting ends. Refrigerate 1 hour before proceeding. (Store in refrigerator up to 2 days or in freezer if not using right away.)

Prepare custard: Heat amasake and salt thoroughly. Stir in dissolved kuzu and cook, stirring, until amasake thickens, about 3 minutes. Remove from heat and stir in almond extract.

To assemble the cake roll, allow cake to come to room temperature. Unroll cake and, if sticky, sprinkle lightly with flour. Reserving some custard to decorate the top of the cake, evenly spread warm custard over surface of cake, leaving about 1 inch all around the edges to avoid squeezing out cream during rolling. Sprinkle with three-quarters of the nuts, reserving the remainder for garnish. Working

from a short side, roll the cake up neatly and firmly. Wrap tightly in waxed paper to keep from unrolling. Transfer to a tray and refrigerate at least 2 hours to set. Refrigerate reserved custard.

To serve: Remove waxed paper from cake, spread top with remaining custard and sprinkle with nuts. Slice into rounds and serve.

Coco-Locos

These cookies are decadent! If you love chocolate (Is there anyone not bewitched by it?), then try these. No one will ever know that you have created sinfully delicious treats with healthy ingredients.

MAKES ABOUT 2 DOZEN

1½ cups rolled oats
1¾ cups whole wheat pastry flour
⅛ teaspoon sea salt
1½ teaspoons baking powder
1 cup unsweetened shredded coconut
½ cup minced pecans
⅔ to 1 cup soymilk
1 teaspoon pure vanilla extract
1 cup brown rice syrup
½ cup avocado or olive oil
1 cup nondairy, grain-sweetened chocolate chips (available at natural foods stores)

Preheat oven to 350F (175C). Line a baking sheet with parchment paper and set aside.

Combine all ingredients, except chocolate chips, in a large bowl until blended. Use enough soymilk to create a soft, spoonable cookie dough. Gently fold in chips and drop by abundant tablespoonfuls onto prepared baking sheet.

Bake 18 to 20 minutes. Cookies should be moist and chewy. Cool on wire racks.

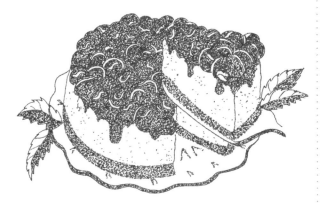

Oatmeal Cookies

These chewy treats are a must in any house with cookie lovers. The lightly fermented dough requires no other leavening, and the delicate sweet taste makes them a real delight.

MAKES ABOUT 2 DOZEN

1½ cups whole wheat pastry flour
1½ cups rolled oats
⅛ teaspoon sea salt
½ cup raisins
½ cup coarsely diced walnuts
1 cup amasake
3 tablespoons avocado or olive oil
¾ cup brown rice syrup
1 teaspoon pure vanilla extract

Combine flour, oats and salt in a large bowl. Mix in raisins and walnuts. Whisk together amasake, oil, rice syrup and vanilla. Fold all ingredients together. Allow to rest, covered with a cloth towel, in a warm place 1 hour or more to allow the dough to ferment slightly so the cookies will rise.

Preheat oven to 375F (190C). Lightly oil a baking sheet. Drop cookie dough by teaspoonfuls onto the prepared sheet, leaving about 1 inch between cookies.

Bake 15 to 18 minutes, until golden and firm to the touch. Do not overbake, or the cookies will be tough. It is better to remove the cookies when they feel a bit on the soft side (they'll firm up as they cool), rather than overbake them.

Viennese Vanilla Crescents

My mother was a great baker. She didn't seem to have a specialty; she just went into the kitchen and created heavenly treats. As a kid, I couldn't resist her cookies, especially at Christmas. This recipe is adapted from one of my holiday favorites.

MAKES 3 TO 4 DOZEN

4 cups whole wheat pastry flour
¼ teaspoon sea salt
¼ cup avocado or olive oil
¼ cup brown rice syrup
About ½ cup spring or filtered water
1 teaspoon pure vanilla extract
1 teaspoon grated lemon zest
2 cups almonds, ground into a fine meal
2 teaspoons baking powder
About ½ cup brown rice syrup, for glaze

Combine all ingredients, except ¼ cup almond meal, in a large bowl. Mix into a stiff dough. Gather into a ball, wrap in waxed paper and allow to rest for 1 hour before proceeding.

Preheat oven to 400F (205C). Line 2 baking sheets with parchment paper and set aside.

Roll dough into ¼-inch-thick ropes and cut into 2-inch pieces. Bend into crescent shapes. Arrange on prepared baking sheets, leaving about 1 inch between cookies.

Bake 10 minutes. Heat rice syrup in a saucepan over high heat until foamy. While cookies are still warm, roll in warm rice syrup and remaining almond meal.

Italian Biscotti

Yes, you read right—biscotti! Now, I know what you're thinking: How can you make biscotti without tons of eggs? Well, frankly, I threw out a lot of cookie batter before I got this one right. All I can tell you is try them; you'll like them. They are a delight with a cup of good, strong espresso.

MAKES ABOUT 2 DOZEN

¾ cup slivered almonds
3 cups whole wheat pastry flour
½ cup ground almonds
1½ teaspoons baking powder
½ cup plus 2 tablespoons brown rice syrup
⅓ cup olive oil
½ teaspoon almond or anise extract
¼ cup spring or filtered water or soymilk

Preheat oven to 275F (135C). Arrange almonds on a baking sheet. Lightly oven-toast almonds until fragrant, about 10 minutes. Reserve ¼ cup for garnish.

Combine flour, ground almonds, remaining ½ cup almonds and baking powder in a large bowl. Combine ½ cup rice syrup, oil, almond extract and water in a small bowl. Stir into flour mixture to make a stiff, kneadable dough.

Preheat oven to 350F (175C). Line a baking sheet with parchment paper and set aside. Divide the dough into 2 equal pieces and shape into 2 logs about 3 inches wide, 1 inch high and long enough to almost equal the length of the baking sheet. Warm the 2 tablespoons rice syrup in a small saucepan. Lightly brush warm syrup on the tops of the logs and gently press in the remaining almonds.

Bake about 20 minutes, until golden brown. Remove from the oven and slice into 1-inch wedges while still warm. Place the wedges back on the baking sheet, cut side up, and return to the oven for 3 to 4 minutes, turn and bake for 3 to 4 minutes on the other side to crisp the biscotti.

Peanut Blossoms

These soft, peanutty cookies are filled to the brim with tart raspberry jam. You can use any peanut butter, but one with a crunchy texture really makes these cookies a real kid (old or young) pleaser.

MAKES ABOUT 3 DOZEN COOKIES

3 cups whole wheat pastry flour
1½ teaspoons baking powder
⅛ teaspoon sea salt
1 cup brown rice syrup
½ cup unsweetened, unsalted peanut butter
2 tablespoons avocado oil
1 teaspoon pure vanilla extract
About ½ cup unsweetened raspberry jam

Line a baking sheet with parchment paper and set aside.

Combine flour, baking powder and salt in a large bowl. Combine the rice syrup, peanut butter, oil and vanilla in a small bowl. Stir into flour mixture and mix just enough to combine ingredients. Overmixing will result in tough cookies, and we want them to be chewy and soft.

Roll the dough into 1½-inch balls. Place about 1 inch apart on prepared baking sheet. Moisten your thumb and press down in the center of each cookie, making a deep indentation. Fill the hole with raspberry jam. Refrigerate the entire tray of cookies 1 hour before baking.

Preheat oven to 325F (165C). Bake 18 to 20 minutes, until cookies are set. Remove from the oven and allow the cookies to cool on the baking sheet. This allows them to finish baking but keeps the cookies soft and chewy.

Raspberry Pinwheels

These delightful cookies are almost as fun to make as they are to eat. A great recipe to get the kids involved in, or to prepare with friends.

MAKES 20 TO 24 COOKIES

2 cups whole wheat pastry flour
1 teaspoon baking powder
⅛ teaspoon sea salt
⅔ cup avocado oil
1 teaspoon pure vanilla extract
¼ to ½ cup cold spring or filtered water
About ½ cup unsweetened or fruit-sweetened
**   raspberry jam**
½ teaspoon grated lemon zest
¼ cup walnuts, pan-toasted (see Note, page
**   46) and minced**

Combine flour, baking powder and salt in a bowl. Blend in oil, vanilla and enough cold water to make a stiff, pliable dough. Gather dough into a ball, wrap in waxed paper and set aside to rest for 30 minutes.

Preheat oven to 350F (175C). Line a baking sheet with parchment paper and set aside. Divide dough into 2 pieces and roll out each between waxed paper into 10-inch squares. Cut each square into 5 (2-inch) squares. Place small squares on prepared baking sheet.

Cut 1-inch slits from each corner toward the center, but not all the way to the center. Place a small amount of jam in the middle of the

square and top with lemon zest and a sprinkling of nuts. Fold every other corner toward the center and pinch, forming the pinwheel shape.

Bake 10 minutes, until lightly golden. Remove from the oven and carefully transfer cookies to a cooling rack.

■ **VARIATION** To glaze the cookies, heat a small amount of rice syrup over high heat until it foams and quickly spoon over the cooling pastries. Allow to stand several minutes to set the glaze before serving.

Almond Custard–Filled Torte

To make this sinfully delicious (and so-o-o-o easy) torte you really need a torte pan, which you can buy at any kitchen shop. You'll know it—the pans usually have scalloped rims with an indentation in the center for the custard or other fillings.

MAKES 1 TORTE, 6 TO 8 SERVINGS

1 recipe Surefire Basic White Cake (page 302)
1½ cups almond-flavored amasake
2 tablespoons kuzu or arrowroot, dissolved in
**   ¼ cup cold water**
Strawberries, sliced, for decoration
Kiwifruit, sliced, for decoration

Preheat oven to 350F (175C). Oil the torte pan well, being sure to get into all the creases so the cake will not stick. Dust the pan with flour. Cut a circle of waxed paper the size of the indentation in the center. Put waxed paper in place and oil it. Set pan aside.

Prepare the cake batter as directed in the recipe. Spoon the batter carefully into the pan without moving the waxed paper around. Bake 30 to 35 minutes, until the center of the torte springs back to the touch.

Meanwhile make the filling: Heat the amasake over medium heat. Add dissolved kuzu and cook, stirring constantly, until thick and creamy, 3 to 4 minutes. (You want the starch of the kuzu to cook completely so that your custard doesn't have a chalky taste.)

Cool cake in pan about 10 minutes before turning out onto a serving plate to cool completely. Fill the indentation with custard and cover the top with concentric circles of strawberry and kiwifruit slices.

- **VARIATION** I like to decorate these cakes with a wide variety of fruits. I decorate the edges of the torte with toasted minced pecans and a thin ring of carefully placed nondairy chocolate chips.

- **NOTE** Don't let the cake cool completely in the pan, as it will stick to the pan and probably break. (The same thing will happen if the cake is too hot.) A good rule of thumb is to remove the cake from the pan when it is still warm, but you are able to hold the pan with no hot pads.

And how exactly do you turn a cake out of a pan? Run a sharp knife around the edge of the pan, then place your serving plate squarely over the cake and, holding the pan and plate firmly on both sides, flip it quickly. The cake should drop onto the plate. If you sense it sticking, gently tap the pan. If that doesn't work, flip it back over, loosen the cake and try again.

Praline Pumpkin Pie

The simple addition of sweet, crunchy pecans gives new meaning to decadent holiday treats. I know it's called pumpkin pie, but winter squash is so much sweeter than pumpkin.

MAKES 6 TO 8 SERVINGS

1 recipe Pastry Dough (page 304)
⅓ cup barley malt
2 tablespoons avocado oil
½ cup pecans, minced
2 cups 1-inch pieces pumpkin (see Note, below) or butternut squash
Sea salt
⅔ cup brown rice syrup
1 teaspoon pumpkin pie spice
½ teaspoon ground ginger
1 cup amasake
4 tablespoons agar-agar flakes
3 tablespoons kuzu or arrowroot, dissolved in ¼ cup cold water

Preheat oven to 400F (205C). Roll out pie dough thinly between sheets of waxed or parchment paper into a 10-inch circle. Lay over a 9-inch pie pan, pressing it into the pan without stretching the dough. Trim the excess dough around the edges, leaving an even ½-inch overhang. Turn the excess dough up toward the edge of the pie and crimp or flute to form a decorative edge. Prick with a fork. Bake the pie shell 10 minutes. This prevents a soggy crust when serving the finished pie. Allow to cool completely after baking.

Combine barley malt and oil in a saucepan and cook until foamy. Immediately stir in the pecans. Spread evenly over the bottom of the pie shell and set aside to cool to room temperature.

Add the squash and ½ inch of water to a pressure cooker. Add a pinch of salt, seal and bring to full pressure over medium heat. Reduce heat and cook squash 20 minutes. Remove from heat and allow pressure to reduce naturally. Puree the squash in a food mill or food processor until smooth.

Preheat oven to 350F (175C). Combine rice syrup, pie spice, ginger, amasake and agar-agar with cooked squash in a heavy pot. Simmer over low heat about 15 minutes, until agar-agar completely dissolves. Stir in dissolved kuzu and cook, stirring, until mixture thickens, 3 to 4 minutes. Pour filling carefully into pie shell over the pecans.

Bake 40 to 45 minutes. The edges should be set, but the center still jiggly. Remove pie from oven, cover completely with foil and allow to cool completely before serving. (Covering the pie while hot prevents the top from cracking as it cools.)

■ **NOTE** The best pumpkin for making pumpkin pie from scratch is the sugar pumpkin. If sugar pumpkins are not available, use a winter squash.

Antico Dolce Torte

An Italian tradition at most Christmas morning feasts, this confection was always a favorite of mine. When my eating habits turned to healthier choices, I couldn't bear to give it up. Here is the result of my experimentation!

MAKES 1 TORTE, 8 TO 10 SERVINGS

DOUGH
3 cups whole wheat pastry flour
Generous pinch sea salt
½ cup brown rice syrup
½ cup olive oil
¾ cup warm spring or filtered water

FILLING
3 cups walnuts, pan-toasted (see Note, page 46) and minced
2 cups raisins
1 teaspoon ground cinnamon
¼ cup olive oil
¼ cup brown rice syrup

GLAZE
1½ cups brown rice syrup
3 tablespoons olive oil

Prepare dough: Place flour, salt, rice syrup and oil in a food processor or heavy-duty electric mixer bowl and mix until blended. While mixer or processor is running, add the warm water to flour mixture. Blend only until the particles begin to cling together. Gather dough into a ball, wrap in waxed paper and set aside to rest for 1 hour at room temperature.

Prepare filling: Process nuts, raisins and cinnamon in a food processor until a fine meal forms. Do not overprocess into flour. Scrape mixture into a bowl. In a saucepan, heat oil and rice syrup until it foams and stir immediately into raisin and nut mixture. Divide the filling into 3 separate bowls and set aside.

To assemble, divide dough into thirds. On a floured surface, roll out 1 portion at a time into a long rectangle, about 30 × 5 inches. Trim strips evenly so the rectangles match.

Preheat oven to 350F (175C). Line a large baking sheet with parchment paper and set aside. Spoon filling from each of the 3 bowls lengthwise over one half of each strip. Fold the other half of the dough over the filling, making 3 filled 30-inch-long strips.

Starting at the end of one strip, roll up tightly into a pinwheel, filling side up. Over-lapping slightly at the end, attach the next strip and continue to roll. Repeat with the last strip. Turn the assembled torte, filling side up, onto the prepared baking sheet. Tie a string midway around the diameter of the torte.

Prepare the glaze: Heat ingredients over high heat until they foam. Immediately brush the sides of the torte with glaze, spooning the remaining glaze over the top. Bake about 1 hour, until golden brown.

When cooled, remove the string from the torte and replace it with a holiday ribbon. Serve sliced in thin wedges with strong espresso or tea for a festive Christmas morning treat.

Cranberry-Pear Relish

A different approach to traditional cranberry relish, this dish combines the natural tartness of cranberries with the delicate sweet taste of ripe autumn pears.

MAKES ABOUT 5 SERVINGS

1 cup brown rice syrup
3 cups fresh cranberries, sorted and rinsed
2 ripe pears, peeled (optional) and cut into
    cubes
½ teaspoon grated nutmeg
½ teaspoon ground allspice
Pinch sea salt
2 teaspoons grated lemon zest

Heat rice syrup in a large saucepan over medium heat until foamy. Add cranberries, pears, spices and salt. Return to a boil and stir in 1 teaspoon lemon zest. Reduce heat and simmer until the cranberries pop, 25 to 30 minutes. Transfer to a serving bowl and chill. Before serving, garnish with remaining lemon zest.

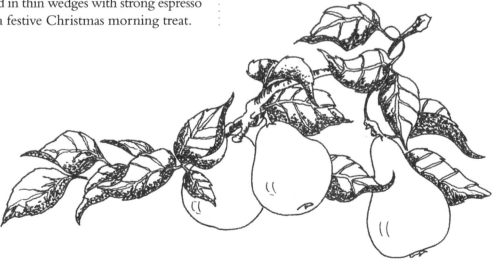

No-Meat Mincemeat Pie

I never liked mincemeat pie when I was a kid, but everyone raved about my mother's version at our Thanksgiving feasts. For Robert's and my first holiday season together, I asked him what pie he'd like and he voted for mincemeat. Well, as anyone who has been in love, and especially in new love, can tell you, you bend over backwards to impress and accommodate. Referring to my mother's recipe and praying for inspiration, I came up with a recipe that still wows Robert to this very day.

MAKES 6 TO 8 SERVINGS

1 cup raisins
1 cup dried apricots
3 cups unfiltered, unsweetened apple juice
Pinch sea salt
4 cups chopped tart apples
2 tablespoons red miso
½ teaspoon ground allspice
2 tablespoons kuzu or arrowroot, dissolved in
    ¼ cup cold water or juice
2 tablespoons grated orange zest
1 tablespoon grated lemon zest
2 tablespoons fresh orange juice
½ cup walnuts, pan-toasted (see Note, page
    46) and broken into small pieces
1 recipe Pastry Dough (page 304)

Soak the raisins and apricots together in the apple juice for 6 to 8 hours. In an uncovered pot, combine the soaked fruit, the soaking juice, salt and apples and cook over medium heat, stirring occasionally, 1 hour. Remove about 2 tablespoons of hot juice and use to dissolve the miso. Stir mixture into the pot and simmer 15 minutes. Stir in allspice, then stir in dissolved kuzu and cook, stirring, until the mixture thickens, 3 to 4 minutes. Stir in the orange and lemon zests, orange juice and walnuts. Set aside to cool as you prepare the pie crust.

Preheat oven to 400F (205C). Prepare pie dough. Roll out thinly between 2 sheets of waxed paper into a 10-inch circle. Lay over a 9-inch pie pan, pressing it into the pan without stretching the dough. Trim the excess dough around the edges, leaving an even ½-inch overhang. Turn the excess dough up toward the edge of the pie and crimp or flute to form a decorative edge. Prick crust with a fork. Bake the pie shell 10 minutes. This prevents a soggy crust when serving the finished pie.

Reduce oven temperature to 350F (175C). Pour filling into pie shell. Bake 30 to 40 minutes, until filling is set.

■ **VARIATION** When making this pie, I like to prepare it as a single-crust pie, but you may also double the pastry recipe and make a lattice top. This recipe also makes really beautiful miniature tartlets.

Would You Believe? Tiramisu

Anyone who has indulged in the real version of this dessert won't be fooled for a minute by this one. A decadent dessert in its own right, it is a spinoff of the original and is so delicious, you will use it to create a new tradition of your own.

Mirin lends the amasake a slight resemblance to mascarpone, the soft, sweet cheese normally associated with tiramisu. Cooking mirin removes just about all the alcohol, leaving you with only its essence.

MAKES 10 TO 12 SERVINGS

2 recipes Surefire Basic White Cake (page 302)
2 cups almond-flavored amasake
2 to 3 tablespoons mirin
3 tablespoons kuzu or arrowroot dissolved in
    ¼ cup cold water
1 cup grain coffee, brewed and cooled
1 cup slivered almonds, pan-toasted (see
    Note, page 55)
¼ cup nondairy, grain-sweetened chocolate
    chips

Bake cake in 2 round cake pans as directed and allow to cool completely before continuing the recipe.

Prepare filling: Mix together amasake and mirin in a saucepan over medium heat and warm mixture thoroughly. Stir in dissolved kuzu and cook, stirring, until thick and creamy, 3 to 4 minutes. Set amasake custard aside to cool. Start assembling tiramisu when the amasake custard has just begun to set.

To assemble: Slice cakes in half horizontally to make 4 layers. To make even layers, insert a serrated knife and turn cake while slicing. Place a cake layer on a serving platter. Spoon grain coffee lightly over it—do not saturate. Top with a layer of amasake custard and sprinkle with almonds. Add the next cake layer and repeat process. The top layer of the cake should be covered with amasake and almonds. If you have enough custard, you may spread it around the sides of the tiramisu as well and then press almonds into the custard as decoration. Decorate the top of the tiramisu with chocolate chips and allow to stand 30 minutes or chill 15 minutes before slicing.

Fresh Fruit Kanten

This basic dessert is a tried-and-true winner. Light and refreshing, it can be simple or profoundly elegant. It's up to you and your imagination.

MAKES 6 TO 8 SERVINGS

3 cups unfiltered, unsweetened apple juice or
    other fruit juice
Pinch sea salt
3 tablespoons agar-agar flakes
1 to 2 cups bite-size pieces seasonal fruit

Combine juice, salt and agar-agar in a saucepan and bring to a boil over low heat. If you boil too quickly, the agar will simply sink to the bottom of the pan and not dissolve. Simmer 10 to 15 minutes, stirring occasionally, until agar-agar completely disappears.

Arrange fruit in individual dessert cups or on the bottom of a 13 × 9-inch dish. Pour juice mixture gently over fruit. It should set up in about 1½ hours, but if you would like to speed up the process, allow to stand 30 minutes at room temperature and then refrigerate at least 30 minutes or until firmly set.

- **VARIATION** A different twist on basic kanten is to simply whip it into a mousse when it has completely set up. This adds a bit of elegance and style to your presentation. Serve garnished with fresh berries and mint leaves.

- **NOTE** If you are using softer fruits, like berries, cherries, melon or peaches, you do not need to cook the fruit in the kanten mixture; if using firm fruit, like apples or pears, you will need to cook them with the agar-agar and juice mixture, so that they soften.

Pear-Almond Clafouti

Clafouti is a traditional French dessert. This version is light and elegant, a joy to create and, of course, eat!

MAKES 6 TO 8 SERVINGS

2 cups whole wheat pastry flour
2½ teaspoons baking powder
¼ teaspoon sea salt
1½ cups almonds, ground into a fine meal
½ cup brown rice syrup
½ cup spring or filtered water
1 teaspoon pure vanilla extract
2 teaspoons fresh orange juice
2 firm pears, cored and thinly sliced
**   lengthwise**

GLAZE
⅔ cup red wine
⅓ cup brown rice syrup
4 tablespoons arrowroot, dissolved in 4
**   tablespoons cold water**

Preheat oven to 375F (190C). Lightly oil and flour a 9-inch round cake or quiche pan and set aside.

Whisk flour, baking powder and salt in a bowl. Mix in almond meal and gently stir in rice syrup, water, vanilla and orange juice, mixing well. Pour batter evenly into prepared pan.

Arrange pears on top of the batter in a decorative spiral pattern. Bake 35 to 40 minutes, until a wooden pick inserted in the cake's center comes out clean and cake springs back to the touch.

Prepare glaze: Heat wine and rice syrup in a saucepan over medium heat until foamy. Stir in dissolved arrowroot and cook, stirring, until the glaze thickens, about 5 minutes. Carefully turn the clafouti out of the pan and brush with glaze while still warm.

Watermelon Freeze

What would summer be without watermelon? Try this refreshing dessert to beat the heat.

MAKES 12 TO 18 SERVINGS

4 cups seeded and cubed watermelon
2 cups cubed cantaloupe
Pinch sea salt
3 fresh mint leaves or 1 mint tea bag
1 cup spring or filtered water
Juice of 1 fresh lemon
Lemon Sauce (opposite) (optional), chilled

Puree the melons in a food processor until smooth. Place in a saucepan with the salt and simmer 15 minutes.

Meanwhile, in another saucepan simmer the mint leaves or tea bag in the water about 3 minutes. Strain and add this infusion to the cooked melons. Turn off the heat and stir in the lemon juice.

Line a muffin pan/s with paper liners, pour

melon puree into each one and freeze. When beginning to firm up, you may insert flat wooden sticks into each treat. Freeze until completely hard or the papers will not peel easily away. Remove papers before serving. I like to serve these frozen treats on a pool of the optional Lemon Sauce.

Light Fruit Crepes

There is nothing more elegant than ending a meal with a light and airy fruit-filled crepe. Mastering the art of crepe making takes a bit of practice, but it is a snap once you've got it down.

MAKES ABOUT 12 CREPES

LEMON SAUCE

1 cup spring or filtered water

¼ cup brown rice syrup

2 teaspoons kuzu or arrowroot, dissolved in ¼ cup cold water

Juice of 2 lemons

CREPES

1½ cups whole wheat pastry flour

½ cup corn flour (not cornmeal)

Pinch sea salt

½ to ¾ cup unfiltered, unsweetened apple juice or water

Avocado or olive oil

CHERRY FILLING

2 cups fresh tart cherries, pitted

Pinch sea salt

½ cup brown rice syrup

2 tablespoons kuzu or arrowroot, dissolved in ¼ cup cold water

Mint leaves or fresh berries, for decoration

Make sauce: Heat water and rice syrup in a small saucepan over medium heat. Stir in dissolved kuzu and cook, stirring, until mixture thickens and clears, 3 to 4 minutes. Turn off the heat and stir in the lemon juice. Cover and chill completely before using.

Make crepes: Dry-roast the flours in a hot, dry skillet over medium heat, stirring constantly so that they do not scorch, until fragrant, about 3 minutes. Whisk together flours and salt in a bowl. Slowly add juice and stir into a thin batter, slightly thinner than pancake batter, but not watery. Set the batter aside at least 1 hour before proceeding.

Heat a small cast-iron skillet or crepe pan over medium heat. Brush lightly with oil, completely covering the bottom and sides. Test the readiness of the pan by dropping a tiny bit of batter in the skillet. If it sizzles and bubbles, the pan is hot enough.

With a small ladle, spoon just enough (about ¼ cup) batter to thinly cover the bottom of the pan, lifting and tilting the pan to evenly distribute the batter over the surface. Cook over medium heat until tiny pin-size bubbles begin to form on the crepe's surface. Remove by simply turning the pan over a towel and letting the crepe drop out. Repeat with remaining batter. Cover crepes and set aside.

Make filling: Combine cherries, salt and rice syrup in a saucepan over medium heat and bring to a boil. Reduce heat and simmer until cherries are just tender. Stir in dissolved kuzu and cook, stirring, until a thick sauce forms around the cherries, 3 to 4 minutes. Allow to cool almost completely.

To serve: Spoon a small amount of filling in the center of each crepe and roll to enclose filling. Whisk the sauce to loosen it up and pool it on small dessert plates. Top sauce with filled crepes. Decorate each plate with fresh mint leaves.

Glazed Apples

This simple dessert of crisp, juicy apples is just delightful after a hearty autumn or winter meal.

MAKES 4 SERVINGS

4 ripe apples
1 cup unfiltered, unsweetened apple juice
Pinch sea salt
1 tablespoon kuzu or arrowroot, dissolved in
3 tablespoons cold water
½ teaspoon fresh ginger juice (see Note, page
164)
Slivered almonds, pan-toasted (see Note,
page 55), for decoration (optional)

Preheat oven to 350F (175C). Cut the apples in half and remove the cores carefully. Lay apple halves in a shallow baking dish, cut sides up, and sprinkle with sea salt. Cover and bake 15 minutes, until tender.

Meanwhile, heat the apple juice over low heat until hot. Stir in dissolved kuzu and cook, stirring, until mixture thickens and clears, 3 to 4 minutes. Add ginger juice and pour over the cooked apples. Increase oven heat to 400F (205C). Return apples to the oven, uncovered, for 15 minutes to set glaze. Serve warm, sprinkled with almonds (if using).

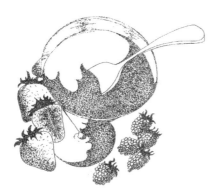

Blueberry Pie

Nothing says summer quite like a pie laden with succulent sweet berries. Serve this pie any time to delight friends, family and, of course, yourself!

MAKES 6 TO 8 SERVINGS

2 recipes Pastry Dough (page 304)
2 pints blueberries, sorted and rinsed
½ cup plus 3 tablespoons brown rice syrup
3 tablespoons kuzu or arrowroot, dissolved in
¼ cup cold water
1 teaspoon fresh lemon juice
1 teaspoon grated lemon zest

Prepare dough and separate into 2 pieces. Roll out thinly between waxed or parchment paper and lay 1 crust over a pie plate. Press into position, without stretching the dough, trimming the excess flush with sides of the pan. Keep other piece of dough wrapped in waxed paper until ready to use.

Preheat oven to 400F (205C). Combine berries and ½ cup rice syrup in a medium saucepan and heat over low heat until hot. Stir in dissolved kuzu and cook, stirring, until the mixture thickens, about 3 minutes. Remove from heat and stir in lemon juice and zest. Spoon into pie shell, filling completely.

Moisten the edge of the bottom crust with water. Lay the other crust over top. Trim excess dough, leaving about ½-inch overhang. Fold the overhang under the rim of the bottom crust and, by pinching dough between your thumb and forefinger, pushing the dough between your fingers with the other forefinger, flute the edge of the crust. Next, with a sharp knife, cut a 4-inch X shape in the center of the top crust. Fold back the points of the X to make a square opening in the center of the pie.

Heat the remaining 3 tablespoons rice syrup in a small saucepan over high heat until it foams. Remove from heat and quickly drizzle over the top of the pie. Bake 40 minutes, until the filling is bubbly and the crust is golden. Cool pie completely before slicing.

Cran-Apple Crumb Tart

The soft pastry dough for this sweet and tangy tart is not rolled but simply pressed into the pan. Rice or maple syrup granules are a great natural alternative to sugar and achieve the same delicious crumb topping that is so traditional in a pastry like this.

MAKES 8 TO 10 SERVINGS

DOUGH
½ cup avocado or olive oil
¼ cup brown rice syrup
1 cup whole wheat pastry flour
⅔ cup semolina flour
Pinch of sea salt

FILLING
1½ pounds Granny Smith apples
1 cup fresh cranberries, sorted and rinsed
2½ tablespoons arrowroot
½ teaspoon ground cinnamon
⅔ cup brown rice syrup

CRUMB TOPPING
1 cup rolled oats
1 cup walnuts, broken into small pieces
¾ cup whole wheat pastry flour
Pinch sea salt
⅔ cup maple syrup granules
6 tablespoons avocado or olive oil

Lightly oil an 11-inch fluted tart pan with a removable bottom and set aside.

Prepare dough: Whisk together the oil and rice syrup. Combine the flours and salt in a bowl and slowly add the liquid, mixing until the dough just comes together. Turn it out onto a lightly floured surface and knead three or four times, just enough to form a soft, smooth ball. Pat the dough gently into a thick round. Press the dough evenly into the sides and bottom of the pan and prick all over the surface with a fork. Refrigerate 1 hour.

Preheat oven to 375F (190C). Place the chilled tart shell on a baking sheet and bake, in center of oven, 10 to 15 minutes, until just beginning to color. Set aside to cool.

Prepare filling: Peel, quarter and core apples and then cut lengthwise into thin slices. Toss the apples and cranberries with arrowroot and cinnamon. Mound the filling into the tart shell and drizzle with the rice syrup.

Prepare topping: Combine oats, walnuts, flour, salt and maple granules in a food processor. Pulse to form a coarse meal. Combine mixture and oil in a bowl and crumble the mixture with your fingers, forming a coarse, sandy texture. Spread topping on top of the apples, covering them completely.

Bake tart about 40 minutes, until the top is golden, the filling is bubbly and the apples are tender when pierced. Cool slightly before serving warm.

■ **NOTE** If the topping is browning too quickly, cover the tart with foil during the last 20 minutes of the baking time.

Chocolate-Hazelnut Torte

This sinful torte is so rich that the tiniest sliver will satisfy your wildest chocolate cravings. Besides, can you think of a better combination than chocolate, creamy custard and hazelnuts? Personally, I can't. Enjoy the indulgence! Go ahead, it's still low-fat. Hard to believe: decadence without guilt.

MAKES 8 SERVINGS

PASTRY DOUGH
½ cup avocado or olive oil
¼ cup brown rice syrup
2 tablespoons almond butter
1 cup whole wheat pastry flour
¼ cup unsweetened cocoa powder, preferably organic and fair trade
Pinch sea salt

CUSTARD
½ cup almond-flavored amasake
2 tablespoons kuzu or arrowroot, dissolved in ¼ cup cold water
½ cup brown rice syrup
1 teaspoon pure vanilla extract

CHOCOLATE CREAM
½ to ⅔ cup nondairy, malt-sweetened chocolate chips
1 teaspoon grain coffee, dissolved in 2 tablespoons cold water
½ cup almond-flavored amasake

1 cup hazelnuts, lightly pan-toasted (see Note, page 46) and minced

Prepare pastry: Beat together oil, rice syrup and almond butter in a bowl. Whisk together flour, cocoa powder and salt and mix into oil mixture. Mix until dough comes together. Gather dough into a ball and flatten it slightly. Wrap in waxed paper and chill for 1 hour.

Preheat oven to 325F (165C). Lightly oil an 8-inch tart pan. Roll out chilled dough into a thick round on a lightly floured surface or between sheets of waxed paper. Transfer the pastry to prepared tart pan, gently pressing the dough into the sides and bottom to create an even crust about ⅛ inch thick. Prick all over with a fork and freeze 10 minutes.

Bake pastry shell 12 to 15 minutes. The crust will still feel soft upon removal from the oven; it will set up as it cools. Set aside to cool.

Prepare custard: Heat the amasake in a saucepan over low heat until hot. Stir in dissolved kuzu and cook, stirring, until mixture thickens, about 3 minutes. In a separate saucepan, heat the rice syrup and vanilla until they foam. Immediately stir into the custard. Set aside to cool.

Prepare chocolate cream: Place the chocolate pieces in a heat-resistant bowl and stir in the grain coffee. In a small saucepan, bring the amasake to a boil and pour it over the chocolate. Whisk until the chocolate melts and the mixture is smooth.

To assemble: Reserve a small handful of hazelnuts for decoration. Pour custard into the tart shell and spread evenly. Sprinkle remaining hazelnuts over custard. Carefully pour chocolate cream on top and spread evenly over custard. Arrange reserved hazelnuts around the edge of the tart to form a decorative edge. Chill until firm, about 1 hour.

Tangy Chocolate Chip Cookies

As a former chocolate addict, I can assure you that, in my past, I mastered just about every chocolate recipe that I could get my hands on. This variation on the classic cookie has stayed with me, changing and evolving as much as my eating habits.

MAKES ABOUT 3 DOZEN

3½ cups whole wheat pastry flour
2 teaspoons baking powder
Pinch of sea salt
1 cup brown rice syrup
⅓ cup fresh orange juice
¼ cup avocado oil
1 teaspoon pure vanilla extract
2 teaspoons grated orange zest
½ cup coarsely diced pecans
1 cup grain-sweetened, nondairy chocolate chips

Preheat oven to 350F (175C). Line 2 baking sheets with parchment paper and set aside.

Mix together flour, baking powder and salt in a bowl. Whisk together rice syrup, orange juice, oil, vanilla and orange zest until creamy and stir into dry ingredients. Fold in nuts and chocolate chips.

Drop cookie dough by heaping teaspoonfuls about 2 inches apart onto prepared baking sheets. Bake 18 to 20 minutes, until cookies are golden and firm. Remove to a cooling rack.

Crispy Chewies

Remember crisp rice cereal treats? Well, they got nothin' on these babies!

MAKES ABOUT 1 DOZEN

1 cup brown rice syrup
½ cup almond butter
½ cup grain-sweetened, nondairy chocolate chips
3 cups crispy brown rice cereal

In a large saucepan, heat rice syrup and almond butter over low heat until creamy. Stir in chocolate chips until they melt. Remove from heat and stir in rice cereal until coated. Press into a shallow, square casserole. Allow to set until firm. Cut into squares and serve.

- **VARIATIONS** Any nut butter is fabulous in this treat: peanut butter, cashew or hazelnut butter—yummy. Omit chocolate and create a decadent nutty-flavored rice treat.

Raspberry Poppers

These light, flaky miniature cookies are the perfect size and the perfect taste to do justice to their name. Once you start popping these bite-size beauties, you'll be hooked.

MAKES ABOUT 3 DOZEN

2½ cups whole wheat pastry flour
⅛ teaspoon sea salt
2 teaspoons baking powder
¼ cup vegetarian buttery spread (like Earth Balance), chilled
2 tablespoons brown rice syrup
⅔ cup soy or rice milk
1 teaspoon pure vanilla extract
About ¾ cup unsweetened or fruit-sweetened raspberry jam

GLAZE
½ cup brown rice syrup
1 teaspoon unsweetened or fruit-sweetened raspberry jam

Combine flour, salt, baking powder, the spread and rice syrup in a food processor. Pulse until mixture resembles coarse cornmeal; do not overmix. Add milk and vanilla and pulse again until dough gathers into a ball. Again, do not overmix, just pulse until the dough gathers.

Preheat oven to 350F (175C). Line a baking sheet with parchment paper and set aside. Place a sheet of waxed paper on a dry work surface. Flour paper lightly. Flatten dough into a rectangular shape. Dust with flour and top with another sheet of waxed paper. Roll dough into a rectangle, about ⅛ inch thick. Remove the top sheet of paper.

With a sharp knife, cut the rectangle in half, lengthwise. Spread both halves with a thin layer of jam. Roll each piece, jelly-roll style, into a long cylinder. Cut into ½-inch rounds and place, cut side up, on prepared baking sheet. Bake 20 to 22 minutes, until puffy and the edges are a bit golden.

Make glaze: Heat rice syrup and jam in a small saucepan over medium heat until they foam. Quickly spoon over warm cookies. Allow to stand until glaze sets a bit before serving.

Blueberry Coffee Cake

I love brunch, especially in the summer because of the abundance of fruit at hand and the fact that we can eat in the garden. Tartlets, strudels, kantens and custards laden with fresh fruit are a tasty addition to any brunch table. But my favorite, really, is coffee cake. And this one, well . . .

MAKES 1 CAKE, 6 TO 8 SERVINGS

1 recipe Surefire Basic White Cake (page 302)
1½ cups fresh blueberries, sorted, rinsed and well-drained

TOPPING
5 tablespoons maple syrup granules
3 tablespoons walnuts, minced
Generous pinch ground cinnamon
2 to 3 tablespoons avocado oil

Preheat oven to 375F (190C). Oil and flour an 8-inch round cake pan and set aside. Prepare cake batter and fold in the blueberries. Take care not to overmix, or cake will become tough. Spoon batter evenly into prepared pan.

Prepare topping: Combine maple syrup granules, walnuts, cinnamon and oil in a small bowl to create a crumbly texture. Sprinkle topping over cake. Bake 35 to 40 minutes, until the top is golden and a wooden pick comes out clean when inserted in the center of the cake. Allow to cool in pan 10 minutes before turning out. Serve warm.

Pear-Spice Coffee Cake

Remember upside-down cakes? In my version, juicy pears are covered with a spicy gingerbread cake. This beautiful dessert will win you raves, and no one has to know how easy it is to make. We love it on crisp, autumn Sunday mornings with hot tea and the newspaper.

MAKES 1 CAKE, 6 TO 8 SERVINGS

1 tablespoon avocado oil
3 tablespoons maple syrup granules
3 firm but ripe Bosc pears
1 tablespoon fresh lemon juice
1½ cups whole wheat pastry flour
Pinch sea salt
1 teaspoon baking powder
2 teaspoons ground cinnamon
½ teaspoon *each* **nutmeg, ginger and allspice**
½ cup brown rice syrup
¼ cup barley malt
½ cup unsweetened applesauce

Place oven rack in the lowest position and preheat oven to 375F (190C). Oil and flour an 8-inch square baking dish.

Drizzle the oil over the bottom of the prepared baking dish and sprinkle with maple syrup granules. Peel, halve and core the pears. Cut a pear half lengthwise, into ⅛-inch-thick slices, leaving the slices attached at the top half of the pears. Keeping the slices together, slide a spatula underneath, invert the pear half onto your hand and press lightly to fan the slices. Place it, cut side up, in the maple syrup mixture in the baking dish. Repeat with the other

pear halves, filling the bottom of the dish. Drizzle with lemon juice. Bake, uncovered, 15 minutes.

Meanwhile, whisk together flour, salt, baking powder and spices in a bowl. Whisk together the rice syrup, barley malt and applesauce. Stir applesauce mixture into flour mixture until just blended. Spoon batter carefully over baked pears, covering them evenly.

Bake 30 to 35 minutes, until a wooden pick inserted in center of cake comes out clean. With a sharp knife, loosen edges of cake from pan. Place a serving platter over pan and invert cake onto platter. Remove any pear slices that adhere to the cake pan and replace them on top of the cake. Allow to cool about 10 minutes before slicing. This cake is really great served warm.

Baked Apples with Creamy Chestnut Filling

This unique twist on a traditional dessert is especially good served with the warm, spicy cooking juices spooned over the top just before serving.

MAKES 6 TO 8 SERVINGS

1 pound fresh chestnuts
¼ cup amasake
⅓ cup unfiltered, unsweetened apple juice
6 tablespoons brown rice syrup
Generous pinch *each* **cinnamon and nutmeg**
⅓ cup currants
6 to 8 Granny Smith apples
Juice of 1 lemon
⅓ cup mirin
1 cinnamon stick

Preheat oven to 350F (175C). Lightly oil a 13 × 9-inch baking dish and set aside.

Make a slit in the flat side of each chestnut. Cook in boiling water over high heat 15 minutes. Drain the chestnuts and run under cool water. Using a sharp knife, peel off the flat top and scoop out the meat.

In a food processor, puree peeled chestnuts, amasake, apple juice, 4 tablespoons of the rice syrup, cinnamon and nutmeg. Fold in currants. Core the apples and, using a spoon, scoop out the insides, leaving a ½-inch-thick shell to stuff. Mince apple pulp and mix into chestnut mixture along with lemon juice. Fill apple shells with chestnut mixture and arrange in prepared baking dish. Pour mirin and remaining rice syrup over apples. Place cinnamon stick in the baking dish.

Bake uncovered 30 to 40 minutes, basting occasionally with the cooking juices, until apples are tender. Place apples on a serving platter. Spoon any remaining cooking juices over apples. Serve warm.

■ **VARIATION** Substitute 4 ounces dried chestnuts for fresh chestnuts. Soak dried chestnuts 6 to 8 hours and pressure-cook in a small amount of water 25 minutes.

Pear Galette

This free-form pie has a delicate crust. Be sure to bring it to the table whole, as it will crumble when sliced. Delicious made with any fruit, it is just the best with the delicate sweetness of ripe pears.

MAKES 6 TO 8 SERVINGS

CRUST
1½ cups whole wheat pastry flour
⅛ teaspoon sea salt

¼ cup vegetarian buttery spread (such as Earth Balance), chilled
2 tablespoons brown rice syrup
¼ cup cold water

PEAR FILLING
⅓ cup maple syrup granules
¼ cup arrowroot
Pinch ground cloves
6 medium ripe Bosc pears

Prepare dough: Combine flour and salt in a bowl. Stir in the spread and rice syrup until mixture resembles coarse cornmeal. Slowly add water, mixing just until dough combines. Do not gather into a ball. Press two-thirds of the mixture into a thick round on waxed or parchment paper and cover with another sheet. Repeat with remaining dough. Roll the larger portion into an 11-inch circle and freeze 5 minutes (to release waxed paper easily).

Preheat oven to 375F (190C). Line baking sheet or pizza pan with parchment paper.

Make filling: Combine maple syrup granules, arrowroot and cloves in a small bowl. Peel, halve and core the pears, then cut into 1-inch wedges. Remove 1 sheet waxed paper, turn dough out onto prepared pan and remove top sheet of paper. Sprinkle dough with one-third of the maple mixture and arrange half the pear wedges over the dough, leaving a 2-inch border around the edge. Sprinkle pears with some of the maple mixture. Layer remaining pears on top and sprinkle with the remaining maple mixture. Roll out remaining dough into a 10-inch round. Freeze 5 minutes and remove 1 sheet of waxed paper. Place dough over pears and remove remaining paper. Pull up edges of bottom dough to meet the top layer. Pinch edges to seal. Cut 6 slits in the top of the galette to allow steam to escape.

Bake 45 minutes or until lightly browned. Allow to cool 20 minutes before slicing.

■ **VARIATION** This galette is even more delicious served with warm amasake and ginger juice (see Note, page 164) spooned over the top.

Apple Focaccia

A dessert pizza that I like to make during the holiday for brunches or other get-togethers when I want a lovely ending to a meal with a minimum of fuss.

MAKES 6 SERVINGS

½ recipe Basic Sourdough Bread (page 282)
1 apple, cored and pureed in a food processor
Pinch ground cinnamon
2 teaspoons brown rice syrup
⅓ cup raisins

FILLING
4 apples, cored and cut into paper-thin slices
Juice of 1 lemon
Pinch *each* ground nutmeg, cinnamon and
  ginger
⅓ cup brown rice syrup
Dash of pure vanilla extract
¼ cup barley malt
1 tablespoon kuzu or arrowroot, dissolved in
  small amount of cold water

GLAZE
2 tablespoons unsweetened apricot or
  raspberry jam
1 tablespoon brown rice syrup

Prepare dough, omitting ¼ cup of the water. Knead in apple puree, cinnamon, rice syrup and

raisins. Knead 10 minutes. Place in a lightly oiled bowl and allow to rise as directed in recipe.

When the dough is ready, preheat oven to 400F (205C). Lightly oil a 13 × 9-inch baking pan. Turn dough onto a floured work surface and knead 1 to 2 minutes. Press dough into prepared pan. Cover with a damp kitchen towel and allow to rise at room temperature while preparing the filling.

Make filling: Toss apple slices in lemon juice to prevent discoloration. Stir in remaining filling ingredients and mix well. Spread filling evenly over surface of dough.

Bake 20 minutes. Reduce oven temperature to 375F (190C) and bake another 20 minutes, until apples are browned and crust is golden.

Make glaze: Heat jam and rice syrup in a small saucepan over high heat until foamy. Immediately drizzle over warm focaccia. Cool slightly before serving.

Apple Pie

Does it get homier or cozier than apple pie? The ultimate comfort food, deliciously made with more healthful ingredients just makes more to love.

MAKES 1 PIE, 6 TO 8 SERVINGS

2 recipes Pastry Dough (page 304)

FILLING
9 tablespoons vegetarian buttery spread (like
  Earth Balance)
3 teaspoons pure vanilla extract
1 cup brown rice syrup
Sea salt
¼ teaspoon ground cinnamon
13 or 14 Granny Smith or Gala apples, peeled,
  cored and thinly sliced into half-moons

Lightly oil a 9-inch deep dish pie plate. Divide pastry dough into 2 pieces, one a little larger than the other. Roll each one between waxed or parchment paper into a thin round, the smaller one about 11 inches in diameter and larger one about 12 inches in diameter. Press pastry into pie plate, using your knuckles to conform the dough to the dish, but do not stretch the dough too much. Let excess hang over the rim. Prick several times with a fork and set aside.

Preheat the oven to 375F (190C).

Make the filling: You will be sautéing apples in 3 batches. Place 3 tablespoons of the spread, 1 teaspoon of the vanilla, ⅓ cup of the rice syrup, a pinch of salt and one-third of cinnamon in a skillet over medium heat. Add one-third of the apples and sauté until the apples wilt and the edges begin to brown, about 7 minutes. Transfer cooked apples to a baking sheet to cool and repeat sautéing process with remaining apples and seasonings. Cool to room temperature.

Spoon cooled apples into pastry shell, mounding them in the center. Lay the remaining pastry over the apples. Using a sharp knife, trim the excess pastry from the rim and gently pinch together the edges of the pastry to seal the crust. Using your thumb and forefinger, crimp the edge to create a decorative crust.

Make 3 to 4 slits in top of pastry to allow steam to escape. Bake 15 minutes, reduce oven heat to 350F (175C) and bake 40 to 45 minutes more. Crust should be golden and filling bubbling. Remove from oven and allow to cool about 15 minutes before slicing.

Orange-Scented Chocolate Cupcakes

Who doesn't love cupcakes? They're small enough to indulge in a whole one; sweet and decadent enough to feel like a real treat and so yummy and comforting that they are nature's perfect food!

MAKES 12 CUPCAKES

1½ **cups whole wheat pastry flour**
½ **cup semolina flour**
½ **cup unsweetened cocoa powder, preferably organic and fair trade**
2 **teaspoons baking powder**
Generous pinch sea salt
½ **cup avocado oil**
1 **cup brown rice syrup**
¾ **cup soy or rice milk**
1 **teaspoon brown rice vinegar**
2 **ounces coarsely chopped nondairy, grain-sweetened chocolate chips**
2 **teaspoons grated orange zest**

CHOCOLATE FROSTING
1 **cup nondairy, grain-sweetened chocolate chips**
Scant ¼ **cup soy or rice milk**
2 **teaspoons brown rice syrup**

Grated orange zest, for decoration

Preheat oven to 350F (175C) and line a 12-cup muffin pan with paper liners.

Whisk together flours, cocoa powder, baking powder and sea salt. Whisk together oil, rice syrup, milk and vinegar until smooth. Mix liquid ingredients into dry ingredients to make a smooth batter. Fold in chocolate and orange zest, spoon evenly into paper liners and bake 20 to 25 minutes, until the tops of the cupcakes spring back to the touch.

Remove from oven and allow to cool enough to handle the cupcakes. Remove from the pan and cool completely on a wire rack.

Make the frosting while the cupcakes cool: Place chocolate in heat-resistant bowl. Bring milk and rice syrup to a rolling boil and pour over chocolate. Whisk until thick and smooth. Cover loosely and set aside for 30 to 40 minutes to set frosting. Whisk to loosen frosting and spread over the top of each cupcake, decorating with a sprinkle of orange zest.

Peanut Butter Cups

It doesn't get better than peanut butter cups . . . and here's a version with no junk, no simple refined sugar, no chemicals, no saturated fat . . . just all the yummy flavor we have come to love.

MAKES ABOUT 24 PEANUT BUTTER CUPS

2 cups nondairy, grain-sweetened chocolate chips
1½ cups creamy, unsweetened peanut butter
3 to 4 tablespoons brown rice syrup or honey
Pinch sea salt

Lightly oil a standard mini muffin pan or line the cups with foil or paper liners.

Melt chocolate in a double boiler or in a glass bowl over a pan of boiling water and stir until chocolate melts.

Fill each cup one-third full with melted chocolate. Place pan in freezer while preparing peanut butter filling.

Combine peanut butter, rice syrup and salt in a saucepan and cook over low heat until the mixture is soft and smooth.

Spoon peanut butter on top of chocolate in

each cup, filling nearly to the tops. Top each cup with chocolate, filling cups full. Place tray in the freezer until set.

Chocolate Decadence Brownies

Decadent, richly chocolate and laced through with nuts. Who says dessert can't be fun *and* healthy?

MAKES 16 BROWNIES

1⅓ cups maple syrup granules
¾ cup unsweetened applesauce
2 tablespoons spring or filtered water
2 teaspoons pure vanilla extract
1 cup whole wheat pastry flour
⅓ cup semolina flour
¾ cup unsweetened cocoa powder, preferably organic and fair trade
½ teaspoon baking powder
Generous pinch sea salt
Plain or vanilla soymilk
1 cup nondairy, grain-sweetened chocolate chips
⅔ cup macadamia nuts, coarsely chopped

CHOCOLATE GLAZE
¼ cup plain or vanilla soymilk
1 teaspoon brown rice syrup or honey
⅔ cup nondairy, grain sweetened chocolate chips, plus ⅓ cup coarsely chopped, for decoration

Preheat oven to 350F (175C), lightly oil an 8-inch-square baking pan and set aside.

Mix together maple syrup granules, applesauce and water in a medium bowl. Stir in vanilla. Fold in flours, cocoa, baking powder and salt, mixing just to combine ingredients.

Stir in soymilk to create a smooth, spoonable batter. Fold in chocolate chips and nuts until well-incorporated.

Bake for 40 minutes for chewy brownies and 45 to 50 minutes for more cakelike brownies. Either way, the brownies should be set when touched.

While the brownies bake, make the glaze: Place soymilk and rice syrup in a small saucepan and bring to a high boil. Pour over chocolate chips in a heatproof bowl and whisk to create a smooth, shiny glaze.

When the brownies have cooled, cut into 16 squares and place on a wire rack with a piece of parchment paper underneath. Spoon glaze over each brownie. Decorate with chopped chocolate chips.

18-Carat Gold Carrot Cake

A classic cake that usually seems healthier than it really is. It's loaded with butter, eggs, sugar and cream cheese; yet the dessert appears to be virtuous because there are carrots. Well, this version has all the virtue and the taste to put it back on the list of options.

Makes 1 (9-inch) cake, 6 to 8 servings

2 cups whole wheat pastry flour
2 teaspoons baking powder
1 teaspoon baking soda
¼ teaspoon sea salt
1¼ cups spring or filtered water
1¼ cups dates, coarsely chopped
1 cup raisins
1 teaspoon ground cinnamon
½ teaspoon ground ginger
Scant pinch ground cloves
Scant pinch ground nutmeg

½ cup shredded carrot
½ cup chopped walnuts
⅓ cup frozen orange juice concentrate, thawed

"CREAM CHEESE" FROSTING
½ cup vegetarian buttery spread (like Earth Balance), softened
¼ cup soymilk, rice milk or other nondairy milk of choice
3 cups maple syrup granules
1½ teaspoons pure vanilla extract

Pan-toasted walnut pieces (see Note, page 46)

Preheat oven to 375F (190C), lightly oil a 9-inch springform pan and set aside.

In a small bowl, sift together flour, baking powder, baking soda and salt. Set aside.

In a small saucepan, combine water, dates, raisins, cinnamon, ginger, cloves, and nutmeg. Bring to a boil, reduce heat and simmer for 5 minutes.

Place carrot in a large bowl, pour hot date mixture over the top and allow to cool completely. Add the walnuts and orange juice concentrate to the carrot mixture and blend well. Add the dry ingredients to the carrot mixture and stir well to combine. Pour the batter into the prepared springform pan and bake 45 minutes, until wooden pick inserted in center comes out clean.

While the cake bakes, make the frosting: Using a handheld or stand mixer, whip the spread, soymilk, half of the maple granules and vanilla in a bowl until smooth. Add remaining maple granules and whip until fluffy.

Allow cake to cool for 10 minutes before releasing pan and carefully transferring cake to a plate. Cool cake completely and frost. Decorate with walnuts.

Blueberry Muffins

Hands-down everyone's favorite, blueberry muffins, have morphed into all sorts of variations. I went back to the classic recipe my mother used (to all our delight) and built up from there to a healthier version of this breakfast classic.

MAKES ABOUT 12 MUFFINS

¼ cup vegetarian buttery spread (like Earth Balance)
½ cup unsweetened applesauce
⅔ cup brown rice syrup
½ cup unsweetened soymilk
1 teaspoon pure vanilla extract
1½ cups whole wheat pastry flour
½ cup semolina flour
Generous pinch sea salt
1 tablespoon baking powder
2 teaspoons grated lemon zest
2 cups fresh blueberries, sorted, rinsed and drained

Preheat oven to 350F (175C) and line a standard muffin pan with paper liners or lightly oil and flour.

Whisk together the spread, applesauce, rice syrup, soymilk and vanilla until blended. In a separate bowl, whisk together flours, salt and baking powder. Fold in applesauce mixture

to make a smooth batter. Fold in zest and berries. Divide batter evenly among the muffin cups, filling each about three-quarters full. Bake about 35 minutes, until centers of muffins spring back to the touch. Cool on a wire rack.

Watermelon Water Ice

Living in Philadelphia I discovered that the summer tradition of water ice was something of a phenomenon. *Granitas,* the Italian word for water ice, are simply fruit-flavored ices, different from sorbet; water ice is chunky, coarse and incredibly sweet. Here is my version of a summer favorite taught to me by Eric Lechasseur, an amazing whole food chef and cookbook author.

MAKES 4 OR 5 SERVINGS

24 ounces seeded watermelon
1 tablespoon fresh lemon juice
½ cup brown rice syrup
Lemon slices, for garnish

Place watermelon in a blender and puree until smooth. Add lemon juice and rice syrup and blend to combine. Transfer mixture to a large freezer container and freeze. Using a fork, stir the mixture every 30 minutes until it is frozen; it will take about 1½ hours. Once frozen, rake the water ice until it is loose and coarse, like rock salt. Keep frozen until ready to serve.

To serve, scoop into individual bowls and garnish with lemon slices.

■ **NOTE** You can vary the flavors of the water ice, by simply varying the fruit. Use 24 ounces of berries, cantaloupe, peaches, cherries . . . all will make lovely water ices.

Better Than Milk Shakes

When I was a kid, chocolate milk shakes were my favorite treat. We weren't allowed a lot of them. My mother was pretty ahead of her time about health and milk shakes, and well, they didn't make the cut. But when she let us indulge? It was a good day. These treats come s-o-o-o-o-o close to the real deal, and with no saturated fat and sugar they come with a lot less guilt!

MAKES 1 SHAKE

½ cup nondairy, grain-sweetened chocolate chips
½ cup unsweetened soymilk
3 tablespoons brown rice syrup
1 cup chocolate soy or rice nondairy frozen dessert
½ cup chocolate soymilk

Place chocolate chips in a heat-resistant bowl. Bring unsweetened soymilk and rice syrup to a boil and whisk into chocolate to create a smooth syrup. Cool to room temperature before proceeding.

Place all ingredients in a blender and beginning on low and gradually increasing to high, whip to creamy perfection.

■ NOTE Vary the flavor of the shakes. Replace chocolate with frozen strawberries, vanilla nondairy frozen dessert and soymilk. Make a vanilla shake by using vanilla nondairy frozen dessert and soymilk, 1 teaspoon pure vanilla extract and 1 cup ice cubes.

Lemony Cheesecake with Raspberry Glaze

I'm not a big fan of fake types of dishes, like tofu meat loaf and all that, but sometimes, you stumble on an idea that results in a recipe so richly flavored and creamy that you just have to share it.

MAKES 6 TO 8 SERVINGS

ALMOND-OAT CRUST
2 cups finely ground blanched almonds
1 cup finely ground rolled oats
Pinch sea salt
2 ounces nondairy, grain-sweetened chocolate chips, melted
2 tablespoons avocado oil (if needed)

FILLING
2 pounds firm tofu, coarsely crumbled
1 cup brown rice syrup
1 tablespoon pure vanilla extract
2 tablespoons cashew butter
Pinch sea salt
⅓ cup fresh lemon juice
Grated zest of 1 lemon
⅔ teaspoon turmeric
3 tablespoons arrowroot
3 tablespoons agar-agar flakes
¼ cup vanilla soymilk

GLAZE
⅔ cup Suzanne's Specialties Raspberry Rice Nectar or ⅓ cup brown rice syrup simmered 15 minutes with ⅓ cup fresh or frozen raspberries
Juice of ½ lemon
Pinch sea salt

Preheat oven to 350F (175C), lightly oil a 9-inch springform pan and set aside.

Make crust: Combine almonds, oats and salt in a mixing bowl with chocolate. Mix well to create a moist texture. If the crust mixture seems dry, add oil, by the teaspoon, until the texture is moist. It should gather and not stick to your fingers, but crumble easily.

Press crust evenly into prepared springform pan, covering the bottom and up the sides as much as your quantity will allow. Bake for 10 minutes, remove from oven and cool completely before filling. Leave oven on.

Make filling: Place all ingredients in a food processor and puree until smooth and creamy. Spoon ingredients into the cooled crust and bake about 1 hour, until the edges of the filling are set, even though the center will still be loose. Set aside until cooled to room temperature and then place the cake in the refrigerator and chill completely.

Before serving, make glaze: Place rice nectar, lemon juice and a pinch of salt in a small saucepan and cook over low heat for 10 minutes. Spoon over the cake and serve.

Tuscan Foccacia with Grapes

This seasonal delicacy is made in Tuscany when the grapes are in full ripeness, the autumn, and it is anticipated like a holiday. My mother (even though she was from southern Italy) made this every fall as a way to stay connected to the seasons and our heritage.

MAKES 8 TO 10 SERVINGS

2½ teaspoons (1 package) active dry yeast
3 tablespoons Chianti wine
1 tablespoon brown rice syrup
¾ cup warm spring or filtered water
2 cups whole wheat pastry flour
1 cup semolina flour
¼ cup extra-virgin olive or avocado oil
½ teaspoon sea salt
3 to 4 cups Concord or wine grapes
½ cup maple syrup granules

Stir together yeast, wine, rice syrup and warm water in a large bowl until the yeast is dissolved. Let stand until the yeast is bubbly, about 10 minutes.

Mix flours together. Stir 1 cup of flour into yeast mixture (the mixture will be lumpy), cover bowl with plastic wrap and a kitchen towel and let rise in a warm place until doubled in size, about 40 minutes.

Stir in oil, 1½ cups of flour and salt and mix until a sticky dough forms. Flour a dry work surface and knead dough (gradually adding up to ½ cup more flour to keep dough from sticking) until dough is elastic, but still soft, 8 to 10 minutes.

Transfer dough to a large, oiled bowl and turn to coat with oil. Cover bowl with plastic wrap and a towel and let rise until doubled in size, about 1 hour.

Lightly oil a 10 x 15-inch baking sheet with sides and set aside. Turn out dough onto a lightly floured work surface and knead briefly to release any air trapped in the dough. Cut the dough in half. Keeping one half covered, roll 1 piece of the dough with a lightly floured rolling pin into a rough 10 × 12-inch rectangle. Transfer dough to a prepared baking sheet with sides and gently stretch dough to cover as much of the pan as possible. Scatter the dough with half of the grapes and sprinkle with ¼ cup of the maple syrup granules.

Roll out remaining piece of dough to match the first and lay it on top of the grapes, stretching to cover them. Scatter remaining grapes over the top and sprinkle with remaining maple syrup granules. Press grapes gently into dough. Cover pan with plastic wrap and a kitchen towel and let rise in a warm place for about 1 hour.

Preheat oven to 400F (205C). Bake foccacia on the middle oven rack about 45 minutes, until well-browned and firm in the middle. After baking, loosen the sides with a spatula and transfer from the pan to a wire rack to cool. Serve warm or at room temperature.

Sweet Strawberry Pie

Raw cuisine is all the rage . . . so I decided to play with it. A total raw approach doesn't work for me personally, but I think it has definite value to a healthy life. I think we all need some raw foods for enzymes, to create a light, fresh energy and for digestion. I love to make this pie when strawberries are in their full season of sweet ripeness.

MAKES 6 TO 8 SERVINGS

**2 pounds fresh strawberries, tops removed
 and berries quartered
Juice of ½ lemon
1 teaspoon pure vanilla extract
½ cup brown rice syrup
Sea salt
2 cups raw almonds
1¾ cups pitted dates
Spring or filtered water**

Combine strawberries, lemon juice, vanilla, rice syrup and a pinch of salt in a bowl and toss to combine. Set aside while you make the crust.

Place almonds in a blender and pulse on high until they resemble bread crumbs. Transfer to a 9-inch pie plate. Place dates in blender

with about 1 teaspoon water and pulse on high until well-chopped; mixture will be a little clumpy. Combine almonds and dates until they hold together and then press evenly onto the bottom and sides of pie plate to form a crust. Spoon berries generously into the crust, discarding any remaining liquid. Refrigerate for 2 hours before slicing into wedges and serving.

Candied Apples

I am totally serious. Remember those bright red, jaw-breaker candied apples we all loved so much as kids? Here is my healthier version . . . just as yummy, and a bit easier on our teeth.

MAKES 6 APPLES

6 Red Delicious or Granny Smith apples, rinsed well and left whole
About 1½ cups Suzanne's Specialties Raspberry Rice Nectar or brown rice syrup
Coarsely chopped macadamia nuts or peanuts
6 flat wooden sticks

Place apples on a tray, top sides down. Cook rice nectar in a deep saucepan over medium-low heat until it adheres to the surface of a spoon, about 15 minutes.

Push a wooden stick into each apple. Holding the apple by the stick, roll it around in the pan of rice syrup to coat the whole apple. Quickly dip in macadamia nuts and place on a sheet of waxed paper until it sets.

Chocolate Red Velvet Cake

You think I'm kidding? Wait until you taste this cake and then we'll just see . . .

MAKES 8 TO 10 SERVINGS

1½ cups chopped beets
2 cups whole wheat pastry flour
½ cup semolina flour
5 tablespoons unsweetened cocoa powder, preferably organic and fair trade
Generous pinch sea salt
3 teaspoons baking powder
3 tablespoons beet powder
1½ cups beet cooking water or spring or filtered water
2 teaspoons pure vanilla extract
¼ cup avocado oil
1½ cups brown rice syrup
2 teaspoons brown rice vinegar

FROSTING
¾ cup nondairy, grain-sweetened chocolate chips
½ cup vegetarian buttery spread (like Earth Balance)
½ cup soymilk
2 tablespoons brown rice syrup
½ teaspoon pure vanilla extract

Place beets in a pot with several cups of water and bring to a boil. Cook until tender, about 15 minutes. Drain beets, reserving 2 cups of cooking water. Cook this water over medium heat until it has reduced to 1½ cups.

Preheat oven to 350F (175C). Lightly oil and flour 2 (8-inch) springform pans and set aside.

Whisk together flours, cocoa, salt, baking powder and beet powder. Place cooked beets and beet water in a food processor and puree until smooth. Whisk together, in a separate bowl, vanilla, oil, rice syrup and vinegar. Mix beet mixture and oil mixture into flour mixture to make a smooth batter. Spoon batter evenly into prepared pans. Bake on the center rack 50 minutes, until tops of cakes spring back to the touch or a wooden pick inserted in the center comes out clean. Cool on a wire rack 10 minutes before releasing cakes from pans. Cool completely before frosting.

Make the frosting while the cakes bake: Place chocolate in a double boiler or in a glass bowl over a pot of boiling water and whisk until smooth. Mix in the spread and whisk until smooth. Whisk in soymilk, rice syrup and vanilla until smooth. Transfer to a glass bowl, cover and chill completely. Whisk briskly to loosen before using.

When you are ready to frost the cake, shave the top of one of the cakes to create a flat surface. Place on a platter and spread frosting over the top of the layer. Place remaining cake on top of the frosting and frost the entire cake.

Vegan Baklava

Not a tough one to adapt, really. But just getting rid of the butter that usually saturates this delicacy results in a delicious dessert with no saturated fat . . . and since we use rice syrup in place of honey, it is completely vegan and less calorically dense, too. Yummy.

MAKES 20 TO 24 DIAMONDS

4 cups coarsely chopped walnut, hazelnut or pistachio pieces
½ cup maple syrup granule
2 teaspoons ground cinnamon

Scant pinch ground nutmeg
Pinch sea salt
1 (1-pound) package phyllo pastry sheets, thawed in the refrigerator for several hours before use (see Note, page 176)
1 cup avocado or olive oil

ORANGE SYRUP
2 cups brown rice syrup
Grated zest of 1 orange
Pinch sea salt
2 tablespoons fresh orange juice

Preheat oven to 350F (175C), lightly oil a 13 × 9-inch baking dish and set aside.

Combine walnuts with maple syrup granules, cinnamon, nutmeg and salt. Set aside.

On a dry, flat work surface, remove sheets of phyllo and lay them flat. Cover phyllo with a damp towel while you work (so it doesn't stiffen). Fold a sheet of phyllo in half so it is the size of the baking pan. Lay it in the bottom of the pan and brush lightly with oil. Repeat with 3 more sheets of phyllo, brushing each layer with oil, creating a base of 8 layers of dough. Sprinkle half the walnut mixture evenly over the dough. Create another 8 layers of phyllo as you did at the base. Brush lightly with oil. Sprinkle the remaining half of walnut mixture evenly over dough. Create a final 8 layers of phyllo, brushing each layer as you have done twice before. Bake, uncovered, 35 to 45 minutes, until the top layer of phyllo is lightly browned.

Prepare syrup when baklava has about 5 minutes left to bake: Combine rice syrup, orange zest and salt in a saucepan and bring to a boil. Remove from heat and whisk in orange juice. When you take the baklava from the oven, spoon the orange syrup over the entire pan and cool on a wire rack before slicing into diamond shapes.

Resource Guide

I AM SURE you have noticed unfamiliar ingredients in more than a few recipes. So rather than leave you dazed and confused as to where you might find these more exotic foods, I thought I would provide you with a comprehensive list of mail-order companies that can easily supply the ingredients in question. See? I told you I would make this painless. Just call or visit the website of the company of your choice. Place your order and get on with your healthy new way of living. No excuses anymore . . . it couldn't be easier.

BOB'S RED MILL NATURAL FOODS
Milwaukee, Oregon
800-349-2173
www.bobsredmill.com
> **SUPPLIES:** packaged and bulk whole grain products, beans, stone-ground flours, gluten-free products, spices, baking supplies

CHRISTINA COOKS
Philadelphia, PA
800-939-3909
www.christinacooks.com

DI BRUNO BROTHERS ITALIAN MARKET
Philadelphia, PA
888-322-4337
www.dibruno.com
> **SUPPLIES:** Italian products, olive oil, dried beans, vinegars, pasta, sauces, specialty, condiments

DIAMOND ORGANICS
Freedom, California
800-922-2396
www.diamondorganics.com
> **SUPPLIES:** organic produce, shipped direct to customer

EDEN FOODS, INC.
Clinton, Michigan
888-424-EDEN
www.edenfoods.com
> **SUPPLIES:** organic grains, organic beans, canned organic beans, condiments, organic tomato products, pasta products, imported Japanese products

GOLD MINE NATURAL FOOD CO.
San Diego, California
800-475-FOOD, 619-234-9711
www.goldminenaturalfood.com
> **SUPPLIES:** macrobiotic and natural food items, non-food items

KUHN-RIKON SWITZERLAND
Corte Madera, California
415-924-1125 or 800-662-5882
www.kuhnrikon.com
> **SUPPLIES:** cookware, pressure cookers, utensils

KUSHI INSTITUTE STORE
Becket, Massachusetts
413-623-5741
www.kushiinstitute.org
> **SUPPLIES::** macrobiotic and natural food items, non-food items

MAINE COAST SEA VEGETABLES
Franklin, Maine
207-565-2907
www.seaveg.com
> **SUPPLIES:** American and imported dried sea plants

NATURAL LIFESTYLE SUPPLIES
Asheville, North Carolina
800-752-2775
www.natural-lifestyle.com
> **SUPPLIES:** macrobiotic and natural food items, non-food items

SOUTH RIVER MISO
Conway, Massachusetts
413-369-4057
www.southrivermiso.com
> **SUPPLIES:** organic miso products

SUZANNE'S SPECIALTIES, INC.
New Brunswick, NJ
800-762-2135
www.suzannes-specialties.com
> **SUPPLIES:** natural sweeteners (brown rice syrup, honey, agave and more), toppings, spreads, sauces

Recommended Reading

TO **FURTHER YOUR** study of macrobiotics, whole foods cooking, vegetarianism and other holistic practices, please check out any or all of these volumes.

Books

The Art of Indian Vegetarian Cooking by Yamuna Devi

The Artful Vegan by Eric Tucker

Aveline Kushi's Complete Guide to Macrobiotic Cooking with Wendy Esko

The Cancer Prevention Diet by Michio Kushi

Chez Panisse Vegetables by Alice Waters

Confessions of a Kamikaze Cowboy by Dirk Benedict

Diet for a New America: How Your Food Choices Affect Your Health, Happiness and the Future of Life on Earth by John Robbins

Diet for a Poisoned Planet by David Steinman

Diet for a Strong Heart by Michio Kushi

Eco-Cuisine by Ron Pikarski

Energetics of Food by Steve Gagne

Love, Eric by Eric Lechasseur

The Macrobiotic Diet by Michio and Aveline Kushi with Alex Jack

Macrobiotic Home Remedies by Michio Kushi with Marc Van Cawenberghe, M.D.

The Macrobiotic Way by Michio Kushi

The Magic Mirror by William Tara

The Natural Gourmet by Annemarie Colbin

Practically Macrobiotic by Keith Mitchel

Recalled by Life by Anthony Sattilaro, M.D., with Tom Monte

Recipes from an Ecological Kitchen by Lorna Sass

The Rise and Fall of the Cattle Culture by Jeremy Rifkin

Sugar Blues by William Dufty

The Venturesome Vegetarian by Jason Hirsch and Michele Hirsch

You Are All Sanpaku by George Ohsawa

Magazines

Christina Cooks
www.christinacooks.com

E, The Environmental Magazine
www.emagazine.com

Natural Health magazine
www.naturalhealthmag.com

Veg News
www.vegnews.com

Vegetarian Times
www.vegetariantimes.com

Bibliography

THE FOLLOWING BOOKS have served me well over these last years—and for this work—for information, facts and statistics, and inspiration.

Abehsera, Michel, *Cooking for Life* (New York: Avon, 1970).

Baggett, Nancy, *Dream Desserts* (New York: Stewart, Tabori and Chang, 1993).

Blackman, Jackson F., *Working Chef's Cookbook for Natural Whole Foods* (Morrisville, VT: Central Vermont Publishers, 1989).

Colbin, Annemarie, *The Natural Gourmet* (New York: Ballentine, 1989).

Gagne, Steve, *Energetics of Food* (Taos, NM: Redwing Book Co., 2006).

Kushi, Aveline, *The Complete Guide to Macrobiotic Cooking* (New York: Warner, 1985).

Lechasseur, Eric, *Love, Eric* (Santa Monica, CA: Eric Lechasseur, 2005).

Levy, Faye, *Sensational Pasta* (New York: HPBooks, 1989).

Pikarski, Ron, *Eco-Cuisine* (Berkeley, CA: Ten Speed Press, 1995).

Rubin, Maury, *Book of Tarts* (New York: William Morrow and Co., 1995).

Somerville, Annie, *Fields of Greens* (New York: Bantam, 1993).

Spencer, Colin, *The Heretic's Feast*: A History of Vegetarianism (London: Fourth Estate, 1993).

Steinman, David, *Diet for a Poisoned Planet* (New York: Ballantine, 1990).

Metric Conversion Charts

Comparison to Metric Measure

When You Know	Symbol	Multiply By	To Find	Symbol
teaspoons	tsp	5.0	milliliter	ml
tablespoons	tbsp	15.0	milliliters	ml
fluid ounces	fl. oz.	30.0	milliliters	ml
cups	c	0.24	liters	l
pints	pt.	0.47	liters	l
quarts	qt.	0.95	liters	l
ounces	oz.	28.0	grams	g
pounds	lb.	0.45	kilograms	kg
Fahrenheit	F	5/9 (after subtracting 32)	Celsius	C

Fahrenheit to Celsius

F	C
200–205	95
225–229	105
245–250	120
275	135
300–305	150
325–330	165
345–350	175
370–375	190
400–405	205
425–430	220
445–450	230
470–475	245
500	260

Liquid Measure to Liters

¼ cup	=	0.06 liters
½ cup	=	0.12 liters
¾ cup	=	0.18 liters
1 cup	=	0.24 liters
1¼ cups	=	0.30 liters
1½ cups	=	0.36 liters
2 cups	=	0.48 liters
2½ cups	=	0.60 liters
3 cups	=	0.72 liters
3½ cups	=	0.84 liters
4 cups	=	0.96 liters
4½ cups	=	1.08 liters
5 cups	=	1.20 liters
5½ cups	=	1.32 liters

Liquid Measure to Milliliters

¼ teaspoon	=	1.25 milliliters
½ teaspoon	=	2.50 milliliters
¾ teaspoon	=	3.75 milliliters
1 teaspoon	=	5.00 milliliters
1¼ teaspoons	=	6.25 milliliters
1½ teaspoons	=	7.50 milliliters
1¾ teaspoons	=	8.75 milliliters
2 teaspoons	=	10.0 milliliters
1 tablespoon	=	15.0 milliliters
2 tablespoons	=	30.0 milliliters

Index

About the Author

CHRISTINA PIRELLO, Emmy Award–winning host of the national public television series *Christina Cooks* (airing weekly on more than 150 public television stations nationwide and daily on CN8, the Comcast network in the Mid-Atlantic and New England regions), found her way to Philadelphia by opening a map and dropping a pin. Her relationship with food began at a young age, cooking with her mother and later, while she was living in Florida, working as a caterer and pastry chef. But the real pivotal point in her life came at age twenty-six, when after being diagnosed with terminal leukemia, she decided to forgo conventional medical therapies and turned to a nutritional approach and whole foods, and cured herself. The passion and commitment that made that happen is what makes her so good and inspirational at what she does.

For the last seventeen years, Christina has been teaching whole foods cooking classes, conducting lifestyle seminars and lecturing nationwide on the power of food in our lives, in a variety of settings from natural food stores to corporate boardrooms. No lives are left unchanged when she leaves the room. Even if they think that she's nuts (but nice), they'll never think of food in the same way again, which is her goal.

She and her husband publish a bimonthly whole foods magazine, *Christina Cooks*, with national distribution and circulation, as well as operating Christina Trips, a travel company that specializes in healthy vacations to exotic destinations. Christina also wrote *Cook Your Way to the Life You Want*, *Glow: Your Prescription for Radiant Health and Beauty* and *Christina Cooks: Everything You Always Wanted to Know About Whole Foods, But Were Afraid to Ask.*

In addition, she is on the faculty of Drexel University, where she serves as a professor of culinary arts. She also serves on the board of the Farm Market Trust, the Fair Food Project, and the Green Council of Philadelphia and holds memberships in both the International Association of Culinary Professionals (IACP) and Women Chefs and Restaurateurs, as well as the Green City Youth Council of Philadelphia and C-CAP (a culinary program for urban high schools). She also serves on the Chefs' Council for Chefs for Humanity.